Pauline Theology, Volume II
1 & 2 Corinthians

PAULINE THEOLOGY

Volume II:
1 & 2
Corinthians

Edited by

David M. Hay

Fortress Press   Minneapolis

PAULINE THEOLOGY, VOLUME II
1 & 2 Corinthians

Scripture quotations, unless otherwise noted, are from the New Revised Standard Version of the Bible, copyright © 1989 by the Division of Christian Education of the National Council of Churches of Christ in the United States of America.

Interior design and typesetting: The HK Scriptorium, Inc.
Cover design: Ned Skubic

Library of Congress Cataloging-in-Publication Data
(Revised for vol. II)

Pauline theology.

    Vol. II edited by David M. Hay.
    Includes bibliographical references.
    Contents: v. I. Thessalonians, Philippians, Galatians,
Philemon—v. II. 1 & 2 Corinthians.
    1. Bible. N.T.—Epistles of Paul—Theology. I. Hay,
David M., 1935–.
BS2651.P284 1991   227′.06   91-17665
ISBN 0-8006-2488-2 (vol. I: alk. paper)
ISBN 0-8006-2489-0 (vol. II: alk. paper)

Manufactured in the U.S.A.   AF 1-2489
97   96   95   94   93   1   2   3   4   5   6   7   8   9   10

▣ Contents

▣ Preface

THERE HAVE BEEN many attempts to define the theology of Paul, but this volume is somewhat novel because it focuses on the theologies of two of his major epistles, 1 and 2 Corinthians. It is the second in a series of volumes, the first of which treated the theologies of the shorter letters[1] and the third of which will concentrate on Romans.

Like those other volumes, this one has grown out of discussions in the Pauline Theology Group of the Society of Biblical Literature. Most of the essays printed here are revised versions of papers originally presented at the group's annual meetings in 1989, 1990, and 1991. Nearly all the authors have been participants in the group's discussions since its formation in 1986, and they were often prompted to make changes in their original papers by conversations in group sessions. Decisions about which essays would be published in this volume were made by members of the steering committee of the Pauline Theology Group, composed of Professors Paul J. Achtemeier, Jouette M. Bassler, Victor P. Furnish, Richard B. Hays, Robert Jewett, Pheme Perkins, and Calvin J. Roetzel. I participated in those decisions and took responsibility for the final editing of each contribution.

Members of the Pauline Theology Group agreed at the outset that one fruitful way to approach our task would be to study the theology of each of Paul's letters separately as though no other letters were known. We thought that each letter should first be viewed as an individual communication in its own right and its distinctive themes and assertions interpreted without seeking to explain them or explain them away by trying to "harmonize" them with everything else he wrote. Rather than seeking to read between the lines

---

[1] Jouette M. Bassler, ed., *Pauline Theology, Volume I: Thessalonians, Philippians, Galatians, Philemon* (Minneapolis: Fortress, 1991). This work will hereafter be cited simply as *Pauline Theology I.*

of an individual letter, we resolved to focus primarily on the actual text of each letter. This decision also reflected a consensus among the group members that the religious thought of Paul should not be conceived first of all as a set of his answers to questions raised by systematic theologians of later centuries. Finally, we did not want to obscure real differences of theological thought or expression that may be found in the letters.

In probing the nature and content of Paul's theological thought, some of the essays in this volume (by agreement) treat 1 and 2 Corinthians in isolation from each other and from the other letters. Other contributions have a synthesizing character, holding several epistles in view in relation to a major theme or issue. Still others concentrate on methodological issues.

The anthology begins with essays by Jouette Bassler and Steven Kraftchick (his written in response to hers) that seek to clarify what it means to identify the theology of a Pauline letter; their statements about "what we are looking for" were written after the group's discussions of the shorter epistles and thus form an appropriate bridge to the explorations of the Corinthian letters. Calvin Roetzel's article deals with the grammar of election language and calls attention to the different meanings that language takes on in 1 Thessalonians, Philippians, Galatians, and 1 Corinthians. William Campbell responds to Roetzel and elaborates a fresh view of how Paul reshaped traditions in formulating his own theological ideas.

Gordon Fee and Victor Furnish offer quite comprehensive studies of the major theological convictions that surface in 1 Corinthians. Fee stresses that the Corinthians have failed to grasp the gospel's transformational implications for behavior; he proceeds to analyze the letter according to the topics of God, Christ, the Spirit, the human predicament, salvation, ethics, the church, and eschatology. Furnish urges that Paul's theology be defined as his critical reflection about the gospel and that it is particularly well illustrated in three major sections of the letter (1:18–2:16, 12:4–13:13, and chap. 15). Charles Cousar's essay responds to both positions and argues that 1 Corinthians has a unifying theological purpose in its advocacy of a distinctive religious epistemology.

Steven Kraftchick and I contribute essays on the theology of 2 Corinthians that focus more on the processes than the products of Paul's thought. Kraftchick discusses the general metaphorical nature of Pauline thought and then examines the dominant role of the death-and-resurrection motif in the letter. My own essay is largely concerned to identify and classify the varied convictions, doubts, and warrants that serve as dynamic components of the letter's arguments. Beverly Gaventa critiques both essays, pointing out some limitations in our approaches. She then proceeds to argue that a vital element in the theology of 2 Corinthians is its delineation of the relationship between apostle and church.

To balance these relatively comprehensive studies of the two letters, there are two exegetical essays focused on brief passages. Troels Engberg-Pedersen explores 1 Cor 11:17–34, maintaining that Paul's actual train of theological thought has often been misunderstood by readers anxious to peer behind or beyond what he actually says about the Eucharist. N. T. Wright offers an investigation of 2 Cor 5:21, urging that in its context this pivotal statement about reconciliation is more self-referential than most exegetes have realized.

All the contributors touch on issues of method, often overtly seeking to show why older approaches to Paul's theological thought are unsatisfying. The Pauline Theology Group has deliberately sought to chart a new course, and each of the essays has an exploratory tone. Several explicitly bring insights from contemporary philosophical analysis and literary criticism to bear on the task. The influence of J. Christiaan Beker's thesis about a polarity of coherence and contingency in the Pauline correspondence[2] may be discerned in several of the essays, but nowhere is it accepted without modification.

The volume concludes with lengthy bibliographies prepared by Professors Fee and Furnish on recent scholarship dealing with 1 and 2 Corinthians. The bibliographies are restricted to articles and books directly related to theology.

The abbreviations used in this volume are taken from the *Society of Biblical Literature Membership Directory and Handbook 1991:* 196–210.

---

[2] Stated most fully in Beker's *Paul the Apostle: The Triumph of God in Life and Thought* (Philadelphia: Fortress, 1980).

▣ Contributors

Jouette M. Bassler
  Professor of New Testament
  Perkins School of Theology
  Southern Methodist University

William S. Campbell
  Director of Religious and Theological Studies
  Westhill College
  University of Birmingham

Charles B. Cousar
  Samuel A. Cartledge Professor of New Testament
  Columbia Theological Seminary

Troels Engberg-Pedersen
  Professor of New Testament
  Institute of Biblical Exegesis
  University of Copenhagen

Gordon D. Fee
  Professor of New Testament
  Regent College

Victor Paul Furnish
  University Distinguished Professor of New Testament
  Perkins School of Theology
  Southern Methodist University

Beverly Roberts Gaventa
    Professor of New Testament
    Princeton Theological Seminary

David M. Hay
    Joseph E. McCabe Professor of Religion
    Coe College

Steven J. Kraftchick
    Assistant Professor of New Testament
    Princeton Theological Seminary

Calvin J. Roetzel
    Arnold Lowe Professor of Religious Studies
    Macalester College

N. T. Wright
    Fellow, Tutor in Theology, and Chaplain
    Worcester College
    University of Oxford

Part I

Methodology

1 PAUL'S THEOLOGY: WHENCE AND WHITHER?

Jouette M. Bassler
Perkins School of Theology

IN RETROSPECT, of all the words that have been written for the Pauline Theology Group, among the most significant and prophetic are those tucked into a footnote of one of the earliest papers: "It is . . . crucial that we carefully define just what is and is not meant by 'theology,' for until we do so each of us will be looking for something different and our conversations with one another will be all the more precariously grounded."[1] Since those words were first penned in 1986, the struggle to define what exactly this group is looking for has continued unabated. The struggle is compounded by the fact that we have been, by agreement, looking for two different things: the theologies of the individual letters and an ongoing synthesis of these theologies. Not only, however, are we not in obvious agreement over precisely what is meant by the theology of a particular letter; we are also not in obvious agreement on how a synthesis of the theologies of the various letters should be construed. Does a synthesis seek to find patterns through a summation of the individual theologies, or does it seek somehow to find a locus of commonality *behind* the divergent expressions of Paul's thought?

Enough papers of both types — individual theologies and ongoing syntheses — have now been written for us to assess the various approaches that have been recommended and tried.[2] Indeed, such an assessment seems timely, for if our conversations are to continue to be fruitful, we need to reach clarity, if not agreement, on how we should define the theology of a particular letter and what we can hope to achieve through a synthesis of these theologies. What, then, do we mean when we speak of the theology, for

---

[1] J. Paul Sampley, "From Text to Thought World: The Route to Paul's Ways," in *Pauline Theology I,* 4 n. 4. The essay was first presented to the Pauline Theology Group at the 1986 annual meeting of the Society of Biblical Literature.

[2] See the various essays in *Pauline Theology I.*

3

example, of 1 Thessalonians or of Philippians? What should a synthesis of these theologies focus on? And how are these entities — the theology of a given letter and the synthesis of the various theologies — related to our larger goal of a fresh understanding of Paul's theology in general? At stake here is not only a sense of definition but also a sense of direction; for when we have answered these questions we will be able to see more clearly where our work seems to be headed. Let us review first the ground we have covered.

I. WHENCE? THE INDIVIDUAL LETTERS

It was agreed in principle, if not always rigorously actualized in practice, that those of us working on this project would define the theology of each individual letter without reference or recourse to the other letters of the Pauline corpus.[3] Each "word on target"[4] would be approached separately and in isolation from words Paul targeted for different audiences. It was further agreed that this phase of the task would be descriptive — but descriptive of what? Most contributors have assumed that the theology of a given letter is to be located somehow in that letter's argument, but is it in the surface structure of the argument, as Edgar Krentz and Robert Jewett have argued (albeit in their own separate ways) for 2 Thessalonians, and as J. D. G. Dunn has argued for Galatians?[5] Or is it in a *deep* structure of binary opposition, such as the conflict between Christ and cosmos that Beverly Roberts Gaventa has presented as the basic theological structure of Galatians?[6] Actually we have not yet achieved complete agreement that the theology of a given letter is to be equated without remainder with its argument. J. Paul Sampley, for example, has reminded us that each letter was written to restore a theological *balance* that had been "twisted askew" by the congregation. Thus the "theology" of a given letter cannot, in Sampley's view, be read directly out of its argument. It lies rather in the tension between the community's misplaced emphasis and Paul's often deliberately exaggerated response.[7] J. Louis

---

[3] See *Pauline Theology I*, ix–x.

[4] This helpful phrase is J. C. Beker's; see "Recasting Pauline Theology: The Coherence-Contingency Scheme as Interpretive Model," in *Pauline Theology I*, 15.

[5] The essays are found in *Pauline Theology I*: Edgar Krentz, "Through a Lens: Theology and Fidelity in 2 Thessalonians," 52–62; Robert Jewett, "A Matrix of Grace: The Theology of 2 Thessalonians as a Pauline Letter," 63–70; James D. G. Dunn, "The Theology of Galatians: The Issue of Covenantal Nomism," 125–46.

[6] Beverly Roberts Gaventa, "The Singularity of the Gospel: A Reading of Galatians," in *Pauline Theology I*, 147–59.

[7] Sampley, "From Text to Thought World," 6–7.

Martyn also takes seriously the tension between Paul's argument in a given letter and the addressees' situation, but he locates the "theology" of a letter somewhat differently from Sampley. According to Martyn, the argument of Galatians was intended to generate an "aural event" when it was read aloud to the Galatian congregations, and the "theology" of the letter is to be identified not with the argument of the letter itself nor simply with the tension between the letter's argument and recipients' stance but with the theological *event* precipitated by its argument.[8]

Three related but nevertheless distinct definitions have thus been proposed for the theology of a given letter: (1) the theological argument of that letter (variously defined), (2) the tension between the argument of the letter and the theological position of the community, and (3) the theological event evoked by the argument of the letter. Definitions 1 (theology as argument) and 2 (theology in tension) can be reconciled by insisting that the task of describing the argument of a letter *includes* defining carefully the context in which that particular argument has been formulated. The event aroused by the theological argument of a letter, however, seems logically distinct from the letter's theology. The one was rooted in Paul's thought and thought world and was communicated by a letter. The other was generated by this letter and arose in the community. The letter links them but does not permit equating them. Nevertheless, the aural event that Martyn refers to should be recoverable from our understanding of the argument of the letter and the situation to which it was directed, and it could serve as a legitimate pointer to the larger entity that is the ultimate goal of our quest: Paul's theology.

II. WHENCE? ONGOING SYNTHESES

If the quest for the theologies of the individual letters has been plagued with conceptual difficulties, the attempts to generate a gradual synthesis of these theologies have faced even greater problems. Not only does the lack of agreement concerning the definition of a given letter's theology generate problems for the synthetic task, but the amount of data to be synthesized, though manageable in the early stages of our work, has rapidly become overwhelming. Even more problematical, however, is the fact that here too there is no agreement on what precisely is the object of this synthesis and what its relationship is to the larger task of defining Paul's theology. We may still be debating, for example, exactly what we mean by "the theology of

---

[8] J. Louis Martyn, "Events in Galatia: Modified Covenantal Nomism versus God's Invasion of the Cosmos in the Singular Gospel: A Response to J. D. G. Dunn and B. R. Gaventa," in *Pauline Theology I*, 160–63.

Philippians," but however this theology is defined, it is at least controlled by the argument of the canonical letter to that church. But what do we mean when we speak of "Paul's theology" in general?

Thus far two things are clear. First, Paul was *not* a systematic theologian. Thus, we are not looking for a theological or doctrinal system to emerge from his letters, nor are we seeking to impose such a system on them. Yet the deconstructive analyses of recent years that deny all coherence to Paul's thought seem to go too far in the opposite direction.[9] If Paul was not a *systematic* theologian, there seems nevertheless to be a pattern, a center, a commitment, a conviction, a vision, an underlying structure, a core communication, a set of beliefs, a narrative, a coherence — something — in Paul's thoughts or behind them that dispels any abiding sense of mere opportunism or intellectual chaos on the part of the apostle. Yet nowhere, it seems, does this core, center, vision, etc. come to expression in a noncontingent way.[10] All of Paul's words are words on target, addressed to and shaped for particular communities and their needs. Is it the goal, then, of a synthesis to summarize and systematize these words on target, or should it attempt to get behind the contingent expressions instead? If so, how far behind them dare we or need we go, and how shall we get there?

Actually the first question to be asked is whether it is *possible* to get behind Paul's specific words and reconstruct the center of his thought. An affirmative answer is, of course, the presupposition of Rudolf Bultmann's magisterial work, and Ernst Käsemann, though so often in disagreement with his former teacher, here concurs.[11] Others, however, are not as sanguine about the task. J. Christiaan Beker, for example, derides its artificiality. While arguing vigorously for the existence of a coherent center to Paul's thought, he questions on principle any attempt to construe this coherence with "linguistic precision." Any "attempt to go 'behind the text' . . . means that we reduce Paul's apostolic intent of proclaiming an intelligible and clear gospel . . . to some sort of 'psychological *Mitte*.'"[12] Robin Scroggs, on the other hand, challenges the very possibility of fulfilling the task because the contingent nature and limited number of Paul's letters preclude easy identification of the core. "As 'Pauline theologians' *we* may find coherence," he says, "but we

---

[9] See esp. Heikki Räisänen, *Paul and the Law* (Philadelphia: Fortress, 1986).

[10] See, e.g., Paul J. Achtemeier's comments in "Finding the Way to Paul's Theology: A Response to J. Christiaan Beker and J. Paul Sampley," in *Pauline Theology I*, 28–30.

[11] Käsemann argues that the center of Paul's theology can be precisely defined, but he uses only Romans and 2 Corinthians to locate it ("Spirit and Letter," in *Perspectives on Paul* [Philadelphia: Fortress, 1971] 138).

[12] Beker, "Recasting Pauline Theology," 22–23.

should not claim that that coherence represents the core of Paul."[13] Finally, John Reumann has argued that while the quest for the center of Paul's thought may be possible, it is not timely: "At this stage it is work enough to try to be somewhat descriptive."[14]

Such statements should give pause to anyone still convinced that the center of Paul's thought will be easily — or ever — recovered. Yet the sense of a center remains, and it does not seem fully satisfied by summaries of the theological statements in the various letters. But if we continue our quest for the "heart and driving force"[15] of Paul's theology, what exactly is it that we are looking for? Various suggestions have been made: Paul's beliefs or conceptions, his convictions, or a foundational story.[16] Let's consider first the recent proposal that the guiding center of Paul's thought is a narrative.

III. WHITHER? NARRATIVE OR THEOLOGY?

Richard Hays has proposed that "the ground of coherence in Paul's thought is to be found not in a system of theological propositions . . . but in the kerygmatic story of God's action through Jesus Christ."[17] Only allusions to this foundational story can be found in Paul's letters, but out of these Hays has pieced together the outline of a narrative that runs from God's initial promise to Abraham to the parousia of the Lord Jesus. Between these points the story includes the fulfillment of the promise in the death and resurrection of Jesus and the present life of the community in the power of the Spirit. According to Hays, this foundational story guides Paul's thoughts and

[13] Robin Scroggs, "Salvation History: The Theological Structure of Paul's Thought (1 Thessalonians, Philippians, and Galatians)," in *Pauline Theology I*, 214.

[14] J. Reumann, "The Theologies of 1 Thessalonians and Philippians: Concerns, Comparison and Composite," in *Society of Biblical Literature 1987 Seminar Papers* (ed. Kent H. Richards; Atlanta: Scholars Press, 1987) 532.

[15] N. T. Wright, "Putting Paul Together Again: Toward a Synthesis of Pauline Theology (1 and 2 Thessalonians, Philippians, and Philemon)," in *Pauline Theology I*, 184.

[16] Wright suggests that we are looking for Paul's beliefs or conceptions ("Putting Paul Together Again," 184). V. P. Furnish thinks it is Paul's convictions ("Summary Remarks in Response to Paul Sampley, Norman Petersen, J. Christiaan Beker, and Paul Achtemeier," paper distributed to members of the Pauline Theology Consultation in 1986). Furnish acutally refers somewhat more expansively to "the presuppositions, convictions, and concerns which inform and thereby distinguish Paul's interpretation of the gospel"; see also Krentz, "Through a Lens," 52. Richard B. Hays looks for a foundational story ("Crucified with Christ: A Synthesis of the Theology of 1 and 2 Thessalonians, Philemon, Philippians, and Galatians," in *Pauline Theology I*, 227–46).

[17] Hays, "Crucified with Christ," 231–32.

provides the basis for their essential coherence: "As he [Paul] confronts pastoral problems in his churches, he responds to them by thinking through the situation in the light of the story, plotting the community's place within the unfolding narrative."[18] The diverse emphases of the various letters arise, then, because Paul appeals to different parts of the story to address different situations. The essential coherence of that story, however, remains unchanged and provides the unifying thread to Paul's thought.

Now it is not to be doubted that Paul would agree to the truth of the narrative that Hays has extracted, both as a whole and in all of its particulars. Whether, however, we are justified in regarding this narrative as the primary seat of the coherence of the Pauline corpus remains, I think, an open—and important—question. I raise the following points.

Hays himself concedes the allusive quality of the narrative in Paul's letters.[19] This does not, of course, constitute sufficient grounds for challenging its centrality to Paul's thought, for the narrative could be so foundational that it only rarely comes to explicit expression. Yet the allusive quality of the story does generate difficulties, for it means that we are looking for something that Paul does not fully articulate. This has led Hays to some cross-referencing among the letters that seems occasionally to force the foundational story on them instead of locating it in them. Hays, for example, was not exactly *incorrect* when he identified the "living and true God" of 1 Thess 1:9 as "surely the God of Abraham,"[20] but would we ever know that from reading 1 Thessalonians? The actual issue in this verse is the true God versus false gods—monotheism—and not the God of Abraham. The influence of the story on the argument seems here, at least, to be questionable.

This leads to a second point. In discussing the concept of "theology as narrative," G. W. Stroup points to what he sees as a frequent methodological defect: "At best they offer a vague description of 'story' and then use it as an excuse, rather than as a systematic principle, for the discussion of other themes."[21] I have much the same feeling about Hays's proposal, though *his* description of the story is quite detailed. Nevertheless, his fine discussions of "Israel, Gentiles, election," "The Messiah and the people of God," and "The community's cruciform role in the drama" do not seem to depend on the identification of a narrative *qua* narrative as the infrastructure of Paul's thought. Indeed, I have the uneasy feeling that this proposed narrative foundation fits a bit too comfortably with the current interests of contemporary theology. Are we not running the risk of having later generations accuse us of forcing our own agenda on Paul, much as the Reformers did in the past?

---

[18] Ibid., 233.
[19] Ibid., 232.
[20] Ibid., 235.
[21] G. W. Stroup, "A Bibliographical Critique," *TToday* 32 (1975) 134.

If we have deemed it illegitimate of the Reformers to have imposed the categories of their debate on Paul's thought, we should be very cautious when today we find in Paul evidence of an interest in story similar to our own. Thus, I still need to be convinced that Paul approached the problems in his churches "by thinking through the situation in the light of the (foundational) story." We really *do not know* if Paul did that or if that was the *only* way Paul approached problems; and, if it was not, then it is difficult to justify on the basis of the letters themselves the claim that a foundational *story* provides the ground of coherence in Paul's thought.

There is another problem as well. The ultimate object of our research is Paul's theology. There has been some discussion over whether "Paul's thought" is not a more valid label for what we are seeking to define,[22] but "Paul's thought" and "Paul's theology" (if not "Pauline theology," which is seen by some as a label best reserved for contemporary systematizations of what the apostle wrote) are viewed by most as essentially interchangeable labels to describe the presuppositions, convictions, and concerns that inform and distinguish Paul's interpretation of the gospel.[23] It changes the nature of our quest in fundamental ways to speak of a search for the foundational story, especially since Paul's presuppositions, convictions, and concerns have already operated on the story. That is to say, the narrative that Hays has outlined is probably not the story that Paul received. It seems to bear clear traces of Paul's contributions to it. Are, for example, the universal implications of the Abrahamic promise part of the pre-Pauline tradition, or do they derive from Paul? How much of the theological reflection on the death of Jesus antedates Paul, and how much of it is Paul's own? Is the understanding of the significance of Jesus' faithfulness (or faith in Jesus) Paul's own insight or an insight that he received from others? It seems to me that the story does not simply influence Paul's theological statements to the various churches, but Paul's theology or thought has influenced the story itself. If that is the case, then Paul's theology or thought lies behind this version of the foundational story and remains, I think, the valid object of our quest. With this "foundational story," then, we have not yet reached the foundation. Indeed, we need to visualize the situation in a somewhat different way.

IV. ANOTHER MODEL
FOR CONSTRUING PAUL'S THEOLOGY

Various models or metaphors have been proposed to help clarify our understanding of Paul's theology. Some suggestions, like ellipses, binary

---

[22] See, e.g., Sampley's essay, "From Text to Thought World."
[23] This definition is Furnish's; see n. 16 above.

stars, and electromagnetic fields, have had short but useful life-spans.[24] Two images, however, keep coming back into the conversation, suggesting perhaps their greater pedagogical or hermeneutical potential: a jigsaw puzzle and a lens. These two images have been used in very different ways in the rhetoric of the papers. The puzzle image was used to underscore the very real difficulty of the task of delineating Paul's theology, if not to indicate a growing sense of despair. Thus, for example, Scroggs spoke of missing pieces of a puzzle impressed with a vague picture, while William Baird warned us that the pieces keep changing shape even as we try to fit them together.[25] The lens image, however, has been put to more positive use to convey an understanding of Paul's theology as an *activity,* for something *passes through* a lens and is transformed by it.

This understanding of Paul's theology as an activity is, I believe, crucial to our task, though occasionally it tends to be obscured. Thus, for example, when N. T. Wright defined Pauline theology as "that integrated set of beliefs which may be supposed to inform and undergird Paul's life, mission, and writing" and then specified the content of this set of beliefs,[26] a static view of theology was conveyed. Later in his paper, however, this gave way to a larger vision: "What, if anything, did Paul *do* with these beliefs? . . . How has he *modified* the Jewish doctrine of election? . . . How has the Pharisaic attitude to the Gentiles . . . *been taken up and reshaped,* and why has it been done like this? Questions such as these . . . are the stock-in-trade of what 'Pauline theology' is all about."[27] Likewise, Krentz has defined the theology of 2 Thessalonians as "a *response* to human need, hope, and aspiration in a time of persecution," and Hays has pushed us "to study the hermeneutical *transformations* that Paul performs."[28] All of these statements point to a construal of theology as an activity, but an activity more complex than the rather simple optical images have thus far conveyed.

The images that have been presented so far have been of simple optical systems with a single "lens" or "prism." Krentz, for example, defines apocalyptic conviction as the lens that focuses "the letter's theology on the traumatic situation of the church," while Hays refers to "the hermeneutical lens through which Paul projects the images of the community's symbolic

---

[24] See, e.g., *Pauline Theology I,* 6, 66.

[25] Scroggs, "Salvation History," 215; William Baird, "Response to Richard B. Hays," paper distributed to members of the Pauline Theology Group in 1988.

[26] Wright, "Putting Paul Together Again," 184.

[27] Ibid., 196 (emphases mine). If one puts Wright's two comments together, this suggests that what Pauline theology is *about* is different from what Pauline theology *is.*

[28] Krentz, "Through a Lens," 52 (emphasis mine); Hays, "Crucified with Christ," 246 (emphasis mine).

world."[29] Yet it is becoming increasingly clear that this metaphor, with its single optical device (lens or prism), does not adequately or accurately construe the full range of activities that constitute Paul's theology. It is necessary to think in terms of a more complex series of activities, *all of which contribute to Paul's theology and none of which in isolation is* Paul's theology. If we retain the optical metaphor for a moment longer, we might begin to imagine the following.

The *raw material of Paul's theology* (the kerygmatic story, scripture, traditions, etc.) passed through the *lens of Paul's experience* (his common Christian experience as well as his unique experience as one "set apart by God for the gospel") and generated a *coherent (and characteristic) set of convictions.* These convictions, then, were refracted through a prism, Paul's *perception of the situations that obtained in various communities,* where they were resolved into specific *words on target for those communities.*[30]

Even this model distorts terribly. It is clear, for example, that Paul's convictions continued to shape his understanding of the kerygmatic story, and that this shaped story, along with the convictions and theological conceptions that arose from it, was brought to bear on specific situations. Nevertheless, the model helps to locate the various aspects of Paul's theology that have been discussed. It also emphasizes the shaping role of experience in the process and formally acknowledges "theology" as an activity rather than a set of theological propositions or presuppositions. Indeed, it suggests a working definition of Paul's theology as his critical appropriation and application of the Christian witness,[31] a definition that embraces not only Paul's thought world, his thoughts, and his targeted communication of them,[32] but also the process of movement from one to the other.

If this is a reasonable definition of Paul's theology, then it raises serious questions about the way we have envisioned our task. According to the

[29] Krentz, "Through a Lens," 52 (in an earlier version of this paper, Krentz spoke of a "prism through which the illumination of a theologian's thought is reflected"); Hays, "Crucified with Christ," 228.

[30] No one, of course, has done more work on defining Paul's theology in terms of a coherent center and contingent expressions than J. Christiaan Beker, and this model owes much to his work. (See, e.g., his recent clarification of his coherence-contingency scheme in "Paul the Theologian: Major Motifs in Pauline Theology," *Int* 43 [1989] 352–65.) The present model, however, encourages us (among other things) to describe more closely the nature of the convictions that derive their coherence from what Beker calls the apocalyptic "substratum of Paul's thought."

[31] I have found very helpful here C. M. Wood's comments in *Vision and Discernment* (Atlanta: Scholars Press, 1985) 21–35.

[32] See Sampley, "From Text to Thought World," 4. Scroggs has questioned whether this triadic formulation does not imply more rigid distinctions than were actually operative in Paul's theology ("Salvation History," 213). By emphasizing theology as an activity that involves movement from one category to another, I have hoped to overcome that problem.

original plan, explorations of the theologies of various letters were to be accompanied by ongoing synthetic work, in which the elements of Paul's thought identified in the individual letters were summarized and organized into coherent and appropriate patterns. Yet it is not clear that such a synthesis contributes significantly to an understanding of Paul's theology as I have defined it here. Overarching patterns may become visible, but there is always a danger that these patterns are our own creation. More seriously, the discrete circumstances of each instance of Paul's theologizing will be lost, and the activity that is Paul's theology will be replaced by superimposed patterns of possible outcomes. In fact, this activity cannot be effectively addressed by summarizing or synthesizing the work on the theologies of the various letters. We need to go back to the texts themselves and ask a somewhat different set of questions of them. What resources has Paul used, and how has he used them? What theological conceptions and religious convictions have consistently structured his arguments, and how have they structured them? If the papers on the individual letters focus on the specific arguments Paul has crafted for particular congregations, these papers will seek, among other things, to understand the fundamental presuppositions or convictions that lie behind and influence all the arguments.

Clearly this is not something that can be accomplished in a brief paper such as this. What is called for is a series of studies focusing on texts that can reveal the different aspects of Paul's theologizing. Here I can only begin to explore one aspect of the investigation: the presuppositions and convictions that underlie and undergird the arguments of Paul's letters. This should involve not speculations about what *could* have informed Paul's arguments but a careful analysis of the convictions that do, in fact, inform them.

Daniel Patte's work suggests a helpful approach. Beginning with a definition of faith as "nothing other than holding to a system of convictions or, better, being held by a system of convictions," Patte explores the nature of convictions and the way one might uncover them in Paul's argument. "A conviction," he says, "is a self-evident truth." One can thus locate convictions in an argument by determining what is "established as self-evidently good and desirable." One can also look for convictions "about what is real and what is illusory" in the situation under discussion.[33] Patte raises these questions — and others — in the interest of a structural reading of Paul's letters, and his analysis moves on to consider the interrelationship of the convictions and their pair-wise arrangement. Yet his questions are also helpful, it seems to me, to those of us who would ask more simply about the convictions that inform Paul's letters to various communities.

---

[33] Daniel Patte, *Paul's Faith and the Power of the Gospel: A Structural Introduction to the Pauline Letters* (Philadelphia: Fortress, 1983) 11, 17, 19.

I propose to begin with the opening verses of 1 Thessalonians (1:2–5). (The text was chosen for its simplicity, not its theological significance.) Once the underlying convictions of these verses are uncovered, we can determine whether these same convictions appear to any significant degree in the rest of the argument of this letter or in the other Pauline letters. Piecemeal analyses of this sort would slowly build up a mosaic of the theological convictions that undergird the arguments in Paul's letters.

V. 1 THESSALONIANS: A QUEST FOR CONVICTIONS

When one asks about what is assumed as self-evidently good and desirable in this portion of the argument, the participial clause in v. 3 provides an answer: "Remembering before our God and Father your work of faith and labor of love and steadfastness of hope in our Lord Jesus Christ." Faith, love, and hope are assumed to be self-evidently good, for Paul regards these attitudes or activities to be worth mentioning in his prayers of thanksgiving to God. Later, of course, Paul will clarify in a rather pointed way precisely what aspects of faith, love, and especially hope are appropriate to the Thessalonians' situation. Yet the conviction Paul brings to the argument at this point (and the structure of the argument implies that Paul assumes that the Thessalonians share this conviction) is that faith, love, and hope are good and desirable attitudes for the Thessalonians to hold. One cannot draw any prioritizing conclusions from the sequence of the three items or from the rhetorical weight that the piling up of liturgical language seems to place on the third. An analysis of the rest of the letter confirms that the Thessalonian situation has influenced how Paul has presented—and ranked—the elements of this triad.

Convictions concerning what is good and desirable will influence, above all, the shape of Paul's exhortations. At a somewhat more fundamental level, at the level of the "heart and driving force" of these letters, will be those convictions that fall into Patte's category of "what is real," for here Paul's "symbolic universe" is revealed. Paul's comment in v. 4 seems rooted in this sort of conviction: "For we know, brothers and sisters beloved by God, that he has chosen you." Paul's conviction concerning the reality of the Thessalonians' existence is that they are beloved and chosen by God. This conviction, however, does not stand alone. Paul describes what led him to that conviction— the demonstrations of power that accompanied his preaching to them, the presence of the Holy Spirit, and his own boldness (v. 5a)—and he attempts to convince the Thessalonians of this interpretation of reality by appealing to their recollection of how he behaved among them (v. 5b). The basic convictions thus seem to be, first, the conviction concerning the Thessalonians' election and, second, the conviction that this election is evident in the spiritual signs that accompanied Paul's preaching among them, including the sign of his own Spirit-inspired boldness.

Elsewhere in the letter these two convictions (election and the confirming presence of the Spirit) reappear in the argument. Thus, in 1:6b Paul interprets without further explanation the Thessalonians' joy in the face of tribulation as deriving from the Holy Spirit (μετὰ χαρᾶς πνεύματος ἁγίου), and in 2:2 he affirms without further comment that his own courage in the face of affliction came from God (ἐπαρρησιασάμεθα ἐν τῷ θεῷ ἡμῶν). A few verses later (2:4) Paul asserts as part of his defense that he has been approved by God (καθὼς δεδοκιμάσμεθα ὑπὸ τοῦ θεοῦ), and later in the same chapter (v. 12) he suggests essentially the same thing of the Thessalonians, when he reminds them of his admonishments to walk worthily of *the God who called them* (ἀξίως τοῦ θεοῦ τοῦ καλοῦντος ὑμᾶς). Paul's subsequent reference (v. 13) to God "who is working in you" (ὃς καὶ ἐνεργεῖται ἐν ὑμῖν) fits this pattern of assertions, though here it again receives further grounding by a reference to the Thessalonians' experience (v. 14). On the other hand, a later reference to "God, who also gives his Holy Spirit to you" (4:8) stands without further confirmation.

These statements asserting that God (through the Holy Spirit) is the power behind Paul's proclamation of the gospel and the Thessalonians' life in it and, further, that Paul has been elected to his task as the Thessalonians have been elected as God's beloved seem to function at a fundamental level in the argument. Though an affirmation of God's election and presence is appropriate to any situation of persecution (and certainly the Thessalonian church was in such a situation), these assertions are not the argumentative goal of the argument but serve repeatedly to undergird it. It is important to note how they function in the argument. God's election of the Thessalonian Christians, their status as "beloved by God," is the primary ground for Paul's expression of thanksgiving. The presence of the Holy Spirit is regarded as proof of this status, and this presence can be detected in the (unspecified) nature of Paul's actions (1:5) and in the joy and courage both Paul and the Thessalonians exhibit in the face of affliction (1:6; 2:2). Somewhat later in the letter Paul uses the concept of election to ground his ethical exhortations (2:12) and, in a subtle shift from his earlier argument, finds evidence of God's presence with the Thessalonians in the suffering which aligns them with the other churches in Christ Jesus (ἐν Χριστῷ Ἰησοῦ, 2:14). Thus the election of the Thessalonian Christians and the sealing of that election through the presence of the Holy Spirit in their congregation emerge as fundamental convictions through which Paul consistently interprets their world and motivates their behavior.

It should not be difficult to demonstrate that the same convictions can be found in the other letters under our purview. Indeed, to demonstrate this is probably an exercise in stating the obvious. In Phil 1:7, for example, Paul again grounds his thankfulness for the church in his conviction of their election ("All of you share in God's grace with me"). Ethical admonitions to the Philippians are grounded by the conviction of God's presence in or among them (2:13), and Paul cites the example of his own life to support this point: "I press on to make it my own, because Christ Jesus has made me his own" (3:12).

In Galatians the thread is somewhat clearer. There is, of course, no expression of thanksgiving in this letter, but the opening statement of astonishment is rooted in the same conviction of election: "I am astonished that you are so quickly deserting *the one who called you*" (1:6). Similarly, Paul's vigorous defense of his gospel appeals to his *own* sense of election (1:15). Later in the argument of the letter, as Paul seeks to convince the Galatians of the efficacy of grace appropriated through faith, it becomes clear that here too the conviction of the experience of God's grace rests, or ought to rest, on the detection of the active presence of the Spirit within the community. No "evidence" is presented here to demonstrate the presence of the Spirit, but the shared conviction of its presence functions at the basic, taken-for-granted level of the argument in 3:1–5:

> You foolish Galatians! Who has bewitched you? It was before your eyes that Jesus Christ was publicly exhibited as crucified! The only thing I want to learn from you is this: Did you receive the Spirit by doing the works of the law or by believing what you heard? Are you so foolish? Having started with the Spirit, are you now ending with the flesh? Did you experience so much for nothing?—if it really was for nothing. Well then, does God supply you with the Spirit and work miracles among you by your doing the works of the law, or by your believing what you heard?

The issue of election is particularly strong in 1 Corinthians. Paul opens the letter by affirming not only his call ("called to be an apostle of Christ Jesus by the will of God") but also that of the Corinthians ("called to be saints," 1:2). This conviction reappears in the final verse of the thanksgiving, functioning there as part of the ultimate ground for Paul's confidence (1:9): "God is faithful; by him you were called into the fellowship of his Son, Jesus Christ our Lord." When the issue surfaces again a few verses later with renewed rhetorical emphasis (1:24, 26–30), it becomes clear that the concept of election or call no longer merely undergirds Paul's argument; it has instead become the focus of this argument. The Corinthians, it seems, have not grasped what election means. Since the significance of election is so prominent a part of the problem Paul faces with this church, and since election is quite regularly confirmed by the Spirit, it is not surprising that there is also evidence of a dispute over the significance of the presence of the Spirit within the community (chaps. 12–14).

The conviction of an election sealed by the presence of the Spirit is thus not only in many ways the basis for what Paul has to say; it is also the basis for the act of writing itself. It is out of Paul's own sense of election that he writes, and he writes to the various churches, not simply because he is interested in their welfare (though he is), but because he knows that they also are elected and beloved by the God who called him. Not only is this obvious from the letters themselves, but in various ways the same points have been highlighted in earlier papers. Thus, Krentz mentioned the primacy of the concept of call in 2 Thessalonians, and Wright focused on monotheism and election as emerging centers of Paul's theology (as did Hays).[34]

Clearly, we are beginning to achieve some consensus on at least one important component of Paul's theology or theological activity. I would, however, like to use the model I have tentatively proposed in order to change somewhat the way we construe this. Wright, for example, has presented election and monotheism as a set of beliefs that functioned as "boundary markers," first within Judaism and then in the Pauline communities.[35] It seems to me that the evidence suggests, when you start with 1 Thessalonians, that these did serve as boundary markers when the circumstances of the community required it, but this was an application of these convictions, not an inherent aspect of them. Rather, a sense of call and a sense of God's presence were basic convictions that Paul brought to his pastoral task of writing letters, and there they could undergird the argument in various ways.

The centrality of the convictions of divine call and presence also sheds light on the significance of the kerygmatic story that Hays has emphasized.[36] The story is important to Paul and his churches not simply because it was the *kerygmatic* story but because it was *their* story. By God's election they had been grafted into it, and their sense of being a part of this story of God's presence with God's people is the only reason for remembering the story and writing to the churches. It is the conviction in this form, and only more

[34] Wright, "Putting Paul Together Again," 184; Hays, "Crucified with Christ," 235–38.

[35] Wright, "Putting Paul Together Again," 195: "Monotheism and election served not so much as abstract beliefs, mere propositions to which intellectual assent should be given by the thinking Jew, but as truths to be celebrated, as boundary markers round the community, as symbols of national and racial solidarity." Earlier (p. 185) he emphasized the importance of these boundary markers for Paul: "This is so [the vital importance of faith], not because he [Paul] is an idealist wishing to achieve a coherence of abstract thought for its own sake but because he is anxious about the boundary markers of the communities he believes himself called upon to found and nurture."

[36] See above, 7–8.

distantly the story itself, that is part, at least, of the "heart and driving force" behind the various letters.

VI. CONCLUSION

I make no claim to have uncovered *the* center of Paul's theology. It no longer seems completely accurate to speak of his theology in this way. I have argued that instead we should self-consciously begin to construe Paul's theology as an activity, and that way of construing it should change somewhat how we approach our task.[37] Instead of focusing exclusively on the outcome of this activity or seeking to isolate a core of his theology, instead of looking for a set of doctrines, for example, or theological propositions, we need to address the far more complicated question of how Paul theologized. Paul certainly brought the kerygma to bear on his arguments, in the form of both narrative and appeal. He gave ethical instructions (rooted in his convictions of what is good and desirable), and he cited and interpreted scripture. We need to investigate more closely how he used these resources in his letters. But if the phrase "heart and driving force" has any significance for construing his theology, and if by this phrase we mean that which *compelled* him to write as he did, then it seems to me that the convictions Paul held about what is real are a legitimate and important object of our quest. In this brief paper I have focused on one of the convictions Paul brought to this activity. Surely there are more, and these too need to be analyzed. A tidy summary of "Paul's theology" will not do. We need to look instead at the rather messy topic of Paul's theologizing.

[37] I find exceedingly interesting Furnish's suggestion that "while Paul's letters do not yield any kind of a comprehensive theological system, they do introduce us to Paul the theologian" ("Theology in 1 Corinthians," p. 61 below). This seems entirely compatible with my recommendations here.

2 SEEKING A MORE FLUID MODEL

A Response to Jouette M. Bassler

Steven J. Kraftchick
Princeton Theological Seminary

I. INTRODUCTION

PROFESSOR BASSLER'S OPENING REMARKS indicate that she has taken an alternative direction in this paper — an approach I think is helpful and provocative because it provides us with an opportunity to reflect on our procedures and because it can prevent us from succumbing to forms of theological or methodological myopia.

Bassler notes that since 1986 there has been a continual struggle to define the object of the group's search. In her view the lack of definition of the term "theology" is especially troublesome because we are searching for two different forms of theology: (1) the theologies of the individual letters and (2) the theology that results from an ongoing synthesis of these individual theologies (p. 3). The initial problem is that the lack of clarity concerning theology is compounded when we move to the synthesis level. A second and equally crucial problem has materialized because we have not agreed on the ways in which we will produce these synthetic theologies. Hence, she asks, "Does a synthesis seek to find patterns through a summation of the individual theologies, or does it seek somehow to find a locus of commonality *behind* the divergent expressions of Paul's thought?" (p. 3). In other words, is a theology of Paul to be found in the letters, or is it the material/essence which generates the letters?

For Bassler, addressing these problems should precede the actual analyses, if possible. One could argue, as the group has done (at least implicitly), that definitions and procedures could be worked out in the process of doing the analytical and synthetic work. However, Bassler suggests that this has not been the most fruitful way in which to proceed, and so she has chosen to ask us to focus on definitions and procedural matters. Thus she poses three questions for the group's consideration: (1) What are we talking about when we refer to a theology of a letter? (2) What should a synthesis of these theologies focus on? And (3) How are these two entities related to the larger goal of "a fresh understanding of Paul's theology in general?" (p. 4).

In answering these questions Bassler proceeds along two lines of critique. First, she exposes a problem that arises out of her examination of individual papers (e.g., Sampley, Krentz, Gaventa, Martyn), that is, the use of the term "theology." Because there is no agreement on the term, Bassler concludes that vast differences exist between the procedures adopted for the analysis of individual letters. Since the target is viewed differently by various writers, their methods and results are significantly different—so much so that it is difficult to assess them individually and even more difficult to synthesize them. Second, she questions the process of the group as such and doubts the wisdom of keeping our present format of synthesis. If Bassler had stopped here, she would have provided enough fuel for heated discussion, given the cruciality of the above questions. However, the paper goes further: it suggests an alternative conception of theology and a process of analysis commensurate with it.

By way of response I will give an overview of what I consider to be the main thrust of her paper, ask some questions of clarification concerning her proposed model of theology, and then offer some reflections on the implications of such a proposal for the ongoing seminar.

II. OVERVIEW

Bassler asks two questions of the group's activity: Whence? and Whither? Under the rubric of "Whence?" she raises questions about interpreting the individual letters of Paul and the attempts to write ongoing syntheses of these individual analyses. When she turns to "Whither?" she offers a critique of Hays's proposal to view Paul's use of the kerygmatic narrative as a key for unlocking his theology. Finding significant problems with such a narrative approach, she returns to the idea of theology and offers her own proposal— to view theology as an activity, which she then demonstrates by an analysis of 1 Thessalonians.[1]

---

[1] Bassler understands that theology incorporates form, content, and activity. I should think that a coined term such as "theologizing" rather than theology would be to her liking since she wishes to stress the activity in this equation.

"Whence?": Individual Letters

Bassler observes that the initial task defined by the consultation was a descriptive one, but she asks "descriptive of what?" (p. 4). In other words, if we do not know the goal of our search, how can we determine which tools will help us discover it, and how will we know the goal if and when we find it? Moreover, she asks, Where is the theology of the letter located? On the surface or in the deep structure? (p. 4). The lack of guidelines for answering these questions has led the consultation to three related but distinct definitions of the letter's theology: (1) the theological argument of the letter (Krentz, Gaventa); (2) the tension between the argument of the letter and the theological position of the community addressed (Sampley); and (3) the theological event evoked by the letter (Martyn).[2]

This unclarity evokes an obvious question: Can there be helpful analyses (in the sense of the overall goal of the group) if the term "theology" is given this range of connotations? Analyses based on such diffuse definitions of theology will be extremely difficult to review and synthesize. In this context she correctly reminds us that defining terms is an essential part of the investigatory process. She is also correct in proposing this lack of definition as a prime culprit in the previous analyses we have received. However, I think that other culprits for these variations suggest themselves with equal if not more potency for trouble. For instance, three quickly come to mind:

(1) An initial desire to proceed from the individual letters outward to a Pauline theology was generated by the concern not to allow preconceived notions of that theology to color our deliberations. However, despite our intentions this has not proved very effective since hidden assumptions of how the larger picture of Paul's thought is construed and related to his individual letters still come into play in the investigations.

(2) We agree that historical context is important for our investigations, but because of the inherent difficulties of producing historical scenarios for the letters, there are differing degrees of confidence in the reconstructions of the settings and the portraits of Paul's conversation partners. These reconstructions have affected our conceptions of the main topics of discussion in the letters and hence those points which are most crucial in them.

(3) There is the difficulty of establishing what the proper means of

---

[2] Bassler suggests, rightly, that definitions 1 and 2 are related, and here she reflects the concern of J. C. Beker throughout his work that the argument of the letter is conditioned by the contingent circumstances in which it takes place. Further, she is correct in distinguishing the response, hoped-for or actual, from the letter's theology, for the two are not necessarily the same (p. 5).

investigation will be, that is, which methods are necessary *and* sufficient to explore the initial letters. These difficulties would obtain even if there were agreement on the definition of the term "theology" among us.

"Whence?": Synthesis

Bassler recognizes that the quest for individual theologies is a minor aggravation in comparison to the synthetic task. She states, "the attempts to generate a gradual synthesis of these theologies have faced even greater problems. Not only does the lack of agreement concerning the definition of a given letter's theology generate problems for the synthetic task, but the amount of data to be synthesized, though manageable in the early stages of our work, has rapidly become overwhelming" (p. 5). Even more of a problem is the lack of agreement about the object of the syntheses and their relationship to Paul's theology as a whole (pp. 5–6). The combination of these factors makes the enterprise extremely difficult.

She notes that the group has thus far agreed on two things: (1) Paul is not a systematic theologian; and (2) deconstructive analyses of recent years do not pass the "test of satisfaction" proffered by R. B. Hays (p. 6).[3]

---

[3] Here I want to register a mild voice of dissent. Perhaps those forms of deconstruction offered by Räisänen and others have not met this criterion; however, this should not rule out deconstructive work per se. In this regard we need only note the deep temptation to self-deception which befell those researchers in the nineteenth century who sought the essence of Jesus' thought. A strong dose of deconstruction would have proved quite helpful there. Note here the comments of Werner Kelber:

> Deconstruction draws attention to the negations with which all affirmations of value are pregnant, and which we tend to suppress. It enables us to explore the hidden contradictions and coverups, the displacement features and narrative mislocations on which the gospels are thriving. Last but not least deconstructionism can help expose our multiple logocentric escapes from the realities of the gospels, whether it be the positivity of revelation in our historical, theological readings, the imposition of unqualified unity and coherence in the New Criticism, the phenomenology of human consciousness in reader-response criticism, or the prestige of stable foundationalism in structuralist thought" ("Gospel Narrative and Critical Theory," *BTB* 18 [1988] 135).

Paul may not write a gospel, but the idea that he is dependent on a narrative suggests that Kelber's remarks apply both to Paul's letters and to us. Further, one might raise a figure such as Wittgenstein, a thinker at least as cryptic as Paul, who proposed to make himself heard through discourse rather than letter. Even so, he has proved notoriously difficult to systematize, and most attempts have reflected the concerns of the interpreters rather than Wittgenstein's own. Nevertheless, even though his work resists essential characterization, it has been extremely influential for subsequent philosophy. Could it not be the case that Paul too is unable to be categorized and that the attempts to do so are our own constructions rather than his? See A. C. Grayling, *Wittgenstein* (Oxford: Oxford University Press, 1988) 116–19.

Granting that Paul is not a systematic theologian, we are fairly confident that there is some form of material to be found in the letters which "dispels any abiding sense of mere opportunism or intellectual chaos on the part of the apostle" (p. 6). We also agree that this thing never comes to expression in a noncontingent manner. In this context Bassler raises the question: "Is it the goal, then, of a synthesis to summarize and systematize these words on target, or should it attempt to get behind the contingent expressions? If so, how far behind them dare we or need we go, and how shall we get there?" (p. 6). More to the point, Bassler wonders if synthesis is possible. Reviewing the work of Beker, Scroggs, and Reumann, she notes that the question of the possibility of synthesis remains a matter of debate for the group, although the group has proceeded as if the answer is yes (pp. 6–7).

At this level the problems become even more complex than at the level of individual letter analysis. For instance, is this synthesis to be found in, under, or above the texts? And is it found in beliefs, conceptions, convictions, or a story (p. 7 n. 16)? But I would suggest that the matter is even more complicated. Even if answers to these questions should be forthcoming, we would still have to determine the relative weight of the individual letters and their respective expressions. We cannot move to a synthesis until the prior question of the relative weight of the letters is settled, because the proportionate mixture of the letters is unclear. Any synthesis could be, and in all likelihood would be, unduly biased. To change the illustration, we cannot simply place all the letters in a large pot, boil them for a specified length of time, and arrive at Paul's theology. There is the problem of how much 1 Corinthians, or Romans, or another letter should be added to the recipe. Should the expressions of Philemon or those parts of Corinthians that are situational and socially bound have equal strength in the mixture? Do we add equal amounts of 1 Thessalonians and Romans, or do some ingredients play a more important role in the final product? Such questions preclude a quick move to syntheses, even if we agree about their goal or the manner of reaching it.

Whither? Narrative or Theology?

On this issue Bassler supplies us with a pithy and significant critique of R. B. Hays's proposal. She makes forceful points with her comments about the term "story" (e.g., its neat fit with current trends within theology), its allusive nature, and its influence (pp. 7–9). Her questions about the relationship of the story to the traditions Paul has inherited and the matter of *how* he uses the story are especially acute. She notes:

Thus, I still need to be convinced that Paul approached the problems in his churches "by thinking through the situation in the light of the (foundational) story." We really *do not know* if Paul did that or if that was the *only* way Paul approached problems; and, if it was not, then it is difficult to justify on the basis of the letters themselves the claim that a foundational *story* provides the ground of coherence in Paul's thought. (p. 9)

In other words, the theology of Paul is not found in the narrative, nor in "thinking through it" (Hays) but rather in why at certain points he stresses one aspect of the narrative and at other instances another (pp. 11, 16–17). Bassler is correct when she, while positing that a "foundational story" is part of Paul's raw material, points out that Paul's theology resides in his use of such material and his reworking of it. Thus the question is why he invests certain characters within the story with specific traits, qualities, functions, and actions.

Bassler's Activity Model

As an alternative to the current approaches, Bassler proposes another model for investigation of the letters.[4] Her model has two crucial points: (1) theology as activity and (2) the double lens of the process. It comprises the following elements: (1) raw material; (2) the lens of Paul's experience; (3) a coherent set of convictions; (4) the prism of Paul's perceptions of the community addressed; and (5) specific expressions found in letters.[5]

Bassler's model is a significant advance over previous constructs because it shows that Paul's theology is not composed of a set of static beliefs and so on, but is an activity, influenced as much by his experience as by his interpretative framework. Since the model emphasizes theology as activity, it reminds us that failure to attend to the circumstances in which Paul wrote distorts our perceptions and makes the discovery of his thought impossible (as Beker has demonstrated). Bassler's model shows that the key question about Paul is not so much *what* as *how*.[6] Thus she calls the viability and legitimacy of the synthesis process into question (pp. 11–12).

---

[4] Bassler notes that the realization of *process* within Paul's letter production was incipient within the work of Wright, Krentz, and Hays, but she wishes to be more intentional about the exploration of theology as activity than they were (pp. 10–11).

[5] Bassler, following Beker, uses the term "words on target." I would like to suggest that we resist the use of this term because it seems to me to prejudice the case. The words may have been words on target to Paul; they may not be to us or to his recipients. In other words, it is quite possible that Paul may have misconstrued the target and so would have missed the mark with his response.

[6] Note here Beker's idea that the theology of Paul is his hermeneutics. The question is whether that hermeneutics is situated in apocalyptic thought or elsewhere. On this point, see

III. QUESTIONS ABOUT THE MODEL[7]

In Theory

(1) The first thing that strikes me is that, although the model is fluid, it is probably not fluid enough. This is due to the lens metaphor and the linear construction of the model. Moreover, the model suggests that the expressions (element 5 above) are the result of a prior imaginative process and that they arrive on the scene whole cloth. However, we should notice that in some instances (Romans 9–11?) the expressions seem to arise in the very process of writing. Such a process is one with which all of us are familiar, especially when we deal with complex issues. Sometimes Paul discovered where he wanted to go during the act of composition rather than prior to it. Thus, in keeping with the concept of theology as activity, I suggest that this more responsive conception of the expressions be adopted.

(2) The model appears to point in one direction only, but is it not possible that it also returns upon itself, not only after a letter is composed but during the composition? For instance, in the process of writing to the Galatians or the Corinthians, Paul may get a clearer picture of what he believes than when he began, which causes a reshaping of the expressions within the letter. In other words, something triggered Paul's response, and perhaps at one stage he could not positively identify it. He just knew that a certain behavior or expressed belief was incompatible with what he perceived Christianity to be — so that in the process of writing he was able to give expression to his feeling with greater and lesser degrees of satisfaction. In my opinion, Bassler's model should include something about how the "set of convictions"(element 3 above) undergoes modification in the process of Paul's writing. Thus the direction of movement is not a one-way path but a bi-directional one, which means that the lens of Paul's convictions should be perceived as a fluid one.

(3) Furthermore, once Paul found an expression that fitted one situation, is it not possible that he used it in situations where it did not fit? To harp upon

---

H. Boers, "The Foundations of Paul's Thought: A Methodological Investigation." *ST* 42 (1988) 55–68. Note further J. D. Crossan's response to John Gager's question "What went wrong with early Christianity so that it not only survived the failure of its initial prophecies but did so in spectacular fashion?" Crossan says: "My answer to Gager's question is that paradox was even more fundamental than apocalyptic in the tradition and that the latter's failure merely emphasized and enhanced the former's presence and dominance. Following Käsemann's image [that apocalyptic is the mother of Christian theology], as long as the father is paradox, the failures of the mother can hardly stunt the growth of the child." See J. D. Crossan, *Finding Is the First Act* [Philadelphia: Fortress, 1979] 107; John Gager, "Functional Diversity in Paul's Use of End-Time Language," *JBL* 89 (1970) 325–37.

[7] I understand Bassler's intention that this model be taken as a prototype. The modifications that follow are offered in that vein.

my colleague's work, it seems possible that Beker has applied the coherency/contingency schema to situations where it was not suitable, simply because he has become comfortable with it. If so, and if Paul is no less wedded to favorite expressions than Beker, we must admit that the expressions of one letter may have become the raw material (element 1) or lens (element 3) for another and that at times he produced "words off target."

(4) The contents of the model's components must be delineated. For instance, Bassler includes the kerygmatic story, scripture, traditions, and so on under element 1 (raw material), and the combination of Paul's unique and common Christian experience under element 2 (the lens of his experience). This makes sense, but it also raises the question of what constitutes the distinction between the common Christian experiences and the kerygmatic story or traditions. That is, element 1 differs from element 2, but element 2 seems to include it as well.

(5) The ranking of the contents of these components must be considered. For instance, should the impact of the kerygmatic story rank over scripture, or, to the contrary, should scripture rank over the kerygmatic story, since, at least in part, the story is derived from it. Similar questions of rank apply to the other components as well, especially element 3.

(6) Further, should we not distinguish between those traditions which Paul brings forward without modification (e.g., the sovereignty of God) and those which he reformulates (the promises to the ancestors, election, covenant)? And should we not also consider those traditions which he was willing to leave behind so that we may ascertain what he found deficient or unnecessary about them?

(7) Although I, with Bassler, want to include Paul's experience in the mix, we must remember that experiences do not occur without prior interpretative frameworks.[8] The reciprocal function between them needs more

---

[8] See the refutation of the fact–value dichotomy in Hilary Putnam, *Philosophical Papers: Reason, Truth and History* (Cambridge: Cambridge University Press, 1981) 127–49. His arguments apply to the idea of a dichotomy between experience and interpretation as well. He notes:

> We use our criteria of rational acceptability to build up a theoretical picture of the "empirical world" and then as that picture develops we revise our very criteria of rational acceptability in light of that picture and so on and so on forever. . . . What I am saying is that we must have criteria of rational acceptability to even have an empirical world, that these reveal part of our notion of an optimal speculative intelligence. In short, I am saying that the "real world" depends upon our values (and, again, vice versa) (pp. 134–35).

See also G. A. Lindbeck, *The Nature of Doctrine: Religion and Theology in a Postliberal Age* (Philadelphia: Westminster, 1984). He sees a religion as a

> kind of cultural and/or linguistic framework or medium that shapes the entirety of life and thought. . . . It is not primarily an array of beliefs about the true and the good (though it may involve these), or a symbolism expressive of basic attitudes, feelings, or sentiments (though these will be generated). Rather, it is similar to an

attention. Just as interpretive frameworks evoke experiences, so experiences reorient the frameworks, which in turn evoke other experiences. Paul would not have had the experience of "being set apart by God" unless he had some prior sense of God as the one who sets apart. Likewise *his* experience of being set apart served to reframe his interpretative framework and conception of God. Thus, his initial ability to interpret the raw material enabled him to interpret certain experiences as a special call, but that call caused him to revamp his interpretative framework and so view scripture and kerygma differently from his prior conceptions.

(8) Finally, we should note also that Paul's expressions are limited by the historical and rhetorical situation in which he found himself and not only by his perception of that situation. Thus, the sides of the prism (element 4) must be increased. There are instances when Paul's lexicon is limited by the choice of terms his "opponents" have taken over as their own or to which his audience has already assigned a specific meaning. In those instances he can say less than he might wish or he is forced to choose terms that he would not ordinarily use. In other words, the contingent setting is a mixture of historical circumstances, rhetorical device, and Paul's perceptions of the problem at hand.

In Practice: 1 Thessalonians, Philippians, Galatians, and 1 Corinthians

General comments. Some other questions about the model arise when one considers its practical application. In her analysis of 1 Thessalonians Bassler suggests that the presuppositions and the convictions that undergird an argument are good places to begin an analysis of Paul's theologizing. Convictions that underlie the texts need to be uncovered (this in a necessarily piecemeal fashion) and then considered as they play different roles in the letters. She defines convictions (following Daniel Patte) as those statements that are held as self-evident truths and can be established as self-evidently good and reliable (pp. 12–13).

With respect to 1 Thess 1:2–5 Bassler suggests that Paul shows dual convictions: of the Thessalonians' election and of his own Spirit-directed mission (pp. 13–14). These dual convictions "seem to function at a fundamental level in the argument" (p. 14) and "emerge as the fundamental convictions

---

idiom that makes possible the description of realities, the formulations of beliefs, and the experiencing of inner attitudes, feelings and sentiments (p. 33).
Moreover, Lindbeck realizes that the direction is not unilateral, from religion to experience; rather, the causality is reciprocal (pp. 33–34).

through which Paul consistently interprets their [the Thessalonians'] world and motivates their behavior" (p. 14). Thus, one might summarize the convictions that seem to undergird this letter, its language, and its logic in the following way: "God (through the Holy Spirit) is the power behind Paul's proclamation of the gospel and the Thessalonians' life in it" (p. 14). Further, this call is not only a call of election but also a call to community and to holiness; hence, the convictions undergird Paul's exhortations and serve as evidence in his discussions about suffering in the churches (p. 14). Bassler also finds similar convictions in Philippians, Galatians, and 1 Corinthians, but in these letters the convictions take on different functions (pp. 15–16).

In principle this seems a quite reasonable procedure to follow, but I wonder about three things. First, although I know that Bassler does not want to consider them and is not using them in this way, nevertheless Patte's structural theory suggests that "self-evident truths" have some real status in and of themselves. That is, they exist in some foundational sense, whether as structural theories or systems of belief. This causes me to pause because the structural theory necessitates a set of axiomatic truths which are being called into question by contemporary philosophers and theologians who wonder about the existence of such absolutes.[9] I have no doubt that Paul considered certain "truths" to be self-evident, but I hesitate to use the language of "self-evident" lest we start to assign metaphysical status to the label when it is better understood as the believing community's shared conviction about its claims. Second, granting that such convictions existed for Paul, I am not as sanguine as Bassler that Patte's methods for uncovering them are all that helpful. Thus, while I share the desire to clarify the convictions that Paul held and their relationship to one another, I think we will have to spend more time discussing how they are found in his letters.

Third, while the general direction of her inquiry seems correct to me, the issue of whether Bassler's discovery of these convictions is (a) the same as uncovering Paul's fundamental convictions and (b) a sufficient basis for explaining "the how" of Paul's way of doing theology remains an open question. Bassler has uncovered some important *data* for Paul, but I am not sure that they are foundational convictions; nor am I sure that such data, while necessary for investigating Pauline theology, can accomplish the task of accounting for them. In other words, despite her desire to maintain fluidity, her own description may be too static.

---

[9] Thus the place of Derridean critiques, but also those critiques internal to the theological discipline, such as those offered by Mark C. Taylor's *Deconstructing Theology* (New York: Crossroad, 1982) and *Erring: a postmodern a/theology* (Chicago: University of Chicago Press, 1984) or Kevin Hart's very dense but suggestive book *The Trespass of the Sign* (Cambridge: Cambridge University Press, 1989).

The foundational convictions. When Stephen Toulmin describes an argument, he suggests that it is like an organism, and this suits Bassler's idea of theology as activity quite well.[10] However, in order to consider an argument in this manner, Toulmin differentiates between levels of argument. As he studies argumentation, he realizes that an argument is composed on two levels: a presenting level, the macro-argument, and a finer level, the micro-argument that lies underneath the presented argument.[11] It appears to me that Bassler has not sufficiently noted this distinction, and because of this she equates the statements of the surface argument with those "convictions" of the finer level. However, what Toulmin has in mind with his description is an analysis of the finer level. Hence, to do what Bassler is suggesting we must not only concentrate on data and backing but move from the surface statements of the argument to its micro-level.

Moreover, Bassler suggests that those statements which can be made without further requirement as self-evident truths are conviction statements. Sometimes this is true, but there are other reasons that such statements can be made. Chaim Perelman's discussion of "Agreement" in *The New Rhetoric: A Treatise on Argumentation* shows this clearly.[12] Agreements are the starting points of arguments, the premises which serve as the initial basis of the argument and to which the speaker believes the hearers will adhere from the start. Objects of agreement fall into two classes: *the real,* "comprising facts, truths, and presumptions," and *the preferable,* "comprising values, hierarchies, and lines of argument relating to the preferable."[13] My point here is that many statements which meet Bassler's definition of "statements that are so basic that they can support an argument" fall into the category of agreement: they are those points which Paul and his audience agree on from the start. Sometimes these are foundational convictions, but sometimes they are not.

In other words, what Bassler has found in 1 Thessalonians does not yet constitute the fundamental part of Paul's theology. Although these statements are crucial to Paul, at times they function as claims made on data

---

[10] Stephen Toulmin, *The Uses of Argument* (Cambridge: Cambridge University Press, 1958) 94.

[11] Attention to this difference may help in determining how the theology of a letter is and is not coextensive with the argument of the letter. Noticing this means that we must admit that there is a distinction between the argument presented in 1 Thessalonians and the arguments on which that argument is based. To be sure the two are necessarily linked, but they are not the same. I think that much about the seminar's course will be determined by noticing this differentiation and deciding where we seek to investigate the argument. See pp. 12–13 of Bassler's paper.

[12] C. Perelman and L. Olbrichts-Tyteca, *The New Rhetoric: A Treatise on Argumentation* (South Bend, IN: University of Notre Dame Press, 1969).

[13] Ibid., 66.

(i.e., you are called because you manifest the activities of called people, 1:4–5) and at other times as data on which he makes further claims (i.e., since you are called by God you should walk worthily of that call, 2:12). In either case, it is not quite correct to refer to these ideas as fundamental convictions, because the terms are a bit too broad. To be sure, election is important to Paul, a part of his inherited religious belief; but, as Bassler notes in her statements about the arguments in Galatians, the things that were important to both Paul and his congregations were matters of debate. Thus, they were required to call into question the "self-evident" truth of such conceptions, even those as important as election. Since what is under discussion is not election, nor the power of the Spirit, nor Paul's call, but rather how these realities obtain in the light of harassment and strife, the fundamental conviction lies in why Paul wanted to make this connection. With the discovery of Bassler's convictions we are only part way to our goal. Let me be clear, I am not disputing Bassler's analysis per se nor rejecting her suggestions about election, so much as I am calling for a further reflection on the idea of convictions and the definition she has supplied—something that seems to be in the spirit of her paper.

Along the same lines, although the same data reappear in different letters, they are used quite differently in the different contexts. Thus, while election is a starting point in 1 Thessalonians, it is a matter of debate in 1 Corinthians, as Bassler has noted (p. 15). This shows that such material may be part of Paul's convictions or part of his raw data, but not necessarily the trigger mechanism for his theologizing. Although the convictions Bassler describes are necessary parts of Paul's arguments, they are not the foundation of his theologizing but rather its presuppositions or products. This leads me to think that Bassler's analysis does not reach the depths sufficient to uncover the activity of Paul's theology.

Thus, even though these convictions are present in many letters, are they the compelling force that prompts Paul to write? Since this cannot be demonstrated easily, we must ask two questions: (1) Can these convictions be called foundational convictions, in the sense that they are generative of other convictions? (2) Are not such statements better seen as part of Paul's raw material, since they are used in a different manner in various letters? For example, the ideas of election and God's working through the Holy Spirit are not particular to Paul since they were part of the common traditions of early Christianity. Thus, finding such convictions in Paul does not answer the question of Paul's theologizing. Rather, given the model Bassler has provided, the issue is determining *how* they are located in and used by that model.

IV. THEOLOGY AS ACTIVITY

Bassler makes an important suggestion concerning theology as activity. It appears to me that theology is, in many ways, a function of irritation. Sometimes the irritants arise from outside in the form of recalcitrant congregations, opposing voices — both within and outside of the community. Other times they are irritants internal to the author which arise from the realization that two equally upheld convictions are contradictory. Again, this may occur when two convictions produce a third which is incompatible with a fourth. In any of these cases the theologian must engage in explanatory activities, both for the self and for others.[14] It seems to me that Bassler's plan suggests at least five other areas of further exploration.

Analysis or Construction?

If our conception of the task is analysis, then we assume that there is an entity called "Pauline theology" which can be discovered. However, if we conceive of the task as construction, then we assume that the theology is something we build either on the basis of the letters or as something resident underneath them. In the first instance (analysis), the theology would reside *in* the letters. In the second case (construction) the theology resides *below or above* them and is the result of our construal. We should clarify for ourselves which we think is appropriate, but in either case the following matters should be considered.

Attention to the historical context. Here the enterprise must consider the constraints in which Paul worked as they are defined by circumstances. That is, Beker's insistence on attention to the contingent situations is crucial. This observation raises severe doubts about the possibility of the synthetic approach. In this context I want to raise two points:

(1) As much as the contingent situation affects the expression of Paul's gospel, there is an equal, perhaps greater, effect which *his conception* of the gospel has on *his understanding* of the contingent situation, which is all that we have at our disposal. A neglect of this fact will cause us to forget that the historical situation, including both the direct and indirect recipients of the

---

[14] We should explore therefore what we mean by the term "coherent." If we mean some form of logical compatibility, then "coherent" may not apply to Paul's thought. But if we are suggesting that there are forms of connections and structure, then perhaps it does.

letter, are "Pauline constructs."[15] (Bassler notes this in her discussion of the second lens.)

(2) A greater distance between the description of and the actuality of the historical situation must be allowed because of the rhetorical nature of the letters. I am not proposing that Paul was a trained rhetorician, but rather that he was engaged in argument and that often his construction of a situation facilitates his position. In other words, he often reframes his audience's questions or positions in order to expose the inherent flaws of their positions and to set the terms of the argument so that they are manageable. Moreover, he also uses such situational descriptions as part of his argument, as G. Lyons has noted about the autobiographical remarks in Galatians.[16] Thus, we should distinguish between the rhetorical situation that is presented by Paul in the letter and the actual situation that gave rise to it. It is necessary to remind ourselves of these matters because, when we mistake rhetorical verisimilitude for actual settings, we warp our construction of the setting of Paul's remarks and thus engage in a commensurate warping of his thought.

Further delineation of the levels of convictions. When Bassler speaks of convictions, a further inquiry is needed not only with respect to the hierarchy of convictions but also concerning the difference between the deep convictions of the micro-arguments and the convictions expressed in the macro-argument of the surface text.[17] Are these convictions caused by internal or external irritants, or are they perhaps trigger convictions that may have been unknown to Paul until he was engaged in the process of writing? There are, indeed, places in the letters which appear as experimental expressions rather than Paul's last word. They were extralinguistic, more intuition than thought, until he was forced to write them down. In some cases these expressions were only temporarily satisfying, and it is possible that what he has said in a given place may have been reworded or reconfigured in another instance. For example, if the letter to the Galatians failed in its purpose, would Paul stick to those arguments and expressions elsewhere? This consideration may help us to clarify the distinction between the theology of *the letters* and that of *the person*.

Mode of argument from tradition. The difference between modes of argumentation and Paul's free formulation *of the argument* must be clarified. That is,

---

[15] See here L. T. Johnson, "On Finding the Lukan Community: A Cautious Cautionary Essay," in *Society of Biblical Literature 1979 Seminar Papers* (2 vols.; ed. P. J. Achtemeier; Chico, CA: Scholars Press, 1979) 1:87–100.

[16] George Lyons, *Pauline Autobiography: Toward a New Understanding* (SBLDS 73; Atlanta: Scholars Press, 1985).

[17] Once more reflecting Toulmin's distinction. See here also Daniel Patte, *Paul's Faith and the Power of the Gospel: A Structural Introduction to the Pauline Letters* (Philadelphia: Fortress, 1983).

there are occasions when Paul uses a stock-in-trade formulation, derived from rabbinic forms of exegesis, Hellenistic philosophy, or rhetorical techniques, as part of his overall argument. Such types of argument follow particular arrangements which were accepted as such.[18] Failure to note these matters results in falsely attributing to Paul a perspective which is primarily that of the form of tradition. In other words, we must be sensitive to the fact that Paul uses argumentative forms in a manner similar to the way he uses and modifies traditional hymns, songs, prayers, and so on.

Relationship of the person to the writings. Despite the polemic against psychologizing, we cannot ignore the fact that the letters were written by a peculiar — if not altogether strange — person, whether we describe him as a mystic, an apostle, an apostate, or the like. We may lose a key that is vital for understanding the *specific* nature of a Pauline letter if we divorce the man from his writings. Part of Paul's lasting influence may reside in his idiosyncrasies. If we forget this, we simply domesticate the letters. In other words, if the specificity of the person of Paul is omitted, then the resistant nature of his letters can be too easily ignored. The letters are *Paul's expressions,* not ours. Forgetting the person makes it too easy to make his thoughts our own and to forget the alien nature of that thought. We may achieve a form of generalization and application of the letters, but this will be at the expense of their own voice and vitality. We must make sure to guard against making the *theology* of Paul the theology of *Paul.*

Propositional and poetic language. Although propositional language is indeed a necessity for our construal of Paul's theology, there is still an acute question about the sufficiency of such language. We have often noted that no single statement encapsulates all of Paul's theology, and when we move to a set of statements we find ourselves baffled by their relationship and ordering. Thus, no propositional form of Paul's theology has until now proved adequate in explaining the generation of the letters.

Moreover, such a practice assumes the primacy of the literal expression over the nonliteral and implies that the affective forms of language can be replaced by, or are in opposition to, cognitive forms of expression. However, in many semiotic and linguistic circles these assertions have been overturned.[19] In other words, does the attempt to explain such affective, nonliteral

---

[18] See, e.g., the argument in 1 Thess 2:1-12, which A. Malherbe recognized in "'Gentle as a Nurse': The Cynic Background to I Thess ii," *NovT* 12 (1970) 203-17. Consider also the rhetorical techniques followed in the letters which H. D. Betz and others have pointed out.

[19] See here the remarks of Max Black in "Metaphor" in *Models and Metaphor* (Ithaca, NY: Cornell University Press, 1962) 25-47, and the more recent book of Janice Soskice, *Metaphor and Religious Language* (Oxford: Clarendon Press, 1985). Soskice argues:

language by means of propositional statements not amount to an impoverishment of it?

When one consults the letters, it is apparent that Paul often utilizes both poetic images and metaphors to express himself. Since Paul himself found it necessary to combine the two forms of language, perhaps his resort suggests that limiting ourselves to nonmetaphorical language is imprudent. Can we afford to deflate this combination of speech and still arrive at an analysis of Paul that adequately reflects his own theology? To put it more boldly, can there be any sufficient expression of Paul's theology that does not incorporate the use of nonliteral expressions?

To be sure, a turn to imaginary language might result in a form of anarchy. The problem of hermeneutics returns at this point: Do we need a form of *Sachkritik* in order to replace those Pauline metaphors which are misleading or incomprehensible at the present time? If so, how will we construct meaningful metaphors without falling into Bultmann's danger of reductionist schemes?

V. SOME FINAL THOUGHTS CONCERNING THE SEMINAR'S PROCEDURE

We all agree that Paul is an interesting and important thinker, but we must also admit that there is a complexity to his thought and manner that should

---

No metaphor is completely reducible to a literal equivalent without a consequent loss of content. . . . The demand for complete redescription is, in fact, a stipulation that only those metaphors which are direct substitutes for literal descriptions (those which are the least interesting and most dispensable sorts of metaphors) have cognitive significance. But there is no particular virtue in literal language for literal language's sake; we may need to use metaphor to say what we mean and particularly so . . . when we are seeking terminology to deal with abstract states of affairs, entities, and relations (pp. 94–95).

More radical is the statement by T. Jenkins in "Review Article: Janice Martin Soskice. *Metaphor and Religious Language*," *Journal of Literature and Theology* 3 (July 1989) 219–41. There he suggests that metaphor must be considered not as purely ornamental but rather as a fundamental part of speech which makes communication possible:

My concern is with what I call the "vertiginous" quality of metaphor. By using metaphors, we are able to mean more than we say, and sometimes to say more than we mean. Metaphors lie at the "boundary" of communication, where meaning is made possible and, at the same time, its possibility is undermined. This makes for a particular interest, for it may be impossible to discuss anything without resorting to metaphor: there is a whole vision of language implicit in the question of metaphor (p. 219).

Even if one adopts the perspective of Donald Davidson that metaphors have no cognitive meaning other than their literal sense, one must recognize with him that they are functionally different from nonmetaphoric expressions. See Donald Davidson, "What Metaphors Mean," in *On Metaphor* (ed. S. Sacks; Chicago: University of Chicago Press, 1979) 29–45. For a response to and rebuttal of Davidson's positions, see Frank Farrell, "Metaphor and Davidsonian Theories of Meaning," *Canadian Journal of Philosophy* 17 (1987) 625–42.

not be lost since it may be a key to why he remains interesting and important. Indeed, it is stimulating for us to uncover the salient parts of Paul's thought. However, regardless of the methods of inquiry we have adopted, the full recovery of Paul's thought has remained beyond our collective grasp. The complexity of this process may find its origin not in the vagaries of the letters or the murkiness of their historical origin but in the complexity of the human being who wrote them. Lamentably we have few avenues of access open to us which reveal that person. Bassler's paper suggests that our present procedure will not get us to our goal and that, even at the risk of anarchy, we should allow other procedures to supplement the search.

Perhaps it will be necessary to break into smaller task forces, each group focusing on a different aspect—the person, the situation, the traditions, modes of interpretation available to Paul. We must do these things not in order to avoid doing Pauline theology but rather to clear a path to this goal. Thus, we should not mistake the smaller enterprises for the larger one, as we have in the past. Rather, keeping the larger endeavor before us, we can participate in smaller intermediate steps in order to accomplish the full task.

Finally, I want to bring to the surface a question that underlies Bassler's entire paper in order to express my appreciation once more. She wonders if and why the group should continue if it follows its present course of analyzing Pauline texts. Moreover, she is concerned that, while the present procedure will result in a number of papers, many of which may be interesting and valuable in their own right, the larger goal of discovering Paul's theology/theologizing process will be forfeited. I share her concerns and think that it will be helpful for the seminar if we call for a moratorium on such papers until questions of definition and procedure are more fully agreed on. If we ignore her advice, then we can be sure that within a short time a paper similar to hers with similar questions will arise.

Part II

The Theology of 1 Corinthians

3 TOWARD A THEOLOGY OF 1 CORINTHIANS[1]

Gordon D. Fee
Regent College

IT SEEMS NEITHER possible nor desirable to analyze the theology of a letter like this without some degree of "mirror reading" of the historical situation presupposed by the text.[2] Thus my own views on this matter, which at times will color my understanding: (1) this is the third in a *series* of letters between Paul and this church; (2) the letter basically reflects *conflict between Paul and the church* on most of the issues addressed; (3) the basic theological point of tension between them is over what it means to be πνευματικός (a Spirit person); (4) their view of being πνευματικός involved a "spiritualized escha-

---

[1] The tentative nature of my title is related to the fact that of all the literature on 1 Corinthians (some 2,500 journal articles alone), there is not a single piece known to me that attempts this particular task: to deal with the theology of the letter as a whole. The reasons for this are obvious. Our interests in this letter tend to reflect Paul's in writing it—the behavioral aberrations he addresses. There are, of course, scores of items that deal with various aspects of its theology; and several of the commentaries (Barrett, Fee, etc.) offer an introductory section on theological contributions, but these tend to highlight the unique contributions of this letter to Paul's overall theology.

All translations of Pauline texts but one are my own; the solitary exception is 1 Cor 13:4, where I deliberately follow the KJV.

[2] A few words are also in order about basic assumptions: (a) In keeping with the ground rules of the seminar, I have tried to write this paper as if 1 Corinthians were Paul's only extant letter. This is an especially difficult exercise, since one is regularly tempted to point out what Paul does *not* say here in light of other letters (e.g., the relatively sparse use of δικαι- words). And how does one make sense of 15:56 ("the power of sin is the law") without outside help? (b) My task is primarily descriptive; at times, however, such description must consider Paul's assumed symbolic universe—both his own and that shared with his readers. Otherwise, one is bound to create distortions. (c) In keeping with these assumptions, I have approached the task inductively, trying to look at the theology of 1 Corinthians on its own grounds. I have therefore, and without apology, purposely avoided much interaction with the work of others. (d) In much of what follows I assume the exegesis of my recent commentary (NICNT; Grand Rapids: Eerdmans, 1987). In the interest of space, I do not here repeat arguments that appear there; hence the embarrassingly high incidence of footnotes to that work (hereafter cited simply as "Fee").

tology,"[3] wherein because of their experience of glossolalia they considered themselves to be "as the angels" and thought they needed finally only to slough off the body; (5) their false "theology" was informed by popular philosophy tainted with Hellenistic dualism; (6) the net result was a "spirituality" and a "higher wisdom" that were generally divorced from ethical behavior, at least as Paul perceived it.

I. THE CENTRAL ISSUE

Because Paul primarily, and in seriatim fashion,[4] addresses *behavioral* issues, it is easy to miss the intensely *theological* nature of 1 Corinthians. Here Paul's understanding of the gospel and its ethical demands — his theology, if you will[5] — is getting its full workout.

What is at stake is Paul's singular urgency, the gospel itself,[6] which from this letter may be defined as "God's eschatological salvation, effected through the death and resurrection of Christ, and resulting in an eschatological community who by the power of the Spirit live out the life of the future in the present age as they await the consummation."[7]

The *way* the gospel is at stake is in their non-Christian *behavior,* which completely misses its redemptive, transformational nature. More simply, then, the central issue in 1 Corinthians is "salvation in Christ as that manifests itself in the behavior of those 'who are being saved.'" This is what the Corinthians' misguided spirituality is effectively destroying.

Thus three phenomena must be reckoned with in attempting a theology of this letter: (1) Behavioral issues (= ethical concerns) predominate. Paul is urging, cajoling, remonstrating, using every kind of rhetorical device, to get this community both to see things his way and to conform their behavior accordingly, that is, in keeping with the gospel. (2) Even though Paul is

---

[3] Cf. H. Koester's "radicalized spiritualistic eschatology" as his description of alleged pneumatics in Philippi ("The Purpose of the Polemic of a Pauline Fragment [Philippians iii]," *NTS* 8 [1961–62] 330).

[4] At least apparently so. I have argued that a "crisis of authority and gospel" holds all of chaps. 1–6 together and that "worship" holds chaps. 8–14 together.

[5] With regard to the discussion generated by Sampley's paper at the 1986 meeting, I am still prepared to understand Paul as speaking out of his *theological* convictions; but in this case, as in most cases, what is being explicated is his understanding of the gospel.

[6] See esp. chap. 9, where in defense of his own behavior (apparently regarding the eating of marketplace food), Paul emphasizes that he does all things *for the sake of the gospel* (vv. 12, 16–18, 23).

[7] One will recognize that in its own way, although I will not hereafter make a point of it as such, this view of things further supports Richard Hays's model of the narrative framework that shapes Paul's theological reflection (see "Crucified with Christ: A Synthesis of the Theology of 1 and 2 Thessalonians, Philemon, Philippians, and Galatians," in *Pauline Theology I,* 227–46).

clearly after behavioral *change,* his greater concern is with the theological distortions that have allowed, or perhaps even promoted, their behavior. This alone accounts for the unusual nature of so much of the argumentation. For example, the simple and clear response to "division over leaders" (1:10–4:21) is to prohibit it in the name of Christian unity. But Paul scarcely touches on this; his primary concern is with the Corinthians' radical misunderstanding of the gospel (1:18–2:16), and of the church (3:5–17) and apostleship (4:1–13), which their sloganeering in the name of wisdom represents.[8] (3) In every case but two (11:2–16; chaps. 12–14),[9] Paul's basic theological appeal for right behavior is the work of Christ in their behalf. Such appeal begins in the thanksgiving,[10] and is thoroughgoing thereafter. Note for example how crucial to Paul's response the following texts are to their respective issues:

(a) 1:18–25, 26, 30; 2:1–2; 3:11; and 4:15 ("Christ crucified" as God's "wisdom" which effected their salvation) – to strife, both internal and over against Paul, carried out in the name of wisdom.

(b) 5:7 ("Christ our Passover has been sacrificed") – to the church's complacent attitude toward a brother's incest.

(c) 6:11 ("Such were some of you; but you were washed, sanctified, justified, through Christ and the Spirit") – to the church's failure to arbitrate between two brothers.

(d) 6:20 ("You were bought at a price") – to some men going to the prostitutes (and apparently arguing for the right to do so on grounds that the body is destined for destruction).

(e) 7:23 ("You were bought at a price") – to their considering change of status a matter of religious value.

(f) 8:11 (". . . destroy a brother for whom Christ died") and 10:16 (our "fellowship in the blood of Christ," which makes temple attendance totally incongruous) – to the Corinthians' insisting on the right to continue to eat meals in the pagan temples; and 9:12–23 (Paul's defense of his actions as totally for the sake of the gospel) – to their questioning his authority to prohibit temple attendance.

(g) 11:23–25, 26 (the bread and wine of the table as proclaiming Christ's death until he comes) – to σχίσμα ("division") between rich and poor at the table.

---

[8] So also with sexual immorality in 6:12–20 and with their insisting on the right to attend temple feasts in 8:1–11:1. See below on "The Ethical Response." Even in chaps. 12–14 a theology of church (the need for diversity in unity) and of love precedes the specific correctives in chap. 14.

[9] Both of these involve community worship and thus take on a different form of theological argumentation.

[10] One can scarcely miss the christological emphasis that pervades both the salutation and the thanksgiving. The past, present, and future of salvation dominate the paragraph – salvation that God has initiated and Christ has brought about.

(h) 15:1–5, 11 (Christ's death "for our sins" and his resurrection) — to their denial of a future bodily resurrection of believers.

These texts in particular illustrate that the gospel is the central issue. My concern in this paper is to reflect on the various strands of Paul's understanding of the gospel as saving event, including both its theological basis and its necessary ethical response, which alone bring the experience of the gospel to proper fruition.

II. GOD AND SALVATION

The gospel ultimately has to do with God, who alone stands at the beginning and end of all things. Salvation is wholly the result of God's own initiative and activity; God foreordained it and effected it — through Christ. Both the fact and the way he did so reflect his character. Moreover, God's own glory is the ultimate foundation of Pauline ethics (10:31). Since salvation finally has to do with being known by and knowing God (13:12), what makes the Corinthians' persisting in sin so culpable is that it keeps others from the knowledge of God (15:34).

At the same time, however, Paul's own experience of God's saving activity through Christ (as Savior and risen Lord) and through the Spirit (who appropriated it to his life) meant for him, as for the early church before him, an expanded understanding of the one God as Father, Son, and Spirit.[11]

God the Father[12]

In keeping with Paul's Jewish roots, the one and only God is the primary reality, who stands at the beginning of all things as Creator[13] and at the

---

[11] Several texts suggest or imply that salvation is the joint work of the Father, Son, and Spirit. In 2:1–5, Paul's preaching of Christ crucified came with the Spirit's power, so that faith might rest only in God's power (as defined in 1:18–25). In 6:11 the divine passives point to God as the initiator, while the saving activity is effected "in/by the name of our Lord Jesus Christ and in/by the Spirit of our God." In 6:19–20 the body participates in redemption as the temple of the Spirit, whom God has given to the Corinthians, having been purchased by Christ. And in 12:4–6 the diversity of God, as Spirit, Lord, and God (= the Father), is the theological foundation for the necessity of diversity in the Spirit's manifestations in their midst.

[12] Although Paul does not often so designate God — he most often uses the simple designation "God" when referring to the Father — the fact that Christ is God's Son (1:9; 15:28) means that when the two are spoken of conjointly, either one or the other is often called "Father" or "Son" (1:3, 9; 8:6; 15:28).

[13] Although creation language as such is used only once, in an incidental way in 11:9, creation is the point of 8:6 (ἐξ οὗ τὰ πάντα, "from whom are all things" [against Jerome Murphy-

consummation of all things as their goal (8:6).[14] Even though there is little reflection on God's character as such,[15] the God of grace and mercy is always the cause and goal of the saving event. Thus, for example, in the argument of 1:18–2:16, God the Father is the subject of all the saving activity. Having foreordained (2:7) and purposed salvation (1:21), God thus thwarted human wisdom (1:19–20) by setting forth a crucified Messiah as his wisdom and power at work in the world (1:18–25). God also chose for salvation those of humble origins and status, whose only "boast," therefore, must be God alone (1:26–31). And since God's purposes stand in such bold contrast—indeed, as absolute contradiction—to merely human wisdom, human access to those purposes is only through revelation, which God himself made possible through his Spirit (2:7–13).

Likewise, God's *call* is what initiates the believer's experience of salvation (1:9; 7:17–24). The "divine passives" in 1:4–8 and 6:11 assume God as the one who "washes, sanctifies, justifies, enriches, and confirms" those who are being saved. The resultant church thus belongs to God (1:2; 3:9), who made it grow (3:6–7); and because the church is *his* temple, God will destroy anyone who destroys it (3:16–17). Moreover, it is God's faithfulness that provides escape from too severe testing (10:13); and even the manifestations of the Spirit in their midst are the activity of God, who works all things in all of them (12:6–7). Prayer and thanksgiving are thus primarily directed toward God the Father.[16] Finally, it is God who will judge (5:13) or praise (4:5) at the eschaton.

That the true source of the Corinthians' illicit behavior is bad theology—ultimately a misunderstanding of God and his ways—is evident from the beginning, especially with Paul's use of crucifixion language in 1:10–2:16. This language, which occurs only here, stands in deliberate contrast to the

---

O'Connor; see Fee, 374–75]) and is assumed in the analogies of the body in 12:18 and 12:24 ("God has arranged/composed the body as he willed") and of the seed in 15:38 ("God gives it a body as he willed"). Note especially the aorist ἠθέλησεν ("willed") in both cases, although Paul's interest in the latter instance is in the continuation of the creative activity.

[14] See esp. 15:23–28, where after all things (especially the final enemy, death) are subjected to Christ, then Christ himself is subject to God (= "hands over the rule to God the Father," v. 24), "so that God might be all in all." So also the second half of 8:6, "and we for [*eis* = purpose/goal] him."

[15] The reason for this is simple; this is the symbolic universe that the Corinthian believers, even though Gentiles, share with Paul through both the gospel and the scriptures that had become a fixed part of their religious life. Cf. 15:3, 4 ("according to the scriptures") and the frequent appeals to the OT as the final court of appeal for a point Paul wants to make (1:19, 31; 2:9; 3:19, 20; and passim). The little that is said in this letter that reflects on God's character (that God is faithful [1:9; 10:13], a "God of *shalom*" [14:33], who is the source of grace and peace [1:3], etc.) is especially in keeping with the OT revelation.

[16] For prayer see 14:2, 28; for thanksgiving, 1:4, 14; 14:18; 15:57.

Corinthians' fascination with σοφία ("wisdom") and λόγος ("word").[17] God's choice of the cross as his way of salvation, and the subsequent bypassing of the world's beautiful people for the nobodies, was the deliberate expression of his own wisdom to nullify every human machination and idolatry. To those seeking signs, demanding that God perform powerfully on their behalf, the cross is an egregious scandal; to those seeking wisdom, demanding that God be at least as smart as our better selves, the cross is unmitigated folly. But for Paul a crucified Messiah was God's way of turning the tables on these two most common of human idolatries.

The cross, therefore, turns out to be the ultimate expression of God's power *and* wisdom, because it alone could achieve what the gods of human expectations could never do—redeem and sanctify sinners from all ranks of humanity, who by believing (placing their trust in God's folly and weakness) thus lose their own grounds for boasting before God. Here God "outsmarted" the wise and "overpowered" the strong, with lavish grace and forgiveness, and thereby divested them of their strength (1:25). Thus in his crucifixion Christ not only effected salvation for the "called," but ultimately revealed the essential character of God, which is revealed further in the servant character of Paul's apostleship (3:5; 4:1-2, 9-13), and which stands over against every human pretension and boasting. This is what is at issue in 1:10-4:21, their understanding of God and his ways, not mere sloganeering, with its ἔρις ("strife") and σχίσμα ("division"). These latter but reflect human fallenness that has lost its vision of the eternal God.

At issue, it should be noted further, is not mere belief in the reality of the one God. Paul's argument is made possible, both here and elsewhere, precisely because these former idolators (6:9, 11; 12:2) now share this conviction with Paul. Indeed, in their letter to him they play back the twin themes of "one God" and "no reality to an idol" as grounds for their continuing to attend meals in the idol temples (8:4).[18] At issue is their misapprehension of the *nature* of the one God and the nature of idolatry. Paul's response is twofold and allows us to see how the coherence-contingency model works out in his thinking.

---

[17] That these two terms together form one dimension of the problem is to be seen not only by the contrasts in 2:1-5 but especially in the subtle but significant way the whole argument begins in vv. 17-18. Christ sent Paul to preach the gospel "not with σοφία λόγου (= wisdom characterized by λόγος [reason? rhetoric?])," since that would empty the cross of Christ of its significance. "For" he goes on in v. 18, "there is another λόγος, that of the cross, which is God's power for salvation."

[18] Their point seems to have been that "since there is only one God, and thus no reality to the idol, and since food itself is a matter of indifference to God (8:8), then why can we not continue to join our friends at these feasts? We can scarcely be honoring a god, since the god doesn't exist." See Fee, 361-63.

On the one hand, coherence demands that he agree with the fundamental premise that there is only one God. That is the only *objective* reality. Contingency is found in people's *subjective experience* of a variety of "gods" and "lords" as divine beings; and this, too, is a reality that must be reckoned with — especially in the lives of some converts for whom that "reality" has been a powerful conviction (8:7, 10–12). Thus the gods and lords are "so-called," but there is also reality to them, even though not reality as "gods." Rather, Paul argues, on the basis of the OT, the idols are the locus of demons (10:19–22). Thus, what (for former pagans) was subjective reality as a god is in fact also (for Paul) objective reality as demonic. In that way he not only works within their now-shared — and for him unwavering — monotheism, but provides the ultimate reason for the incompatibility of participation in both Christian and pagan meals.

On the other hand, Paul's experience of Christ as Savior and risen Lord has meant for him an expanded understanding of the one God as Father and Son. Thus, picking up the language of the so-called gods and lords (8:5), Paul affirms that "for us" (in contrast to *them* and their obvious polytheism) there is only *one God* — namely, the Father — the source and goal of all things, including us, and *one Lord* — namely, Jesus Christ — the divine agent of all things, including our redemption (v. 6).

Paul does this in such a way as to affirm two realities simultaneously: first, he speaks of the Father and the Son together in the language of deity (one God, one Lord), and, second, he does so in a context where he is at the same time affirming the strictest kind of monotheism. Which leads us directly to Paul's christology.

Christ the Son, Savior and Lord

This is one of the more complex theological issues in this letter. First, as noted, there is every kind of evidence that Paul's thinking about God has been expanded to include the reality of Christ as Son and Lord. Yet, second, there are texts that also seem to suggest a kind of subordination between Christ and God (3:23; 11:3; 15:27–28). Third, and most problematic, is to determine the relationship between christology and soteriology, which is not immediately discernible. Paul does not himself resolve these tensions, first, because either their resolution or simply their affirmation belongs to his and the Corinthians' shared symbolic universe, and, second, because his interest in Christ in this letter is almost altogether soteriological. Christ both saves and sets the pattern for the ethical life of those who are being saved (11:1).

One can scarcely doubt that Paul sees Christ in terms of deity. The basic appellation is the primary Christian confession of "Lord," whose deep roots in the LXX as the appellation for God,[19] however, allows (causes?) Paul to attribute every kind of divine activity to Christ. Thus, believers pray to Christ;[20] to know the mind of the Lord (from Isa 14:13) is now to have the mind of Christ (2:16). The OT "Day of the Lord" has become the "day of our Lord Jesus Christ" (1:8). The Lord whom Israel "provoked to jealousy" in the Song of Moses (Deut 32:21) is now the Lord Christ, whom the Corinthians are provoking by attending idolatrous feasts (10:22). The divine will is both God's (1:1) and the Lord's (4:19; cf. 16:7); and judgment is now the prerogative of the Lord (4:4–5; 11:31). With fine irony Paul designates the one whom the rulers of this age killed as the "Lord of glory" (2:8), picking up the language "for our glory" in the preceding verse, and thus designating the crucified one as Lord of all the ages and inheritor—as Lord—of the final glory that is both his and his people's.

Moreover, one must take seriously that grace and peace come from both God our Father *and* the Lord Jesus Christ (1:3), since one preposition controls both nouns. Thus the Father and Son (and Spirit) cooperate in the saving event. The Father calls; the Lord assigns (7:17); God washes, sanctifies, justifies by the authority of Christ and by the Spirit (6:11); everything God does is "in/by Christ Jesus."[21]

All of this is unthinkable language for a strict monotheist such as Paul and can only be explained in light of his own encounter with the risen Christ. He had "seen Jesus our Lord" (9:1), which serves as the basis for his christology.[22] The resurrection and the designation "Son of God" probably lead to Paul's conviction of Christ's preexistence, which is implied by the affirmation that "all things are through him" (8:6).[23] In any case, this is almost certainly their shared conviction.

[19] There have been occasional objections to this (see P. E. Kahle, *The Cairo Geniza* [Oxford: Basil Blackwell, 1959] 222; G. Howard, "The Tetragram and the NT," *JBL* 96 [1977] 65), but the evidence from the independent use of the LXX in Paul, Luke, Hebrews, and Matthew seems overwhelmingly in favor of the commonly held understanding.

[20] By "calling on the name of the Lord," 1:2; cf. the early Aramaic prayer to Jesus recalled in 16:22 (Μαρανα θα, "Come, Lord").

[21] This formula occurs some twenty-two times in the letter; its precise nuance is especially difficult to pin down. Sometimes it seems to be clearly locative (Christ is the sphere of their new existence); but in other cases it seems just as certainly instrumental (God has acted "in" Christ Jesus). In both cases the high christology is unmistakable.

[22] As well as for much else, I would argue, especially his understanding of grace and apostleship.

[23] So also with "and the Rock *was* Christ" (10:4), which probably intends to designate Christ not simply typologically as the rock at Horeb that "followed them" but also as the Lord, their Rock, whom Israel rejected in the wilderness (cf. Deut 32:4, 15; etc.). On the other hand, 15:47, which is often seen this way, almost certainly refers to his present resurrection existence as "of heaven (=heavenly)" rather than "from heaven" in terms of his origins (see Fee, 792).

What, then, does one do with, "and Christ is God's" (3:23) and "even the Son will be subjected to him . . . so that God might be all in all" (15:28)? The answer seems to lie in Paul's primary interest in soteriology. Whenever he uses Father and Son language (1:9; 8:6; 15:28), his interest is in salvation, which lies ultimately in the one God. Hence, the language of subordination is primarily functional, that is, referring to Christ's function as savior, not to his being as God. In any case, these two realities hold together for Paul: God the Father is the source and goal of all that is; Christ the Lord functions as savior, who effects the saving work of God in human history.

Although Paul does not *explicitly* make this point, Christ the Lord's role as savior further establishes the connection between theology, gospel, and ethics. This is surely the way we are to understand the "hardship catalogue" of 4:11–13. Here is Paul's theology of the cross being applied to Christian life: the whole point of the next paragraph (vv. 14–17) is to urge them to "follow his way of life *in Christ Jesus.*" So also with his "not seeking his own good but the good of the many" as his way of "imitating Christ," which they again are commanded to follow. The life of the Son of God on earth, exemplified ultimately in his crucifixion, serves as the basis and goal of Christian ethics; this is to do all things for God's glory (10:31–11:1).

The Role of the Spirit

More than any other issue, the Corinthians and Paul are at odds over the role of the Spirit. For them "Spirit" has been their entrée to life in the realm of σοφία ("wisdom") and γνῶσις ("knowledge"), with their consequent rejection of the material order, both now (7:1–7) and for the future (15:12), as well as their rejection of the Christian life as modeled by Paul's imitation of Christ (4:15–21). Their experience of tongues as the language(s) of angels had allowed them to assume heavenly existence now (4:8), thought of primarily in terms of nonmaterial existence, rather than of ethical-moral life in the present. Thus Paul tries to disabuse them of their singular and overly enthusiastic emphasis on tongues (the point of chaps. 12–14); but in so doing, he tries to retool their understanding of the Spirit so as to bring it into line with the gospel. There are therefore three emphases concerning the role of the Spirit.

First, despite an emphasis on sanctification, Paul only twice uses the full designation, *Holy* Spirit (6:19; 12:3). Most often he refers to the Spirit *of God* (2:11, 14, 16; 6:11; 7:40; 12:3) or the Spirit who is *from God* (2:12; 6:19). Thus the Spirit's activities are first of all the activities of God. With especially pointed irony Paul argues in 2:6–16 that since the Corinthians are πνευματικοί (Spirit people), they should have understood the cross as God's wisdom; for the Spirit alone knows the mind of God and has thus revealed what was formerly hidden. Since "like is known by like," the Spirit, who alone knows the thoughts of God and whom they have received, becomes the link on the human side for their knowing the thoughts of God. Moreover, by "the Spirit of our God" they have been washed, sanctified, and justified (6:11); only by the Spirit of God is the basic confession made as to the lordship of Christ (12:3); and through one and the same Spirit God gives to the church the variety of manifestations for their common good (12:7–8). Thus Paul thinks of the Spirit not as some energy or influence but as God's own presence at work in their midst.

Second, and related to the first, the Spirit effectively appropriates the work of Christ to the life of the individual believer and the community. Paul's preaching in weakness a message of "divine weakness" brought about their conversion—through the power of the Spirit (2:4–5; cf. 4:20). It is the prophetic Spirit, who reveals the secrets of the heart, that leads to conversion (14:24–25). Hence it was by the Spirit that they themselves were converted (6:11); and by the Spirit they confess Jesus as Lord (12:3). On the analogy of the one-flesh relationship in sexual intercourse, the believer has been so joined to the Lord as to become one S/spirit with him.[24] Furthermore, the Corinthians together became the one body of Christ by their common, lavish experience of Spirit (12:13);[25] and the Spirit's presence in/among them forms them into God's temple in Corinth (3:16).[26] Thus the Spirit belongs to the gospel, not to σοφία ("wisdom") or γνῶσις ("knowledge")[27] or nonmaterial existence.

Third, the Spirit is also the key to ethical and community life. It is especially because they have received the Spirit of God, who is *in you* and makes the body a temple of the Spirit, which thus disallows sin against the body in the form of sexual immorality. This becomes the more pronounced in chaps. 12–14, where the key to true Spirit manifestations among them is to be found in the language of οἰκοδομή ("building up"). After the description of love in chap. 13, which is first of all a description of the character of God and Christ

---

[24] On this translation of this term, see Fee, 204–5.

[25] As noted in the commentary (Fee, 603–6), the basic issue in this text is not how people become believers, but how the many of them (Jew, Greek, slave, free) became the one body of Christ.

[26] Thus the two basic images of the church in this letter (body, temple) are tied directly to the activity of the Spirit.

[27] Surely Paul's heading the list of Spirit manifestations in 12:8 with the λόγος σοφίας ("word/message of wisdom") and λόγος γνώσεως ("word/message of knowledge") is another moment of irony. These "gifts" that are their special province are thus reshaped in terms consonant with the gospel (= message of wisdom, etc.).

(see how it begins with "love [= God] suffereth long and is kind"),[28] he urges that they pursue love and in that context eagerly desire the things of the Spirit, especially intelligible utterances, because they *build up.*

Thus, "salvation in Christ" is the great concern in this letter, because such salvation is at once God's activity in their behalf and the revelation of his character. Therefore, salvation calls them to conform their own behavior to God's, as it is reflected and modeled by Christ and made effective by the Spirit.

III. SALVATION AND ETHICS

The gospel that effects eschatological salvation also brings about a radical change in the way people live. That is the burden of this letter and the theological presupposition behind every imperative. Therefore, although apocalyptic-cosmological language is also found, salvation is expressed primarily in ethical-moral language.

The Human Predicament

In a former day Paul had divided the world into two basic groups: Jew and Gentile. As a Christian he still divides the world into two groups: "us who are being saved" and "those who are perishing" (1:18), the latter now including both the former groups, seen in light of their basic idolatries (power and wisdom) and in terms of their response to the cross as God's saving event (1:20–24). For Paul the preaching of the gospel is intended to save people *from* the one existence and *for* the other. "Such were some of you," he says to them, following a major sin list (6:11); "when you were pagans," he says in 12:2 of their former life in idolatry.

Given the eschatological framework of Paul's thinking (see below), one is not surprised to find him at times referring to human fallenness in apocalyptic-cosmological terms. Idolatry is fellowship with demons (10:20–21); Satan tempts those who lack self-control (7:5); death is the final enemy, obviously one of the ἀρχαί, ἐξουσίαι, and δυνάμεις ("principalities, authorities, and powers") that Christ will destroy at his parousia (15:24–26). Likewise the five items mentioned in 3:22 (world, life, death, present, future) are best under-

---

[28] Here is one of the places where the "rules" of the seminar are especially constricting, since in Rom 2:4 Paul specifically refers to God's character in terms of these two words; but I am unfortunately not supposed to know that, so this matter cannot be further pursued here.

stood as the tyrannies to which people are in lifelong bondage as slaves, and over which Christ has already taken jurisdiction.

The human predicament is also expressed in terms of people's living in the present age, apart from, and over against, God. Three terms describe this existence: The ψυχικοί ("natural persons"), because they do not have the Spirit of God, cannot know what God is about in Christ (2:14). They are also σάρκινοι/σαρκικοί ("made of flesh/of the flesh")[29] — still in the physical body, and as such giving way to the flesh (= sinful nature).[30] The ultimate censure of such people is that they are living κατὰ ἄνθρωπον (as "mere human beings," 3:3–4).

In each case this depiction of the fallen condition stands in contrast to those who are Spirit people, who have thus entered the realm of eschatological existence that stands in contradiction to what is merely human. What is "merely human" belongs to "this world/age" that is passing away (2:6–8); the "disputer of this age" and the "wisdom of this world" do not know God (1:20–21), just as the "rulers of this age" did not understand God's wisdom revealed in Christ crucified (2:8). Because they lack the Spirit, such people have eyes that cannot see, ears that cannot hear, nor can their (merely) human minds conceive what God has done in Christ (2:9).

Despite such ways of expressing the human predicament, however, and because the letter deals mostly with behavioral aberrations, salvation is most often seen as God's response to moral failure. People are sinners, and what God has provided in Christ is salvation from sin. Sin is the deadly poison that leads to death (15:56). Christ died "for our sins" (15:3); and to deny a future resurrection means to deny Christ's resurrection, thus leaving the living still in their sins and the dead without hope (vv. 17–18). Even though ἁμάρτ-("sin") language does not abound,[31] *sin* is the burden throughout the letter. The ultimate exhortation is to "sober up as you ought and stop sinning," precisely because others *do not know God* (15:34). Those who are perishing are thus described as ἄδικοι ("wicked," 6:1, 9) or ἄπιστοι ("unbelieving").[32] If the latter term is most often descriptive, for Paul it is never merely descriptive. People are "wicked," not simply overtly so, but also because they do not believe.

---

[29] I have argued that Paul uses these terms with precision in 3:1–3, to refer to physical existence (3:1, σαρκικός) and to the "sinful nature" (σάρκινος, 3:3), as a twin blow against their false spirituality (see Fee, 121–24).

[30] I would also include here the usage of σάρξ ("flesh") in 5:5. On this much-debated text and reasons for seeing it as referring to the incestuous man's sinful nature, see Fee, 208–12.

[31] ἁμαρτία ("sin," 15:3, 17, 56 [bis]); ἁμάρτημα ("sinful deed," 6:18); ἁμαρτάνω ("to sin," 6:18; 7:28 [bis], 36; 8:12 [bis]; 15:34).

[32] 6:6; 7:12, 13, 14 [bis], 15; 10:27; 14:22 [bis], 23, 24.

The specific forms of wickedness that lead to the world's being condemned (11:32) are many and varied. Often they reflect Paul's Jewish view of the pagan environment of Corinth: idolatry (5:10–11; 6:10; 8:10; 10:7, 14); various forms of πορνεία ("sexual immorality," 5:1–2, 10–11; 6:10 [several words]; 6:18; 10:8); greed (5:10–11; 6:1–6, 10); robbery (5:10–11; 6:10); drunkenness (5:11; 6:10); and delighting in wickedness (13:6). But just as often it includes particularly self-centered sins: pride (4:6, 18–19; 5:2, 6; 8:1; 13:4); seeking one's own interests (10:33; 13:5); shaming those who have nothing (11:22); keeping records of the evil done by others (13:5); and various sins of discord (σχίσμα, "division" [1:10; 11:18], ἔρις, "strife" [1:11; 3:3], ζῆλος, "envy" [3:3; 13:5], λοιδορία, "abuse" [5:11; 6:10], ἀποστερεῖν, "to defraud" [6:8; 7:5], γογγύζειν, "to murmur" [10:10]).

People are wicked and sinful; they do not know God. But Christ died "for our sins," not only to forgive but also *to free people from their sins.* Hence Paul's extreme agitation at the Corinthians' sinfulness, because they are thereby persisting in the very sins from which God in Christ has saved them. This, after all, is what most of the letter is about.

The Saving Event

The focus of Paul's gospel is on the saving event effected by Christ's death (8:11; 11:26; 15:3), and especially on his *crucifixion* (1:13, 17, 18, 23; 2:2, 8; cf. 5:7), which is variously asserted to be "for you" (ὑπὲρ ὑμῶν; 1:13; 11:24) or "for (ὑπέρ) our sins" (15:3). In the words of institution the wine represents "the new covenant in my blood" (11:25), and those who partake of the table are thus said to "share in the blood of Christ" (10:16).

Despite the frequency of these references, it is not easy to determine how Paul understood Christ's death as "for us." The combination of 5:7 (Christ as the sacrificed paschal lamb), 11:24–25 (my body "for you"; the new covenant in my blood), and 15:3 (Christ died for our sins) suggests a much richer understanding than is actually spelled out. Most likely, this language reflects Isaiah 53 (LXX), where God's suffering servant bears the sins of the many. In any case, this is the language of atonement, in which a combination of motifs from both the exodus and the sacrificial system combine into a rich tapestry. It presupposes alienation of God and humans because of human sinfulness, for which the just penalty is death. The death of Christ "for our sins" means that one died on behalf of others to satisfy the penalty and to overcome the alienation. For Paul this almost certainly includes not only forgiveness of past sins, but in a very real sense deliverance from the bondage of one's sinfulness as well. That, at least, is what the primary metaphors for salvation in this letter suggest, especially so in light of the overall concern of the letter.

It is not surprising, therefore, that the predominant metaphors for salvation all touch on the ethical sphere. At issue is human sinfulness; not only in its boasting over against God but also in the various forms of behavior that reflect that boasting. Salvation involves both deliverance *from* sin and *for* righteousness. This is especially true of the two sets of three metaphors in 1:30 (as nouns: righteousness, sanctification, redemption) and 6:11 (as verbs: washed, sanctified, justified [made righteous?]). Thus:[33]

Δικαιοσύνη (1:30; cf. ἐδικαιώθητε, "you were made righteous/justified," 6:11) most likely places emphasis on "righteousness," as both gift and requirement, rather than on rightstanding before the Law. Nothing else in the letter suggests a forensic metaphor, whereas, especially in the context of 6:1–11, the verb seems to be used in a kind of wordplay over against the ἄδικοι (the unbelieving "wicked," vv. 1, 9) and the one who by "wronging" (ἀδικεῖσθε, vv. 7–8) his brother is acting just like the ἄδικοι. "Such *were* some of you," Paul says, "but you ἐδικαιώθητε (have been made right[eous])."

Sanctification is also a metaphor for conversion in this letter (1:30; 6:11; cf. 1:2). In calling people to himself, and in effecting their salvation through Christ's death, God has determined to set them apart for himself as his "holy people," which in this letter regularly entails observable behavior.

Redemption, which occurs as a noun in 1:30, also occurs as a full metaphor in 6:20 and 7:23 ("You were bought at a price"). The noun most likely reflects exodus imagery, thus the deliverance of slaves held in bondage to sin. But the usage in 6:20 (and partly so in 7:23) seems to put emphasis on being purchased *for* God, so that one is now his "slave," to walk in his ways.

Washing (6:11), although very likely also referring to Christian baptism, in the context of 6:1–11 refers primarily to being "washed" from the sins just mentioned in vv. 9–10.

Thus God's aim in salvation is not merely to create a people for his name who will inherit his kingdom, but to create a people for his name who will be "sanctified," that is, who will be like Christ himself and thus live and behave in the present in ways that will glorify God's name.

---

[33] Since the emphasis throughout is on God's initiative and Christ's redemptive work, there is very little emphasis on the believer's own response. Most often Paul refers simply to their "believing" (1:21; 3:5; 15:2, 11; cf. πίστις, 2:5; 15:14, 17); but the near equation of "your faith" in 15:14 and 17 with "having put our hope in Christ" in v. 19 suggests that "faith" means to respond to Christ's saving activity with full trust, including a total confidence that he has secured the believer's future.

The Ethical Consequence[34]

1 Corinthians emphasizes that the gospel issues in transformed lives, that salvation in Christ is not complete without God/Christlike attitudes and behavior. This is assumed at every point; it is also frequently stated. In the context of demanding that the church members exclude the incestuous man, Paul asserts that they are a "new lump" because "Christ our Passover has been sacrificed." That is, the sacrifice of Christ for sin is the basis of their transfer from the old to the new. "So then," he concludes, still playing on Passover imagery, "let us keep the feast without the old leaven of κακίας καὶ πονηρίας ("malice and evil," two synonyms which gather under their umbrella every form of iniquity), but with the new leaven of sincerity and truth (fully authentic behavior, without sham or deceit, that can stand the light of day)."

Likewise, in 6:11, after a severe warning, which includes a considerable sin catalogue describing the ἄδικοι ("unrighteous") who will *not* inherit the eschatological kingdom, Paul reasserts with equal vigor, "And these things are what some of you *were;* but you were washed, etc." Paul simply cannot let warning be the final word; but neither will he allow the warning to be taken lightly.[35] It is precisely this tension that needs theological resolution. What seems to miss Paul's theology are resolutions that either turn the imperatives into "Christian rules," on the one hand, or effectively emasculate them, on the other. That is, whatever else, the "imperative" in this letter is never simply imperative — either as "Christian Torah" or "calculated response" to God's gift of salvation; but neither is there anything close to genuine salvation that does not take the Spirit-filled, Spirit-led life seriously as simultaneously expressing both gift and demand.

The classic expression of Paul's understanding of the relationship between gospel and ethics (indicative and imperative) is to be found in 5:7. With reference to the incestuous man, he commands the church, "Cleanse out the

[34] I am especially indebted to Professor William A. Beardslee, in his formal response at the seminar, both for his insightful critique of this section of the paper and for the fact that he took this matter seriously as the central issue of Pauline theology in the letter. Some of his observations and suggestions have been incorporated into the present paper. In particular Professor Beardslee expressed concern over (1) the paradigm of "indicative/imperative" that I had set forth (too neatly, I would agree, even if unintentionally), which seemed to make ethics too consequential and not sufficiently transformational as gift and Spirit activity, and (2) the eschatological paradigm of "already/not yet," which I use to "resolve" this tension. Since I tend to agree with much of his critique, though not all (I think the tension "resolves" itself in Paul more than Professor Beardslee appears to), I have adjusted the wording at several places, so as to reflect this more "transformative" view of the ethical imperative in this letter.

[35] Cf. esp. the combination in chap. 10 of warning (vv. 6–12), affirmation (v. 13), and imperative (v. 14).

old leaven, in order that you might become a new batch of dough." But that comes perilously close to sounding as if the imperative preceded the indicative, so he immediately qualifies, "even as you really are." Thus "become what you are" is a basic form of Pauline parenesis.

But to say the imperative now follows the indicative is not quite adequate, since there are different kinds of imperative, both before and after the indicative. What Christ has done is forever to abolish the old imperatives, the Jewish boundary markers of circumcision (7:18–19) and food laws (9:19–22; 10:23–11:1), which gave privilege. These may *not* be placed after the indicative, as imperatives, either in their Jewish form or in any new Christian form. Neither circumcision *nor* uncircumcision counts for anything (7:18); and food will not commend us to God (8:8). Since in Christ neither kosher nor nonkosher has significance, Paul eats or does not depending on context (9:19–22). Likewise Jewish Christians may continue to eat as Jews. What they may not do is to impose these regulations on the one who is free in Christ.³⁶

On the other hand, because Paul dismisses all such boundary markers as totally outside questions of Christian conscience (10:25), one may not infer that for Paul there are no absolutes with regard to conduct. Paul warns that those who persist in the sins of 6:9–10 will not inherit the kingdom; they are commanded to stop sinning in 15:34. While it is true that neither circumcision nor uncircumcision counts for anything, something does count, namely, "keeping the commandments of God"! (7:19). If Paul eats as one who is ἄνομος ("outside the Jewish law") with those outside the Law, this does not mean he is truly ἄνομος (= "lawless"). To the contrary, he is ἔννομος Χριστοῦ ("under Christ's law," 9:21). Both of these phrases ("keeping the commandments of God" and "under Christ's law") must be understood as requiring obedience to the Christian imperatives, in the form of Pauline parenesis.³⁷

Thus, idolatry in the form of attendance at idol meals is incompatible with life in Christ, absolutely (10:14–22); sexual immorality is wrong, absolutely (6:18–20). And so also are strife and slander and greed, and all those other

³⁶ Which, of course, is what makes the whole argument of 11:2–16 so surprising, the best solution to which is not Paul's basic cultural conservatism but their apparent disregard for sexual distinctions in the present age. They are not yet as the angels!

³⁷ Which, in response to Professor Beardslee, is precisely where the theological tensions lie. The person "in Christ" is expected to act like/reflect Christ's own character/activity; thus Paul can speak of "Christ's law" and "keeping the commandments of God." But these are not now encoded in some form of "rules for believers to live by." Salvation as gift and the transformed life as Spirit indwelt are always the predicates for such behavior. Ideally, perhaps, the latter should eliminate the imperative altogether (as Professor Beardslee would seem to urge). But that is precisely what awaits the final consummation. For the present the imperative, which reflects the character of God, thus "describes" the life of the future that is to be lived out in the present. The reason for its being imperative (so it would seem) is precisely as a reflection of the tension of the "already/not yet."

sins mentioned in this letter. Ethical living is not optional; it is the only viable fruition of the work of the gospel.

But even here, Paul never begins with the imperative. For him it must be the living out of the gospel as grace and gift of the Spirit, or it is nothing at all. That is why so much of the content of this letter, in all of the behavioral sections, takes the form of theological argumentation. The divine order still has moral and ethical absolutes; there is conduct that is totally incompatible with God's own character and therefore with "being in Christ." But Paul never begins here. Going to the prostitutes (6:12–20) is wrong first of all because the Corinthians have a faulty view of ἐξουσία ("authority, rights") and the body and they exhibit an invalid understanding of the nature of the sexual relationship. But it is finally prohibited because the body, which is destined for resurrection, has been redeemed by Christ and invaded by the Holy Spirit. Going to the temples is prohibited because the Corinthians' argument for their case is based on a false view of idolatry and an incorrect basis for conduct (γνῶσις, "knowledge"), but it is finally prohibited because fellowship with demons is incompatible with fellowship with Christ at his table, where one reaffirms the benefits of the new covenant (8:1–13; 10:1–22).

But all has not been said. Ethics for Paul is ultimately a *theological* issue pure and simple. Everything has to do with God and with what God is about in Christ and the Spirit. Thus (1) the *purpose* (or basis) of Christian ethics is the glory of God (10:31); (2) the *pattern* for such ethics is Christ (11:1); (3) the *principle* is love, precisely because it alone reflects God's character (8:2–3; 13:1–8); and (4) the *power* is the Spirit (6:11, 19). Since we have already made note of items 1, 2, and 4, a further word is needed about love.

Although Paul clearly understands that the gospel sets one free and thus gives one ἐξουσία ("authority, rights," 6:12; 9:1–2, 19; 10:23), this is not for him the basis of ethical conduct—because as in the case of the Corinthians it can be abused (6:12–20; 8:9). So also with γνῶσις ("knowledge")—Paul is not against it;[38] it simply fails as the predicate for behavior in the "new age." In both cases it leads to abuse of others (8:7, 9); indeed, ethics predicated on γνῶσις invariably "puffs up," gives one too high a view of oneself and a correspondingly too low a view of others.[39]

Love, on the other hand, is the ultimate expression of the character of God. Therefore, it "builds up" (8:2); indeed, the one who loves is the truly "knowing [or known] one."[40] The basis of Christian conduct is what is beneficial,

---

[38] See esp. 12:8; 13:2; 14:6.

[39] See esp. the biting rhetoric of 4:7, "What have you that you have not received?" expressed in the context of condemning their pride. Such people fail to see everything as gift; hence they also fail to live out of gratitude.

[40] See my argument for this as the original text of 8:2–3 (Fee, 367–68).

what builds up; therefore, it does not seek its own good but that of the other
(10:23–24, 33; 13:5). And this, of course, is what God himself is all about
in the gospel.

The Church, the Sphere of Salvation

Finally, 1 Corinthians is about the church, the local community of
believers, who live out the gospel in relationship to one another and over
against the world. If the gospel is at stake by the Corinthian theology and
behavior, so also is its visible expression in the local community of redeemed
people. This is made clear both by Paul's basic images for the church (temple
of God, body of Christ) and by the nature of the argument in several sections,
especially 5:1–13 and 6:1–12.

Two great images predominate. First, the local church is God's temple in
Corinth (3:16–17). With this imagery Paul makes several points: (a) As the
temple of God Christians are expected to live as his alternative both to the
pagan temples and to the way of life that surrounds them. Indeed, this is
precisely the concern throughout so much of the letter, that there are too
many gray areas so that Christians are hardly distinguishable from the
Corinth in which they live (cf. 5:1; 6:7; 10:32; 14:23). (b) What makes them
God's temple is the presence of the Holy Spirit in their midst. Thus, in contrast to the mute idols around them, Christians are themselves the sanctuary
of the living God by his Spirit. And when God's Spirit is manifested among
them by prophetic utterance, pagans will have their hearts searched and
judged and they will come to recognize that God is among his people
(14:24–25). (c) So sacred (ἅγιος) to God is his temple that those who would
destroy it — as they are doing by their quarrels and worldly wisdom — will
themselves be destroyed by God (3:17). This understanding of their existence
as a people among whom God is powerfully present by his Spirit makes
possible our understanding of 5:1–13, where the church is purified by
removing the incestuous man; yet he himself will experience salvation from
such an action. Apparently being removed from such a community will lead
to his repentance.

Second, the church is the body of Christ (10:17; 11:29; 12:12–26). With
this image Paul makes essentially two points: (a) Underlying the imagery is
the necessity of unity. As with the preceding image, the key to this unity is
their common, lavish experience of the Spirit (12:13). Whether Jew or Greek,
slave or free, they are one in Christ through the Spirit. Precisely because they
are *one* body in Christ, the rich must cease abusing the poor at the Lord's
table (11:22, 29); and those who are more visible may not say to the less

visible, "we have no need of you" (12:21–26). God has so arranged the body that all the members are essential to one another. (b) But his greater concern with this imagery is the concomitant necessity of diversity. Rather than the uniformity that the Corinthians value, Paul urges that they recognize the need for all the various manifestations of the one Spirit. Otherwise there is no body, only a monstrosity (12:15–20).

Therefore, neither the gospel nor its ethical response is individualistic. God is not gathering individuals into his kingdom; he is saving a *people* for his name. Above all, it is as a people that they must live out the gospel. Thus, every argument is aimed at their becoming this people. This is especially spelled out in the most highly unusual arguments of 5:1–13 and 6:1–11, where in both cases the sins of individuals, grievous as they are and as strongly as Paul condemns them, play a secondary role to his consternation with the church.

In 5:1–13 the argument is addressed almost entirely to the church and its arrogance. What is at issue is not simply a low view of sin; rather, it is the church itself: Will it follow Paul's gospel with its ethical implications? Or will it continue its present "spirituality," one that tolerates (or condones) such sin and thereby destroys God's temple in Corinth?

In 6:1–11 the two great urgencies, besides his concern over the two men themselves (taken up in vv. 7–11),[41] are the church's self-understanding as God's eschatological people (vv. 2–4) and its witness before the world (vv. 5–6). Their existence as an eschatological people, who are to judge both the world and angels, trivializes all matters that belong merely to this present age. But what concerns him in this is their "defeat" before the world, their shooting down the gospel and its "new-age" behavior "in front of un-believers" (v. 6; cf. 15:34).

And so it goes throughout. God's eschatological salvation is creating a new people, who collectively must live the life of the future in the present age, as they await its consummation. This leads to the final matter—the eschatological goal of salvation.

IV. THE ESCHATOLOGICAL GOAL OF SALVATION

It is now time to return to the longer definition of the gospel suggested earlier "God's *eschatological* salvation, effected through the death and resurrection of Christ, and resulting in an *eschatological community* who live out *the life*

---

[41] See Fee, 240–42, for the argument that these verses speak in turn to the one who was wronged and the one who perpetrated the wrong in the first place.

of the future in the present age by the power of the Spirit, as they *await the consummation.*" Salvation is not simply a matter of changed behavior in the present. The absolutely essential framework of all of Paul's theological thinking, as well as the goal of God's saving event, is eschatological. This note is struck at the beginning in the thanksgiving (1:7–8, they "await the revelation of our Lord Jesus Christ" at which time God "will confirm them blameless on the day of our Lord Jesus Christ"), and it is the final note before the concluding grace-benediction (16:22, Μαρανα θα, "O Lord, come"). So, too, it is the assumption of the theologoumenon in 8:6 ("one God, the Father, from whom are all things and we *for* him"). Since salvation is essentially eschatological, always pointing toward its final consummation at the parousia, the future is understood to condition everything in the present. This is why ethical life is not optional; life in Christ in the present age is but the life of the future already begun.

The Framework Itself

Paul's eschatological thinking has its focus in the event of Christ, his death and resurrection, and the subsequent gift of the Spirit. Christ's resurrection marks the turning of the ages (15:20–23; cf. 10:11); the subsequent gift of the eschatological Spirit is the certain evidence that the end has begun (cf. 1:7; 13:8–13). But the facts that believers still live in bodies subject to decay (15:49–53), that the χαρίσματα ("gracious endowments") are *only* for the present (13:8–13), and that there is yet a future parousia of the Lord (11:26; 15:23) with a subsequent resurrection (15:20–28), also offer clear evidence that what has begun has not yet been fully brought to consummation. Thus, salvation is both "already" and "not yet."

This framework is thoroughgoing: God's Rule, begun by Christ who *now* reigns until his parousia (15:24–25), is both present (4:20) and future (6:9–10; 15:50). At the Lord's table they proclaim his death until he comes (11:26). Judgment belongs essentially to the future (4:4–5; 5:13), but the death of some is God's "judgment" at work now so that they will escape final condemnation (11:30–32).

The Future as "Already"

This perspective can be seen especially in Paul's ethics. The believer's present existence is entirely determined by the future that has already been set in motion ("the time has been foreshortened," 7:29–31). God's people live "as if not"; they are not, as others, conditioned by the present order that is passing away.[42] Such a point of view controls Paul's ethical imperatives at every step. Believers may not take one another to pagan courts, because their lives are conditioned by eschatological realities that render the redressing of one's grievances a mere triviality (6:1–6); believers may not attend pagan feasts because the judgments against idolatry of a former time have been written down to warn those upon whom the end of the ages has come (10:11). All merely human values and behavior have already been judged by God in Christ; already the present age is passing away (1:26–28; 7:31). Thus believers must exercise internal judgments in the present (5:12–13); the church must cleanse out the old leaven so that it might be a new loaf (5:7–8).

The Future as "Not Yet"

Yet the future that has begun and absolutely conditions present existence still awaits its final consummation. In contrast to the Corinthians' overly spiritualized present realization of future realities,[43] Paul frequently reminds them that they still await the revelation of the Lord (1:7); that they themselves must yet face the day of the Lord (1:8; 3:13–15); that they are to withhold judgment until the appointed time, when the Lord will come and will expose hearts (4:5); that even though Christ reigns now (15:25) and death is already theirs (3:22), only at the still-future parousia will all the powers finally be destroyed (15:23–26).

Such a future is as certain as life itself. Being Christ's means that both life and death, both the present and the future belong to those who are his (3:22–23). Again, this certainty has been guaranteed by the resurrection. Just as God raised up the Lord, so he will raise up believers (6:14; 15:1–28). Christ is the firstfruits, God's own surety of the full harvest (15:20). When Christ comes again, not only will he raise the dead and transform the living, but by these events he will also have finally destroyed the last enemy, death itself

---

[42] Paul uses the terms "this age" and "this world" somewhat interchangeably (cf. 1:20 and 3:18–19). The use of the demonstrative "*this* age/world" (1:20; 2:6 [bis]; 2:8; 3:18/3:19; 5:10; 7:31) tends to emphasize its present character in contrast to that to come, while the use of the verb καταργεῖν ("abolish, do away with") especially emphasizes that this present age and that which belongs to it have been judged and rendered ineffective through the cross and resurrection (see 1:28; 2:6; 6:13; 13:8 [bis], 10, 11; 15:24, 26; cf. παράγει ["is passing away"] in 7:31).

[43] Despite some demurrers, both the nature of the rhetoric and the combination of "already" and "ruling" in 4:8 seem to reflect Paul's own view of their present perspective. Whether this is a carefully thought through position and whether it is an overrealized eschatology in a linear sense of time are more debatable. Most likely their experience of Spirit has simply put them "above" the present age, having already assumed angelic existence.

(15:24–28, 54–57). So certain is Paul that Christ's resurrection guarantees the future of believers that he finally taunts death in the language of Hos 13:14 (15:55). When death is thus rendered helpless by resurrection, then salvation will have reached its conclusion; and the present reigning Lord, having destroyed all other dominions, will hand over the rule to God the Father, so that the God who initiated salvation will be "all in all."

But even here the final word is one of exhortation (15:58). Despite the magnificent crescendo with which Paul brings the argument of chap. 15 to its climax, the last word is not the sure word of future hope and triumph of vv. 50–57; rather, in light of such realities, the last word is an exhortation to Christian living (v. 58). Thus, eschatological salvation, the great concern of the epistle, includes proper behavior or it simply is not the gospel Paul preaches.

4 THEOLOGY IN 1 CORINTHIANS[1]

Victor Paul Furnish
Perkins School of Theology
Southern Methodist University

I. PRELIMINARY CONSIDERATIONS

IT IS IMPORTANT to indicate at the outset how the term "theology" is being used here, especially with reference to Paul, and also to suggest how it is proposed to gain access to theology in 1 Corinthians.[2]

"Pauline Theology"

In its original and most literal sense, the term "theology" (θεο-λογία) refers to any account about the gods. Within the specifically monotheistic framework of Judaism and Christianity, theology would be thought and speech about the one God "than whom none greater can be conceived" (Anselm). In Western Christianity since the Enlightenment, the fundamental task of theology has been understood to be *critical reflection* about this one God, whose reality is unsurpassable and from whom all other realities derive their existence and their meaning. This task is appropriately extended to include critical reflection about all beliefs and rites in which particular understandings of God's reality come to expression, and about the social structures within which those beliefs and rites are continued and interpreted.[3]

---

[1] The present study builds on but is much more than just a revision of my earlier paper "Theology in 1 Corinthians: Initial Soundings," in *Society of Biblical Literature 1989 Seminar Papers* (ed. David J. Lull; Atlanta: Scholars Press, 1989) 246–64.

[2] See also my essay "Paul the Theologian," in *The Conversation Continues: Studies in Paul and John in Honor of J. Louis Martyn* (ed. Robert T. Fortna and Beverly R. Gaventa; Nashville: Abingdon, 1990) 19–34.

[3] For this understanding of theology I am indebted to the writings of and conversations with my colleague Schubert M. Ogden. In addition to his collection of essays, *On Theology* (San

The process of theological reflection may or may not lead to the production of *a* "theology," in the form of *a* comprehensive, systematic statement of beliefs about what is ultimately real and significant. Yet wherever theological reflection has proceeded in a genuinely critical way, one may infer some degree of theological intentionality and may thus refer to the work of a "theologian."

When asking in what respect, if at all, it is appropriate to speak of "Pauline theology" or of Paul as a "theologian," one must take account both of his own sense of vocation and of the nature of our sources. With reference to the first, it is clear that Paul understood his vocation to be that of an apostle, not that of a theologian. Thus the task to which he was committed above all else was the *proclamation* of the gospel, not critical reflection about it. This is evident in the nature of the sources at our disposal, which are not theological treatises or essays. They are apostolic letters, occasioned by particular situations and influenced in both their objectives and content by particular circumstances, as well as by Paul's own theological understandings and faith commitments.

Nonetheless, it is not only possible but necessary to regard Paul's letters as in part theological documents. They are theological in the general sense that they are written to support a ministry that presupposes a certain understanding of God, as well as various beliefs, rites, and social structures deemed appropriate to that understanding. But they are also theological in a narrower sense, for Paul's concern to clarify and commend the gospel sometimes leads him to deliberate, serious reflection about its truth and meaning. Of course he is not a *critical* theologian in the modern Western sense. Yet neither does he simply make assertions about the gospel or just recite the "story of salvation." When he interprets the gospel and argues for its truth he is thereby conceptualizing it in ways that he presumes will be meaningful to his readers. One sees this going on, especially, where he is interpreting the church's traditions (scriptural, creedal, liturgical, catechetical), where he is interpreting his own experience of the resurrected Lord and of Christian community (these two are inseparable), and where he is engaging opposing interpretations of the gospel to which he is committed.[4]

Francisco: Harper, 1986), see "Doing Theology Today," in *Doing Theology in Today's World: Essays in Honor of Kenneth S. Kantzer* (ed. J. D. Woodbridge and T. E. McComiskey; Grand Rapids: Zondervan, 1991) 417–36; and "Must God Be Really Related to Creatures?" *Process Studies* 20 (1991) 54–56.

[4] The interpretive character of Paul's theology has been rightly emphasized by J. Christiaan Beker; see, e.g., *Paul the Apostle: The Triumph of God in Life and Thought* (Philadelphia: Fortress, 1980) 109–31; idem, "The Faithfulness of God and the Priority of Israel in Paul's Letter to the Romans," in *Christians Among Jews and Gentiles: Essays in Honor of Krister Stendahl on His Sixty-Fifth Birthday* (ed. G. W. E. Nickelsburg, with G. W. MacRae; Philadelphia: Fortress, 1986) 10; idem,

In brief, while Paul's letters do not yield any kind of a comprehensive theological system, they do introduce us to Paul the theologian, to a person engaged in earnest theological reflection. Hence, the subject of the present essay is not "*the* theology *of* 1 Corinthians," but Paul's theological reflection as that is evident *in* this letter.[5]

Theology in 1 Corinthians

Paul's theological reflection should be clearly distinguished, although it must not be separated, from his proclamation of the gospel (his κήρυγμα).[6] The apostle's kerygmatic affirmations and appeals, whether traditional or of his own creation, are formulated as direct address and are invitations, either explicit or implicit, to receive (or remember) and commit (or re-commit) oneself to the gospel. In 1 Corinthians there are examples of such kerygmatic formulations in 1:30; 6:11b, 14 (cf. 15:15b); 6:19b–20a/7:23a; 11:12b; 12:27; and 15:3–5, 20, 22 (cf. 15:49). The apostle's theological statements, however, are formulated as teaching and, along with his moral counsels, serve to explicate the truth and meaning of the gospel. All kerygmatic statements are implicitly theological, of course, because every summons to the gospel implies and requires some understanding of it. Similarly, insofar as Paul's theological statements lead to an understanding of the gospel, they serve as an indirect summons to it. Nevertheless, the distinction between kerygma and theology remains: Paul's kerygmatic affirmations and appeals constitute a summons to "believe in the gospel," while his theological statements seek to clarify what it means to do so.

"Recasting Pauline Theology: The Coherence-Contingency Scheme as Interpretive Model," in *Pauline Theology I,* 15–16; and idem, "Paul the Theologian: Major Motifs in Pauline Theology," *Int* 43 (1989) 353.

[5] In what follows I presuppose the literary integrity of this letter. Although some have argued that 1 Corinthians is a composite of several originally distinct letters (e.g., Robert Jewett, "The Redaction of I Corinthians and the Trajectory of the Pauline School," *JAAR* 44 Supplement B [1978] 389–444; Gerhard Sellin, "Hauptprobleme des ersten Korintherbriefes," in *ANRW* 2.25.4 [1987] 2964–86), I regard arguments for the letter's integrity as more compelling. For the latter see esp. Helmut Merklein, "Die Einheitlichkeit des ersten Korintherbriefes," *Studien zu Jesus und Paulus* (WUNT 43; Tübingen: Mohr-Siebeck, 1987) 345–75; and Wolfgang Schrage, *Der erste Brief an die Korinther, 1 (1 Kor 1,1–6,11)* (EKKNT 7/1; Zurich and Braunschweig: Benziger Verlag; Neukirchen-Vluyn: Neukirchener Verlag, 1991) 63–71. I do not, however, exclude the possibility that the letter contains interpolations or glosses (one likely instance is 14:34–35).

[6] For this distinction, see Rudolf Bultmann, "Church and Teaching in the New Testament," in *Faith and Understanding* (1929; ed. Robert W. Funk; trans. Louise Pettibone Smith; New York and Evanston: Harper, 1969) 208, 213–14, 218–29.

If Paul's theology is to be identified with his reflection about the truth and meaning of the gospel, then it follows that one can gain access to that theology only where this reflection has become "public"—in the apostle's *exposition* of his gospel. This does not mean that the exposition itself constitutes "a theology," or that it reflects a theology that underlies or somehow transcends the texts of his letters. Rather, if Paul's theology is to be understood as his reflection about the gospel—hence, as a process—then it can only be found as one follows and engages the dynamics of his argument, including the movement back and forth between proclamation and exposition.[7] This has to be done exegetically, letter by letter, for only in this way can one take account of the circumstances that have occasioned and helped to shape Paul's theological reflection.[8]

The theology in 1 Corinthians cannot be engaged apart from some understanding, however tentative, of the particulars of the situation Paul is confronting in his congregation. That situation remains partly veiled to us, not least because we are totally dependent on Paul's own perception of it. Yet some things are reasonably clear. (a) The divisiveness in the congregation, to which there are references especially in chaps. 1–4, suggests that some in Corinth have called Paul's own status and authority into question and, along with these, also the gospel that he has proclaimed to them. (b) This divisiveness is manifested in sharply differing judgments about what is and is not appropriate Christian behavior (5:1–11:1) and is evident as well in the congregation's disorderly worship (11:2–14:40). (c) Insofar as this situation may have been due to or fueled by a particular ideology, that is perhaps best described as a kind of proto-gnostic spirituality, according to which the "not yet" of salvation is largely collapsed into the "already" of a pretentious religiosity. One catches sight of this in some of Paul's reprimands (especially in 4:7, 8, 18–21; cf. 3:18; 5:2, 6; 8:1, 11) and also in his discussions of Christian community (chaps. 12–13) and the resurrection of the dead (chap. 15).[9]

Theological exposition occurs throughout 1 Corinthians, at various points and in various forms. For example, it may be concentrated in just a sentence

---

[7] In assessing the dynamics of Paul's argumentation one must also take account of the fact that he *dictated* his letters. Emphasizing this, Kurt Niederwimmer observes that, in a letter like 1 Corinthians, one sees "not the *finished* but the *evolving* theology of the apostle" ("Erkennen und Lieben: Gedanken zum Verhältnis von Gnosis und Agape im ersten Korintherbrief," *KD* 11 [1965] 77–78 n. 9).

[8] Similarly, Georg Eichholz, who properly insists, "We must engage the texts" (*Die Theologie des Paulus im Umriß* [2d ed.; Neukirchen-Vluyn: Neukirchener Verlag, 1977] 7). My own thoughts on exegesis as the only proper method for approaching Pauline theology are developed more fully in "Paul the Theologian," 27–30.

[9] Schrage's overview of the situation in Corinth is particularly convincing, both because he recognizes the difficulty of assessing the evidence and because he does not try to fill out the picture in every detail. See *Der erste Brief an die Korinther*, 38–63.

or two, as in the brief comment on the Lord's Supper tradition in 11:26. Or it may be more extensive, as in 3:5–4:5, where scattered reflections about God and the role of God's servants are combined with some rather pointed admonitions. There are, however, three particularly important expository passages in 1 Corinthians. They may be regarded as the letter's principal theological discourses and as such deserve special attention.

These three key discourses deal, respectively, with the wisdom of the cross (1:18–2:16), the nature of Christian community (12:4–13:13), and the resurrection of the dead (chap. 15). In each instance Paul's reflections on the topic are deliberate and focused, and lead him to develop a more or less extended and coherent argument. Moreover, each of these passages occurs at an important point within the overall structure of the letter. The discourse on wisdom, situated prominently at the beginning of the letter, supports the apostle's urgent appeals for unity (1:10–4:21). It can be argued that the discourse on Christian community undergirds, directly or indirectly, all of the counsels and instructions in chaps. 8 through 14. And the discourse on resurrection, a response to those who claim that "there is no resurrection of the dead" (15:12), is located prominently at the end of the letter.

Ideally, a study of theology in 1 Corinthians should proceed in a series of distinct steps. First, each of the principal theological discourses would be examined within its own literary and situational contexts, and its particular function(s) within those assessed. Second, the argument of each of these passages would be thoroughly analyzed. Third, the controlling ideas of each, most especially the key theological conceptions, would be identified. Fourth, one would consider how the controlling theological conceptions in these passages may have informed the overall contents and argument of the letter. Fifth, the various theological statements found in essentially nonexpository passages would be taken into account.[10] Finally, with the results of these discrete inquiries in hand, one might be able to venture some generalizations about the theological orientation of the letter as a whole.

It is of course impossible to carry out all of these procedures within the scope of a single essay.[11] Here only two things can be attempted. First, the three principal expository passages will be examined in turn (sections II, III, and IV). The concern will be to delineate the main lines of the argument and to identify the pivotal theological conceptions in each of them. Second, and with reference as well to certain other important passages, some preliminary

[10] For example, theological statements in which Paul intends to elucidate some particular tradition, or that he offers as summaries of his own preaching, convictions, etc. (See point 8 in my essay "Paul the Theologian," 29.)

[11] I have been able to explore the topic more fully in *The Theology of the First Letter to the Corinthians* (New Testament Theology 7; Cambridge: Cambridge University Press, forthcoming).

suggestions will be offered about the overall theological orientation of the letter (section V).[12]

II. 1 CORINTHIANS 1:18–2:16

The first main subdivision of 1 Corinthians extends from 1:10 through 4:21, a section framed by the appeals of 1:10 (παρακαλῶ δὲ ὑμᾶς . . .) and 4:16 (παρακαλῶ οὖν ὑμᾶς . . .). Here Paul's chief concern is with the profane and arrogant boasting (note 1:29–31; 3:21–23; 4:6–7) that he believes not only poses a serious threat to the unity of the congregation (1:10–12; 3:4, 21, etc.) but is evidence of a fundamental misunderstanding of his gospel and ministry (thus 1:18–2:16; 3:5–4:5). Within this section 1:18–2:16 stands as a kind of excursus, one formal marker of which is the shift from the first person singular (1:10–17) to the first person plural.[13]

The Argument

Paul's overall topic in 1:18–2:16 is the wisdom of the cross, a subject evidently occasioned by the distinction that he has made, at least implicitly, between preaching "with eloquent wisdom" (ἐν σοφίᾳ λόγου) and preaching "the cross of Christ" (1:17).[14] He comments first of all on the apparent foolishness of God's wisdom (1:18–2:5), and then on its essential hiddenness (2:6–16).

---

[12] In accordance with the aims and methods of the larger project to which this study is a contribution, passages from other Pauline letters will not be invoked, even where they almost certainly could be of assistance. Also, while I have benefited greatly from numerous scholarly studies, including the major commentaries, references to these have been kept to a minimum. My major concern here is not with what other interpreters have said about Paul, but with the apostle's own thought.

[13] Within 1:18–2:16 the singular appears only in 2:1–5, and this is because of the subject matter.

[14] For two of the more recent and significant studies, see Charles B. Cousar, *A Theology of the Cross: The Death of Jesus in the Pauline Letters* (OBT; Minneapolis: Fortress, 1990), esp. 27–36; Peter Lampe, "Theological Wisdom and the 'Word About the Cross': The Rhetorical Scheme in I Corinthians 1–4," *Int* 44 (1990) 117–31. It should perhaps be remarked that where Lampe uses the terms "theology" and "theological" I would use the terms "religion" and "religious," reserving the word *theology* for the specific discipline of critical (and therefore always necessarily *self*-critical) reflection about God. In any case (and regardless of the definition), I certainly agree with him that, from Paul's standpoint, "any human theology is moved into constant crisis by its own subject . . ." (p. 122). This of course includes the apostle's theology, as well as the theologies of his readers, both ancient and modern.

(1) *The "foolishness" of God's wisdom, 1:18–2:5.* In this part of the discourse the argument proceeds in three steps: Paul makes his main point in 1:18–25, confirms it in 1:26–31 with an appeal to the Corinthians' own situation, and then further confirms it in 2:1–5 with reference to what and how he had preached in Corinth.

The apostle's thesis is registered first in 1:18 and then twice restated (in 1:21 and 1:23–24). According to the initial formulation, the proclamation of the cross is bound to seem like foolishness to "those who are perishing" (non-believers), for they are by definition alienated from its saving power. This is supported with a citation from Isa 29:14 (which follows generally the LXX), to the effect that God opposes and destroys what human beings ordinarily think of as wisdom (v. 19). After glossing the citation with a series of four rhetorical questions (v. 20),[15] Paul restates his point in a way that emphasizes the purposefulness of God's foolish wisdom (v. 21):

> For since, in the wisdom of God, the world did not know God through wisdom, God regarded it as good [εὐδόκησεν] to save those who believe through the foolishness of our proclamation [κήρυγμα]. (My translation)

In yet a third formulation of his point (vv. 23–24) Paul adds a reference to the σκάνδαλον that a crucified Christ poses for Jews, even as he affirms that all who are *called,* whether they be Jews or Greeks, have encountered in this Christ "the power of God and the wisdom of God." The sum of the matter is set forth in v. 25, which declares, in effect, that God's wisdom and strength are utterly beyond compare.

Paul extends his argument, first, by reminding the Corinthians that God's foolish wisdom has been demonstrated in their own experience (1:26–31). They have not embraced the gospel because of any wisdom, power, or status they can claim for themselves (v. 26), but solely by reason of God's call. This note is sounded in the threefold "God chose" (ἐξελέξατο ὁ θεός, vv. 27–28), and again in the statement that their being "in Christ Jesus" derives entirely from God (ἐξ αὐτοῦ δὲ ὑμεῖς ἐστε ἐν Χριστῷ Ἰησοῦ, v. 30a). The point is underscored in the statement that *Christ* has become their "wisdom . . . from God" (v. 30b; cf. v. 24), and again in the scriptural warning (Jer 9:22, 23) that one's boast must be only in the Lord (v. 31).

As a further demonstration of the character of God's wisdom, the apostle points to the content and manner of his initial preaching in Corinth (2:1–5). He had come in weakness and with fear and trembling, proclaiming only "Jesus Christ, and him crucified" (vv. 2–3) — simply the cross, with none of the high-flown speech or clichéd wisdom of sophistic oratory (vv. 1, 4a).

---

[15] The first three questions anticipate the affirmative answer presupposed by the fourth.

Thus the Corinthians' faith is founded not on what the world regards as wisdom but on the inherent saving power of the kerygma itself, on God's own power (v. 5).

(2) *The hiddenness of God's wisdom, 2:6–16.* Paul's concern to show how radically "the word of the cross" challenges all human notions of wisdom, power, and status is by no means left behind in 2:6–16, even though it comes to expression in a rather different line of argument.[16]

First, perhaps responding to Corinthian critics, Paul maintains that his preaching does in fact convey wisdom (vv. 6a, 7). This is, however, the wisdom of God, thus absolutely distinct from merely human wisdom and in principle beyond the reach of any human inquiry or conceiving (v. 9).[17] God's wisdom is not only represented "in a mystery" (ἐν μυστηρίῳ); it "remains hidden" (v. 7; note the perfect tense, τὴν ἀποκεκρυμμένην).[18] It is nothing else than the proclamation of "Jesus Christ, and him crucified," which Paul has already described as "the mystery of God" (2:1–2),[19] and which the world regards as foolishness (1:18). "The rulers of this age" are mentioned as an example of the world's response (vv. 6b, 8): knowing only the wisdom of this age, they "crucified the Lord of glory" and are themselves "doomed to perish."[20]

Two further points follow in quick succession. Since this wisdom is in principle beyond the reach of merely human inquiry, whatever can be understood about it must be revealed by the Spirit of God (vv. 10–11). This means, in turn (vv. 12–13), that only those who have received the Spirit (οἱ πνευ-ματικοί) are able to understand what God has granted (τὰ ὑπὸ τοῦ θεοῦ χαρισθέντα).[21] The reference here is not to the spiritual gifts (τὰ χαρίσματα) on which Paul comments later (chaps. 12–14). In the present context he is

---

[16] I find no compelling reason to question the authenticity of this passage or its original positioning here (*pace* Martin Widmann, "1 Kor 2 6–16: Ein Einspruch gegen Paulus," *ZNW* 70 [1979] 44–53). That 2:6–16 continues and supports the argument of 1:18–2:5 is ably shown by Peter Stuhlmacher, "Zur hermeneutischen Bedeutung von 1 Kor 2,6–16," *TBei* 18 (1987) 133–58.

[17] The source of the citation in v. 9, introduced as a statement drawn from scripture (καθὼς γέγραπται), remains as mysterious as the wisdom of which Paul writes.

[18] Thus Schrage, *Der erste Brief an die Korinther,* 251; contrast Gordon D. Fee, *The First Epistle to the Corinthians* (NICNT; Grand Rapids: Eerdmans, 1987) 105.

[19] Although there are arguments for reading μαρτύριον instead of μυστήριον (thus, e.g., Fee, *First Epistle to the Corinthians,* 88 n. 1), arguments for the latter are, on the whole, more weighty (thus, e.g., Schrage, *Der erste Brief an die Korinther,* 226).

[20] Whether Paul is thinking of political or cosmic rulers does not affect the main point: they are ignorant of God's wisdom as that is represented in the kerygma.

[21] The use of the aorist ἐλάβομεν suggests that Paul has reference to one's receiving the Spirit at the time of baptism.

evidently thinking of everything that is granted those who have been graced and claimed by the saving power of God in the kerygma.[22]

In conclusion, Paul underscores three points which, in a way, summarize the entire discourse. First (v. 14), humanity in its "natural" state (ψυχικὸς ἄνθρωπος)—without the Spirit—is unable to receive and know what God in God's wisdom has granted in the kerygma, for apart from the Spirit the wisdom of the cross seems like foolishness. Second (v. 15), one who has received the Spirit (ὁ πνευματικός) discerns everything (which God in God's wisdom has granted in the kerygma) and is not himself or herself subject to scrutiny by anyone (who has not received the Spirit).[23] Third, although God's wisdom is in principle past finding out—even by those who have received the Spirit,[24] those who have accepted the kerygma "have the mind of Christ" (specifically: the mind of "Jesus Christ, *and him crucified*").[25] This means that their faculties for critical thought and reasoned action are informed and guided by the wisdom of the cross.[26]

Pivotal Theological Conceptions

The single most fundamental theological conception here—no less clear for having been left unexpressed—is the existence of one God whose reality transcends and surpasses all other realities. What does come to expression, however (because it is germane to Paul's concerns for his congregation), is a certain understanding of the nature of God—or perhaps one should say, of the *meaning* of God. This understanding may be summarized as follows.[27]

(1) The whole of Paul's argument here is predicated on the sovereignty (δύναμις, 1:18, 24; 2:5) and unfathomable wisdom (1:21, 24–25; 2:6–7, 9, 16a) of God. God's power and wisdom are presented not merely as superior to the world's but as belonging to an entirely different order. Two closely related

---

[22] Thus also Fee, *First Epistle to the Corinthians*, 113; cf. Schrage (*Der erste Brief an die Korinther*, 260), who believes nonetheless that the χαρίσματα mentioned in 1:7 would be included.

[23] Contrast Richard Horsley ("Wisdom of Words and Words of Wisdom in Corinth," *CBQ* 39 [1977] 224–39), who argues that in 2:15 Paul is citing a Corinthian principle that he cannot himself accept (p. 238).

[24] The question as posed in Isa 40:13 and adapted by Paul in v. 16a admits of but one answer: "Nobody!"

[25] In v. 16b, as in vv. 7, 10, and 12, the first person plural (ἡμεῖς . . . ἔχομεν) embraces the whole Christian community.

[26] Schrage's comments on v. 16 are especially insightful (*Der erste Brief an die Korinther*, 266–68). See also Wendell L. Willis, "The 'Mind of Christ' in 1 Corinthians 2,16," *Bib* 70 (1989) 110–22.

[27] Cousar offers a rather similar, seven-point summary of "God's purposes" as he finds Paul expressing those in 1 Cor 1:18–2:5 (*Theology of the Cross*, 35–36).

conceptions also find expression. The existence of this sovereign God must perforce transcend the finite limits of time and space. Thus Paul thinks of God as one who is active "before the ages" and who, unlike "the rulers of this age," will not cease to exist (2:6–7). Moreover, this sovereign, eternal God is also eminently free, for example, to save—or to destroy (note especially 1:21 [εὐδόκησεν], 27–28 [ἐξελέξατο ὁ θεός]).

(2) Indeed, God's purpose is to save. Although Paul believes that God's reality transcends both time and space, thus surpassing all other realities, he clearly does not conceive of God as existing apart from these other realities. He in fact associates God's wisdom principally with God's beneficent purposes for humankind (e.g., 1:21; 2:7), and God's power specifically with the fulfillment of those (e.g., 1:18; 2:4–5). At least in this passage, Paul is thinking about God only from the standpoint of the meaning of *God's* existence for *human* existence.

(3) God's saving power has been given an effective historical presence in "Jesus Christ and him crucified," and in the kerygma through which this Christ is proclaimed. Paul stresses this repeatedly in the first part of the discourse (e.g., 1:18, 21, 23–24; 2:2) and clearly presupposes it throughout the second part (hence his remark in 2:8). It is evident that he is attaching special importance to the fact that Jesus was crucified (thus the distinctive locution in 2:2, καὶ τοῦτον ἐσταυρωμένον), and that Christ in fact continues to be the crucified one (thus the perfect tense in both 1:23 and 2:2). Yet Paul is not interpreting Jesus' death on the cross as an act of atonement for sins, even though such an idea surfaces elsewhere in the letter (15:3; cf. 8:11; 11:24).[28] Rather, his point is that specifically the *crucified* Christ discloses the nature of God's power and wisdom. The cross is thus definitive for a properly Christian understanding of God.

(4) God's self-disclosure in the cross places all human pretensions to power and wisdom under judgment, including, quite particularly, all religious claims and expectations. This is the point Paul is making when he contrasts the kerygma's offer of "Christ crucified" with the religious "signs" and "wisdom" so esteemed in the world (1:22–25).[29] If this cross—in the world only a sign of shame and weakness—is indeed the defining event of God's power and wisdom, then every merely human notion about these is turned completely upside down (thus 1:26–31).

(5) No less certainly, from Paul's point of view, God's self-disclosure in the cross establishes a radically new norm and context for life in this age. These

[28] The occurrence of the term ἀπολύτρωσις in 1:30 is only a hint of the notion that Christ's death has "purchased" freedom from sin for those who believe (6:20; 7:23).

[29] See Lampe's excellent discussion in "Theological Wisdom and the 'Word About the Cross,'" 119–25.

are given in and with the crucified Christ himself. Thus Paul can describe those who accept this kerygma as being "in Christ Jesus" (ἐν Χριστῷ 'Ιησοῦ), who has become their "wisdom from God" as well as their "righteousness and sanctification and redemption" (1:30). That this is understood to be by God's own initiative is clear. Those in Christ are "the *called*" (οἱ κλητοί, 1:24; cf. 1:26–28), are "*being saved*" (οἱ σῳζόμενοι, 1:18), and have "*received* . . . the Spirit that is from God" (2:12), through which they perceive the meaning of God's gifts. But they are at the same time "those who *believe*" (οἱ πιστεύοντες, 1:21), since God's call requires the response of faith (ἡ πίστις ὑμῶν, 2:5). It is on behalf of this believing community that Paul affirms, "We have the mind of Christ" (ἡμεῖς δὲ νοῦν Χριστοῦ ἔχομεν, 2:16b), meaning that the lives of believers are both formed and informed by the wisdom of the cross.

III. 1 CORINTHIANS 12:4–13:13

From 12:1 through 14:40 Paul's subject is "spiritual gifts" (12:1), a topic he has taken up because of his concern about the factiousness in Corinth and, in particular, the disruptions in worship caused by those who speak in tongues.[30] He introduces the larger subject in 12:1–3[31] but gives no actual directives until chap. 14. Nonetheless, the particulars of the Corinthian situation are by no means forgotten as, in chaps. 12 and 13, he lays the foundation for the subsequent direct appeals (14:1–25) and specific instructions (14:26–36).

The Argument

Chapter 13, most scholars agree, is to be read as an integral part of the discussion of spiritual gifts. Even if some preexisting document lies behind the chapter, Paul has significantly adapted it to meet the needs of his argument in this particular context.[32] Indeed, chap. 13 both crowns the discussion

---

[30] I am thus reading τῶν πνευματικῶν in 12:1 as neuter, an interpretation supported by the subsequent discussion of χαρίσματα in 12:4–11 and, especially, by the appeal in 14:1 concerning "the spiritual gifts" (τὰ πνευματικά).

[31] The formulary "Now concerning" (περὶ δέ) in 12:1 could mean that here, as in 7:1, Paul is turning to a subject about which the congregation itself has written him. It does not necessarily indicate this, however, either here or in the other occurrences where there is no specific reference to a letter (e.g., 8:1; 16:1); see Margaret M. Mitchell, "Concerning ΠΕΡΙ ΔΕ in 1 Corinthians," *NovT* 31 (1989) 229–56.

[32] See the important study by Oda Wischmeyer, *Der höchste Weg: Das 13. Kapitel des 1. Korintherbriefes* (SNT 13; Gütersloh: Mohn, 1981) esp. 27–38. Further, Ralph P. Martin, *The Spirit and*

of Christian community in chap. 12 and sets the course for the appeals and
directives in chap. 14. Thus, with the appeal in 12:31a to "seek the greater
gifts," exposition has given way to exhortation,[33] and the appeal in 14:1a to
"pursue love" only makes explicit what is implicit throughout chap. 13.[34] Yet
chap. 13 itself is still expository,[35] and the particular understanding of love
offered there also significantly undergirds what has been said in chap. 12
about Christian community.

The expository section that opens in 12:4 proceeds from a point which
Paul has just stated as axiomatic: "no one can say 'Jesus is Lord' except by the
Holy Spirit" (12:3). Put otherwise, *everyone* within the believing community
has received the Spirit and is "spiritual" (cf. 2:12) — not just some, as the
Corinthians seem to have thought. Paul's understanding of what this implies
about Christian community is the subject of the following paragraphs. Here
it is possible to identify only the three main points of his argument.

(1) Those who confess Jesus as Lord have been graced with different kinds
of gifts, although one and the same Spirit has bestowed them all; and further,
these diverse manifestations of the Spirit have been granted "for the common
good" (πρὸς τὸ συμφέρον, v. 7), 12:4–11.

(2) Because of their diverse gifts, the members of this believing community, like the different parts of the human body, are totally interdependent
and, as a consequence, necessary to one another (12:12–30). The analogy is
introduced in vv. 12–13 (where a traditional baptismal formula is adapted to
help make the point, v. 13; cf. Gal 3:27–28; Col 3:10–11) and is then spelled
out in vv. 14–26. Its applicability to the church is summarized in v. 27 ("Now
you are the body of Christ and individually members of it," v. 27; cf. v. 12)
and is then concretely illustrated in vv. 28–30.

(3) What is definitive for the life of this community, and is indeed the *sine*

---

the *Congregation: Studies in I Corinthians 12–15* (Grand Rapids: Eerdmans, 1984) 39–56;
Margaret M. Mitchell, *Paul and the Rhetoric of Reconciliation: An Exegetical Investigation of the
Language and Composition of 1 Corinthians* (HUT 28; Tübingen: Mohr [Siebeck], 1991) esp.
165–71, 266–79. For representative dissenting views, see the studies by Jewett and Sellin
mentioned above in n. 5.

[33] With most translations and commentators, I am reading ζηλοῦτε in v. 31a as an imperative.
Alternatively, one could interpret it as an indicative, so that Paul would be making a statement
about what the Corinthians actually do — to his dismay. The case for the imperative, however,
is stronger; thus Fee, *First Epistle to the Corinthians*, 623–25.

[34] The parenetic character and function of chap. 13 are shown very well by Carl R. Holladay,
"1 Corinthians 13: Paul as Apostolic Paradigm," in *Greeks, Romans, and Christians: Essays in Honor
of Abraham J. Malherbe* (ed. D. L. Balch, E. Ferguson, and W. A. Meeks; Minneapolis: Fortress,
1990) 80–98.

[35] This holds true even though, particularly in vv. 1–3, Paul seems to be presenting his own
ministry as a "paradigm" (Holladay, "1 Corinthians 13") or "example" (Mitchell, *Paul and the
Rhetoric of Reconciliation*, 58, 273–74, 277–78) of love's way.

qua non of its existence, is nothing else but love (ἀγάπη), 12:31–13:13. Paul reflects, in turn, on the necessity of love (vv. 1–3), its qualities (vv. 4–7), and its distinctive permanence (vv. 8–13).

Pivotal Theological Conceptions

The tattered fabric of Christian community in Corinth is no less in view where Paul writes about love (chap. 13) than where he writes about the body (chap. 12). Indeed, he specifically sets love over against the spiritual gifts that are so prized (and he believes so misunderstood) in the Corinthian congregation, portraying it as that apart from which none of the spiritual gifts has meaning.

The pastoral and polemical aspects of Paul's argument must be set to one side, however, as we attempt to focus on the theological conceptions that lie at its heart. These are not confined to chap. 12, where Paul describes the community of believers as one body instituted by God through the Spirit. They also lie at the heart of the exposition in chap. 13, where his comments about love and knowledge clearly presuppose what he has said about these in 8:1–6, an explicitly theological passage.[36] Read together, then, chaps. 12–13 yield several significant theological points.

(1) Baptism marks one's incorporation into a community whose members, having received the Spirit, participate in a reality that is more than the sum of its individual parts (12:12–13). Because Paul understands this to be a community of those who confess Jesus as Lord (12:3), he can describe the "one body" into which they have been baptized as "the body of Christ" (12:27). Their life together is understood to be defined and sustained by the common life they share in him (e.g., 12:14–26). That Paul could be thinking of Christ as the "head" of this body, perhaps in the sense of ruling over it, is excluded by 12:21.[37]

(2) There is but one Spirit (12:9, 11, 13), however many and varied the manifestations of the Spirit (12:7); and it is by reason of their common suffusion with this Spirit that those who are baptized into Christ are one in him, whatever their situation in society (12:12–13). However, Paul does not comment (at least not here) on whether or how he would distinguish the Spirit

---

[36] So, e.g., Niederwimmer, who has examined the continuity of Paul's argument in chaps. 1–4, 8, and 13 (esp. 13:8–13) ("Erkennen und Lieben").

[37] As Helmut Merklein has observed, Paul is using this concept of the body of Christ not to explicate his "christology" but to express a certain understanding of Christian existence (and thereby to support his teaching about spiritual gifts); see "Entstehung und Gehalt des paulinischen Leib-Christi-Gedankens," in Studien zu Jesus und Paulus, 319–44, esp. 343.

from God, or on exactly how he conceives the relationship between the Lord (Christ) and the Spirit.[38] There is no reason to think that his successive and parallel references to the Spirit, the Lord, and God (12:4–6) either echo or constitute a specific "trinitarian" formula, or that they represent some incipient Pauline doctrine of the Trinity.[39]

(3) The new reality represented by this community of the Spirit has been established according to the express purpose of God and is God's own doing. This point comes through in various ways. The spiritual gifts have been "activated" and purposefully (καθὼς βούλεται, 12:11) bestowed by God/the Spirit (12:6, 7, 11). Each part of the body is "arranged" according to God's will (ὁ θεὸς ἔθετο . . . καθὼς ἠθέλησεν, 12:18). God intentionally constitutes the separate parts of the body as a unity (12:24b–25). And God has established the members of the church in various needed roles (12:28). This means that God's purposes are understood to be accomplished in relation to individual believers (e.g., "to each," v. 7; "to each one of them," 12:18), yet only as they exist in community with other believers (hence, "for the common good," 12:7; "the same care for one another," 12:25).

(4) Love (ἀγάπη) is utterly distinct from prophecy, tongues, and knowledge. The latter belong only to this age (13:8–10), and are therefore partial ([τὸ] ἐκ μέρους, vv. 9, 10, 12; contrasted with the perfect τὸ τέλειον, v. 10) and ephemeral (vv. 8, 10, 11). In themselves they have no significance (vv. 1–3). But love, as Paul conceives it here, belongs to another order of reality. Love does not end (13:8a), is itself of unsurpassed significance (ὑπερβολή, 12:31b), and is therefore indispensable (13:1–3). This means that love cannot be just a human virtue, or just another spiritual gift, or even the "greatest" of the gifts. To conceive of love as Paul does in this chapter is to understand it as nothing other than an expression of God's own reality—indeed, as God's own love qualifying, norming, and lending meaning to all other realities.[40]

---

[38] For example, the function attributed to God in 12:6 is attributed to the Spirit in 12:11. In the case of the Spirit and Christ, however, more of a distinction seems to be presumed. It is only through the agency of God's Spirit that one can confess Jesus as Lord (12:3); and while believers have been baptized *in* and partake *of* the Spirit (12:13), it is yet *Christ's* body of which they have become members (12:27; cf. v. 12).

[39] I should want to be even more circumspect than C. K. Barrett, who comments that here "the Trinitarian formula is the more impressive because it seems to be artless and unconscious" (*A Commentary on the First Epistle to the Corinthians* [HNTC; New York and Evanston: Harper & Row, 1968] 284), followed by Fee (*First Epistle to the Corinthians,* 588). And I find no exegetical warrant at all for the claim that Paul has "grounded his appeal for diversity in the Triune God himself" (Fee, *First Epistle to the Corinthians,* 588).

[40] The theological character of Paul's exposition of love in chap. 13 has been demonstrated especially by Sigfred Pedersen ("Agape—der eschatologische Hauptbegriff bei Paulus," in *Die Paulinische Literatur und Theologie: The Pauline Literature and Theology* [ed. S. Pedersen; Århus:

(5) The knowledge (γνῶσις) that Paul mentions as one of the spiritual gifts (e.g., 12:8; 13:2) is specifically the knowledge of God (cf. 8:1-6).[41] Like prophecy and tongues, however, it belongs only to this present age and will therefore "come to an end" (13:8b). Moreover, even while it lasts this knowledge of God is indirect and partial, as when something is known only as a reflection in a mirror rather than through direct, personal encounter (13:12a, c).[42]

(6) Paul contrasts this present, incomplete knowing of God (γινώσκειν) with a "full knowing" (ἐπιγινώσκειν) that lies quite beyond this age (ἄρτι . . . τότε, 13:12). Such knowledge is not conceived as merely the completion or perfection of what can "now" be known about God. Because the knowledge to come belongs (like love) to an entirely different order, it will have an entirely different character. It will consist in a personal relationship ("face to face") that cannot be conceived in terms of ordinary "subject–object" knowledge. Even more important, it will be a knowledge of God that depends entirely on the initiative of God, by whom one has already *"been fully known."* It is apparent that the biblical concept of election lies behind this formulation: those who have been "known by God" have been identified and established as God's people, and thereby claimed for God's service (e.g., Gen 18:19; Exod 33:12, 17; Ps 37:18; 139:1-6; 144:3; Jer 1:5; Amos 3:2).[43]

(7) Along with love, Paul regards faith and hope as fundamental for the life of the Christian community. This much at least is clear from his incorporation of the traditional triadic formula in 13:13, even though love is the only term on which he has commented. Yet "faith," when combined with hope and love, must be that believing response to the gospel which, by definition,

---

Aros; Göttingen: Vandenhoeck & Ruprecht, 1980] 159–86) and Wischmeyer (*Der höchste Weg,* esp. 92–116). See also Günther Bornkamm, "The More Excellent Way: I Corinthians 13," in *Early Christian Experience* (New York and Evanston: Harper & Row, 1969) 180–93; Niederwimmer, "Erkennen und Lieben," 98–102; and Holladay, "1 Corinthians 13," esp. 97–98.

[41] The phrase in 13:12, "just as I have been known" (καθὼς καὶ ἐπεγνώσθην), echoes the claim in 8:2 that "anyone who loves God is known by him" (εἰ δέ τις ἀγαπᾷ τὸν θεόν, οὗτος ἔγνωσται ὑπ' αὐτοῦ). See also Gal 4:9.

[42] For the meaning of δι' ἐσόπτρου ἐν αἰνίγματι, see esp. Norbert Hugedé, *La Metaphore du Miroir dans les Épîtres de saint Paul aux Corinthiens* (Neuchâtel and Paris: Delachaux et Niestlé, 1957); and F. W. Danker, "The Mirror Metaphor in 1 Cor. 13:12 and 2 Cor. 3:18," *CTM* 31 (1960) 428-29. The metaphor suggests only that one's knowledge of God is always indirect, not that it is inherently baffling.

[43] Cf. Gerhard Ebeling (*ad* Gal 4:9), in *The Truth of the Gospel: An Exposition of Galatians* (Philadelphia: Fortress, 1984) 223: "With respect to knowledge of God, our grammar, based as it is on a metaphysics of substance, proves totally inadequate and begins to come apart. Knowledge of God is grounded in God's active desire to be known." Similarly, Rudolf Bultmann, "Theology as Science," in *New Testament and Mythology and Other Basic Writings* (ed. S. M. Ogden; Philadelphia: Fortress, 1984) 49–50; his comments on knowing God could almost be an exposition of 1 Cor 13:12 (although no Pauline passages are cited).

characterizes every member of the Christian community (as, for example, in 1:21).[44] "Hope," for Paul, would presumably include one's expectation of ultimately seeing God "face to face" (13:12), but the apostle himself does not bring out the connection. Rather, he is mainly concerned to stress the importance of love, which he therefore names last (thereby altering the logical and probably traditional order, faith–love–hope). How these three may be related, he does not try to explain; nor is it clear in what sense faith and hope "remain" (μένει), as well as love.[45]

IV. 1 CORINTHIANS 15

In this third discourse Paul is responding to "some" in Corinth who say that there will be no resurrection of the dead (v. 12). These deniers apparently believe that those who are truly "spiritual" (in the Corinthians' sense) are already "reigning with Christ" in glory (see 4:8).[46] Here, then, the apostle is dealing with another symptom of the same enthusiast ideology that lies behind the overevaluation of "wisdom" and spiritual gifts.

Paul's critique of this ideology in chaps. 1–2 and 12–14 has been eschatologically oriented. He has argued that God's wisdom (the cross) discloses the wisdom of this age to be foolishness and that God's love (electing grace) discloses even the gifts of the Spirit to be partial and imperfect. Chapter 15, with its discussion of the resurrection of the dead, is not unrelated.[47] Now he claims that faith itself is meaningless if it does not include a hope that looks beyond this age (e.g., vv. 17–19). Although various details of the Corinthians' views, and therefore of Paul's response to them, remain unclear, the main lines of the argument are fairly evident and, within those, several key theological conceptions as well.

---

[44] The "faith" mentioned in 12:9 as a spiritual gift, thus not given to all believers, is doubtless to be understood as empowerment for the performance of extraordinary deeds (as in 13:2).

[45] On the second question see, e.g., Willi Marxsen, "Das «Bleiben» im 1. Kor 13, 13," in *Neues Testament und Geschichte: Historisches Geschehen und Deutung im Neuen Testament: Oscar Cullmann zum 70. Geburtstag* (ed. H. Baltensweiler and Bo Reicke; Zurich: Theologischer Verlag; Tübingen: Mohr [Siebeck], 1972) 223–29.

[46] However, the details of the Corinthian position, as also its religious-historical background, are matters of continuing scholarly debate. See esp. Gerhard Sellin, *Der Streit um die Auferstehung der Toten: Eine religionsgeschichtliche und exegetische Untersuchung von 1. Korinther 15* (FRLANT 138; Göttingen: Vandenhoeck & Ruprecht, 1986). Other important studies of chap. 15 may be found in Beker, *Paul the Apostle*, 163–81, and Martinus C. de Boer, *The Defeat of Death: Apocalyptic Eschatology in 1 Corinthians 15 and Romans 5* (JSNTSup 22; Sheffield: Almond, 1988) 93–140, 181–88.

[47] Correctly, Christian Wolff, *Der erste Brief des Paulus an die Korinther* (2d part [chaps. 8–16]; 2d ed.; THKNT 7/2; Berlin: Evangelischer Verlagsanstalt, 1982) 149.

The Argument

The argument in chap. 15 is framed by a brief introduction (vv. 1–2) and a hortatory conclusion (v. 58).[48] In the introduction Paul alerts his readers to the importance of the gospel on which their faith is founded, and in the conclusion he urges them to excel in the Lord's work, knowing that in him (ἐν κυρίῳ) their labors are by no means pointless. The concluding appeal looks back, especially, to the claim advanced in vv. 13–14 (and implicit throughout the chapter), that if there is to be no resurrection of the dead, nothing one believes or does in this life has any real meaning. The argument thus framed has two main phases, vv. 3–34 and 35–57.

(1) The premise underlying vv. 3–34 is summarized in v. 20: "Christ has been raised from the dead, the firstfruits of those who are asleep."[49] In order to establish the first part of this premise, Paul has started off by reminding the Corinthians of the tradition that underlies their faith, and which includes an affirmation about Christ's resurrection (vv. 3–11). But the second part of the premise simply takes for granted the very point at issue; so the argument, finally, is circular.[50]

Paul's reasoning, insofar as this is evident in vv. 13–19, seems to be as follows: (a) The kerygma that I proclaimed, and on which your faith rests, affirms that "Christ has been raised from the dead." (b) Christ has been raised from the dead as "the firstfruits of those who have died." (c) Therefore, if you deny the resurrection of the dead, you are denying what is essential to a proper understanding of Christ's own resurrection. (d) But if you thus deny Christ's own resurrection, my preaching must have had no meaning. (e) And if my preaching had no meaning, neither does your faith, which is founded on it.

This argument is variously supported in vv. 20–34, first of all by some comments on the "cosmic dimension"[51] of Christ's resurrection (vv. 20–23).

---

[48] Hans Dieter Betz takes 15:58 as concluding the whole argument since 1:10 ("The Problem of Rhetoric and Theology according to the Apostle Paul," in L'Apôtre Paul: Personnalité, style et conception du ministère [ed. A. Vanhoye; BETL 73; Leuven: Leuven University Press/Peeters, 1986] 33, 39; followed by Mitchell, Paul and the Rhetoric of Reconciliation, 290–91). However this may be, the appeals to remain "steadfast" and "immovable" (in the Lord) form a particularly apt conclusion for a discourse that has opened with reference to the gospel "in which you . . . stand." Compare also the concern that the Corinthians may have believed "to no purpose" (εἰκῇ, v. 3) with the assurance that their labor need not be "in vain" (κενός, v. 58).

[49] De Boer goes further, describing v. 20 as the thesis of the whole chapter (Defeat of Death, 109).

[50] Beker, Paul the Apostle, 168.

[51] The phrase is Sellin's (Der Streit, e.g., 261).

With these Paul includes a brief description of "the end" (vv. 24–28), where-
upon the first phase of the argument is concluded with remarks about certain
"existential consequences"[52] of denying the resurrection.

(2) In vv. 35–57, anticipating possible objections, Paul discusses the nature
of the body (σῶμα) with which the dead will be raised, arguing that it is
"spiritual" (πνευματικόν), not "physical" (ψυχικόν) (e.g., v. 44). He supports
this claim with analogies from nature (vv. 36–44a) and with comments about
the significance of Adam and Christ, respectively (vv. 44b–49). His closing
reflections on the "mystery" of God's transforming a perishable body into an
imperishable one (vv. 50–56) are climaxed with an exclamation of thanksgiving (v. 57).

Pivotal Theological Conceptions

The theological platform from which Paul is launching his discussion of
the resurrection of the dead is evident even before the topic itself has been
introduced. It is the tradition which he describes as "of first importance" (ἐν
πρώτοις, v. 3), and which he identifies as the common apostolic kerygma
(v. 11): that "Christ died for our sins . . . and has been raised . . ." (vv. 3–5).
Given Paul's topic here, the second part of this affirmation becomes the
special point of reference. But as the discussion proceeds, other critical theological concepts emerge.

(1) Paul conceives the resurrection of Christ as an event of cosmic and
eschatological significance. His attention is not focused on the *raising* of Jesus,
which is an episode that belongs simply to the past. He is interested in the
present and continuing significance of Christ's resurrection. This is reflected
grammatically in the use of the perfect tense (ἐγήγερται, Christ *has been
raised*), both in the tradition as Paul cites it (v. 4, in contrast with the aorist,
ἀπέθανεν, "died," v. 3) and in the argument proper (vv. 13, 14, 16, 17, 20).[53]
Specifically, Paul understands Christ's resurrection to be representative (the
ἀπαρχή, "firstfruits") of the resurrection of the dead and thus of God's
ultimate victory over death (vv. 20–28).

(2) The resurrection of Christ is of cosmic and eschatological significance
because it is an act of God, a manifestation of God's sovereign power. This
point is registered implicitly wherever Paul uses the passive voice with

---

[52] I have again borrowed a phrase from Sellin (*Der Streit,* e.g., 276).

[53] The only exception is in v. 15, where, as in 6:14, an aorist active form (ἤγειρεν) is used with
reference to God's having raised Jesus from the dead. In Paul's other letters, however, only *aorist*
forms of the verb are used of Christ's resurrection.

reference to Christ's *having been* raised from the dead. It is made quite explicitly where he maintains that if Christ has not been raised those who preach the gospel have misrepresented the truth about God, since they have "testified of God that he raised Christ" (v. 15). The power manifested in Christ's resurrection is therefore the same power of God by which every one of God's enemies, finally even death, will be defeated and destroyed (vv. 24-27, 54-55).

The ultimate victory of this sovereign God will be initiated, according to Paul, with Christ's parousia (mentioned in v. 23). This is the subject of the excursus in vv. 24-28,[54] which must be taken as at least generally representative of the apostle's own views, even though it incorporates various traditional apocalyptic motifs. Paul indicates, on the one hand, that Christ will reign until "every ruler and every authority and power" have been put in subjection to him and destroyed (vv. 24-25, 27a).[55] On the other hand, it is to God—"the Father"—that Christ will deliver the kingdom (v. 24), since it is by God's power that every hostile power will have been put in subjection to Christ (v. 27a).[56] And finally even Christ himself—"the Son"—will be put in subjection, "that God may be *all in all*" (v. 28b), fully sovereign.[57] Here God is conceived as the one who can be put in subjection to nothing, and to whom, in the end, everything will be put in subjection.

(3) According to Paul, it is specifically the life-giving power of this sovereign God that is operative in and through the resurrected Christ. He seeks to establish this point by presenting Christ as the second Adam. In distinction from "the first Adam," who was "a living being" (ψυχὴν ζῶσαν, following Gen 2:7 LXX), "the last Adam" not only lives but has the power to make alive; he is "a life-giving spirit" (πνεῦμα ζῳοποιοῦν, v. 45). Paul's comments about Adam and Christ (vv. 21-22, 44b-49) are aimed at correcting certain notions that seem to have prevailed among the Corinthians, the reconstruction of which is a complex and disputed matter.[58] It is clear enough, however, that Paul's interest here is soteriological as well as eschatological.[59] The power of God by which Christ has been raised from the dead

---

[54] See esp. Andreas Lindemann, "Parusie Christi und Herrschaft Gottes: Zur Exegese von 1 Kor 15,23-28," *WD* n.F. 19 (1987) 87-107.

[55] Taking Christ to be the subject in vv. 24, 25a, and the referent of αὐτοῦ at the end of v. 25 and in v. 27a. It is not clear whether Paul intends Christ or God to be understood as the subject of θῇ (v. 25b); see Lindemann, "Parusie Christi," 96.

[56] Taking God as the subject of ὑπέταξεν.

[57] On Paul's use of this formula, [τὰ] πάντα ἐν πᾶσιν, with reference to God's sovereignty, see, e.g., Hans Conzelmann, *1 Corinthians* (trans. James W. Leitch; Hermeneia; Philadelphia: Fortress, 1975) 275; Lindemann, "Parusie Christi," 102-3.

[58] Sellin's discussion of this includes an extensive investigation of the religious-historical backgrounds (*Der Streit*, 72-209). Cf. de Boer, *Defeat of Death*, esp. 96-105.

[59] De Boer, *Defeat of Death*, 129; Sellin, *Der Streit*, 270-71.

will, through Christ, bestow new life on those who believe (v. 22).[60] Henceforth they will bear the "image" of this "man of heaven" in place of "the image of the man of dust" (v. 49).[61] It is to this kind of a hope, a hope that looks beyond the decay and finitude of "this life" (ἡ ζωὴ αὕτη, v. 19), that Paul is summoning his congregation.

(4) This hope pertains not only to "those . . . who have died in Christ" (v. 18)—that at "the end" they will be raised. It also pertains to those who will remain alive until the parousia, among whom Paul evidently includes himself (v. 51b). They too "will be changed," the "perishable" body (σῶμα) putting on "imperishability" (vv. 50–53). They, along with those who have been raised from the dead, each with this new "spiritual body" (v. 44), will "inherit the kingdom of God" (v. 50). This means that they will be brought fully and finally under the rule of the one who is "all in all" (vv. 24–28), and thereby fully and finally will be delivered from the tyranny of death, sin, and the law (vv. 54–56).

(5) Even hope that looks beyond "this life," as authentically Christian hope does, according to Paul, is itself a phenomenon of this life. Indeed, the apostle is concerned to show that hope, properly conceived, is vital for the present life of the believing community (e.g., vv. 2b, 11, 14, 17). Living with this hope is part of what it means to stand in the gospel, holding fast to its saving word (vv. 1–2); and its absence shows an "ignorance of God" (ἀγνωσία θεοῦ, v. 34).[62] Apart from such a hope there would be no point in taking risks for the gospel, even suffering for it (as Paul has, vv. 30–32a), while with such a hope, one's labor within and for the Christian community "is not in vain" (v. 58).

Moreover, this hope invests the believer's life with a moral seriousness it would not otherwise have; it makes the distinction between good and bad important (vv. 32b–34). Paul does not explain (here) why this is so, but he has left several clues. One of them is his comment that, "if Christ has not been raised, your faith is futile and you are still in your sins" (v. 17). Here he seems to presume what the apostolic tradition says about the saving efficacy of Christ's death ("for our sins," v. 3), even as he implies that it is without saving power apart from Christ's resurrection.

Further clues are given in vv. 56–57. Since Paul can assert that "the sting

---

[60] Taking πάντες in v. 22b to mean "all who believe," as the following statement would seem to require (οἱ τοῦ Χριστοῦ, v. 23).

[61] Reading φορέσομεν (future) in v. 49 (with most interpreters). For arguments in favor of reading the hortatory subjunctive, see, e.g., Fee, *First Epistle to the Corinthians,* 787 n. 5.

[62] The τινες in v. 34 probably corresponds to the τινες in v. 12 (whether Paul employs it with reference only to certain members of the congregation or to the congregation as a whole).

of death is sin, and the power of sin is the law,"[63] he must believe that God's defeat of death will also mean the end of sin and the law. This prompts him to exclaim, "Thanks be to God, who gives us the victory through our Lord Jesus Christ." Here the present tense (διδόντι) expresses not only certainty about God's ultimate victory but also a sense of what is already given to those who are in Christ (note Paul's comments about his own experience of "the grace of God," vv. 8–9). Hence, the faith by which believers live during the interval between Christ's death and his return keeps both of these in view. Something of the dialectical character of Christian existence, thus conceived, is apparent as soon as the indicative implied in v. 17 is put alongside the imperative of v. 34b: "You are no longer in your sins; . . . sin no more."

V. THE LETTER OVERALL

Having now surveyed the principal expository passages, we are in a position to consider whether they exhibit anything like a common theological orientation. It will not be difficult to show that this is indeed the case. There is a significant overlapping and congruence of the key theological conceptions in these three sections of the letter. Given this result, it will be possible to take the further step of considering whether and, if so, how the argument of the letter as a whole is informed by a coherent theological point of view.

The Theological Orientation of the Discourses

Each of the principal expository passages in this letter has its own topic, although Paul discusses each in accord with his understanding of circumstances in the Corinthian church. In addition, the argument in each case is developed theologically, in the specific sense that, as it proceeds, a certain understanding of God and of God's self-disclosure in Christ is being unfolded. As we attempt to probe this understanding, it will not be inappropriate to begin with the first of the discourses and work from there, since that is Paul's own starting point in the letter.

We have seen that in this first expository passage (1:18–2:16) Paul emphasizes the sovereignty and unfathomable wisdom of God. He is thereby conceiving of God, also, as one whose reality, purposes, and freedom to accomplish those purposes are of an entirely different order from anything

---

[63] This is well enough understood as a gloss on the citations in vv. 54b–55 (from Isa 25:8 and Hos 13:14). There is no reason to regard it as an interpolation, as some interpreters have.

that belongs to this age. The viewpoint here is thoroughly eschatological, even though "hope" is not as such the subject. This is especially evident in 2:7, where Paul refers to the wisdom "which God decreed before the ages for our glory." In chap. 15, where hope is specifically the subject, the sovereignty of God also emerges as an important theme. At "the end," says Paul, this sovereign God will defeat every power, including death, by which the present age is tyrannized, and then God will be "all in all" (vv. 24–28).

The apostle's discussion of Christian community is also eschatologically oriented (12:4–13:13). Claiming that this community has been constituted according to God's purpose, he portrays it as living from a reality that is more than the sum of its individual parts. Above all, he cautions that the spiritual gifts with which its members have been variously graced are destined to pass away, that apart from the enduring (eschatological) power of love they have no meaning, and that even the community's present knowledge of God will be superseded by a "knowing" of God that involves participation in another kind of reality.

God's power and wisdom, as these are represented by Paul in chaps. 1–2, have to do with God's beneficent purposes. Here, and also in chaps. 12–13, 15, he writes of God exclusively in terms of these purposes. Thus, when he refers to "the depths of God" which only the Spirit can plumb (2:10; cf. "what belongs to God [τὰ τοῦ θεοῦ]," v. 11b), he is not thinking of God's nature as that exists in and for itself but of the divine counsels according to which God's purpose is to save (2:9). He insists, specifically, that the character of God's power is defined and decisively established in the cross, in "Jesus Christ and him crucified." Christ indeed *continues* to be met as the crucified one in the kerygma through which believers are being saved. Through the agency of the Spirit, they have been able to discern that what the world dismisses as an expression of folly and weakness is actually an expression of God's own wisdom and saving power.

There are no explicit christological affirmations in 12:4–13:13, yet the community of which Paul writes is understood to be one which confesses that "Jesus is Lord" (12:3). This believing community can therefore be portrayed as Christ's body, even though here, for polemical and pastoral reasons, Paul has associated initiation into the body particularly with the enlivening presence of the Spirit (12:12–13). It is not impossible, given earlier comments about sharing in Christ's body at the Lord's Supper (10:16–22; 11:23–29), that Paul wishes the Corinthians to think of themselves as specifically the body of the *crucified* Christ.[64] However, his portrayal of the body as a living

---

[64] For example, Robert G. Hamerton-Kelly suggests that in chap. 12 "the Church is the body of the victim and must take its cue from that fact. The nature of power in the church . . . is

organism (12:15–26) does not lend itself readily to such an interpretation. And even if the description of love in 13:4–7 is implicitly christological, with Christ's own patient suffering and death as part of the background,[65] it is nonetheless love's role in the *life* of Christ's body that Paul has in view.

In chap. 15 Paul cites a tradition that includes a reference to Christ's having died "for [ὑπέρ] our sins" (v. 3). As noted earlier, this interpretation of Jesus' death seems to lie behind the apostle's comments in vv. 17, 32b–34, and 56. Yet in this chapter there is no exposition of the meaning of Christ's death. It is his resurrection, also affirmed in the tradition (v. 4), which is critical for Paul's argument here. Just as Christ is represented in chaps. 1–2 as, through the kerygma, continuingly present as the crucified one, so now he is represented as, through the kerygma, continuingly present as the resurrected one. Whereas in chaps. 1–2 God's power is associated with Christ's death on the cross, now it is associated with the resurrection of the dead ("[a seed/the body] is sown in weakness, raised in power," v. 43), hence with the one whose resurrection is the "firstfruits" of that resurrection. According to chaps. 1–2, Christ's crucifixion discloses the folly of this age and its rulers (e.g., 2:6–8); according to chap. 15, the resurrected Christ, at his parousia, will be God's agent for the destruction of all the powers that tyrannize this age. Thus in this letter Paul seems to be thinking of Christ's death and resurrection as distinct but complementary manifestations of the saving power of God. The corollary of his view that Christ's death has no saving significance apart from his resurrection (15:17) is that precisely "Jesus Christ *crucified*" has been resurrected.

What does it mean, according to Paul, to benefit from the saving power of God that is operative through Christ the crucified and resurrected one? It must be emphasized, first, that nowhere in these three passages, nor anywhere in the letter, is Paul thinking of salvation as something already accomplished. His use of present passive forms of the verb ("being saved," 1:18; 15:2) shows that he regards salvation as in process but not yet fulfilled (the Corinthians probably thought otherwise). For its fulfillment he looks beyond this age.

Chapters 1–2 provide only hints of what Paul thinks is "prepared" for God's people (2:9). In 2:7, employing an apocalyptic term, he writes of this as "our glory" (δόξα), perhaps meaning investment with an imperishable body (as in 15:42, 43, 50–55). That he conceives of salvation as the opposite of annihilation is clear from the contrast he draws between "being saved" and

---

conditioned and controlled by the nature of that body as the body of the victim" ("A Girardian Interpretation of Paul: Rivalry, Mimesis and Victimage in the Corinthian Correspondence," *Semeia* 33 [1985] 80).

[65] Thus Wischmeyer, *Der höchste Weg*, 92–116.

"perishing" (1:18; cf. 15:18; 2 Cor 2:15). From the argument as a whole one may infer that he conceives of it as release from the futile quest for wisdom and power as these are defined in the world. To explain his statement that Christ "became for us [ἡμῖν] wisdom from God," he introduces the terms "righteousness," "sanctification," and "redemption" (1:30). Yet these terms are themselves left unexplained and appear nowhere else in this letter.[66] It is clear only that Paul means to describe what God grants through Christ to those who are in Christ.

In 13:12, as we have seen, Paul refers more specifically to what salvation will finally mean: seeing God "face to face," and a knowledge of God which is of the same order of reality as one's having been known by God. The conception here is of full, personal, and unhindered communion with the one whose reality surpasses and gives meaning to all other realities. It is important to note, however, that this communion is conceived as having the character of a *relationship* with God, not as being somehow taken up "into" God.

The same is true in chap. 15, where Paul uses traditional language about "inheriting the kingdom of God" to describe the ultimate destiny of those who are in Christ (v. 50). In the context, God's kingdom is conceived as the realm where all things, including Christ, will have been put in subjection to the one who can be put in subjection to nothing (vv. 24–28). One may therefore infer that inheriting the kingdom will mean being received into this sphere where God is "all in all," there to be fully subject to God's saving power and purpose. Therefore, a relationship with God is once more in view. Similarly, the mysterious "change" of the perishable body into an imperishable one (vv. 50–55; cf. vv. 42, 43) will mean participation in a new kind of existence, but not the loss of one's "somatic" identity. With this change, in fact, a new freedom will have been bestowed, since it will mean full deliverance from death, sin, and the law (v. 56).

According to chaps. 1–2, God's saving power and purpose are already operative in the word of the cross. "Those who believe" (1:21) can therefore be referred to as "those who are being saved" (1:18), "the called" (1:24; cf. vv. 26–28), and those who have "received the Spirit of [ἐκ] God" (2:12). Although they remain in the world, it is no longer their standing in the world that counts (1:26–28) but their standing "before God" and "in Christ Jesus" (1:29, 30). Their calling is to live in accord with "the mind of Christ" (2:16) as that is disclosed in the word of the cross.

From chaps. 12–13 it is evident that, for Paul, life "in Christ Jesus" is necessarily also life in "the body of Christ," in community with all who confess him as Lord. Here, as in chaps. 1–2, Paul suggests that one's identity

---

[66] But other passages may be compared; for δικαιοσύνη, 6:11; for ἁγιασμός, 1:2; 3:17; 6:11, 19; and for ἀπολύτρωσις, 6:19b–20a; 7:23.

derives not from one's standing in the world but from one's relationship to God (God's Spirit) and to Christ (12:12–13). Within this body, through the express will of God and the agency of God's Spirit, believers are variously graced with gifts to serve the common good (12:7). The appeals of 14:1–5 show that Paul's comments about love in chap. 13 are meant to supplement and support what is said about the body of Christ in chap. 12. He thinks of love as an eschatological reality which, even more than "faith" and "hope," is definitive of life in Christ/the body of Christ. Yet love itself "believes" and "hopes" (13:7), and these two, along with love, characterize the life in Christ (13:13).

Faith and hope (but not love) are also in view in chap. 15. Hope, as Paul presents it here, is founded on faith's encounter with Christ who "has been raised" from the dead. This means that the power of God by which Christ was raised is still and continuingly at work, vitalizing the present life of faith (thus, e.g., vv. 2, 9–10, 14, 17). The appeals to "sin no more" and to "excel in the Lord's work" (vv. 34, 58) derive from this encounter with the life-giving presence of the resurrected Christ. Where faith holds fast to the hope of God's ultimate defeat of death and sin, the power of these over one's present life is already broken (vv. 30–33). Hence the "victory" for which Paul gives thanks (v. 57) is not conceived as just the victory of God's sovereignty in and of itself, as if a victory only for God. The apostle understands it as the victory of God's *saving* power, thus as a victory to be *given*—indeed, as a victory even now under way.

To try to summarize further could be misleading, yet a few general points seem clear enough. First, all three of these passages are *eschatologically* oriented, in the sense that Paul is positing throughout a sovereign God whose power and purpose transcend this age. Second, these passages are all *soteriologically* oriented. It is the saving power and purpose of this sovereign God of which Paul writes. Third, all three passages are *christologically* oriented. Paul understands God's saving power and purpose to be definitively disclosed and operative in Jesus Christ, who is encountered in the kerygma as both the crucified and the resurrected one. Finally, each passage is *ecclesiologically* oriented, in that Paul understands life in Christ to be at the same time life within the believing community (enlivened by the Spirit, nurtured and normed by love, bouyed up by hope).

The Theological Orientation of the Letter

Although 1 Corinthians is not a theological essay but a letter, written to admonish and to instruct,[67] it contains at least three important passages in

---

[67] This general description is sufficient for our present purposes, although some interpreters

which there is significant theological exposition. This much, as well as the generally similar theological orientation of these expository passages, has already been established. Now our task is to consider whether the letter as a whole exhibits anything like a coherent theological orientation. That this is indeed the case is not hard to show, although here we must limit ourselves to just a few observations.

(1) Paul's concern to counteract the "overrealized" eschatology of the Corinthians is apparent not only in chap. 15 but throughout the letter. As a consequence, the entire argument is eschatologically oriented. Already in the thanksgiving he seems to be emphasizing that Christ is to return (1:7-8); his subsequent counsels and directives presuppose that "the present form of this world is passing away" (7:31b; cf. v. 29; 10:11); and in the very last lines he lifts up the prayerful appeal, "Our Lord, come!" (16:22b).[68]

(2) The appeals and affirmations of 3:18-23 are worth special attention, both because they summarize what Paul has been concerned about since 1:10,[69] and because they significantly expand the theological horizon of his argument. He first suggests that the Corinthians may still need to exchange the vaunted wisdom of this age for the apparent "foolishness" of God, the wisdom of the cross (v. 18). In support of this counsel Paul invokes the thesis of 1:18-25, that the world's wisdom is foolishness with God (v. 19a; cf. 1:20b), and two statements from scripture (vv. 19b-20, citing Job 5 and Psalm 94). His second, more concrete appeal to the Corinthians is to give up boasting in human leaders like Apollos and himself (v. 21a), since they are but "servants" of the one who alone is the source of the congregation's life and growth (3:5-15; cf. 4:1).

This second appeal is supported by a series of three assertions (vv. 21b-23): "For everything belongs to you . . . , and you belong to Christ, and Christ belongs to God" (my translation). While the Corinthians seek for status by claiming attachment to particular leaders (1:12; 3:4), Paul affirms that they are, at least in principle, free from control by human beings and also from every other threat that is posed by this age, including death (v. 22). The

---

have identified 1 Corinthians with one or another of the epistolary types described in the ancient rhetorical manuals. Mitchell, for example, has argued that 1 Corinthians is an example of a *deliberative* letter (*Paul and the Rhetoric of Reconciliation,* 20–64). Schrage, however, concludes that it is best regarded as a combination of several letter types, with the "practical-parenetic" predominating (*Der erste Brief an die Korinther,* 84–90). The matter cannot and need not be settled here.

[68] In the earlier chapters the exhortations are frequently sanctioned by references to the coming judgment (3:12-15; 4:4, 5; 5:5, 13; 6:2, 3, 9-10)—which makes it all the more surprising that this is not part of the scenario set forth in 15:24-28.

[69] Betz, too, has remarked on the summarizing function of 3:18-23, but for some reason looks back only as far as 1:18, not all the way to 1:10 ("Problem of Rhetoric and Theology," 39).

freedom to which he refers derives not from the cultivation of an inner serenity but from belonging to Christ (v. 23a), who belongs to God (v. 23b). This conforms to the eschatological perspective of 15:24–28: Christian freedom consists in belonging to the one who, at last, will conquer every hostile power, even death (15:24–26), and who himself belongs ultimately to God (15:28; see also 11:3). Here, as elsewhere in 1 Corinthians, Paul is conceiving of God as utterly transcendent and absolutely sovereign. For him, God is the one who belongs to no other and to whom all else belongs. But it is still the case that God's transcendence and sovereignty are identified less with God's "being" in itself than with God's being for those who need deliverance from the tyrannical powers of this age.

(3) An equally important, closely related conception in this letter is of believers as "the called" (1:24). As early as the salutation Paul describes his readers as "called to be saints" (1:2), by which he means "called" (or "chosen") by God to belong to Christ (1:9, 26–30). Moreover, in accepting this call believers also accept the claim that is given with it, whereby their relationship to the world and all of their relationships within the world are decisively altered (1:26–31; 7:17–24; cf. 7:29–31, 35).

How radical and total Paul conceives this claim to be is apparent from a metaphor he twice employs: believers have been "bought with a price" (6:19b–20a; 7:22–23a). Therefore, accepting God's call does not just mean accepting a new set of orders but the new Lord to whom one's life now belongs.[70] Similarly, when Paul writes of being "in-lawed to Christ" (ἔννομος Χριστοῦ, 9:21) he seems deliberately to avoid suggesting that believers stand under some new law. More radically, their whole existence is claimed as well as graced by belonging to Christ and, through Christ, to God.[71]

(4) The conception of Christian community spelled out in chap. 12 is evident throughout the letter. The question, "Is Christ divided" (μεμέρισται ὁ Χριστός, 1:13a) presumes an understanding of the believing community as Christ's body,[72] and so does the later question, "Do you not know that your bodies are members of Christ (μέλη Χριστοῦ)?" (6:15a). When Paul describes believers as "called into the fellowship (κοινωνία) of [God's] Son" (1:9) he is employing a closely related image, of a reality that is more than the sum of its parts. Those who are set within the sphere of Christ's rule are thereby in partnership with one another as well as with Christ. Indeed, these two

---

[70] Paul's remark in 7:19 about "keeping the commandments of God" is properly understood in the light of the metaphor in 7:22–23, not the reverse.

[71] This point is more fully developed in my essay, "Belonging to Christ: A Paradigm for Ethics in First Corinthians," *Int* 44 (1990) 145–57.

[72] Schrage points out that here, as in 12:12, ὁ Χριστός (employing the article) may be taken as shorthand for "the body of Christ" (*Der erste Brief an die Korinther*, 152).

images (σῶμα and κοινωνία) are combined in 10:16–17, where Paul is remarking on the observance of the Lord's Supper as a sharing of the one (ecclesial) body in the eucharistic cup and loaf. Also, the image of a temple (ναός) inhabited by God's Spirit (3:16), which is indebted to the Jewish apocalyptic tradition (e.g., Ezek 37:26–28; *Jub.* 1:17), shows that Paul conceives of the church as an eschatological community ruled by the power of God's presence. This is at least consistent with the conception of the church presented in chap. 12, even though the matter of spiritual gifts is not specifically in view in 3:16.

(5) Paul's comments in 8:1–6, which provide an important theological basis for the practical directives that follow (8:7–11:1), are congruent with the theological orientation of the letter's principal expository passages. Three points may be noted. (a) In his remark that "anyone who presumes to know something special"[73] does not yet have the necessary knowledge (v. 2), he is bringing forward his earlier distinction between God's wisdom and the world's (1:18–2:16; 3:18–20) in order to apply it to the issue at hand.[74] (b) His distinction between "knowledge" and "love" (vv. 1b–3) anticipates what he will say about these in chap. 13 and underlies the directives in chap. 14 as well as those in 8:7–11:1. (c) What he affirms about God and Christ (v. 6) not only supports and clarifies the statements in 8:1–5 but also coheres with statements elsewhere in the letter, particularly in chap. 15. The first of these points is clear enough, but the other two require some further comment.

The statement that "knowledge puffs up, but love builds up" (v. 1b) is doubtless aimed at those in Corinth who, heedless of what is best for some of their fellow Christians, persist in eating "food sacrificed to idols." They seem to have argued on the basis of the monotheism to which they were converted, as expressed in the *Shema* of Deut 6:4–9, to which Paul alludes in v. 4 ("there is no God but one"). In response, Paul argues (v. 3), evidently with the *Shema* already in mind, that what matters is not knowledge about God but being known by God (cf. 13:12) and loving God in return ("You shall love the Lord your God with all your heart, and with all your soul, and with all your might," Deut 6:5).[75]

Before proceeding with any specific instructions, Paul makes a further introductory point (8:6): for Christians "there is one God, the Father, . . . and one Lord, Jesus Christ . . . ."[76] Whether this is Paul's adaptation of a creedal

---

[73] This is the force of ἐγνωκέναι τι (Wolff, *Der erste Brief des Paulus an die Korinther,* 5).

[74] This is also recognized by Troels Engberg-Pedersen, "The Gospel and Social Practice according to I Corinthians," *NTS* 33 (1987) 567.

[75] Thus N. Thomas Wright, *The Climax of the Covenant: Christ and the Law in Pauline Theology* (Minneapolis: Fortress, 1992) esp. 127.

[76] When God is called "the Father," that implies an understanding of Christ as the Son (cf.

tradition or his own formulation may be left as an open question. In either case, it seeks to retain the radical monotheism of the *Shema* even as it adds a confessional statement about Christ.[77] God is affirmed as creator ("from whom are all things"), as the one in relation to whom life has purpose ("for whom we exist"), and as sovereign over all reputed "gods" and "lords" (see v. 5). Similar or related affirmations are present in 10:26 (where Paul cites the psalmist's declaration that "the earth is the Lord's and all that fills it"), 11:12b ("all things are from God"), and 15:27, 28 (at the end, "all things" will be subjected to God, the "all in all"). The conception of Christ as God's (preexistent) agent in creation ("through whom are all things") is not found elsewhere in the letter. But the affirmation that Christ is the one "through whom we exist" (ἡμεῖς δι' αὐτοῦ) assigns him a soteriological function, as agent also of the new creation.[78] It is not specified precisely how Christ is the agent of salvation,[79] although Paul likely has his atoning death in view, since he refers to that in 8:11 (see also 5:7b; 11:24–25; 15:3; cf. 6:20; 7:23).[80]

The sum of the matter, and the basis on which Paul proceeds to offer some practical counsels, is that to be "known by God" means to be graced by God's love and called to live according to that love, as it is disclosed in Christ.[81] The christological basis of Paul's counsels is evident, for example, in 8:11–12 (those for whom Christ died constitute a family and should care for one another; cf. 12:25–26), at various points in chaps. 9 and 10 (e.g., 9:12, 19–23; 10:16–22), and in the final appeal of the section to imitate Paul as he imitates Christ (11:1). Here, imitating Christ means "not seeking [one's own] advantage" (10:33) but what will benefit others (exactly the counsel of 10:24). This is "the more excellent way" of love as Paul has already characterized it in 8:1b (it "builds up"), as he will describe it in chap. 13 (it is not "puffed up," v. 4; it is not out for itself [οὐ ζητεῖ τὰ ἑαυτῆς], v. 5), and as he urges it upon the Corinthians (10:23; 14:3–5, 12, 17, 26c).

Wright, *Climax of the Covenant,* 130; so also 15:24), yet this title appears only twice in 1 Corinthians (1:9; 15:28). The reference to Christ as the "one Lord" is understandable in view of the mention of "many lords" (v. 5); but also, "Lord" is a frequent christological title in this letter. In addition to the more stereotyped expressions where "Lord" is combined with both "Christ" and "Jesus" (e.g., 1:2, 3, 7, 9, 10), it is sometimes combined simply with "Jesus" (5:4; 11:23; 16:23; cf. 9:1; 12:3). Most frequently, however, it is used alone (e.g., 2:8; 4:4, 5; 6:13, 14; 7:10, 12, 22, 25; 10:21, 22; 11:27; 14:37; 15:58; 16:22).

[77] Wright characterizes the conception here as "christological monotheism" (*Climax of the Covenant,* 129).

[78] Thus, e.g., Rudolf Bultmann, *Theology of the New Testament* (trans. Kendrick Grobel; New York: Scribner's, 1951) 1. 132; Wolff, *Der erste Brief des Paulus an die Korinther,* 7–10.

[79] The means of Jesus' saving work is also left unspecified in 1:2, 4, 30; 6:11; 15:57.

[80] As we have seen, the *atoning* significance of Jesus' death seems not to be in view in Paul's discourse on the wisdom of the cross (1:18–2:16).

[81] Cf. Niederwimmer, "Erkennen und Lieben," 96; Wright, *Climax of the Covenant,* 132–33.

(6) Finally, several points already observed about the overall theological orientation of 1 Corinthians are evident in the way Paul opens and closes the letter. It is addressed to "the church of God that is in Corinth, to those who are sanctified in Christ Jesus, called to be saints . . ." (1:2). Here the conception is of an eschatological community, established by God, which finds its life "in Christ Jesus."[82] This perspective, including the specific idea of a community "called" of God (see also, e.g., vv. 9, 26–29; 7:17–24), is maintained throughout the argument.

In the thanksgiving (1:4–9) Paul mentions God's "grace" that is given "in Christ Jesus" (v. 4; although grace in the general sense is not a special theme in this letter) and also its manifestation in various spiritual gifts (vv. 5–6, 7). But his comments about waiting for the parousia (vv. 7, 8) seem intended to put a brake on the Corinthian enthusiasts, and they thus presage the cautions and counsels of chaps. 12–14. Then in concluding the thanksgiving (v. 9), Paul affirms that "God is faithful" and that "by him [the Corinthians] have been called into the fellowship (κοινωνία) of his Son, Jesus Christ our Lord." Assurance of God's faithfulness (the same formula occurs in 10:23) underlies everything that Paul will be saying about the beneficent purposes of God and about God's power to bring them at last to triumphant fulfillment. And the conception of sharing (κοινωνία) in Christ/in Christian community is of special importance for Paul's entire argument.

The closing, summary admonitions in chap. 16 open with appeals to "keep alert"—for the parousia (cf. v. 22b)—and to "stand firm in your faith, be courageous, be strong" (v. 13). All of these are especially appropriate following chap. 15. But Paul has formulated a further appeal differently, doubtless to make it stand out: "Let everything you do be done in love" (πάντα ὑμῶν ἐν ἀγάπῃ γινέσθω, v. 14). Even if this is not quite "a restatement of the argument of the entire letter,"[83] most of its appeals can be read as expressions of what Paul thinks love requires in particular cases.[84] But this final summons to love also has a theological dimension. We have seen that the love Paul has been commending to the Corinthians is nothing else than God's love as disclosed in Christ (thus 8:1–6, 11–12; 10:31–11:1; chap. 13). For Paul, life "in Christ" is also and necessarily life "in love." Therefore, his appeal is not just to do everything *with* love (μετὰ ἀγάπης), as Chrysostom has it.[85] More

---

[82] Apocalyptic Jewish conceptions of the eschatological Israel lie in the background. Schrage cites as examples *1 Enoch* 62:8; 1QM 3:5; 12:7; 1QSb 1:5; 1QH 7:10; 1QSa 1:9; CD 4:6 (*Der erste Brief an die Korinther,* 103–4).

[83] Mitchell, *Paul and the Rhetoric of Reconciliation,* 94 n. 170; cf. 165 n. 604, 278, 294.

[84] For example, this appeal is closely parallel in both form and content to the admonition of 14:26c, "Let all things be done for building up." Cf. also 14:40.

[85] Cited by Archibald T. Robertson and Alfred Plummer (*A Critical and Exegetical Commentary*

radically, it is to allow one's whole life (πάντα ὑμῶν—literally, "everything that is yours") to be embraced and governed by the love that God has bestowed in Christ.

on the First Epistle of St Paul to the Corinthians [ICC; 2d ed.; Edinburgh: Clark, 1914] 394). They note, correctly: "The change is for the worse."

5 THE THEOLOGICAL TASK OF 1 CORINTHIANS

A Conversation with
Gordon D. Fee and Victor Paul Furnish

Charles B. Cousar
Columbia Theological Seminary

THE PAPERS ON 1 CORINTHIANS by Gordon Fee and Victor Paul Furnish exhibit remarkable similarities. Both take the letter to be a unity, share common assumptions about the circumstances of the church in Corinth, and agree that the letter exhibits a coherent theological orientation. Both underscore the eschatological, soteriological, christological, and ecclesiological dimensions (to use Furnish's helpful summation) of Paul's message to his readers.

The papers, however, differ in striking ways. The prepositions in the titles (Fee: "Toward a Theology *of* 1 Corinthians"; and Furnish: "Theology *in* 1 Corinthians") reveal varying definitions of theology and varying understandings of how one can speak about the theology of Paul. Fee does not provide an elaborate definition of theology, except to say that it is comprised of "Paul's understanding of the gospel and its ethical demands" (p. 38). His systematic presentation of the theology of the letter reveals an assumption of a rather unencumbered access to and comprehensive understanding of Pauline "theology."[1]

Furnish, on the other hand, particularly defines theology in relationship to a process—"critical reflection on the beliefs, rites, and social structures in which an experience of ultimate reality has found expression."[2] In this sense, Paul's letters do not yield a comprehensive system of theology, but they do expose the apostle as he interprets the church's traditions, often in conflict with other such interpretations, or as he interprets his own experience of the resurrected Lord. Furnish invites us to consider Paul as a theologian, to listen

---

[1] Fee can avoid dealing with the details of exegesis and the flow of arguments within the letter because he can presuppose the results of his excellent commentary: *The First Epistle to the Corinthians* (NICNT; Grand Rapids: Eerdmans, 1987).

[2] This definition comes from "Paul the Theologian," in *The Conversation Continues: Studies in Paul and John in Honor of J. Louis Martyn* (ed. Robert T. Fortna and Beverly R. Gaventa; Nashville: Abingdon, 1990) 25, where Furnish provides a fuller definition of Paul's "theology."

in as Paul critically engages in theological reflection about the gospel in relation to the situation of the readers.

The two understandings of theology result in studies structured in sharply different ways. Fee, though always keeping particular immediate contexts in view, provides a topical organization of the theological statements of the letter ("God and Salvation," "Salvation and Ethics," and "The Eschatological Goal of Salvation"). Furnish primarily sticks to the arguments of three particular passages, noting pivotal concepts that emerge from Paul's critical reflection and how the pivotal concepts of the three passages (and to some extent the pivotal concepts of other passages) cohere.

While Fee is not insensitive to Paul's activity as a theologian, his paper is primarily concerned with the content and organization of Paul's theological statements in the letter. Furnish, on the other hand, though by no means avoiding content and willing to venture generalizations about the theological orientation of the letter, is more interested in uncovering the dynamics of Paul's theological reflection on the nature of the gospel.[3]

The primary purpose of this essay is more modest than, and certainly preliminary to, a consideration of the theology in the letter (Furnish) or the theology of the letter (Fee). It is to pose the argument that 1 Corinthians has a unifying theological purpose and that the interpreter is not reduced to ferreting the theology from the principles underlying the various pastoral directives. The theological intent of the letter is to confront the readers with

---

[3] Furnish's definition of theology leads him to plead for a distinction between gospel and theological reflection, between kerygmatic statements and theological statements ("Theology in 1 Corinthians," 61). Two observations: (1) It is not entirely clear what difference the distinction makes in the consideration of passages and pivotal concepts. Furnish provides a list of kerygmatic formulations in the letter, but do they then function as warrants in particular arguments or as texts on which reflection is done? What is the point of the distinction between kerygmatic and theological statements? (2) The distinction derives from Rudolf Bultmann, but with Bultmann the reason for the distinction does not primarily have to do with a method for analyzing New Testament theology. Bultmann draws the distinction in order to ensure that theological statements not be taken as "objectifying kind of thinking," but simply as the unfolding of believing self-understanding. Theological statements present "not the object of faith, but faith itself in its own self-interpretation" (*Theology of the New Testament* [New York: Scribner's, 1955] 2. 237–41). Maybe Bultmann *should* have taken the distinction more as a methodological principle in light of Hendrikus Boers's judgment:

> True, he [Bultmann] did consider Paul's thought to have been formulated from the standpoint of faith, including his thoughts about human existence before faith. Nevertheless, Paul's theology was presented by Bultmann in a way that could very appropriately be called a coherent, logical, necessary system of ideas in terms of which every element of our experience concerning God could be interpreted. His presentation of Paul's theology contradicted what he said about Paul as a theologian" (*What is New Testament Theology?* [Philadelphia: Fortress, 1979] 77).

an alternative way of viewing reality, specifically an alternative way of viewing God, the Christian community, and the future.[4]

Admittedly, a unifying theological intent for the letter is not automatically self-evident. The specific problems addressed and Paul's responses seem to have little consecutive development.[5] C. K. Barrett has commented that "it is a practical letter addressed to a single, though complex, situation, aimed at telling its readers not so much what they ought to think as what they ought to do—or ought not to do."[6] Theology is relegated to the underlying principles that emerge here and there in connection with Paul's reactions to the practical problems. This means that for some 1 Corinthians has a very low theological yield.[7]

Clearly the letter is organized around the particular issues raised by the oral reports (1:11; 16:17) and written communication (7:1) received from the congregation. The letter invites attention to the pastoral predicaments and to the directives Paul offers. There is no shrinking from the community's problems and how the problems are to be dealt with. And yet the way in which the initial problem is addressed (the divisions developing around particular leaders, 1:10–17) indicates that the letter functions as much more than a problem-addressing document or, put more sharply, the behavioral difficulties and theological distortions of the Corinthian community will not be solved until the members learn to think differently.

One methodology occasionally used in approaching the theological task of the letter warrants brief comment. It begins by reconstructing the ideology provoking the problems in Corinth (usually entailing a rather extensive amount of mirror reading) and by letting the reconstruction serve as the integrating focus around which the theology is organized.[8] For example,

---

[4] Karl Barth is the commentator who has argued most decisively for a unifying element to the letter. He located the theological purpose in chap. 15. "It forms not only the close and crown of the whole epistle, but also provides the clue to its meaning, from which place light is shed on the whole, and it becomes intelligible, not outwardly, but inwardly, as a unity" (*The Resurrection of the Dead* [New York: Revell, 1933] 11). See also Margaret M. Mitchell, *Paul and the Rhetoric of Reconciliation: An Exegetical Investigation of the Language and Composition of 1 Corinthians* (HUT 28; Tübingen: Mohr [Siebeck], 1991); she understands the letter as a piece of deliberative rhetoric and a consistent and powerful appeal for ecclesial unity.

[5] See W. G. Kümmel, *Introduction to the New Testament* (Nashville: Abingdon, 1975) 270.

[6] C. K. Barrett, *The First Epistle to the Corinthians* (HNTC; New York: Harper & Row, 1967) 17.

[7] Walter Bauer comments that 1 Corinthians is "that unit among the major Pauline letters which yields the very least for our understanding of the Pauline faith" (*Orthodoxy and Heresy in Earliest Christianity* [Philadelphia: Fortress, 1971] 219; cited by Hans Conzelmann, *1 Corinthians* (trans. James W. Leitch; Hermeneia; Philadelphia: Fortress, 1975] 9n).

[8] For example, see Ernst Käsemann's chapter "For and Against a Theology of the Resurrection," in *Jesus Means Freedom* (Philadelphia: Fortress, 1967) 59–84.

the letter addresses particular problems in the congregation, all or most of which are the result of a spiritualized or overly realized eschatology. What gives cohesiveness to the letter's theology is the target at which it is aimed. All of the theological statements of the letter are interpreted in light of their critique of the ideology that opposes Paul.

There are certainly advantages to an approach like this. 1 Corinthians is obviously written to reprove a congregation, some members of which have embraced a wrongheaded eschatology. Furthermore, in this way the letter can be read as a coherent document, not merely random counsel regarding moral and pastoral problems.

A difficulty, however, arises (1) when challenges are made about the extensive mirror reading necessary to reconstruct the ideology of the readers,[9] or (2) when a case is made that some of the problems in the community derive from socioeconomic conflicts as well as from eschatological misunderstandings,[10] or (3) when the hypothesis of a single front and a single opposition is shown to be inadequate.[11] Any effort to derive the theological intent of the letter primarily from a reconstruction of the ideological stance of the Corinthian community, particularly when that stance is depicted as monolithic or consistently advocated by all the members, becomes shaky. While the interpreter can hardly avoid a certain amount of mirror reading, a more promising strategy is to stick to the argument of the letter itself (which of course contains partial information about the ideology rampant in Corinth), to read it in linear fashion, and from the argument to infer the theological intent.

I. 1 CORINTHIANS 1:10–4:20

The most surprising strategy in the response to the factionalism in the church is that Paul does not take sides in the quarrel nor argue the case of one leader over against another. He eventually gets around to claiming his own voice with the readers (4:14–21), but only after an extensive statement of the word of the cross (1:18–2:5), a clarification of how God is known (2:6–16), and an application of this epistemology to himself and Apollos (3:1–4:13). The whole church, not just one or another faction, has to face what schism implies.

---

[9] See the trenchant critique of mirror reading in Galatians by George Lyons, *Pauline Autobiography: Toward a New Understanding* (SBLDS 73; Atlanta: Scholars Press, 1985) 82–105, 119–21.

[10] See Gerd Theissen, *The Social Setting of Pauline Christianity: Essays on Corinth* (Philadelphia: Fortress, 1982) 145–72; and Wayne A. Meeks, *The First Urban Christians: The Social World of the Apostle Paul* (New Haven: Yale University Press, 1983) 68–72.

[11] See William Baird, "'One Against the Other': Intra-Church Conflicts in 1 Corinthians," in *The Conversation Continues,* ed. Fortna and Gaventa, 116–36.

In this section the critical issue has to do with the way the sharp critique of human wisdom relates to the divisions in the church (1:10–17). The Corinthians are chided for their pretentious wisdom (3:18–20), and their wisdom is linked to their boasting about particular leaders (3:21–22), but this relationship is not spelled out clearly and hardly accounts for the extensive reflections on the wisdom and power of God in 1:18–2:16.

Furnish speaks of this section "as a kind of excursus." But an excursus to what end? Peter Lampe has made the intriguing argument that 1:18–2:16 functions as covert speech. The Corinthian readers are led to accept the statements there as "agreeable and even enjoyable" because they are directed at the "world" and not at them, until 3:1 when the implications are shockingly turned against them. "1:18–2:16 is a 'Trojan horse' with which Paul thrusts himself into the middle of the Corinthian party situation."[12] The Achilles' heel to Lampe's Trojan horse, however, is 1:26–31, which is pointedly directed at the readers, opening with a strong attention-getter ("Consider your own call, brothers and sisters") and closing in 1:30 with an emphatic ὑμεῖς ("From him you are in Christ Jesus, who became for us wisdom . . ." [my translation]). How could the readers possibly imagine, after 1:26, that this is not addressed to them?

What must be taken seriously is the epistemological thrust of 1:18–2:16. The section confronts the readers with a way of knowing God radically different from the way of knowing that has resulted in factionalism. Human wisdom is bound to misconstrue the character of God and how God works in the world, and a community's behavior based on human inclinations, not surprisingly, results in jealousy and division (3:3–4). A strategy of conflict management of the Corinthian divisions would accomplish little. The community must radically readjust its vision. It must come to a different way of viewing God and its life together. Thus Paul points to the message of the crucified Messiah not as a statement of atonement but as a new epistemological focus.

Furnish has in a lucid fashion traced the argument of 1:18–2:16, and his analysis need not be repeated here. I shall offer four brief observations about the passage.

(1) 1:21 presents a rationale for God's decision to thwart the wisdom of the wise. "Since, in the wisdom of God, the world did not know (οὐκ ἔγνω) God through wisdom, God decided, through the foolishness of our proclamation, to save those who believe." God's decision to initiate the saving activity through the message of the cross (and not some other way) is set

---

[12] Peter Lampe, "Theological Wisdom and the 'Word About the Cross': The Rhetorical Scheme in I Corinthians 1–4," *Int* 44 (1990) 124–25.

against the backdrop of the world's failure to know God.[13] The problem of the world is that its norms for knowing have proved inadequate and have resulted in a not-knowing. God eludes the world's various criteria and expectations. Over against the sign-seeking Jews and the wisdom-demanding Greeks is set the message of the cross, providing not new information about God but a decisive act of salvation. Over against the not-knowing of the world is set the believing of those being saved.

What emerges here at the beginning of the section is a way of knowing alternative to that of human wisdom, a new lens through which God and God's community are to be understood. The text draws attention to the foolishness and weakness of the message of the cross, where, by God's design, the idolatrous character of human wisdom is exposed, but salvation is effected.

(2) Following an invitation to the readers to reflect on their own situation as people called of God, Paul offers a reminder of his earlier preaching in Corinth (2:1-5). "For I decided to know (εἰδέναι) nothing among you except Jesus Christ, and him crucified" (2:2). The choice of the infinitive is interesting. Why not "preach" or "declare" or "announce"? Any one of these might read more smoothly than "know," except that "know" more specifically identifies the epistemological dimensions of Paul's preaching. His theological knowledge is rooted exclusively in the message of the cross.[14] The homiletical and pastoral style accompanying such a message is neither eloquent nor confident. Instead, it is marked by weakness, fear, and much trembling — but results in a demonstration of the Spirit and power.

(3) Four times between 1:18 and 2:5 the word "power" occurs, and in each case, explicitly or implicitly, it denotes divine power. The point being made is that God has decisively invaded the world in the crucified Christ, and thus the message of the cross declares God's power (1:18). Persons engaged in a power struggle over leaders need to know that. To quote J. H. Schütz, "It is a restricted view of authority which calls upon the *auctor* to assert not himself and his authority, but the primary source of power. When others perceive this power correctly and act accordingly, they share in the same power with Paul and are themselves authoritative."[15] A power struggle over competing factions is preempted by God's power expressed in the cross.

The text thus prods the readers into recognizing that such power authenticating all ministries belongs to the whole church in the message of the cross.

---

[13] Here I am most tempted to violate the groundrules of the Pauline Theology Seminar and point to Rom 1:18-25 as an elaboration of the first clause in 1 Cor 1:18.

[14] Fee rightly comments that "'to know nothing' does not mean that he [Paul] left all other knowledge aside, but rather that he had the gospel, with its crucified Messiah, as his singular focus and passion while he was among them" (*First Epistle to the Corinthians,* 92).

[15] John Howard Schütz, *Paul and the Anatomy of Apostolic Authority* (SNTSMS 26; Cambridge: Cambridge University Press, 1975) 204.

It is in this context that Paul's comments at the end of the section are to be understood: "I will come to you soon, if the Lord wills, and I will find out not the talk of these arrogant people but their power. For the kingdom of God depends not on talk but on power" (4:19–20).

The authorizing of ministries in light of God's power is further under-girded by the ironic nature of the rhetoric of the passage. The irony functions in two ways. On the one hand, the text exposes, even mocks, self-confident pretensions. The foolishness of God is wiser and the weakness of God stronger than the very best that humans can muster. On the other hand, irony also functions to nurture a group of readers who perceive what is going on. It creates a community of kindred souls who get the point and who are drawn together by their agreement with the text. The "us" of 1:18 reflects a shared understanding between author and at least some of the audience about the decisive character of the cross.[16]

(4) The next section (2:6–16) carries the argument further by making the case that the wisdom of God, already defined in 1:24 as the message of the crucified Messiah, is not an innate property humans possess but a gift of God, a self-revelation taught by the Spirit. Six times in these verses the verbs for "know" (γινώσκειν and εἰδέναι) occur (1 Cor 2:8[bis], 11[bis], 14, 16). The section, with its epistemological focus, reaches a climax with a reworked citation of Isa 40:13, "For who has known (ἔγνω) the mind of the Lord so as to instruct him?" and the claim "we have the mind of Christ" (2:16).

An insight critical for the rest of the letter unfolds in 2:6–8, where this new way of knowing is given an eschatological cast. The secret and hidden wisdom spoken among the mature is not "a wisdom of this age or of the rulers of this age." Since none of the rulers of this age "knew" (ἔγνωκεν), they crucified the Lord of glory. Scholars may debate whether "the rulers" refer to historical figures responsible for the crucifixion or to the demonic powers that lie behind historical figures, but the repeated use of the phrase "of this age" (τοῦ αἰῶνος τούτου) clearly reflects the perspective of apocalyptic dualism. The wisdom decreed "before the ages" cannot be grasped by this age, but is understood only by the way of knowing that comes with the preaching of the crucified Christ.

It is interesting that explicit language of the new age does not appear in 1:18–2:16, which suggests that this "cross" epistemology is a piece of Paul's eschatological reservation and is peculiarly appropriate "at the juncture of the

---

[16] Wayne C. Booth comments: "And every irony inevitably builds a community of believers even as it excludes" (*The Rhetoric of Irony* [Chicago: University of Chicago Press, 1974] 28). The subversive side of the irony is developed by Robert G. Hamerton-Kelly, *Sacred Violence: Paul's Hermeneutic of the Cross* (Minneapolis: Fortress, 1992) 84–85.

ages."[17] In chap. 13 Paul is clear that the knowledge of the present is partial and will yield to a full knowledge only in the new age. "Now I know only in part; then I will know fully, even as I have been fully known" (13:12).[18]

In chaps. 3 and 4, the message of the cross is applied to the ministries of Paul and Apollos (3:5–15; 4:1–13) and to the Corinthians (3:1–4, 16–23). Particularly in regard to the latter, the text pushes the notion of the incompatibility between being spiritual (which now entails a way of knowing via the message of the cross) and being a fractured community (3:1–4)[19] and more directly warns readers about the pretentious "wisdom of this world," which manifests itself in the division over leaders (3:18–23).

The application of this new perspective to the apostolic ministries underscores that the way of knowing being advocated is not merely a new logic, a new cognitive enterprise, but includes living as well as thinking. The ironic statements of the peristasis catalogue (4:9–13) demonstrate what the epistemology consistent with the message of the cross actually implies — not a rich, royal life, marked by wisdom, strength, and honor, but being fools for Christ's sake, a spectacle to the world.[20]

Many things are written in the first four chapters of this letter that relate to the divisions in the community — the straightforward appeal for unity (1:10); the critique of human wisdom (1:18–2:5); the mutuality of the ministries of Paul and Apollos as "God's servants, working together" (3:9); the warning about boasting over human leaders (3:21); the establishing of Paul's authority with the readers (4:14–21). But what is argued *theologically* in this section is a new epistemology commensurate with the message of the cross, appropriate to the eschatological times. In the long run behavior can only be superficially changed unless imaginations are changed, unless angles of vision are renewed. Thus the text confronts readers with an alternative perspective, albeit a radical one, to their way of understanding God and their life in community.

---

[17] The eschatological (as well as the christological) character of Paul's epistemology is developed by J. Louis Martyn, "Epistemology at the Turn of the Ages: 2 Corinthians 5:16," in *Christian History and Interpretation: Studies Presented to John Knox* (ed. W. R. Farmer et al.; Cambridge: Cambridge University Press, 1967) 269–87. As Martyn has noted in connection with 2 Corinthians, Paul is careful to locate this "cross" epistemology "at the juncture of the ages." "The marks of the new age are at present hidden *in* the old age. At the juncture of the ages, the marks of resurrection are hidden and revealed in the cross of the disciple's daily death, and *only* there" (p. 286).

[18] See Furnish's treatment of chap. 13 ("Theology in 1 Corinthians," 71–74). I agree that the "knowledge" spoken of in 13:8–13 is knowledge of God.

[19] Fee notes that in 3:1–4 Paul is seeking to get his readers "to stop *thinking* like the people of this present age" and "to stop *behaving* like the people of the present age" (*First Epistle to the Corinthians,* 122; italics his).

[20] See Karl A. Plank, *Paul and the Irony of Affliction* (Atlanta: Scholars Press, 1987).

II. 1 CORINTHIANS 5:1–14:40

If George Kennedy is correct in arguing that the Bible retains an oral quality for its audience and that its books are to be read primarily as speeches — that is, in a linear fashion so that the argument accumulates from beginning to end[21] — then the epistemology established in the early chapters of 1 Corinthians carries repercussions for the rest of the letter. The readers have not been given handy hints about how to resolve their differences, but have been challenged at a very fundamental level to do their theologizing in a different mode. In terms of the argument of the letter, a critical foundation has been laid for confronting the other problems in the community.[22] It is unnecessary for Paul to recount the new epistemology with every issue that is faced, but here and there statements are made that prod the Corinthians to understand themselves differently, that recall the new way of knowing argued in chaps. 1–4. We shall take note of several of these statements.

(1) The unusual feature of 5:1–13 is the manner in which the community is addressed first and more extensively than the man involved in an incestuous relationship. The congregation is distinguished by its arrogance and boasting and its failure to mourn. At the heart of Paul's rebuke is an urgent plea for a new, communal self-understanding (5:6–8). Mixing the cultic images of unleavened bread and Passover lamb, the text pushes the Corinthians to think of themselves differently — as an unleavened community that demonstrates honesty and dependability, as a community for whom the paschal lamb has been sacrificed. The crucified Messiah lies at the heart of the new perspective, critically needed by the readers.

(2) Something of the same dynamic is at work in 6:1–11.[23] With a string of barbed questions, Paul chides the church for taking its grievances to the public courts. But the congregation's root problem lies in its lack of theological depth. It shames itself by not understanding itself as an eschatological

---

[21] George A. Kennedy, *New Testament Interpretation through Rhetorical Criticism* (Chapel Hill: University of North Carolina Press, 1975) 5–6.

[22] Stanley Stowers comments:

Far from opposing faith and tradition to reason, 1 Cor. 1:18–4:21 criticizes a lack of openness to that which is new and different, as well as epistemic vices such as conceit and bragging. The latter are not only matters of self-deception but also create conditions in the community that make difficult the pursuit of knowledge and the exercise of practical reason" ("Paul on the Use and Abuse of Reason," in *Greeks, Romans, and Christians: Essays in Honor of Abraham J. Malherbe* [ed. D. L. Balch, E. Ferguson, and W. A. Meeks; Minneapolis: Fortress, 1990] 261).

[23] On the importance of including 6:9–11 with 6:1–8, see Peter Richardson, "Judgment in Sexual Matters in 1 Corinthians 6:1–11," *NovT* 25 (1983) 37–58; and Fee, *First Epistle to the Corinthians,* 239–40.

community ("Do you not know that we are to judge angels?") and as a community redeemed by Christ. The structure of 6:11, with a likely reference to baptism, is instructive: once you were this, but now you are that. The demand for a different style of life among the Corinthian congregation must be accompanied by a fresh awareness of its own character as a washed, sanctified, and justified people.[24]

(3) The entire case against frequenting prostitutes (6:12–20) is argued in terms of a theological understanding of the body: the body will be raised by God's power (6:14); the body is united to Christ (6:15–17); the body is the temple of the Spirit (6:19); and the body has been redeemed at a cost (6:20). The reason to glorify God in the body and not engage in sexual immorality is rooted in a new way of understanding the self.

(4) In some respects, the issue of eating food previously offered to idols (8:1–13; 10:23–11:1) presents the most intriguing application of the new epistemology to the life of the community. Any first-time reader of 1 Corinthians, having scanned 8:1–6, would certainly anticipate Paul's siding with those who espouse a correct theology (those who have "knowledge") and settling once and for all the legitimacy of eating the available food. He develops an airtight case based on a solid theological foundation (8:6). But then comes the ἀλλά ("however"), and the argument moves in an entirely different direction.

At issue is the nature of the community. Is it a community where those with a correct theology can ignore others who have an aversion to eating the idol-consecrated food? What must prevail is not the principle of superior knowledge but the realization that those who lack knowledge are those "for whom Christ died" (8:11). Edification takes precedence over freedom; the other person's advantage takes precedence over one's own (10:23–24).[25] The christological epistemology of 1:18–2:16 applied to the controversy over eating food offered to idols calls for a community of sensitivity and love.

(5) Participation in the worship of idols is forbidden because the Christian community is one body that partakes of one loaf (10:17). The text forges a link between sacramental bread, crucified body of Jesus, and ecclesial body, resulting in the affirmation that "participation in Jesus and his body becomes

---

[24] Fee relates the indicative and imperative in Paul's ethics and comments: "Ethics for Paul is ultimately a *theological* issue pure and simple. Everything has to do with God and with what God is about in Christ and the Spirit" ("Toward a Theology of 1 Corinthians," 53).

[25] Stowers examines "the weak" in a variety of Hellenistic sources and concludes that they were not people with false beliefs, but were inconsistent and insecure in what they believed to the point of illness ("Paul on the Use and Abuse of Reason," 278–84). Paul "tells the wise to take seriously the severely ill state of the weak, to be sensitive to the acuteness of the pain that strikes the divided mind of the weak when they are 'wounded' (τύπτειν) by the insensitive behavior of the wise (1 Cor. 8:12)."

identical with incorporation into the church as the body of Christ."[26] Given an identification of itself as a people who share in the Lord's cup and the Lord's table, the community cannot at the same time engage in the worship of pagan gods.

(6) The problems surrounding the practice of the Lord's Supper (11:17–34) no doubt derived, at least in part, from social conventions from the broader culture that had become operative at the Corinthians' community meals.[27] Paul's practical response is rather untheological: "When you come together to eat, wait for one another. If you are hungry, eat at home . . ." (11:33–34). The horrifying specter of some with too much to eat and drink and others hungry, however, demands also a theological response. The liturgy of the Lord's supper is rehearsed, with a Pauline addition clarifying what the church is about when it celebrates communion: "You proclaim the Lord's death until he comes" (11:26).

The "unworthy" or "inappropriate" participation in the Lord's Supper that entails eating and drinking judgment against the participants comes in not "discerning (διαχρίνων) the body" (11:29). How members of the community view one another, whether they are sensitive to the poor and latecomers or whether the prevailing social customs dictate their behavior, becomes the decisive issue.[28] Does the congregation recognize itself as the distinctive body of Christ? In addition to the practical solution to the Corinthians' problems, there is the push for a new communal self-understanding, consistent with the declaration of the Lord's death, whereby each member, regardless of social standing, is honored.

(7) The complex problems that swirl around the worship of the congregation (12:1–14:40) evoke from Paul several specific directions about the ordering of its life. And yet at the center of Paul's directions lie two theological affirmations that recall the christological epistemology being advocated. First, in 12:3 he presents "a radically different perspective" by noting that the simple baptismal confession "Jesus is Lord" can be confessed only under the influence of the Spirit. By binding pneumatology to christology, "Paul undermines any pneumatic elitism" and develops a fresh understanding of spiritual gifts.[29] Second, the Corinthians are confronted with their true

---

[26] Ernst Käsemann, "The Pauline Doctrine of the Lord's Supper," in *Essays on New Testament Themes* (SBT; London: SCM, 1962) 110.

[27] Theissen, *Social Setting*, 145–57; and Meeks, *First Urban Christians*, 68–72.

[28] I take "body" in 11:29 to signify the ecclesial body, in line with 10:16–17 (where "body" shifts from denoting the sacramental body of the crucified Christ to the ecclesial body). For a quite different reading of the text, see Troels Engberg-Pedersen, "Proclaiming the Lord's Death: 1 Corinthians 11:17–34 and the Forms of Paul's Theological Argument" (chapter 6 in this volume).

[29] Jouette M. Bassler, "1 Cor. 12:3 — Curse and Confession in Context," *JBL* 101 (1982) 416;

character as the body of Christ (12:12-24, 27) and with the implications of
that awareness—the variety of gifts given by one Spirit (12:4-11), the
mutuality of a functioning diversity of members within a single body (12:14–
31), the excellency of love (13:1-13), the need for building up (οἰχοδομεῖν) the
church (14:1-40). The directness of 12:27 ("Now you are the body of Christ")
underscores its intent of molding the identities of the Corinthian readers in
line with the way of knowing anchored in the cross.[30]

It becomes evident in chaps. 5 through 14 as specific problems in the Corinthian community are considered and as pastoral directions are given that
at the same time something else is going on. With statements here and there,
the epistemology presented in 1:18-2:16 is kept before the readers. They are
nudged into viewing themselves and their congregational life in new and
different ways, consistent with the message of the crucified Messiah.

III. 1 CORINTHIANS 15:1-58

In 2:6-8 God's wisdom is sharply delineated from "a wisdom of this age
or of the rulers of this age," but no specific statements are made about its
identification with a new age. In 13:8-13 knowledge "now" is partial, but
"then" it will be complete, like the complete way God knows us. This way
of knowing connected to the cross seems excluded from both this age and
the age to come. In chap. 15, however, the eschatological dimension of Paul's
alternative epistemology emerges more clearly as he addresses the matter of
the resurrection of the dead.

Again, since Furnish has succinctly traced the logic of chap. 15, a rehashing
of it is unnecessary.[31] Most instructive for our consideration are the particular argumentative moves made from the basic statement of the gospel
(15:3-4). One could imagine a different construal of the kerygma. For example, the case might be made that since Jesus "died" (aorist tense), "was
buried" (aorist tense), and "has been raised" (perfect tense), then his death and
burial are historical events located in the past and the church encounters him

---

and Paul W. Meyer, "The Holy Spirit in the Pauline Letters: A Contextual Exploration," *Int* 33
(1979) 16.

[30] Furnish is reluctant to acknowledge "that Paul wishes the Corinthians to think of themselves as specifically the body of the *crucified* Christ" in 12:4–13:13 ("Theology in 1 Corinthians,"
80–81), because the body is portrayed as a living organism. The argument of the letter, however,
is cumulative, beginning with 1:16 ("Was Paul crucified for you?") and including the linkages
forged in chaps. 10 and 11 between the crucified body, the sacramental body, and the ecclesial
body. The impact of the argument, together with direct statements like 5:7; 6:11; 8:11, makes
it difficult to avoid associating the church with the body of the crucified Christ.

[31] See also Martinus C. de Boer, *The Defeat of Death: Apocalyptic Eschatology in 1 Corinthians
15 And Romans 5* (JSNTSup 22; Sheffield: Almond, 1988) 105–40.

in the present as one risen from the dead, as the enumeration of appearances indicates (15:5–9). Believers know him as the triumphant figure of Easter morning, and life with Christ means association with one who has transcended death and burial. This is apparently what the authors of Ephesians and Colossians infer from the kerygma when they write that God "raised us up with him and seated us with him in the heavenly places in Christ Jesus" (Eph 2:6; Col 3:1). The present existence of baptized believers then is beyond death.

But of course 1 Corinthians 15 moves in a quite different direction, particularly in 15:20–28. Christ is "the firstfruits of those who have died." The association with him is a *promise* for the future ("all will be made alive"). Only at his parousia are believers raised with him. Between now and then, Christ is engaged in the struggle to destroy "every ruler and every authority and every power," to put all his enemies under his feet. And the life of believers is very much at risk (15:30–34).

The epistemology of the cross then construes the kerygma as warrant not for something concluded but for something decisively begun.[32] The present is a critical moment between Christ's resurrection and parousia, a time when people are "perishing" or are "being saved" (1:18), when Christians live by faith and not by sight, when the inbreaking new age overlaps the old (10:11). The remainder of chap. 15 deals with issues of the future (15:35–37) and their impact on the present (15:58).

IV. CONCLUSION

This paper has sought to make the point that 1 Corinthians is more than a practical letter aimed at telling the readers what to do and what not to do. The letter in fact primarily seeks to influence the minds, dispositions, intuitions of the audience in line with the message Paul had initially preached in the community (2:2), to confront readers with the critical nature of God's saving action in the crucified Christ in such a fashion that it becomes the glasses to refocus their vision of God, their own community, and the future. The advancing of such an epistemology gives the letter a theological purpose that unifies its otherwise unconnected structure. I am grateful for the papers of Fee and Furnish, who have convinced me that the letter in fact has a theology not limited to principles underlying the behavioral issues and a theology with a clear intent.

---

[32] De Boer concludes his treatment of 1 Corinthians 15 by saying, "Paul's argument against the deniers and for the resurrection of the dead with his cosmological-apocalyptic understanding of death is thus an extension of his theology of the cross (1:18ff)" (*Defeat of Death,* 140). On the relation of cross and resurrection in Paul, see Charles B. Cousar, *A Theology of the Cross: The Death of Jesus in the Pauline Letters* (OBT; Minneapolis: Fortress, 1990) 88–108.

6 PROCLAIMING THE LORD'S DEATH

1 Corinthians 11:17–34 and the Forms
of Paul's Theological Argument

Troels Engberg-Pedersen
University of Copenhagen

THE AIM OF THIS ESSAY is threefold: to present a specific way of understanding what we are looking for when we speak of the "theology" of a given Pauline letter, the kind of thing that it is; to make a suggestion about one substantive element in the theology of 1 Corinthians; and to present a regular, exegetical reading of the Eucharist passage referred to in the title.

The three aims are closely connected, though in a slightly complex way. Although my reading of the Eucharist passage is to some extent influenced by my general understanding both of Pauline "theology" and of the theology of 1 Corinthians, the exegesis is intended to stand on its own and to invite acceptance from readers who do not initially share those other presuppositions. That, in fact, is the whole purpose of presenting a piece of exegesis of a particular text in a volume of essays directed toward elucidating Pauline theology as a whole: to employ the results reached in a shared, unprejudiced interpretation of a particular text as a stepping-stone toward reaching wider conclusions. What we want to know in the project reflected in this volume is the kind of thing that Pauline "theology" is and the substantive theology of a substantial piece of Pauline text.

The most logical procedure in the exposition would therefore be first to present the exegesis and then to draw out the consequences for Pauline "theology" and the theology of 1 Corinthians. However, in order to help readers grasp the purpose of some of the questions I raise in the exegesis, I have decided first to sketch the understanding of Pauline "theology" that has framed those questions. Then follows the exegesis. Finally, I turn to my suggestion concerning the theology of the Eucharist passage as seen in relation to that of 1 Corinthians as a whole. The reader is asked, however, to see and acknowledge the exegesis as being as unprejudiced as possible. In the context of this essay at least, my sketches of Pauline "theology" and of the theology

of 1 Corinthians depend on the measure of agreement that I can engender
in my reading of the Eucharist passage.

I. THE "THEOLOGY" OF A PAULINE LETTER

One pervasive trend in the modern understanding of what a "theology" is
focuses on the relationship between what may broadly be called "ideas" and
"practice." The inspiration may be directly philosophical and so derive from
Wittgenstein. Or it may have a more sociological accent and so derive from
P. Berger and T. Luckmann. Or it may finally stem from modern cultural
anthropology and so be influenced, for example, by Clifford Geertz. In all
cases the area that is in focus is that of the relationship between "ideas" and
"practice" in the following fairly specific sense. Whereas everybody will admit
and even insist that ideas are very important tools of orientation on the part
of individuals and groups, we also have to recognize a certain instability in
the ideas. They are not just there in the world with a fixed meaning of their
own independent of all human contingency—like their remote philosophical
ancestors, those of Plato. On the contrary, ideas are heavily dependent for their
very meaning on the wider context to which they belong, the practice.
Moreover, they may change their meaning as that context changes.

In order to make this general insight fruitful for the analysis of Paul, I suggest that we understand Pauline theology in terms of the following two
categories. The first is that of "theological conceptions," that is, explicitly
theological or religious ideas, beliefs, or convictions that are given some
linguistic formulation by Paul in the letters.[1] These theological conceptions
are to be contrasted with a great number of other things that are also treated
in or implied by the letters, for example, particular moral issues, personal
experiences, social conditions, and also such contingent matters as the theological conceptions of Paul's opponents. But the first category is that of *Paul's
own variously formulated theological conceptions.* The other category is that of the
"application" of the theological conceptions to those other things.

Now, when one is looking for the theology of a given Pauline letter, the
traditional approach has been to concentrate on the theological conceptions
and consider their intrinsic meaning and coherence with other theological conceptions purely at the level of ideas. This approach will situate the theology
squarely at one end of the spectrum made up of all the things I listed. It will
not, of course, make the other things totally unimportant. For they come in

---

[1] I take the phrase from Victor Furnish's paper "Theology in 1 Corinthians" (chapter 4 in this
volume).

precisely as those more or less contingent issues to which the theological conceptions are *applied* in the given letter. Still, this approach leans heavily on the one end of the spectrum in the following precise sense: on its understanding of application, the theological conceptions are seen as premises that come with a fully developed content and that are then applied to the contingent issues in such a way that these are simply *subsumed under* those other intrinsically self-consistent premises.

This is one clear and possible understanding of theology and application. It does not, however, generally work for Paul, and this fact is well illustrated by an analysis of the Eucharist passage in 1 Corinthians 11. For in that passage, as we shall see, Paul is precisely not arguing either by developing, purely at the level of ideas, the meaning of a theological conception (the Eucharist) or by just applying such a meaning directly to the particular matter at hand.

There is another understanding of application, however, which will give us a different conception of where the theology of a given letter is to be found—and will also show in a fresh way how the Eucharist passage is highly relevant to the theology of 1 Corinthians as a whole. On this understanding, the theological conceptions still function as premises, but they are not now seen as coming with a full-fledged meaning of their own. They are semantically "underdetermined" in the sense that they do not have their meaning so clearly fixed in advance that one can immediately see how they should be applied in a given situation. Quite to the contrary, they are even taken to get meaning *added* from or *in* the application. Instead of working with one center of gravity on the spectrum I mentioned, we now have two: the theological conceptions themselves *and* those issues to which they are applied.

So, in looking for the theology of a given letter, are we looking for Paul's theological conceptions and how they hang together purely at the level of ideas—and only bringing in any given application of them as a process that does not really touch the theological conceptions themselves? Or are we looking for *what results from* Paul's application *of* the theological conceptions to the various issues that are being addressed? Are we mainly interested in the theological conceptions themselves—and so taking application to be a wholly one-directional process? Or do we believe that whatever theological conceptions Paul brings to the particular situation that he is addressing become so enmeshed in his perception of that situation that we must understand application as a genuinely two-directional process and situate the theology as it were in the mid-area of the suggested spectrum?

These are two logically very different ways of understanding the theology of a given letter and it is important to see that they are so different. This does not mean, however, that, if we come to believe that the second construal of application is in fact of great importance for an adequate grasp of Paul's theology, we should *always* see that type of application at work in his letters. There may be passages where Paul feels justified in *simply* applying a Christian understanding that he has worked out previously to the particular situation he is addressing, without letting himself be influenced by any contingent particularities of the new situation. What matters is that there are these two different construals of application and that we constantly keep ourselves open to the possibility that in a given passage Paul is working in the more complex, two-directional manner.

The distinction between two types of application that I have just drawn goes a long way toward explaining a set of feelings that some students of Paul have recently formulated. Paul's theology, so it is suggested, is to be found in his "theologizing."[2] Yes, for the meaning of his theological conceptions lies in the way in which he *uses* them. Correspondingly, as is often said, Paul was not a "systematic theologian" nor even a "consistent" one.[3] Right, whatever system we shall be able to discover in his letters will lie not in a fully worked out set of ideas but rather in Paul's *handling* of his theological conceptions in the different situations he is addressing.

All this tends to emphasize the dynamic and open-ended character of Paul's theologizing. What we see in the letters is a symbolic universe *in the making*, not a fully worked out, static, and final one. Paul comes to the various epistolary situations he is addressing with a theological perspective that is not sufficiently powerful to shape completely his perception of the world. There are other interpretations around, which Paul cannot neglect: precisely those which account for the fact that the epistolary situation raises certain *problems*. (If everything were easy to settle, there would be no room for theologizing.) Moreover, *these interpretations affect the theological perspective itself*. Paul is trying to *make* the theological perspective sufficiently powerful by, as it were, rubbing his preconceived theological understanding and his perception of the particular situations *against each other* so as to make them fit. What we are witnessing is this process of a symbolic universe *being* made, of its having determinacy added to it from its use.

But this process is also in principle unfinished for the obvious reason that the types of epistolary situation to which Paul's theological conceptions may be applied are virtually limitless. The possibility is always there that a situation will arise which is such that it will influence the way in which a theological conception that has stood its test in many other situations should now be

---

² Jouette M. Bassler, "Paul's Theology: Whence and Whither?" (chapter 1 in this volume).
³ The first claim is pervasive. The second underlies such important recent contributions as Heikki Räisänen, *Paul and the Law* (Philadelphia: Fortress, 1986); and E. P. Sanders, *Paul, the Law, and the Jewish People* (Philadelphia: Fortress, 1983).

understood. A Pauline theological conceptions is not a fixed, stable Platonic idea that is maintained rigidly no matter what the situation looks like to which it is applied. The process is, in principle at least, two-directional, and the meaning of the theological conceptions — and hence the theology — lies at the place of *intersection* between the theological conceptions themselves and Paul's perception of the particular situations to which they are applied, not in the theological conceptions themselves.

There is one component of this proposal that should be made explicit. In looking for the theology of a given passage or letter, one should look for the overall meaning of the entire passage. One should not take it that the theology lies in a particular element in the passage which constitutes its theological "core" and imagine that the rest of the passage can be cut away as so much "mere application." Nor should one understand the theology as a certain set of ideas or beliefs that might be formulated independently of the text on the basis of which it is reconstructed. Nor, finally, is it something that has primarily existed or gone on in Paul's mind and might then be thought to have engendered the text that we have. Rather, it is the overall meaning of the text itself as we have it and as it is accessible to our attempts to elicit that meaning.

Does this idea not make it superfluous to speak of the theology of a given passage? Not at all. For we may still focus precisely on the overall meaning of a passage as opposed to any particular element in it — what the given passage as a whole is apparently saying in response to the particular situation that is reflected in it. What we are looking for, then, is the specific point of the passage, that which Paul has apparently wanted, whether consciously or not, to convey to his addressees through his use of his religious vocabulary in response to that particular situation.

On such an understanding, one will approach any given passage in a Pauline letter with questions such as these. How does Paul use his religious vocabulary here? How does it fit in with the contingent elements of the situation as perceived by Paul? Do these elements result in changes of emphasis in Paul's theological conceptions? What is the overall point that Paul intends to convey to his addressees? And exactly how does this point respond to the situation as apparently perceived by Paul? When I now turn to look at the Eucharist passage in the light of these questions, I shall be exclusively concerned with issues that are directly relevant to determining the overall meaning of the passage. Issues that are outside the present horizon include all broader ones concerning the celebration of the Eucharist in the early church, the history of the various traditions of Christ's words at the Last Supper, and the like. My aim is only to determine what is being said in the passage (in its immediate context and in comparison with a few other passages in 1 Corinthians) and what this shows about Paul's theology here and in the letter as a whole.

For obvious reasons the passage has received its fair share of exegetical attention in modern scholarship. I shall argue, however, that insufficient attention has been paid to the very type of argument that Paul is deploying: what he is doing as opposed to what he is merely saying — and what he is *not* doing (and saying). When the question of type of argument is given its due, we shall see that there are many tempting exegetical moves in dealing with the passage that should in fact be left untaken. For they will result either in overinterpretation or in direct misinterpretation.

II. THE EUCHARIST PASSAGE

The Context

The ties of the passage with what precedes it are very close. At 11:2 Paul has adopted the stance of praising (ἔπαινος) the Corinthians for (1) remembering him and (2) sticking to the traditions (παραδόσεις) that they had received from him. Verses 3–16 are intended by Paul to be understood in the light of such praise — though he is in fact most likely trying, somewhat tentatively and in the end inconclusively, to *correct* the way in which the Corinthians have apparently applied and developed a genuinely Pauline tradition (the "rule of no distinction" that Paul is obliquely referring to in 11:11).[4] By contrast, in 11:17–34 Paul is *withholding* his praise,[5] and precisely because, as the transition from v. 22 to v. 23 makes clear,[6] the Corinthians have *not* stuck to the tradition that Paul had received from the Lord himself and passed on to them.

More detailed analysis of this would, I believe, reveal that Paul's approach here fits in closely in two respects with his argumentative practice in the rest of the letter. First, Paul is constantly showing himself to be highly aware of his own relationship with the Corinthians: whether he is speaking to them in an authoritative tone of voice (e.g., in order to shame them, 4:14; 6:5; 15:34) or appealing to them in family terms (again 4:14; see also 4:21, which explicitly contrasts the two types of address); what his warrants are for his various instructions (chap. 7 passim); and how the Corinthians are likely to react. Second, he appears constantly aware of the relative importance of the issues he is addressing (again chap. 7). Some are more important, some less. Thus, for

---

[4] I argue for this interpretation in "I Corinthians 11:16 and the Character of Pauline Exhortation," *JBL* 110 (1991) 679–89.

[5] Note the emphasis on "not" (οὐκ) in "I do not praise" (οὐκ ἐπαινῶ, 11:17): In giving you these instructions, I can *not* give praise for the fact that you. . . . The idea is repeated at the end of v. 22: on this point I do *not* praise you.

[6] Note the contrastive ἐγώ and γάρ at the beginning of v. 23.

example, the issue treated in 11:3–16 turns out in the end to be less important. In 11:17–34, by contrast, Paul brings his most powerful warrants into action: a tradition from the Lord, which the Corinthians did receive from him (v. 23), but from which they have departed, thereby laying themselves open to clearly implied (vv. 17 and 22) and authoritative (v. 34) blame by one who is most conscious and explicit about the precise character of his stance toward them and the warrants for his various instructions.

In spite of the sharpening of Paul's tone of voice, we should note also a certain circumspection in his manner of speaking. Paul is careful throughout the passage not to write off altogether those members of the Corinthian congregation whose behavior he is criticizing.[7] So, although the issue he is addressing is apparently no small matter, he chooses in relation to it to promote social integration rather than divisiveness. Why? And what is the issue?

The Practical Problem and Its Solution

Paul is sufficiently clear, even to us, on the immediate problem that he is addressing. When the Corinthians came together "as a congregation" (v. 18), that is, for formal meetings of the congregation and in particular in order to celebrate the Eucharist, they divided up into disagreeing groups in such a way that they were not able to eat the Lord's Supper in the manner in which, according to Paul, it should be done. I shall take it, without repeating the argument here, that basically the issue is between certain richer and socially more powerful members of the congregation who are behaving in a way that is shocking to the sensibilities of certain other, less powerful members, the have-nots of 11:22. In this confrontation Paul is siding with the latter group but also doing his utmost to satisfy the former one.[8]

Settling the details of the practical problem that Paul is addressing in 11:21–22 and 33–34 requires a decision on two issues that have been hotly disputed:

---

[7] Cf. "to some extent I believe it" in v. 18 and "my brothers and sisters" (NRSV) in v. 33. Verse 22 is interesting in this respect since it is a mixture of (1) a wry sneer ("Can't you eat and drink at home?"—note the almost proverbial meaning of "eat and drink," for which see also 1 Cor 15:32), (2) irony ("What do you want me to say? Praise you?"), and (3) Paul *not* explicitly stating his blame.

[8] This also explains Paul's integrative manner of arguing in 11:17–34, as noted above. I shall in general refrain from attempting to define a "theology" of the people whom Paul is criticizing in 1 Corinthians (if they are indeed the same throughout the letter). I agree with Alan F. Segal, who has recently re-argued the case for seeing them as in the main Gentile Christians who were not bothered by the issues arising from not applying the ceremonial laws of Torah—for example, in relation to food. See Segal's convincing reading of Paul on the weak and strong in Corinth, in *Paul the Convert: The Apostolate and Apostasy of Saul the Pharisee* (New Haven and London: Yale University Press, 1990) 228–41.

the actual order of the Eucharist, in terms of blessing of bread, blessing of cup, and meal proper, as celebrated in the Corinthian congregation and the meaning of the two connected verbs προλαμβάνειν (usually translated "take beforehand") in v. 21 and ἀποδέχεσθαι (usually translated "wait for") in v. 33. Fortunately, both issues have been settled, to my mind conclusively, by Otfried Hofius:[9] (1) In his rendering of Jesus' words Paul presupposes the following order of Jesus' meal with his disciples: blessing and distribution of bread — δεῖπνον (i.e., the "meal" proper) — blessing and handing around the cup. (2) In Corinth the Eucharist was celebrated in the same order.[10] (3) προλαμβάνειν means just "consume" or (as I have argued independently of Hofius)[11] "take" (or consume) "in preference" or "for oneself." Similarly, ἀποδέχεσθαι means just "receive" or "entertain" and so its present use is closely analogous to προσλαμβάνεσθε ἀλλήλους ("Welcome one another") in Rom 15:7 with the only difference that there Paul is speaking more generally, whereas here he is focusing specifically on the meal.[12]

On this background the practical problem that Paul is addressing is the following. Participants in the Eucharist were expected to bring with them food and drink to be shared by all during the meal, which was part of the Eucharist itself. But some (who had brought much) took for themselves what they had brought of their own[13] and consumed it as a "private meal" (ἴδιον δεῖπνον) in the middle of the Eucharist, the result being that whereas the meal was obviously meant to be a *shared* meal with everybody having the *same* amount of food and drink, some (the have-nots, who had brought little or nothing) would be hungry while others would be drunk.[14]

---

[9] Otfried Hofius, "Herrenmahl und Herrenmahlsparadosis: Erwägungen zu 1Kor 11,23b–25," *ZTK* 85 (1988) 371–408.

[10] This conclusion goes against what was a sort of mid-century scholarly consensus, according to which the situation had changed in Corinth from the order presupposed in Paul's rendering of Jesus' words to an order that placed the sacramental eating of bread and drinking of the cup last, with the meal proper taking place almost before the Eucharist itself. This understanding was eloquently formulated by Günther Bornkamm in "Herrenmahl und Kirche bei Paulus," *ZTK* 53 (1956) 312–49, also in Bornkamm, *Early Christian Experience* (New York and Evanston: Harper & Row, 1969) 123–160, esp. 128.

[11] See my first draft of the present essay, "Proclaiming the Lord's Death: 1 Corinthians 11:17–34 and the Forms of Paul's Theological Argument," in *Society of Biblical Literature 1991 Seminar Papers* (ed. E. Lovering; Atlanta: Scholars Press, 1991) 592–617, esp. 597.

[12] Again noted by Hofius, "Herrenmahl," 389 n. 108. It is interesting to compare and contrast προλαμβάνειν in 1 Cor 11:21 (active voice and with προ- in the sense given above) with προσλαμβάνεσθαι in Rom 15:8 (middle voice and προσ-).

[13] Greek ἐκ τῶν ἰδίων. As Gerd Theissen has suggested, Paul's "private meal" most likely plays on this phrase. See Theissen, "Social Integration und Sacramental Activity," in *The Social Setting of Pauline Christianity: Essays on Corinth* (Philadelphia: Fortress, 1982) 145–74, esp. 148–50.

[14] This again implies a full meal (between the bread and the cup). Some do not even get enough *food* (so they are hungry), whereas others get more than enough even to *drink*.

The practical solution that Paul suggests is twofold. He first states that if the rich want to "eat and drink," they can do it at home (v. 22). The somewhat mocking tone is absent in v. 34, when Paul repeats his suggestion: if they are hungry, they may eat at home in order to still that hunger. The implication is that there may not in fact be enough food (and drink) present at the Eucharist to satisfy the rich people's appetite when the food is divided equally—and so they may make up at home for any deficiencies that they may feel.

This implication shows, however, that there is a second element to Paul's solution: the food and drink brought to the Eucharist *should be equally divided* between all participants. Paul does not explicitly say so, but it is clearly implied. The famous "love-patriarchalist compromise" that Gerd Theissen found in this text is more complex than he suggests.[15] When Theissen says that it would have been more consistent with the idea of fellowship if Paul had demanded an equal sharing of the ἴδιον δεῖπνον (instead of merely instructing the rich to eat *at home*),[16] we should answer that he does demand precisely that—though not in so many words.[17]

The Central Problem of Interpretation

We now know what practical problem Paul is addressing and what his solution is. But this only leads to the central problem of interpretation with regard to the passage: Exactly what is the connection between 11:17–22 and 33–34, on the one hand, and the intervening section, on the other? What does Paul mean by his "Ωστε ("So then") at the beginning of v. 33? How should we spell this out?

There is one way in which this issue should *not* be understood, namely, as concerning two independent spheres or levels, a social one (of vv. 20–22 and 33–34) and a religious one (of vv. 23–32). This is Theissen's interpretation, which he takes over (for his own "love-patriarchalist" purposes) from Johannes Weiss.[18] This interpretation, however, one will not find congenial if one is struck

---

[15] See the closing pages of "Social Integration."

[16] Ibid., 164.

[17] J. Weiss saw this (though on the basis of a false understanding of προλαμβάνειν): "Es folgt also, dass bei den Mahlzeiten die ärmeren Brüder mit verpflegt werden sollten . . . aus den von den Bessergestellten mitgebrachten Vorräten" (*Der erste Korintherbrief* [MeyerK 5; 9th ed.; Göttingen: Vandenhoeck & Ruprecht, 1910) 282. H. Conzelmann declares: "This indeed is the very thing that is *not* demanded."—without argument (*1 Corinthians* [trans. J. W. Leitch; Hermeneia; Philadelphia: Fortress Press, 1975] 195 n. 22).

[18] Theissen, "Social Integration," 164 (referring to Weiss, *Earliest Christianity* [1937; New York: Harper & Row, 1959] 2. 648–49). For Weiss "the real problem of the passage" lies in seeing how the "sacramental perspective" of vv. 23–32 is brought to bear on the "social" issue of the surrounding verses.

by the interpenetration of Paul's religious talk with his perception of the particular situations that he is addressing. It is true that Paul turns to highly charged religious talk (as *we* call it) in 11:23–32. But of course the surrounding, more "social" passages are interspersed with religious conceptions too (God's "congregation," vv. 18 and 22; "the Lord's meal," v. 20; God's "condemnation," v. 34). So the real problem lies not in relating two different spheres or levels to each other, but in seeing exactly how Paul uses his theological conception of the Eucharist as part of his practical argument. How does his argument go?

One Possible Solution

In order to answer this question, almost all interpreters of the passage have looked for indications in it of how certain types of (social) behavior should be seen to follow from, and others conversely to be excluded by, participation in the Eucharist when this is taken to have the *meaning* that Paul (so it is believed) is pointing to in the passage. In other words, interpreters have been looking for a coherent set of ideas centering on the Eucharist that the Corinthians might then keep in sharp mental focus in order to apply its direct social consequences to the issue of the proper behavior during the Eucharist.

That, in fact, is a most sensible approach. Think of 1 Cor 8:11–12, where Paul is backing up his insistence that the strong care for the weak by reminding the latter that the weak person is "your brother for whom Christ died."[19] Or think of 10:14–22, where Paul is emphasizing the idea of "sharing" (κοινωνία) in direct connection with the Eucharist and even stating that "we are all one bread, one body, inasmuch as we all participate in one bread" (10:17).[20] Or think finally of 12:13, where Paul introduces his "baptismal

---

[19] Hofius uses this passage in his attempt to find Paul's theology of the Eucharist expressed in 11:17–34, not least in the "for you" (ὑπὲρ ὑμῶν) of 11:24: "Rücksichtslosigkeit, Gleichgültigkeit und Lieblosigkeit gegenüber dem »Bruder, für den Christus gestorben ist«, sind deshalb nichts Geringeres als die Leugnung des ὑπὲρ ὑμῶν, – eine unerhörte Missachtung des heilschaffenden Sühnetodes Christi" ("Herrenmahl," 407). Hofius goes on to speak persistently (pp. 407–8) of the importance, according to Paul in 11:17–34, of understanding properly the *meaning* ("Wesen" and "Bedeutung") of the sacramental acts – since this will imply that one cannot in principle act in the way criticized by Paul. He thereby exemplifies directly the approach I am describing (and eventually rejecting).

[20] In his attempt to develop Paul's theology of the Eucharist as contained in 11:17–34, Ernst Käsemann took his point of departure precisely here, in the motif of the Body of Christ ("The Pauline Doctrine of the Lord's Supper," *EvT* 7 (1947–48) 263–83; also in *Essays on New Testament Themes* (SBT; Naperville: Allenson, 1964) 108–35, esp. 108–14. When Käsemann finally turns to 11:17–34 (pp. 119–35) he notices (pp. 132–33) that the emphasis on the bread formula is strangely missing here. (Though not quite; witness 11:29 "discern the body" – which fits in: "The element of the body in the Supper has a deeper significance for Paul himself than that of

reunification formula,"[21] or "rule of no distinction," possibly with a play on the Eucharist and certainly with emphasis on the single body that all Christians are.[22]

So is it not possible to formulate a Pauline "theology of the Eucharist" that combines in a precise conceptual way a number of different ideas: that of Christ's death (and possibly his resurrection), which is celebrated in the Eucharist, and that of ἀγάπη ("love") viewed as a social norm that consists in not seeking one's own but that of others (to quote 10:24)? Moreover, would such a theology not fit in with what one might well term Paul's theology in 1 Corinthians as a whole: the religious *cum* social "vision" that Paul *formulates* in 2:2 as the only content of his knowledge (when he came to Corinth for the first time) and the meaning of which he *develops* in chaps. 1–4 as an introduction to his discussion in the rest of the letter of how to *apply* this vision in the actual Corinthian practice—the vision, namely, that Jesus is Christ and that he (i.e., Jesus *as* Christ) was crucified?

To these two questions I will answer yes. But if it is then suggested that this supposed theology of the Eucharist is present also in 11:23–32 as something that Paul is either developing further or at least recalling, then my response will be no. In 11:23–32, as I shall try to show, Paul is presupposing at one turn of his argument that his addressees *already* know that other "theology of the Eucharist." But he is not trying to teach them anything new, nor even (as he might well have done) just reminding them of what he has previously taught them, in the form of a set of ideas or beliefs, a doctrinal, cognitive understanding of the (religious *cum* social) meaning of the Eucharist. If "theology" is understood in this somewhat detached sense as the name for a comprehensive understanding of the Eucharist that Paul is trying to impart to his addressees, then he is not "doing theology" in 11:17–34. Nothing can be learned from that passage for an understanding of Paul's "theology of the Eucharist" in that sense. And if one approaches the passage with such an aim (as almost all scholars have done), one will invariably misinterpret it. Here, then, is a case where a traditional, more or less purely cognitive construal of "theology" has led interpreters astray. Conversely, a new look at the passage will strengthen the suggestion that there is also another type of "theology" to be found in Paul.

---

the blood because it affords him a better foundation for his own conception of the Supper" [p. 127].) Instead Paul seems to emphasize the cup formula. However, this only gives Käsemann additional material for a rich development of his *own* theology. For "the *objective content* of the new *diatheke* ["covenant"—which is, of course, introduced by the formula of the cup] is the *Body* of Christ" (p. 131; my italics). Argument?

[21] In the felicitous formulation of Wayne A Meeks, *The First Urban Christians: The Social World of the Apostle Paul* (New Haven and London: Yale University Press, 1983) 161.

[22] See again Käsemann, "Doctrine," 113–14.

No Solution

I shall begin by registering the negative results of my own initial search for clear and unmistakable indications in the passage of a Pauline theology of the Eucharist in the sense just given: a more or less coherent understanding of the meaning of the Eucharist, which brings together a number of ideas in some kind of system.

(1) Is Paul describing Jesus' last meal with his disciples in terms that unmistakably identify it as a Passover meal, with all the connotations this might have for ascribing to Jesus' death a sacrificial meaning (cf. 1 Cor 5:7) and with whatever implications this latter idea might then have for the social issue? No.[23]

(2) Is the phrase τὸ ὑπὲρ ὑμῶν ("which is for you") an unmistakable hint in the same direction?[24] No. Evidently, the phrase does introduce the idea of atonement, but there is no emphasis on it to show that it is intended by Paul to be in any special way significant. The same holds of everything said in the rest of vv. 24–25[25] (not least when this is compared with Luke's version) — until one comes to "as often as you drink it" in v. 25.

(3) "As often as you drink it" looks significant. (i) It has no counterpart in the Synoptic Gospels. (ii) Syntactically, it is noteworthy, if not awkward, since it breaks up the neat sentence "Do this in remembrance of me," which was used straightforwardly in v. 24. (iii) It is taken up most emphatically in v. 26, which is Paul's own comment on the tradition that he has just recapitulated.[26] So "as often as you drink it" probably *is* significant. But it goes no way toward hinting at a Pauline theology of the Eucharist in the above sense.

(4) Apart from the repeated emphasis on "as often as" in Paul's comment in v. 26, the meaning of "this" (in "this bread") is intriguing. It evidently takes up the idea contained in "Do this in remembrance of me" (and so goes closely with "as often as you drink/eat it"), but it does not thereby introduce any theology of the Eucharist in the sense specified.

---

[23] Compare Hofius's careful discussion of the passage in relation to the Passover meal ("Herrenmahl," 379–82).

[24] As claimed by Hofius ("Herrenmahl," 407).

[25] Fortunately, I am not alone in having this feeling: "The section contains theological ideas which Paul certainly takes over from the tradition, but which he does not himself introduce and develop: atonement, substitution" (Conzelmann, *1 Corinthians,* 197 n. 41). Käsemann's terribly contrived interpretation ("Doctrine," 127–35) of the implications of Paul's reference to the new covenant in v. 25 seems to support this view *e contrario.*

[26] It is highly unlikely that v. 26 is intended by Paul as part of Jesus' speech. It would be very strange if Paul suddenly had Jesus speak of himself in the third person ("the Lord" and "he comes"). See Gordon D. Fee, *The First Epistle to the Corinthians* (NICNT; Grand Rapids: Eerdmans, 1987) 556 n. 58. On "as often as you drink it" I agree with Fee's suggestion (p. 556) that these words "are in fact a Pauline insertion into the words of command to bring out his own special emphasis."

(5) But what about the rest of v. 26: "you proclaim the Lord's death until he comes"? It is likely that the phrase is highly significant inasmuch as it expresses the central core of Paul's comment on the tradition that he has just recapitulated, his spelling out (indicatively) the very meaning of participation in the Eucharist as Christ wanted this to be understood.[27] And indeed, the violent, almost oxymoronic phrase "you proclaim the Lord's death" cannot but be potent with meaning.[28] It strongly brings to mind Paul's claim in 2:2 about knowing only that Jesus is Christ and that he was crucified. Still, it is far from immediately obvious that the phrase actually introduces a Pauline theology of the Eucharist in the earlier sense. (More on this below.)

There are other important issues in this verse. (a) "proclaim": Is Paul saying that when the Corinthians eat "this" bread and drink the cup ("this" cup, no matter which text one prefers), they are *eo ipso* proclaiming the Lord's death? Or is he referring to some kind of *verbal* proclamation that may have accompanied the eating and drinking? The first must be right.[29] There is an additional problem, however, stemming from the fact that καταγγέλλειν ("proclaim") is most often used of making a verbal proclamation toward *outsiders* (cf., e.g., Rom 1:8), which cannot be what Paul is directly thinking of here. But that precisely gives added point to his use of the term: when the Corinthians eat and drink from the consecrated bread and cup, they are *doing* something *within* the group which *equals proclaiming* the Lord's death toward *outsiders.* They are not just having a pleasant in-group meal together.

(b) "until he comes": What is the point? The idea seems to be that the kind of proclamation of the Lord's death that goes into participating in the Eucharist is an interim phenomenon only, which will end at the parousia. But why should that be important? Presumably because it puts into perspective and qualifies what Paul says is taking place when the Corinthians participate in the Eucharist: their proclamation of the Lord's death. The reference to the parousia thus softens, to some extent, the harsh idea of proclaiming the Lord's death.[30]

---

[27] The importance of 11:26 as the verse on which the whole passage turns is well brought out by Beverly R. Gaventa in her brief but excellent paper "'You Proclaim The Lord's Death': 1 Corinthians 11:26 and Paul's Understanding of Worship," *RevExp* 80 (1983) 377–87; she states (p. 378) that "verse 26 serves not simply as the recapitulation of the tradition but as the basis for the connection between the tradition and the difficulties in the Corinthian congregation's practice of the Lord's Supper." I was not able to get a copy of Gaventa's paper until I had virtually finished this paper. The amount of substantial agreement that I shall note is reassuring.

[28] As Gaventa notes, the fact that Paul has reversed normal word order here suggests that "the phrase 'the death of the Lord' receives special stress" ("You Proclaim," 380).

[29] For arguments, see my "Proclaiming," 603. Gaventa too argues carefully ("You Proclaim," 380–83) for the conclusion that "Paul understands the Supper itself as an act of proclamation" (p. 383).

[30] I cannot, however, find any indication whatever that ἄχρι οὗ should have a purposive as

But only to some extent. In fact, the reason why Paul has felt the need to soften the idea of proclaiming the Lord's death is precisely the harshness of that idea. This harshness, then, presumably gives us a clue to the point Paul is making by recapitulating Jesus' words and explicating them in the way he does in v. 26.

This reading of v. 26 implies that Paul is not trying to develop, or even merely referring to, a theology of the Eucharist in the sense in which I have used it: a connected set of ideas that the Corinthians might then come either to understand for the first time or at least to reactivate in such a way that they will now see or remember that a different kind of behavior is required at the Eucharist than the one they have hitherto displayed. It is true that "the Lord's death" recalls 2:2, but Paul does not use the idea at all as he does there, where he is extensively elaborating and developing the meaning of the "word of the cross." In 11:23–26 he is doing something else. He is going back to "the night in which the Lord Jesus was betrayed"; he is quoting Jesus' own words, which contain clear references to his death (the "body that is for you," "remembrance," "in my blood"); he is emphasizing (by inserting "as often as you drink it" in v. 25) those words of Jesus which provide a bridge between the situation in which Jesus said those words and the Christian reenacting of that situation in the Eucharist; and he is commenting that *whenever* Christians eat *this* bread and drink *this* cup, they are proclaiming the Lord's death. In short, Paul is doing one thing and one thing alone. He is impressing on the Corinthians the tremendous importance of doing just this: eating *this* bread and drinking *this* cup. It is, after all, a matter of celebrating the Lord's *death*.

If I am right here, the consequences for evaluating scholarly efforts in relation to the passage are momentous. Any attempt to find hints in the passage of a Pauline "theology of the Eucharist" (in the above sense) is misguided. It will either overinterpret formulations in the text that remind scholars of formulations in other passages where something like a theology of the Eucharist is in fact being developed (see those mentioned above, pp. 112–13), or else it will directly misinterpret what Paul is saying.[31] When reading the

---

opposed to a purely temporal meaning here, as claimed by Hofius ("Herrenmahl," 405–6, following Joachim Jeremias).

[31] This is most clearly so in the case of the phrase "until he comes" in v. 26, but the reference to the new covenant in v. 25 is also a frequent victim. The most dangerous temptation lies in bringing in the ideas of Christ's resurrection and return and the salvation of humanity implied in these events. This whole side of the Christ-event is decidedly not in focus in Paul's text. On the contrary, Paul wishes to talk about the Lord's death and just that. It is difficult, however, to find a commentator who does not speak of the other side too. Even Gaventa, who is right on target with statements like this one: "The community's celebration of the Lord's Supper is not a time for rejoicing in one's salvation. Instead, the celebration of the Lord's Supper proclaims the death of Jesus," adds to the last sentence "and awaits his return" ("You Proclaim," p. 385),

scholarly literature on the passage one should mark in red any passage which implies that in the present text too Paul is either developing or referring to his developed "theology of the Eucharist." There will be a lot of markings!

Ritualization

In view of the content of Paul's application in vv. 27–32 of what he has said in vv. 23–26, it is necessary to look at a few more, well-known issues in these earlier verses. (1) How are we to understand Jesus' claim (according to Paul) that "this" (τοῦτο, i.e., the bread that Jesus has taken, blessed, and broken) "is" his body? (2) What is the referent of "this" (τοῦτο) in "Do this"? (3) What is the character of the "remembrance" that Jesus is talking about? (4) Finally, what is meant by "*this* bread" in v. 26?

(1) Scholars often try to explicate "is" (ἐστιν) in v. 24 by referring back to Paul's question in 10:16: "The bread that we break: is (ἐστιν) it not a sharing (κοινωνία) of the body of Christ?" But first, in 10:16 Paul is talking not of a thing (the bread) but of an act (the bread that we *break,* i.e., breaking the bread). Second, the grammatical predicate too is of an entirely different type (sharing versus body). Perhaps, then, 10:17 is a better parallel, since here Paul is saying that "we are all one bread, one body"? However, Paul goes immediately on to explain this claim: "for we all partake of a single bread." Here the idea of "partaking" of the bread is presumably a quite straightforward one. What makes the case special is just that what we partake of is in some sense *one.* So what does this tell us about a special sense of "is" (ἐστιν) in 11:24?

The point is this. Both 10:14–22 and 11:29–32 show that in Paul's universe there is a lot of power around, which is activated at the Eucharist (and similarly in rituals for other [quasi-]divine beings, 10:14–22), but there is no indication that this fact is tied specifically to an infusion of power into the "elements" *independently of* the whole ritualized setting to which the bread and the cup belong. *In itself* a phrase like "partaking of (the) one bread" has no additional meaning compared, for example, with "partaking of one meal" (as said of several people). "All being one bread or body" similarly equals "all being one family" (or the like). The verb "is" in "This (bread) is my body" similarly means simply "signifies," "stands for," "represents," "pictures," "images," or the like. *When the* whole ritualized setting is introduced, however, one may well locate "in" the

---

and elsewhere speaks of believers proclaiming the death of the Lord (when celebrating the Eucharist) "in its eschatological significance" (p. 383). The scholar who fares best on this point is probably Johannes Weiss, but see also Victor Furnish, "Theology in 1 Corinthians," in this volume, 59–89, esp. 68. See, further, his essay "Theology in 1 Corinthians: Initial Soundings," in *Society of Biblical Literature 1989 Seminar Papers* (ed. David J. Lull; Atlanta: Scholars Press, 1989) 260.

"elements" (or the acts performed in relation to them) the power that is being activated — and understand the phrases just quoted accordingly. There is nothing intrinsically wrong with this, and it ties in with the fact that Paul connects the point of the Eucharist as brought out in vv. 23–26 very emphatically with the concrete acts of eating and drinking. But locating the power "in" the "elements" (or the accompanying acts) is in no way required by the Pauline text, and it is potentially dangerous since it runs the risk of removing attention from the *overall* ritualization that seems to be in focus.

What is the form and character of this overall ritualization?

(2) The question of the referent of "this" in "Do this" is relevant here. What Paul is referring to must be at least taking the bread, blessing it, breaking it — and handing it around for consumption (as we may conclude from the repeated references later in the passage to eating). Will it also include saying what Jesus "said" (cf. εἶπεν in v. 24) on that night? The answer must be positive. Indeed, the fact that Jesus' words are so clearly given by Paul in a way that makes them bridge the gap between the "original" situation and any later ones virtually demands that they will have been repeated in those later situations. Furthermore, *if* these words were actually spoken as part of the Eucharist as it was celebrated at Corinth, then Paul's rehearsal of them becomes a powerful rhetorical device to impress upon the Corinthians his point that when they celebrate the Eucharist they are themselves, *through* those words, doing no less than proclaiming the Lord's death.

On this background it will be clear what I meant by an overall ritualization. Jesus' words, as quoted by Paul, not only speak into the particular situation in which they were spoken but also in themselves contain a bridge to future situations where they will again be spoken ("Do this" etc.). They thereby set up or even create a ritual (and so are genuinely "institutional"), since this is defined precisely by the fact that a later set of activities is understood as *reenacting* an earlier one.

But then we can also see that what Paul is himself doing in formally repeating those words is *re-ritualizing* the Eucharist by reestablishing the link with their first use. If, then, as I urged at the beginning, doing theology should be taken to cover any handling and use of a religious vocabulary, we can conclude that one significant way in which Paul is doing theology in our passage is by re-ritualizing the Eucharist. He is invoking a specifically religious (because ritual) character of a certain activity so as to impress its importance on his addressees.

(3) With such an understanding of the overall strategy of vv. 23–26 there is little difficulty in answering the questions relating to the meaning of "remembrance" and "*this* bread." As commentators usually stress, the remembering of Jesus that is part of the Eucharist is not just any ordinary thinking back on something or other. For it is precisely *ritualized* "remembering." And

similarly, the meal that is being eaten "in memory of Jesus" is not just any ordinary *Gedächtnismahl.* For it is heavily ritualized.

(4) Finally, *this* bread that Christians are eating during Eucharist (and *the* one bread of which they partake, 10:17) is nothing but bread that has been ritualized by being inserted into the overall framework that Paul has restated in vv. 23–25.

Paul's Application

In 11:23–26 Paul has re-ritualized the Eucharist and impressed upon his addressees that participation in the Eucharist is a matter of life and death— the Lord's *death.* In vv. 27–32 he draws out the consequences that will accrue if one does not participate in the Eucharist in a manner that conforms with this content. The first half of v. 27 expresses this line of thought with total precision: "*So that* the one who eats the bread and drinks the Lord's cup *inappropriately* . . . ." What are these consequences and how do they follow from the character and content of the Eucharist as stated by Paul in vv. 23–26?

Before turning to these questions we should note how exceedingly strongly Paul carries his general ritualization of the Eucharist (as given in vv. 23–26) over to the concrete situation of each Corinthian individual eating "the" bread and drinking "the" cup. Thus in the three verses of 27–29, "eating (the bread) and drinking (the cup)" makes its appearance four times as an almost haunting refrain. Even if Paul had not explicitly said so, no one could miss that there is a need to "discern the body"! Nor should it come as a surprise when Paul states that one may even *eat and drink* judgment upon oneself. Clearly Paul is wanting to concentrate all the weight he has attributed to the Eucharist on those very acts that each individual participant in the Eucharist will personally do.

There are two consequences of eating the bread and drinking the Lord's cup inappropriately: (1) being "answerable for the body and blood of the Lord" (v. 27) and (2) "eat and drink judgment upon oneself" (v. 29). What do the two formulations mean and how are they related?

(1) "Answerable" (ἔνοχος) is a powerful word, which expresses that by participating inappropriately in the Eucharist one becomes logically "liable to action," that is, *responsible,* for the Lord's death.[32] How? Paul's intended logic is not difficult to grasp. If, as he has just reminded the Corinthians, participation in the Eucharist means proclaiming the Lord's death, and if one participates in a proclamation with this radical content without oneself *conforming* to it,

---

[32] Thus also Käsemann, "Doctrine," 123.

then one will immediately move over to the other side and belong to those
of "the present world" who actually crucified the Lord (1 Cor 2:8) and are
therefore responsible for his body and blood. In other words, participation
in the Eucharist appropriately or inappropriately is a matter of no less a thing
than either being or not being "in Christ." It is no wonder, therefore, that at
the beginning of the passage (11:19) Paul almost welcomed the divisions in
the Corinthian congregation over how to celebrate the Eucharist on the ground
that they would show who among them were "genuine" (δόκιμοι), that is, who
could pass the test.[33]

Verse 28 goes immediately on to bring in the notion of "test" (δοκιμασία):
"Let everyone test himself and then (only then!) eat from the bread and drink
from the cup." This is apparently the positive counterpart to the negative "inappropriately" of the preceding verse. But exactly what is the connection? Will
a test by itself ensure that one eats and drinks appropriately? Hardly. Rather,
what one must test is whether in eating and drinking one is oneself in fact
proclaiming the Lord's death. There is something one should test, and if one
does pass the test then one may eat and drink without risking becoming
responsible for the Lord's death. By contrast, Paul continues (v. 29), eating
and drinking is eating and drinking judgment upon oneself if one does *not*
"discern the body."

The logic, then, appears to be this: If one eats and drinks inappropriately,
one will *eo ipso* fall away from being in Christ. One must therefore test oneself
before eating and drinking. (What one should look for is whether or not one
will be proclaiming the Lord's death in eating and drinking. If one will, then
one can go on to eat and drink without risking falling away from being in
Christ.) By contrast, if one does eat and drink *without* discerning the body,
one will eat and drink judgment upon oneself.

I shall return to the judgment and the question of the mutual relationship
of the two consequences of eating and drinking inappropriately distinguished
above. First we should consider the notion of "discerning the body." By now
some of the mystery that has surrounded this famous phrase should be dis-
pelled. For we already know that no matter how the phrase should be understood in detail, the general sense will be that of attending to the overall point

---

[33] δόκιμος/δοκιμή ("tested"/"test") is a key word. Whereas in ordinary Greek δόκιμος has the
somewhat generalized sense of "acceptable," "approved," or "esteemed" (see LSJ s.v.), in Paul
the meaning is closer to the basic sense of the parallel verb, δοκιμάζειν, "assay," "test," "put to
the test" (LSJ s.v.). δόκιμος in Paul is one who has passed the test, to be contrasted with the one
who turns out ἀδόκιμος or "disqualified" (NRSV), e.g., Paul himself in 1 Cor 9:27). Similarly,
the substantive δοκιμή is not so much a "tried *or* approved character" (LSJ s.v. 2, with reference
only to Phil 2:22 and 2 Cor 2:9) as "proof" or "test" (LSJ s.v. 1) or at most a *"tried"* character."
It is not surprising, therefore, that δοκιμάζειν turns up again in 1 Cor 11:28 or that Paul elsewhere
(2 Cor 13:5) glosses ἑαυτοὺς πειράζετε as ἑαυτοὺς δοκιμάζετε.

of the Eucharist acts and "elements," namely, that *in* eating *this* bread and drinking *this* cup one is proclaiming the Lord's death. But exactly what, on this understanding, is the "body"?

Many commentators take it to refer specifically either to the bread (as opposed to the cup) or to Christ's body (again as opposed to his blood) and therefore suggest that "discern" should mean either "distinguish" (or "separate") the body, namely, the consecrated bread, from other types of food, or else "pay attention to" the body, namely, Christ's body *in* the consecrated bread. There is one grave obstacle to either suggestion, which is that it is not at all clear why Paul should have decided to concentrate on the *bread* or on Christ's *body* alone when in the very same verse he speaks, even twice, of eating *and drinking*. Therefore, if there is any way at all in which the "body" can be taken to refer to both what is eaten and what is drunk, that way will be intrinsically preferable. Note, however, that if there is such a way, then on that reading the word for "body" will no longer be able to stand for *Christ's* body or blood for the simple reason that it is highly unlikely that there should be any viable sense of "body" that would also cover Christ's *blood*. So is there a viable sense of "body" in the Greek of the period that will allow the word to cover both what is eaten (the bread) and what is drunk (the cup with its content: wine)?

Indeed there is. For "body" is very often used in philosophical and philosophically influenced literature to stand for a "body" in the sense of "any corporeal substance" (LSJ s.v. III) — as opposed, for example, to the void or to such entities as place and time (if these were not also construed as corporeal).[34] Stoicism in particular had given currency to this sense, since the Stoics were famous for being "materialists" precisely because they insisted that only those things that are bodily or corporeal (τὰ σώματα, "bodies") really exist.[35] But the Stoics may be even more relevant, since they also reckoned with something which, though not an "existent" in this more restricted sense, is still very much part and parcel of the world —"sayables" (λεκτά) or meanings, that is, whatever is or may be said *of* "bodies."[36] So could it be that Paul uses the term σῶμα to stand for that "body" (the bread and the wine) to which a certain meaning is attached when it forms part of the Eucharist? Without in any way implying that Paul is taking up here philosophical, or even specifically Stoic, language, we may at least consider whether understanding him to be using σῶμα in this general sense will fit the passage as a whole — in

---

[34] For an example of this use of "body," see Sextus Empiricus, *Adversus Mathematicos* 10.215–18.

[35] Cf., e.g., Plutarch, *De Communibus Notitiis* 1073E: "They say that only bodies are existent" (ὄντα).

[36] See again the passage in Sextus Empiricus referred to in n. 34.

spite of the fact that two verses earlier he has used the word to stand for Christ's (dead) body?[37]

I think it will. Johannes Weiss paraphrased "discern" in the phrase we are considering as "grasping and handling something correctly in accordance with its specific value,"[38] and this is exactly the sense that will make the whole phrase fall into place. What Paul is demanding is that the person who eats and drinks from the consecrated bread and cup "discern" or "pay attention to" the "body" in the sense of the concrete, corporeal stuff that he or she is actually eating and drinking, so as to remember *its* meaning — namely, that in eating and drinking from the consecrated bread and cup one is (or should be) proclaiming the Lord's death. There are two things involved: what is consumed (the "body" or corporeal substance) and the ritual meaning that it has. That meaning is the one that Paul has been trying to bring out in vv. 23–27, and he now states that if one does not pay attention to that meaning as attaching to the "body," that is, to the bread and the wine, then one eats and drinks judgment upon oneself. What, then, does the latter claim mean?[39]

(2) Paul is quite obviously and explicitly referring to God's exercising his power so as to punish the offenders with illness or even death — for pedagogical purposes (v. 32), but presumably also due to the fact that God has been provoked by a nondiscerning participation in the Eucharist in the same way that Christ would be provoked by Christian participation in non-Christian cults (10:22 with 10:9). The *literal* sense of this is clear, and the same goes for its function, which from a rhetorical point of view is quite straightforwardly to threaten the Corinthians into celebrating the Eucharist appropriately — by "discerning the body."[40]

We should ask: Are God's judgment and punishment, as consequences of eating and drinking inappropriately, related to the first consequence (that one becomes responsible for Christ's death) in such a way that what one is punished *for* is precisely that one has become responsible for Christ's death? The

---

[37] This, however, has not kept scholars from taking the "body" in v. 29 in other ways.

[38] Weiss, *Der erste Korintherbrief,* 291: "eine Sache in dem ihr eigentümlichen Wert richtig erkennen und behandeln."

[39] The only other viable way of understanding the "body" in 11:29 that I know of is that of taking it as a reference to the eucharistic congregation, on the basis of the reference to the "one body" in 10:17. This interpretation has close affinities with Käsemann's view (see n. 20 above), and it suffers from the same defect of having to bring in a highly specific understanding of the "body" from outside the passage itself. By contrast, the understanding that I have suggested fits in immediately with the heavy emphasis from 11:23 up to this very verse on the concrete stuff that must be handled properly, that is, in accordance with its actual meaning as part of the ritual itself.

[40] For the notion of threat, compare v. 34: "lest when you come together, it will be for your condemnation."

question may seem contrived, but it has often been raised and it will turn out to be quite important.

The correct answer is no. For in spite of the fact that the reference to God's punishment is clearly meant as a threat, it is, in a sense, the *least* awful consequence: becoming responsible for Christ's death is worse. Whereas the latter means falling completely out of being in Christ, the former means staying in (though also being mercifully chastised by God). This means that the reference to God's judgment is introduced in vv. 29–32 in order both to point to one further — and as Paul believes quite concrete and tangible — consequence of not celebrating the Eucharist appropriately, a consequence with which Paul may directly threaten the Corinthians precisely because of its concrete and tangible character — and also to *soften* the harshness both of the threat and of the fatal consequence introduced in v. 27. Metaphorically speaking, in vv. 29–32 Paul is applying both the stick and the carrot in order to make the Corinthians come over to a proper way of celebrating the Eucharist.

We may conclude that in his remarks about the consequences of celebrating the Eucharist inappropriately, the basic issue and the basic consideration to which Paul is appealing and which he is impressing on his addressees are *staying in* (and hopefully only being chastised if one has already been celebrating the Eucharist inappropriately) or *falling out completely* with all the dire consequences of that (including, presumably, being "condemned along with the world," as opposed to merely "disciplined" by the Lord).

Summary

What, then, does "Ὥστε ("So then") in v. 33 mean? That is, exactly how is what Paul says in the central part of the passage (vv. 23–32) relevant to the concrete issue he is addressing of social behavior during the Eucharist?

Paul, I have argued, is not trying to show his addressees that the Eucharist *means* something that implies the need to "wait for" the other participants in the Eucharist in the sense that we saw this term to have: sharing equally with each other the food which some (the rich) had brought to the common meal. Such a "theology of the Eucharist" may be developed on the basis of other passages in 1 Corinthians, though even there one should very carefully note the exact use that Paul makes in each particular passage of any given idea in that general "theology." One may also attempt to show how Paul's "theology of the Eucharist" ties in with the richly varied way in which he develops and makes use of the notion of ἀγάπη throughout the letter. Still, that "theology" itself is neither developed nor just recalled in the Eucharist passage itself. Here

Paul presupposes it only at one turn of his argument without either spelling it out or even mentioning it directly.

Thus the line of thought underlying the "So then" in v. 33 runs thus: You behave in a certain way during Eucharist (vv. 17–22). Now the Eucharist has the following point (proclaiming the Lord's *death* [vv. 23–26], which is such a startling thing that either you do it or you don't). Participation in it *therefore* requires total commitment *lest* you fall away altogether from being in Christ (vv. 27–28) or at least be chastised by God (vv. 29–32). But *since* being in Christ (to which you must be dedicated while participating in the Eucharist) *requires* (*here* comes the presupposed "theology") agapic behavior, *therefore* . . . (vv. 33–34).

Or in a shorter version: If you do not behave in the way that goes with being in Christ while participating in the ritual that *defines* Christian existence, then you *stop* being in Christ. Therefore . . .

III. ONE ELEMENT IN THE THEOLOGY OF 1 CORINTHIANS

The Eucharist Passage as Theology, I

If the Eucharist passage, as I have interpreted it, is relevant to the theology of 1 Corinthians as a whole, then we must not construe Paul's theology merely as a more or less clearly worked out set of beliefs. For if we consider the direction of Paul's argument in the passage, then, as we have seen, there is no theology in that sense in sight as the goal that the passage is working toward. Admittedly, Paul does presuppose at a particular point in his argument a theology of the Eucharist in that sense. But he is not driving toward that point. Instead he is doing something else.

This means that while one may well formulate a Pauline theology of the Eucharist in the form of a certain set of beliefs and refer to 1 Cor 11:17–34 in support of this, such a procedure will not do justice to that particular passage. Indeed, as I have claimed, such a theology could never be formulated on the basis of that passage alone. And so, if we want the theology of that very passage, where should we find it?

I need a distinction here between two general types of argument that may be used in order to convince other people of some favored way of understanding the world or acting in it. One is the type that goes into teaching people something new or reminding them of something they already know. What defines this mode of argumentation is that it is an appeal to the understanding in the sense that the interlocutors must, in a way that is unfortunately far from easy to define, *by themselves* come to see what the teacher wishes to convey to them. Similarly, when they are reminded of something, an appeal is made to *their own* previous understanding. In both cases the presupposition is that if they come to see "by themselves," then they will also act on their understanding. The other type of argument is the one that goes into threatening people into complying with some favored understanding or practice. Here too the understanding of the interlocutors is being addressed, but there is no appeal, no wish that the interlocutors should become convinced as it were by themselves in such a way that they would themselves adopt that way of seeing even if no pressure were put on them. Here, then, we may speak of forcing them (by cognitive and emotional means) into compliance.

If we apply this distinction to 1 Cor 11:17–34, we should say that its argumentation belongs basically under the mode of forcing the Corinthians into compliance. Paul is re-ritualizing the Eucharist and threatening the Corinthians with God's punishment. He is not teaching them anything new, nor is he primarily reminding them of something they already know. However, this is not all there is to be said. On the contrary, although I have insisted that in 11:23–32 Paul is not primarily appealing to the understanding in the above sense, it is worth noting, and in fact highly revealing for a broader grasp of Paul's theologizing, that his argument runs in such a way that the distinction between appealing and forcing becomes relevant again *within* Paul's use of rhetorical force in the passage.

The point is this. We saw earlier that in vv. 27–32 Paul develops two different consequences of not participating in the Eucharist appropriately, the first of which (stated in v. 27) is apparently the one that Paul has been driving at since v. 23. We also saw that throughout vv. 23–28 (in fact even including v. 29 with its repeated refrain of "eating and drinking") Paul is ritualizing participation in the Eucharist and so using rhetorical force. But now we should also notice that in vv. 26 and 27 Paul is also appealing to his addressees' understanding in a different way from what we find in vv. 29–32. For even though he is certainly not developing or hinting at the *wider* meaning of the Eucharist, he *is reminding* them of its most immediate and obvious point (that celebrating the Eucharist is proclaiming the Lord's death) and making direct use of this reminder in his statement of the first consequence of not celebrating the Eucharist appropriately. So, although Paul is ritualizing in vv. 23–28, he is also here appealing to the understanding of his addressees: they must themselves make up their minds whether they want to stay in or not—now that Paul has made clear to them (by rhetorical means) what is at stake. It is no wonder, therefore, that he goes on to exhort them *individually* to test their attitude before participating in the Eucharist (v. 28).

By contrast, in his statement of the second consequence of participating inappropriately Paul is not so much appealing to his addressees' own understanding of what is involved in the Eucharist and their own decision for or against staying in. Rather, he is threatening them with consequences of their acts which are outside their own control, tangible and concrete. Here, then, there are very few traces of an appeal to the understanding in the more specific sense.

If this is right, then it is also noteworthy. For there can be little doubt that it is the line of thought leading to Paul's formulation of the *first* consequence of celebrating the Eucharist inappropriately which is the basic one. In fact, his argument would have been complete had he moved on directly from v. 28 to v. 33 (and reformulated the "so that"-clause in v. 34 accordingly). I am not suggesting, of course, that "these verses are not part of the original text" (or something similar). Nor am I saying that Paul's use in vv. 29–32 of the religious vocabulary he had at his disposal is uncharacteristic of him. On the contrary, we shall see that it is in fact rather characteristic. But we shall also see that his primary impulse is to be less overtly rhetorical and that he uses the other approach only in special cases like the present one. Before I finally attempt to formulate the theological point of Paul's use in the Eucharist passage of these two types of approach, we should consider a few other passages in 1 Corinthians in which we find the same mixture of appeal and threat.

Crucial and Less Crucial Issues

(1) In chap. 5 Paul addresses the issue of an especially offensive case of sexual immorality in the Corinthian congregation. His reaction is violent. He calls on the Corinthians, when assembling together with him "in the name of our Lord Jesus" (though Paul himself is in fact only present "in the spirit"), to hand over the offender "through the power of our Lord Jesus"—to Satan for the destruction of his body. Here there is no genuine argument and appeal to the understanding, only a direct use of the idea that Christians are in contact with more-than-human powers which define and circumscribe their sphere of action. Gradually, however (from v. 6), a more reasoned language takes over, from the use of a proverbial saying (v. 6 — though still with a play on the idea of pollution, v. 7) to a sort of "moral translation" of the saying (v. 8) and a calmer reasoning (v. 9ff).

What we learn from this is that when Paul feels that he is, as it were, standing against the wall, he lashes out by making direct use of the belief in a *Geisterwelt* that he shares with his addressees. But his wish lies in arguing, in making his addressees see *for themselves.*

Why does Paul react violently to that particular case of sexual immorality at Corinth? The chapter itself shows why: not so much because of the offense itself as because the Corinthians have *not* reacted to it in the way Paul ends up by saying they should—namely, by neither mixing with such a person nor (certainly) eating with him (presumably at the Eucharist). In other words, what is at stake is not just a case of sexual immorality (however heinous) but the identity of the group. Boundaries must be respected. Otherwise Paul will attack—but he will also step down quickly from using that type of argument.

(2) In 10:14–22 Paul again invokes the *Geisterwelt*. In spite of its complexity the passage is so revealing for my purpose that I need to spend a few (relatively unargued) words on it.

In warning against idolatry, is Paul here (and right from the beginning of chap. 10) speaking of a different topic from the one he addresses in chap. 8 and 10:23ff., namely, the eating of idol meat? No. In all three passages he is addressing exactly the same topic: the eating of idol meat. Only his form of argument changes.

Paul is addressing certain religiously, and presumably also socially, "strong" people in the Corinthian congregation. His main argument is that by *refraining* from enforcing their own freedom with regard to the consumption of idol meat, these people will be *practicing* that freedom, which (Paul claims) is the freedom of love. He also introduces his own behavior in relation to the Corinthians and others as a prime example of such a practice of Christian freedom (chap. 9). But he also does something else, in 10:1–22. He impresses on the strong the fear of running a severe risk. Suppose they eat meat bought in the market (which is all right in itself, 10:25–26); suppose they accept an invitation from a non-Christian (which in itself is all right too, 10:27); suppose they eat meat that they *know* to be idol meat (again, this is all right in itself, 10:28–30); suppose, finally, that they lie down for a meal in a heathen *temple* (where lots of heathen ceremonies will be taking place—but again, having a meal there is in itself *also* all right, 8:10): in all these cases they run a severe risk of switching over from doing those things for purely social purposes (without paying any attention to their religious content, that is) to being ensnared by that very content. For that content is actually present because it is attributed to the meat by those non-Christians of whose religious ceremonies eating the meat is part. What Paul is doing, in other words, is trying to scare the strong Corinthians away from practicing the freedom which on Paul's own principles (and "theology") they do have. They risk being ensnared in non-Christian religious ceremonies (if they "forget" their own sound principles that will otherwise dissociate them from what they are participating in)—with the dire consequences that this will have when they will in this way put Christ to the test (10:9) and provoke the Lord to jealousy (10:22).

If this account is anywhere near the truth, then Paul is both arguing (extensively and ingeniously, chap. 9) for his claim that in the given situation the strong should abstain (certainly from the more obvious situations of being in contact with idol meat) out of concern for their weaker brothers, but he is also using a somewhat more indirect type of "argument": using the *Geisterwelt* to scare the Corinthians away from applying their (in themselves correct) principles to the issue of eating idol meat.[41]

Since 10:14–22 is so highly relevant to 11:17–34, it is worth noticing one point of detail about the passage. Paul's argument in it evidently turns on the notion of "sharing" (see 10:16, 18 and 20). The point of this term might be to emphasize the community *of believers* that comes from their all sharing in Christ's blood and body. The statement in 10:17, which commentators often see (rightly to my mind) as a sort of explanatory parenthesis, suggests this understanding — and then the road would be open for finding the full, Pauline theology of Christ's death and love developed in the passage in confirmation of Paul's plea for restraint out of concern for one's brother. Clearly, however, that is not in fact the sense of "sharing" that is operative in the verses surrounding 10:17, but a different one, according to which one shares with *Christ* or with *demons* when one is participating in a religious ceremony, no matter what one's relation is with other *people*. (This type of sharing might in principle be a wholly individual matter.) This observation shows particularly strikingly that what Paul is up to in 10:14–22 (going back to 10:1) is not developing any further his "theology" proper; instead he is using the notion of the *Geisterwelt,* for the same purpose (of making the strong Corinthians refrain since their behavior has proved offensive to the weaker people), but in a quite different type of argument.

Why, then, does Paul turn also to this rhetorical argument as part of chaps. 8–10? Again the reason appears to be that Paul saw the issue that he is discussing

[41] With this interpretation I in effect applaud the position against which Hans von Soden argued famously in "Sakrament und Ethik bei Paulus," *Marburger Theologische Studien* 1 (1931) 1–40; also in von Soden, *Urchristentum und Geschichte 1* (ed. Hans von Campenhausen; Tübingen: Mohr [Siebeck], 1951) 239–75, from which I quote. In essence von Soden attempted to show that in 10:14–22 Paul is *not* playing on a second motive (as against the demand of love) for complying with his instructions, namely, a spiritual δεισιδαιμονία or a superstitious, magical fear of their personal danger in not complying (p. 259). But that is precisely what Paul *is* doing. Behind the whole of von Soden's ingenious argument lie two unargued assumptions, one concerning the kind of sacramentalism that we should ascribe to Paul the Christian (see, e.g., a clear formulation of it on p. 274, where von Soden glosses "der volle, sakramentale Sinn des Paulus" as follows: "dass man mit Gottes Handeln und Wirken als einem gegenwärtigen und freien ernsthaft rechnet"!) and one concerning the kind of sacramentalism among the Corinthian, "Hellenistic gnostics" whom Paul is arguing against (for this see, e.g., pp. 259 and 262, where von Soden speaks of those people, without any argument whatever, as "überspannte Enthusiasten des Pneumaglaubens" and of their sacramentalism as "der mehr oder weniger sublimierte, animistische Naturalismus"). The fact that von Soden repeatedly states (p. 264 n. 32, p. 266 n. 38, p. 267) that *Paul did not himself clearly distinguish between the two supposed types of sacramentalism* should have made him pause. In fact, as we can now see, von Soden was reading his own theology into Paul.

(of irresponsible use of one's freedom) as a crucial one, one so divisive that it risked tearing the congregation apart. In such a situation, not only did Paul develop a whole "theology" of abstaining from exercising one's freedom; he also attempted to *scare* his addressees into compliance.

(3) Finally, consider 11:2–16, dealing with women's head-covering during service. I have argued elsewhere for my understanding of this passage.[42] What we see is Paul starting out making grandiloquent use of farfetched religious imagery in support of a type of behavior that goes against his own "rule of no distinction" (vv. 2–10), then abruptly introducing a form of that very rule (v. 11), and finally backing down step by step from his initial instruction (vv. 12–15) so as in effect to leave the matter, at the very end, to the decision of his addressees (v. 16). Why such reasonableness in the end when Paul did start out making authoritative use of a potent weapon in his religious armory? Obviously because the issue was *not* crucial to the continued existence of the group.

The Eucharist Passage as Theology, II

Returning now to the Eucharist passage, how should we finally understand its theology? Can we see a distinct and characteristic point to Paul's theologizing in that passage, one which possibly fits into his approach elsewhere in the letter?

We may take as our starting point the idea that I presented at the beginning of this essay: that what we find in the Pauline letters is a genuine interplay between certain more general theological conceptions and the particularities of the situation that is being addressed, with movements going back and forth between the two. One example in 1 Corinthians of such a theological conception is the "word of the cross" (1:18), the claim that Jesus is Christ and that Jesus the Christ was crucified (2:2). If we then follow the picture I drew of Paul's theologizing, we should expect to see him (i) develop this seminal idea in the light of his perception of the specific letter situation (so that his precise way of spelling it out is also influenced by that perception) and (ii) apply it directly to the particular issues he is addressing, thereby helping to solve these. That, of course, is what we do find. And so, formulating the theology of 1 Corinthians is (among other things) a matter of grasping and seeing the relationship between the many different ways in which Paul does this.

We find both (i) and (ii) in chaps. 1–4 of the letter. Here Paul develops the word of the cross at the level of ideas by bringing it together with the notion

---

[42] See n. 4 above.

of wisdom (1:18–25; 2:6–16) and a cluster of ideas surrounding that notion. He also combines it with the concrete experience of the Corinthians when they were originally called (1:26–31) and with his own kerygmatic practice among them when he visited them for the first time (2:1–5), thereby helping to clarify the content of the "word." When he then applies all this to the present situation in Corinth as he understands it (chap. 3), Paul in fact provides a complete redefinition of wisdom as, basically, love; and this sets the scene for his use of love as a comprehensive religious *cum* social norm throughout the letter, for example, in such a centrally placed maxim as 10:24 ("each should look after the interests of the other, not his own") or in his idea of the congregation as a single body.[43] This is obviously a set of ideas that Paul develops in order to impart to the Corinthians a certain understanding of the content of Christian existence that they may then apply for themselves in practice. I have only referred intermittently to this whole set of ideas here, partly because it is well known in itself and partly because I have been wanting to show that it is decidedly not in the forefront in 11:17–34. Still, it *is* strongly present elsewhere in the letter (and, as we know, is presupposed at a certain point in the argument of 11:17–34 itself).

In chaps. 1–4, however, we also see Paul apply his norm to his own practice in addressing the Corinthians. This happens, and surely not accidentally, at the very end of these introductory chapters. Here Paul explicitly contrasts ἐντρέπειν ("putting to shame")[44] the Corinthians with "admonishing" them (νουθετεῖν) "as my beloved children" (4:14) and asks them whether they want him to come with a rod in his hand or with love and the spirit of gentleness (4:21). Paul obviously preferred the latter method of approaching the Corinthians, and there can be no doubt that he did this because he saw it as an application of the gospel as he has developed its meaning up to that point in the letter: in its basic form of an appeal to the understanding of his addressees it expresses the attitude of "not looking to one's own interests but to those of the others."

All of this is quite straightforward once one keeps in mind the importance of the particular situation for the way in which Paul spells out the meaning of his message, that is, his theology. In 1 Cor 11:17–34, however, Paul follows a different track. It is true that here too he does remind his addressees of the

---

[43] I have argued for this in "The Gospel and Social Practice according to I Corinthians," *NTS* 33 (1987) 557–84, where I discuss chaps. 1–4 in some detail and attempt to show their relevance for the rest of the letter, including Paul's favoring the argumentative mode of appealing to his addressees' understanding.

[44] The basic meaning of ἐντρέπειν appears to be "make somebody turn about or hesitate" by impressing something on him, hence "make him feel misgiving or compunction" (LSJ s.v. I 2 and II 1). Cf. Sextus Empiricus, *Pyrrhoneae hypotyposes* 3.135, where ἐντρέπειν parallels δυσωπεῖν, "put out of countenance, abash" (LSJ s.v.) or "make (visibly) uneasy."

meaning of something to which he expects them to be committed: the Eucharist as a proclamation of the Lord's death. It is also noteworthy that this claim brings in the very same theological conception that Paul was working with in chaps. 1–4. But the purpose of Paul's argument is not now primarily to appeal to the understanding and independent judgment on the part of the Corinthians. Rather, it is to scare them into compliance. Here Paul in fact both puts them to shame (in 11:22) and comes with a (metaphorical) rod in his hand (in 11:26–32). Thus in the Eucharist passage we find the same combination of two very different types of argument that we also noticed in chaps. 5, 8–10 and in 11:2–16.

How, then, should we understand this combination of the two approaches? In particular, where does Paul's use of threats fit in? I suggest the following answer. Paul's basic drive in writing, reflected even in a passage like 11:17–34, is toward arguing his case, toward making the addressees see the connections of meaning and make up their minds for themselves. Thus in his writing he goes as far as he can in the direction of giving up his own apostolic claim to superior knowledge. For insisting that he as an apostle knows best is an authoritarian move that undermines the genuine freedom of decision Paul wants his addressees to have. However, where there is a genuine risk that giving up the claim to knowledge would mean jeopardizing the Christian faith of the Corinthians, there Paul insists on the claim.

What we have, then, is an interplay between the two modes of argumentation that is not just accidental or basically innocuous. Rather, it constitutes a genuine tension. Apparently, Paul is not prepared to give up either mode. Quite to the contrary, we saw that toward the end of chap. 4 he expressly mentions both. Similarly we can now see that the way in which Paul has set up the whole argumentative framework for his discussion in 1 Cor 11:17–34 falls neatly into place. He had wished to be integrative (by giving praise), but felt forced by the gravity of the matter to be authoritative—though he is also careful to specify in some detail his justification for such an approach. That tension, then, seems constitutive of Paul's argumentative practice.

But then comes the crucial question: *If* Paul does resort, from time to time, to using argumentative force instead of making a genuine appeal to the independent judgment and understanding of his addressees, does this approach not belong under his "rhetorical strategy" as *opposed* to his "theology"? Is there at all anything *theological* about it? By now we can see that there is. What we have found to be special and characteristic about 1 Cor 11:17–34 is, first, the idea that proclaiming the Lord's death is constitutive of the Eucharist understood as a ritual, participation in which even defines a person as "belonging to Christ," and, second, a certain argumentative practice on Paul's part that aims at being integrative but also makes use of an authoritative type of approach. On the basis of the other passages in 1 Corinthians that I have briefly reviewed we can see that the latter part of this, the practice, does serve to express what according to Paul defines Christian existence, and moreover that it does this in direct response to the particular situation as apparently perceived by Paul.

The resulting picture of Christian existence is the following. Belonging to Christ, says Paul, is a matter of all or nothing. So boundaries must be sharply maintained. But as Paul develops the content and meaning of belonging to Christ in chaps. 1–4 and in other chapters of the letter there is also an intrinsic openness to it, the openness of love. And so there is also a tendency to break down boundaries, certainly between the apostle and his hearers and between the strong and the weak within the congregation, and to some extent also between those inside and outside of it. There is a tension, then, at the very heart of Paul's understanding of Christian existence, a tension between openness and closure, between removing boundaries and insisting on them. But this tension is not just built into a sort of theological cognitive system. It is also reflected in Paul's own argumentative practice. Indeed, that is the place where it comes out most clearly. Moreover, Paul is himself *explicit* about the tension at this very level of his own argumentative practice, his own direct relationship with his addressees. Why, then, should we not include this whole side of 1 Corinthians in its *theology?* The modern understanding of theology from which I started suggests that we should. And the Eucharist passage itself will be relevant to the theology of 1 Corinthians only if we do.

Part III

The Theology of 2 Corinthians

7 THE SHAPING OF THEOLOGY IN 2 CORINTHIANS

Convictions, Doubts, and Warrants

David M. Hay
Coe College

IN 2 COR 10:1–6 PAUL pictures himself as appealing to his readers with the humility and gentleness of Christ and yet as also destroying every argument and capturing every idea necessary to bring about their complete submission to Christ. The apostle's goals are as definite and as aggressively pursued as those of any soldier or general.[1] Still, since Paul's arguments in 2 Corinthians, especially chaps. 10–13, have often been characterized as a defense of his apostolic ministry, it is worth noting at the outset that Paul says that he fights not for himself but for the Corinthians' relationship to God and Christ. He insists he will not be using "worldly"(σάρκικα) weapons but rather ones possessing divine power, although he does not directly explain the meaning of this distinction.[2]

The present essay seeks to explore structural elements in the argumentative theology of 2 Corinthians. I call it "the shaping of the theology" of the epistle because I think we do well to think of the theological thought of Paul as

---

[1] An earlier form of this essay appeared in *Society of Biblical Literature 1990 Seminar Papers* (ed. David J. Lull; Atlanta: Scholars Press, 1990) 257–72. The discussion of that paper in the SBL Pauline Theology Group, and especially the critical response of E. Elizabeth Johnson, were most helpful to me as I prepared this revised version.

[2] George A. Kennedy urges that by "worldly arguments" Paul means rational rhetoric, as opposed to intuitive rhetoric based on religious authority and revelation; he thinks the combination may have disturbed the Corinthians but that Paul claims that in his case both rhetorical styles come from God (*New Testament Interpretation through Rhetorical Criticism* [Chapel Hill: University of North Carolina Press, 1984] 93–96). On the philosophical traditions behind the military imagery, see Abraham Malherbe, "Anthisthenes and Odysseus, and Paul at War," in his *Paul and the Popular Philosophers* (Minneapolis: Fortress, 1989), 91–119. Malherbe remarks that for Paul "the issues at stake are cognitive and volitional" (p. 95; cf. 118). On this imagery, see further Frederick W. Danker, *II Corinthians* (Augsburg Commentary on the NT; Minneapolis: Augsburg, 1989) 86, 148–51.

developing as he acts, thinks, and writes in relation to specific situations.[3] Theology as Paul practices it is an activity, an ongoing process. The theological activity that is 2 Corinthians may usefully be analyzed in terms of three dynamic components: convictions, doubts, and warrants. The components are dynamic because they are continually interacting and are not absolutely fixed, even within a single letter (let alone an amalgam of letters like 2 Corinthians). By speaking of "the activity that is 2 Corinthians" I imply that it is useful and possible to focus on the text of 2 Corinthians as "theology in the making," without inquiring into Paul's theological thinking in other epistles or apart from any extant Pauline writings.[4] I thus focus on theologizing in the form of arguments stated in the text of the epistle.[5]

To emphasize the significance of argumentation is not to insist that Christian faith for Paul is a purely cognitive enterprise. Faith involves will and emotion, trust and loyalty, as well as belief and affirmation.[6] Yet the apostle's expressions of emotion rarely seem bereft of thought or rhetorical purpose, and his exhortations to confidence and faithfulness are often accompanied by cognitive discriminations concerning the proper norms of faithfulness and the suitable objects of trust.

At several key points in 2 Corinthians Paul himself seems to reflect on the nature of Christian knowing. He contrasts the veiled minds of Israelites with the unveiled ones of those who know the glory of the Creator in the face of Christ (3:12–4:6). The coming of Christ or faith in Christ has effected a revolution in epistemology (5:16–17).[7] The paradoxical hardship catalogues in 4:7–12

---

[3] Cf. the concerns of Jouette M. Bassler, "Paul's Theology: Whence and Whither?," and Steven J. Kraftchick, "Seeking a More Fluid Model: A Response to Jouette M. Bassler" (chapters 1 and 2 in this volume). See also D. Georgi's remarks about Paul's "experimental theologizing" marked by openness to dialogue (*The Opponents of Paul in Second Corinthians* [Philadelphia: Fortress, 1986] 342–43).

[4] Of course Paul probably had some "unpublished" theological ideas, but we can only speak of them insofar as they can be inferred from our written evidence. What Paul writes in 2 Corinthians can and must at some levels be interpreted in the light of his other writings; but we can analyze how its theological arguments develop without much reference to his other writings, and this procedure allows us to see more clearly some distinctive features of epistle.

[5] In this respect I feel close to the approach of Victor Furnish, "Theology in 1 Corinthians" (chapter 4 in this volume). To view the letter as rhetorical and argumentative does not, however, imply that Paul simply accepts the framework of thought of his critics or opponents in Corinth; on this point, see J. Louis Martyn, "Events in Galatia: Modified Covenantal Nomism versus God's Invasion of the Cosmos in the Singular Gospel: A Response to J. D. G. Dunn and B. R. Gaventa," in *Pauline Theology I*, 162–63.

[6] A powerful analysis of the complex ways in which religious belief is intertwined with trust and loyalty is offered in H. Richard Niebuhr, *Faith on Earth: An Inquiry into the Structure of Human Faith* (New Haven: Yale University Press, 1989); see esp. pp. 4–5, 83–101.

[7] See J. Louis Martyn, "Epistemology at the Turn of the Ages: 2 Cor 5:16," in *Christian History and Interpretation: Studies Presented to John Knox* (ed. W. R. Farmer et al.; Cambridge: Cambridge University Press, 1967), 269–87.

and 6:3–10 emphasize contrasting perceptions. Paul's self-defense in chaps. 10–13 repeatedly implies distinctive criteria of religious truth; and Paul claims that, whatever his shortcomings in speech, there is nothing defective in his knowledge (11:6).[8]

Like "faith," "doubt" has multiple meanings.[9] In terms of Paul's rhetoric in 2 Corinthians, *a doubt can be defined as an underlying problem or concern (perhaps not directly stated) that gives rise to arguments (based on warrants) designed to persuade persons to move toward new or stronger convictions.* Thus, in the present essay doubts, warrants, and convictions will generally be understood to belong to a common framework of discourse (or language game system) within which they take on significance in relation to each other.[10] Doubting, expressed with various words, can involve general uncertainty or perplexity or specific questions about particular convictions. It may express distrust of God or other persons (oneself, other individuals, or an entire church community). In 2 Corinthians there are frequent indications that some Corinthians distrusted Paul and that he questioned their loyalty to Christ and to himself. Yet most or all of the expressions of doubt in the epistle have a persuasive purpose, as opposed to a simple or naïvely autobiographical one.

To be persuaded means to have *convictions.* To know what you are convinced about implies that you discriminate between some matters you consider certain and others you regard as uncertain — matters of *doubt.* To make meaningful distinctions between convictions and doubts, one needs further to have a sense of how things doubted might cease to be doubted; that is, one needs a concept of *warrants,* of what may be persuasive. People can be in doubt about something and feel unsure *if* or *how* it can ever become for them a matter of conviction or certainty. Part of the achievement of effective communicators lies in their persuading their audiences that stepping-stones (warrants) do exist by which they can move from doubt to conviction.

In seeking to identify the doubts Paul attributed to the Corinthians, we need not attempt to piece together an overall position or ideology advocated by

---

[8] The terms γινώσκω and γνῶσις occur more often in 2 Corinthians than in any other Pauline letter with the exception of 1 Corinthians.

[9] A pattern of doubting not much in evidence in 2 Corinthians but present in other epistles is explored in my essay "Job and the Problem of Doubt in Paul," in *Faith and History: Essays in Honor Paul W. Meyer* (ed. J. T. Carroll, C. H. Cosgrove, and E. E. Johnson; Atlanta: Scholars Press, 1990) 208–22.

[10] Religious argumentation can be meaningful only within a framework of shared assumptions according to which some things are not doubted (convictions), other things can be doubted, and it is understood that in principle warrants may exist that can justify replacing doubts with convictions. See L. Wittgenstein, *On Certainty* (San Francisco: Harper & Row, 1969) 16–21 (esp. §§105, 115, 126, 141).

Paul's opponents, hints of which are scattered through 2 Corinthians.[11] Of course the historical situation behind 2 Corinthians must be considered, but I propose here to limit myself quite severely to doubts directly expressed or implied in the letter, without assuming that all the doubts were tucked into a "system" or that Paul was facing a single coherent pattern of doubt.

As I will use the term, "warrant" refers to any explicitly stated basis for an argument or appeal. A warrant is a stepping-stone by which the apostle seeks to transport his readers from uncertainty or doubt regarding some issue to a position of conviction. The term then pertains to logic and persuasion. Paul may cite the Jewish scriptures, essentials of the Christian kerygma, past experiences of the Corinthians, or other grounds. Stephen Toulmin recommends that warrants be distinguished from two other elements in arguments: data and backings.[12] I suspect that such distinctions will not fit Paul very well because in his arguments "data" conceived as "facts we appeal to as a foundation for the claim" cannot be tidily disentangled from interpretations that function as warrants. Likewise, a simple distinction between warrants and more fundamental "backings" (defined as "assurances, without which the warrants themselves would possess neither authority nor currency") is hardly one which study of Paul's paragraphs will encourage. It seems more likely that the warrants Paul brings forward to support his contentions fit together more or less coherently; some are mentioned more than others, but the picture of a fairly fixed hierarchy of primary and secondary grounds seems inappropriate.[13] It is also well to bear in mind that, although 2 Corinthians presents an apostle who has to argue earnestly about his own authority and about the essential meaning of the Christian message, it is nevertheless a communication between persons who know each other well and have trusted each other as fellow church members. Paul assumes that extensive misunderstanding and mistrust exist

---

[11] See, e.g., J. Christiaan Beker, *Paul the Apostle: The Triumph of God in Life and Thought* (Philadelphia: Fortress, 1980) 294–96, building on the work of Georgi.

[12] S. Toulmin, *The Uses of Argument* (1958; Cambridge: Cambridge University Press, 1990), 97–107.

[13] As an alternative to applying Toulmin's logical theory to religious discourse, one may recommend John H. Whittaker, *Matters of Faith and Matters of Principle: Religious Truth Claims and Their Logic* (San Antonio: Trinity University Press, 1981). Such statements as the following are suggestive for analyzing Pauline arguments:

> Even when the air is full of reasonable suspicions and some defense of a principle is badly needed, a truly fundamental principle can never be justified as an inference from prior, more certain grounds. The only defense of such principles is a counter-argument against the reasoned grounds for unbelief, so that the capacitating effect of a principle can be left to believers and potential believers to judge for themselves. (p. 144)

The notion of a "capacitating effect" is somewhat vague on the phenomenological level, but that may be inevitable; Paul might speak of the evident presence of the Spirit.

in the congregation; but he also assumes that he and they still have many things in common, along with considerable mutual respect and confidence. He is an apostle addressing a church he has founded and nurtured, not a stranger attempting to win an impersonal debate.

There are some fundamental convictions that Paul maintains throughout the epistle, some of which he assumes and does not argue for, others for which he argues strenuously so as to persuade the readers to embrace or re-embrace them. For our purposes a "conviction" may be understood as a self-evident truth, bearing in mind that what is self-evident to one person may not be so to another.[14] Of course a conviction can also be deliberately used as a warrant if the writer thinks his readers probably or certainly share it.

What is desirable, then, is a close examination of the workings of all the individual arguments in 2 Corinthians. As a first move in that direction, I offer an analysis of the kinds of convictions, doubts, and warrants expressed in those arguments.[15] I will not attempt a general systematization of Paul's thought in the epistle, but some effort will be made to identify primary and recurring elements.

We must further bear in mind that "Paul" in this paper means generally "Paul as he presents himself to the readers in 2 Corinthians" (implied author), while the readers are really "the implied readers." Paul may not be so sure of everything as he presents himself as being, and the original readers of 2 Corinthians probably differed somewhat from Paul's implied portrait of them in the letter (and there must have been many differences among individual church members as well).[16]

Finally, there is the difficult question of the literary integrity of 2 Corinthians. I view it as a combination of Pauline letter fragments: 1:1–6:13 + 7:2–16; 6:14–7:1; 8–9; 10–13.[17] My approach in this study does not, however, essentially depend on any particular theory about the history of the formation of 2 Corinthians, although it may shed light on the problem. The doubts, convictions, and warrants vary in different parts of 2 Corinthians, but a single

---

[14] The definition is taken from Daniel Patte, *Paul's Faith and the Power of the Gospel* (Philadelphia: Fortress, 1983) 11. Patte remarks that 2 Corinthians 10–13 "aims at converting the Corinthians from their new idolatry and thus at freeing them from the power of their system of convictions" (p. 313).

[15] It will be obvious that the analysis is illustrative rather than exhaustive and that many exegetical details could be debated.

[16] In contrast to 1 Corinthians, 2 Corinthians hardly suggests that the congregation is marked by divisions. Yet every congregation has differences; that Paul does not stress this point in 2 Corinthians is no reason for us to ignore the probability that there were pronounced variations on all sorts of issues in the Corinthian church.

[17] The authenticity and meaning of 6:14–7:1 remain uncertain; see Victor Paul Furnish, *II Corinthians* (AB 32A; Garden City, NY: Doubleday, 1984) 371–83.

general concept of Christian knowing seems presupposed throughout;[18] and this suggests that all (or nearly all) parts of 2 Corinthians were written within the same general period of Paul's career.

I. CONVICTIONS

Convictions are certitudes, things held without doubt. They are, then, the antithesis of doubts, but they also give doubt meaning and support. If everything were doubted, nothing believed with certainty, the meaning of doubt itself would become obscure.

The language of conviction includes words like βέβαιος ("unshaken," 1:7) as well as terms for knowing (οἴδαμεν, γινώσκετε, etc.). Convictions may be divided into two classes, those that are taken for granted and not argued for at all (hence things that both Paul and the Corinthians agree on as beyond question) and matters about which Paul is sure but knows the Corinthians are not.

Sometimes Paul employs the language of certitude and yet does so in a way that suggests serious doubt. Such is the case with his expressions of confidence in the Corinthians, especially in chaps. 8–9 (9:2, 11–15). Paul has boasted of their readiness to contribute (9:3). His expression of conviction involves implicit exhortation, demanding that the Corinthians live up to his expectations or hopes.

What are Paul's working assumptions in 2 Corinthians? We may begin by noting that he everywhere presupposes that God exists and acts (or has acted) in a decisive and reconciling way in Jesus, especially through his death (5:14–15, 18, 21). Paul further assumes that believers look forward to a bodily resurrection and divine judgment according to works (5:10). He assumes that the Corinthian church is functioning and has a general sense of Christian purpose and awareness of ties with other Christian communities. He assumes that some forms of church discipline exist, including exclusion or excommunication. Paul also takes for granted an involved history of previous interactions between himself and the Corinthians, including communications via associates and agents. He assumes that the Corinthians recall much about his previous preaching and conduct in their midst. Paul throughout assumes without argument that the Jewish scriptures have continuing authority for Christians, and that the Corinthians can recognize all or many of his references to those scriptures (and perhaps to special exegetical traditions). On the other hand, there

---

[18] Though there are significant variations especially on the theme of appearance and reality (see n. 51 below).

are convictions that Paul holds firmly but which he thinks some or all of the Corinthians doubt. These are the convictions for which he argues. These include Paul's God-given apostolic authority, his consistent integrity in dealing with the Corinthians, his interpretation of the kerygma as a word of love and reconciliation for the world, and his ideas about glory and suffering in the Christian life.

Perhaps we should place in a special category the emphatic assertions, in various sectors of the epistle, that cluster around the principle of divine power revealed in weakness. In 1:8–11 and 12:8–10 Paul implies that in the past he was not himself certain of the truth of this principle (or aware of all its applications), but that it has gradually become more meaningful to him through his own experiences (including experiences of prayer). Clearly he wants the Corinthians to become convinced of this principle.

Closely related to this is the concept of appearance in contrast to reality. What appears weak, contemptible, sinful (10:10; cf. 5:21 and 11:7!), transient (4:18) or false to human eyes and minds is not necessarily so in God's sight; and what finally matters is reality as God sees it. Paul assumes without argument that the Corinthians will understand this general principle.[19] What he argues about with them is particular cases in which appearances are potentially or actually deceptive.

In 2 Corinthians Paul and his apostleship are spotlighted, and the epistle offers an unusually revealing portrait of its author. Yet at the last Paul steps aside and says, what matters is not what you think of me, but whether you are obedient to Christ.[20] Christ, however, is understood to be represented in both Paul's message and life, not least as these are now re-presented to the Corinthians in Paul's letters; hence a decision against Paul implies a rejection of the Jesus and the God whose ambassador Paul is. The apostle pictures himself as an earthen vessel, in himself nothing at all; yet he demands that the Corinthians acknowledge the glory of God glistening in his ministry. So it is in a dialectical sense that Paul repeatedly and confidently stresses that he himself is not the issue.[21] Although he does not directly say so, perhaps the supreme instance for Paul of confusing appearance with reality is the Corinthians' pre-

---

[19] Both pagan and Jewish traditions would support the general idea. On the latter, see my article (centered on Gal 2:6) "Paul's Indifference to Authority," *JBL* 88 (1969) 36–44, esp. 39–42.

[20] This point is well worked out in contrast to traditional rhetorical guidelines in J. Paul Sampley, "Paul, His Opponents in 2 Corinthians 10–13, and the Rhetorical Handbooks," in *The Social World of Formative Christianity and Judaism: Essays in Tribute to Howard Clark Kee* (ed. J. Neusner et al.; Philadelphia: Fortress, 1988) 162–77, esp. 172–75.

[21] See John Schütz, *Paul and the Anatomy of Apostolic Authority* (SNTSMS 26; Cambridge: Cambridge University Press, 1975) 178, 183–84; see also Ernst Käsemann, *Die Legitimität des Apostels* (Darmstadt: Wissenschaftliche Buchgesellschaft, 1956) 31.

occupation with the apostle's status and behavior while, from his standpoint, the real issue is the church's relation to Christ. It is all a matter of perception.

II. DOUBTS

Probably the most important single expression of doubt appears in the *peristasis* catalogue of 4:7–12:

> But we have this treasure in clay jars, so that it may be made clear that this extraordinary power belongs to God and does not come from us. (8) We are afflicted in every way, but not crushed; *perplexed, but not driven to despair* (ἀπορούμενοι ἀλλ' οὐκ ἐξαπορούμενοι); (9) persecuted, but not forsaken (ἐγκαταλειπόμενοι); struck down, but not destroyed; (10) always carrying in the body the death of Jesus, so that the life of Jesus may also be made visible in our bodies. (11) For while we live we are always being given up to death for Jesus' sake, so that the life of Jesus may be made visible in our mortal flesh. (12) So death is at work in us, but life in you.

The term ἀπορέω has the general meaning of "being uncertain."[22] In Gal 4:20 (Paul's only other use of the term) the apostle writes "I wish I were present with you now and could change my tone, for I am *perplexed* about you (ἀποροῦμαι ἐν ὑμῖν)." In that passage Paul makes it clear that his doubts pertain to the Galatians, but he does not specify a precise object of his doubting (the whole letter of Galatians suggests he had multiple doubts about the Galatian Christians). In 2 Corinthians 4 Paul does not indicate at all the object of his doubting. The succeeding clause about "persecuted but not abandoned" suggests that Paul is thinking in part about experiences of suffering, in line with 1:8–9. In that passage we find the only other use of ἐξαπορέομαι in the New Testament:

> (8) We do not want you to be unaware, brothers and sisters, of the affliction we experienced in Asia; for we were so utterly, unbearably crushed that we despaired of life itself (ἐξαπορηθῆναι ἡμᾶς καὶ τοῦ ζῆν). (9) Indeed, we felt that we had received the sentence of death so that we would rely not on ourselves but on God who raises the dead. (10) He who rescued us from so deadly a peril will continue to rescue. . . .

---

[22] It occurs four times in the New Testament apart from the Pauline letters, each time with a fairly specific indication of an object of doubt: Mark 6:20 (Herod was greatly *perplexed* when he listened to John the Baptist); Luke 24:4 (the women were *perplexed* at discovering the body missing); Acts 25:20 (Festus was *at a loss* about how to investigate the charges against Paul); John 13:22 (the disciples *were uncertain* of whom Jesus spoke). The single use of ἀπορία in the New Testament (Luke 21:25) gives it the meaning "perplexity." In the LXX the verb occurs fourteen times, in each case with a fairly clear indication of a source of doubt (or distress).

What exactly does "despaired of life" mean in this context? Presumably Paul thought his physical death was imminent, and this caused him to feel "utterly, unbearably crushed." But how could the threat of physical death drive into total despair one who speaks so buoyantly about Christ's victory over death and the Christian hope of resurrection—for example, in 5:1–6? How can Paul have been in absolute despair if he believed in a "God who raises the dead"? Perhaps the language of despair here is meant to recall the LXX's solitary use of the verb (Ps 87:16): "I have been poor and troubled since my youth; having been exalted, I have been humbled and caused to despair (ἐξηπορήθην)." It is also noteworthy that in the context Paul speaks about remembering to trust in God rather than himself and of being *certain* that God will provide deliverance in the future. This certainty, which should bring comfort to the Corinthians as it does to Paul (1:7), consists in confidence that God will offer Paul (and other Christians—"us") deliverance even after or in spite of physical annihilation. The general point of 1:8–11, then, is to inform the Corinthians that Paul suffered terribly at some point in Asia but that his despair was overcome by a specific event of deliverance and by Paul's remembering to trust in God absolutely.[23] That he had to learn anew to rely on God suggests that for Paul every day can offer a fresh occasion to believe—or to doubt. The confidence in deliverance he now announces to the Corinthians is open-ended: God will always in the future deliver Paul (and presumably the Corinthians). This confidence is partly warranted by Paul's experience of deliverance in Asia (and by other past events, presumably, above all the events concerning Jesus of Nazareth); but this hope of future deliverance clearly goes beyond all past experiences of narrowly avoiding death.

It is noteworthy that Paul's description of his time of despair is framed by assurances to the Corinthians (1:3–7, 12–22). He intends that they should recognize, first, that God's comforting of Paul implies a promise that they, too, are and will be comforted (both by Paul's deliverance and by the security they themselves have in Christ). Paul expresses himself as perfectly confident of the purity of his conduct toward the Corinthians; he implies that their doubts of him arise from their failure to understand him fully (vv. 12–14). Then he describes how he intended to visit them, sure of giving them a double pleasure, and then changed his mind. They are inclined now to view the change as a token of ambivalence on his part. He insists, however, that his conduct and attitude toward them have always been "Yes," just as and just because God's word to them in Christ is consistently yes. The implication is that the Corinthians must learn to trust in a yes despite all ambiguity and apparent

---

[23] See C. K. Barrett, *A Commentary on the Second Epistle to the Corinthians* (HNTC; New York: Harper & Row, 1973) 64–66.

ambivalence on the part of Paul (and the God Paul has proclaimed to them). Later on (12:7–10) Paul will explain how in another situation he learned to be content (to say yes) despite suffering because the Lord taught him that divine power comes not instead or in spite of but through experiences which humans could interpret as only evil.

In 4:8, the affirmation is "perplexed, but not driven to despair." The thought may be that Paul suffers perplexity but, since God does not abandon him,[24] he does not fall into despair. The object or objects of the doubting are not stated, and he may be thinking about a kind of general uncertainty that marks his ministry. On the other hand, there is no suggestion here or elsewhere that Paul has any doubts about the kerygma or his apostolic mission. Probably we should think of the kind of physical suffering alluded to in 1:8–9 and the dangers and sleeplessness mentioned in 11:26–27,[25] but the doubting probably also includes anguished uncertainty about the condition of the churches (μέριμνα, 11:28), not least the church in Corinth. We may reasonably guess that part of Paul's frustration and anxiety in writing 2 Corinthians stems from uncertainty about exactly what the experiences of the Corinthians have been with the false or superlative apostles and their partisans.

At all events, Paul suggests in this passage that doubt is his constant companion, like affliction and persecution; it manifests his vulnerability, weakness, and participation in the death of Jesus. He does not enjoy it, but has learned to bear it. He does so not out of his own powers of endurance but by the miraculous strength of the God who does not abandon him (4:9).[26] Does this passage reveal in Paul an ability to tolerate doubts and ambiguity, a "negative capability" in Keats's sense? He may not bear uncertainty with delight (any more than he does his "thorn in the flesh"), but he at least has learned to accept the fact that some so-called Christians consider him a fraud. He has also come to realize that he must live with uncertainties about the Corinthians' loyalty to himself and to Christ, uncertainty about how well they will support him in the future and how much they will contribute (if at all) to the collection for the Jerusalem church.

It is also apparent that we should interpret both 1:8–11 and 4:8–9 in relation to Paul's rhetorical objectives. In the first chapter he wishes to convince

---

[24] So Furnish, *II Corinthians,* 255, 280–82. Danker suggests that the wordplay in 4:8 might be rendered, "sometimes at a loss, but not a loser" (*II Corinthians,* 66).

[25] R. P. Martin, *2 Corinthians* (WBC 40; Waco: Word Books, 1986) 86; John T. Fitzgerald, *Cracks in an Earthen Vessel: An Examination of Hardships in the Corinthian Correspondence* (SBLDS 99; Atlanta: Scholars Press, 1988) 175: Paul and his cohorts "may be distressed as a consequence of being oppressed (θλιβόμενοι) but they are not desperate or in despair!"

[26] See Fitzgerald, *Vessel,* 174–75; Rudolf Bultmann, *The Second Letter to the Corinthians* (trans. Roy A. Harrisville; Minneapolis: Augsburg, 1985) 114: Paul's meaning is that "in all affliction things do not really and finally go badly for us."

the Corinthians that suffering (his and perhaps theirs) leads to the reception of divine comfort; in the fourth he is concerned to argue the validity of his apostolic ministry, as attested in part by his sufferings. The point in neither case will be to emphasize Paul's doubt in itself but rather to stress how divine glory and life are manifest in the midst of his experiences of human and apostolic weakness. Perhaps a special concern with doubt while writing 2 Corinthians led Paul to insert the theme into the *peristasis* passages in 4:8 and 11:27-28.[27]

Occasionally Paul expresses some doubt about himself. In 12:2-3 he stresses that he does not know if his heavenly vision took place while he was in or outside his body. This expression of doubt accompanies and supports what he says he is sure about, that God granted him an ascent into paradise where he received secret revelation.[28]

When Paul speaks of himself as "losing heart" (4:1, 16), can this mean he was sometimes himself tempted to preach with timidity? Is not confidence (as opposed to being ashamed of the Gospel—Rom 1:16) essential to faith for Paul, and does not confidence in faith for him involve full assurance of the truth of what is believed? Paul never accuses himself of sin (including sinful doubt) in this letter; he has a "robust conscience" as an apostle and is sure that God approves of him and that the Corinthians would, if their perceptions were accurate. Nevertheless, passages like 1:8-9 and 4:1, 16 suggest that Paul wishes the Corinthians to realize that he himself is not above doubting, and the intent may be pastoral: just as Paul has struggled against despair despite special revelations and a commission from Christ, so they in spite of their doubts can "improve" in the sense of moving toward greater and more adequate faith (13:9).[29]

Apart from 4:8 and 1:8-9, the language of doubting in 2 Corinthians varies greatly. Doubt can be expressed directly in a question or statement of concern. It can be implied in a Pauline assertion or string of arguments.

Quite often Paul seems not to define a doubt very specifically. This may in part be a rhetorical tactic, reflecting a desire not to give undue attention to opponents' opinions.[30] But partly it probably reflects the diffuseness of

---

[27] The theme of Paul's own doubts is not directly expressed in the other Pauline *peristasis* paragraphs.

[28] James D. Tabor, *Things Unutterable* (Lanham, MD: University Press of America, 1986) 121. Furnish thinks that Paul stresses his uncertainty on the point because he doesn't care about it (whereas presumably some Corinthians do (*II Corinthians,* 545).

[29] Cf. Philo's insistence that even Abraham's faith could falter, since he was only human (*De Mutatione Nominum* 181-87).

[30] Sampley, "Paul, His Opponents," 176 n. 8 (citing Quintilian 5.13.27). Perhaps for a similar rhetorical reason Paul does not *name* his opponents.

doubting in Corinth: there were probably many different doubters and doubts in that church, and not all their doubts may have crystallized or been formulated in discrete propositions. Likewise Paul's doubts about the Corinthians extend beyond a series of specific worries or questions. Cognitive disbelief and personal distrust slide into one another. There are specific and general doubts.

The doubts of the Corinthians seem to have dealt mainly with Paul. They doubted his love for themselves (1:24; 11:11), his knowledge and speech as an apostle (especially by comparison with other leaders 11:5–6), they questioned his honesty and candor, particularly in relation to money (1:18; 4:2; 6–8; 8:20; 10:9–11; 11:7–12; 12:13–16). They felt that his weaknesses and sufferings rendered his apostolic claims dubious (4:7–11). They wondered if he was sufficiently sober or ecstatic (5:13) and if his proofs of charismatic power were adequate (12:12; 13:3). They questioned what they saw as his arrogance (2:4, 16; 3:5). They raised doubts about his self-commendations (3:1; 4:5–6; 5:12; 10:9; 11:16; 12:19) and assumed that he needed letters of recommendation from others (3:1). Perhaps we may infer from 3:7–18 that some in Corinth had doubts about the Christian message, especially insofar as it claimed superiority to the Mosaic revelation. Yet for the most part the Corinthians' doubts converged on Paul. In their own minds they did not doubt God or Christ. But they did not completely trust Paul or fully accept his claim that Christ was speaking to them through him.

Paul's doubts about the Corinthians extend further. Of course he knows their doubts about his legitimacy as apostle and ongoing spiritual guide for the church (1:24; 2:4). He also doubts their love for himself (6:11–13) and his associates in mission. He doubts that they have understood him in the past, especially in his previous letters (1:13; cf. 5:11). He expresses doubts about their readiness to participate in the collection (9:3–5).[31] If he wrote 6:14–7:1, he must have thought their association with non-Christians would endanger their morals and faith. When he appeals to the Corinthians to be reconciled with God and not receive grace in vain (5:20; 6:1), he implies that their faith regarding Christian fundamentals is in jeopardy.[32] The anxious uncertainty expressed in 1:12–23 and 7:5 probably pertains to the Corinthians' response to Titus as Paul's representative.[33]

But it is especially in chaps. 10–13 that Paul indicates grave doubts about the Christian faith of some or all in the church. He tells them they may not

[31] The length and variety of arguments brought forward throughout chaps. 8–9 suggest that he thought he had strong reasons to doubt their readiness.

[32] As opposed to viewing the expression as simply a standard component of Paul's missionary message. See Furnish, *II Corinthians*, 341, 352–53; Martin, *2 Corinthians*, 166–67.

[33] So Furnish, *II Corinthians*, 170–72, 394.

pass the "test" of faith (13:5). He says he fears they have been seduced and corrupted by Satan (11:3, 13–15). He says they readily accept "another Jesus," "a different Spirit," and a "different gospel" (11:4), and he seems to imply here (as in Gal 1:8–9) that this means apostasy and damnation (cf. 11:15). Doubt carried to the extreme of rejection of Christ is mentioned in 4:3 and is ascribed to the work of the "god of this world" (cf. 2:15–16; 3:14), just as the work of the false apostles is said to be performed at the behest of Satan (11:14; cf. 11:3). In good measure Paul interprets the Corinthians' doubt of himself as a rejection of Christ. In such passages there seem to be virtually no limits to Paul's doubts about the Corinthians.

Yet Paul in chaps. 12 and 13 emphasizes his plans to return to Corinth soon and exercise his authority there to discipline offenders.[34] Although he expresses fear that the Corinthians and he will be mutually disappointed (12:20–21) and says he hopes he will not have to use his authority severely (10:2; 13:10), Paul seems sure he can wield effective power over the church once he arrives (13:1–4). He says he will be exercising the power of Christ (13:3–4), but on a social level he will need the backing of many, probably a majority, in the congregation to make good his threats of discipline.[35] So Paul, despite his many doubts about the Corinthians, seems confident (or at least hopeful) that he can count on the support of many in the church.

He also ends the letter with an exhortation "Heed my appeal!" alongside blessings and greetings. He could be "whistling in the dark," but it is more likely that Paul expects a large number in Corinth to "come around" to his way of thinking. So Paul's doubts about the church, while serious enough to prompt passionate words and sustained argumentation, do not engender despair. Perhaps this is part of the meaning of 4:8.

In several passages (esp. 4:1–12; 5:16; 6:8–10) Paul writes as though Christian faith is a "point of view" or "way of seeing things"—as opposed to a human (κατὰ σάρκα) view. In these passages he pits faith against unfaith as antitheses as though there are only two options, assuming a binary logic or rhetoric.[36] The apostle emphasizes how faith leads him to think one way rather than

[34] Note that he does not tell the Galatians he expects to visit them and bring rebels into line there. Does he doubt his ability to exercise authority in that church?

[35] See Thomas W. Overholt, *Channels of Prophecy: The Social Dynamics of Prophetic Activity* (Minneapolis: Augsburg Fortress, 1989), esp. 69–72. Cf. Furnish, *II Corinthians,* 464 (on 10:6); Wayne A. Meeks, *The First Urban Christians* (New Haven: Yale University Press, 1983) 124; Bengt Holmberg, *Paul and Power* (Philadelphia: Fortress, 1978) 76–77. Otherwise: Bultmann, *Second Letter,* 243: Paul's third visit will result either in the repentance of the Corinthians and the excommunication of some individuals or, if the community is obdurate, the entire church will be handed over to divine punishment.

[36] Recently a number of British and American philosophers of religion have discussed religious faith as a distinctive way of interpreting or seeing the world. See John Hick, *Philosophy of Religion* (4th ed.; Englewood Cliffs, NJ: Prentice Hall, 1990) 100–108.

another (3:5; 10:2; 11:5) and that his readers must choose to think in one way rather than another (λογίζομαι, 10:2, 7, 11; 12:6). Those who engage in worldly comparisons are choosing to think mistakenly (10:12, 18). The thorn in the flesh was given him lest he think wrongly about himself (12:7). In all such passages faith is construed as a way of thinking or reckoning that involves a deliberate repudiation of one or more opposed ways of thinking or perceiving. Faith assumes doubt—or at least the possibility of doubt. Faith intrinsically involves an element of "nevertheless."

Does a person choose the faith way of seeing things? In 4:3–4 Paul suggests that unfaith is forced by the blinding activity of "the God of this world" (cf. the predestination overtones in 2:14–15). But Paul's appeals to "Be reconciled" imply the opposite, that after all the Corinthians and others are free to choose. Bultmann's view of faith as a decision that must be made over and over fits many passages of exhortation in 2 Corinthians,[37] and that implies that all Christians are recurrently offered the option (or temptation) of disbelief (doubt in its most radical form). Faith's recognition of the power and love of God in Christ is a judgment (5:14) made in the face of ambiguous evidence (cf. 5:7).

What does one do with doubts? Some cannot be resolved, at least in this world (such seems the case with Paul's doubts in 12:2–3).[38] Others must be resolved by events: a deliverance by God in 1:8–10; a demonstration of acceptance by other people (e.g., the welcome Titus received from the church, 7:5–15). But other doubts can and, in Paul's view, must be met by argument: they are obstacles to be overcome, negative thoughts to be taken prisoner for the cause of Christ.[39]

III. WARRANTS

The concept of warrants is central to the concept of argument—or it presupposes the idea of arguing toward a conclusion. It also presupposes a framework of convictions (which implicitly define what will be a persuasive warrant) and doubts (which occasion the arguments).

---

[37] See Bultmann, *Second Letter*, 164.

[38] A general claim about the limitations of Christian knowing before the eschaton is offered in 1 Cor 13:12. See Paul W. Gooch, *Partial Knowledge: Philosophical Studies in Paul* (Notre Dame, IN: University of Notre Dame Press, 1987), esp. 142–61.

[39] Romans 14:23 addresses a related issue of doubt, but one that does not seem prominent in 2 Corinthians: the need of the individual believer not to act contrary to her or his personal convictions. See especially Paul Sampley's discussion of doubts as providing "the individuated fence within which one may act" in his essay, "Faith and Its Moral Life," in *Faith and History*, ed. Carroll et al., 233–236.

There are indications in the epistle that Paul has reflected on the general nature and value of verification in relation to Christian faith. He tells the Corinthians to "Give proof" of their commitment to the collection. He promises that when he comes again he will give proof of his authority to those who doubt it. Paul also says he needs no letter of recommendation to or from the Corinthians. They themselves are a letter from Christ to humanity that somehow offers a good reference statement about their founding apostle. But of course 2 Corinthians as a whole (in all its parts) is a long and strenuous letter of self-recommendation offering a stream of warrants intended to convince the readers to rely on Paul. He says he is not commending himself again and adds that all his deeds commend him. He points out that the only commendation that counts is not self-commendation but commendation from God. He argues to persuade the Corinthians that he is not at all inferior to the "superlative apostles," but then adds that he is really nothing and that all these arguments have been "foolish." He asks, "Have you been thinking all along that we have been defending ourselves before you?" (12:19).

In his debate with opponents, especially in chaps. 10–13, Paul clearly demands that his readers reconsider what constitutes real "proof of apostleship."[40] He urges the Corinthians to "test" themselves, evidently assuming that they know some true criteria for testing Christian faith. Then he goes on to suggest the possibility that he may in their eyes seem a failure but that that does not matter so long as they themselves "do what is right" and "improve" (13:5–9). The implication is not that Paul has really failed but only that the Corinthians may perceive him as ἀδόκιμος ("unproved").

He says that on the basis of faith he seeks to persuade others that salvation comes through Jesus, but he readily admits that to some people his preaching has the stench of death, that some cannot respond to what he preaches because the god of this world has blinded them.

The upshot of all this is that a letter full of argument sets serious, not quixotic or simply paradoxical, limits to the value of argument. Paul does not pretend

---

[40] So Furnish, *II Corinthians,* 579. Furnish goes on to remark: "For Paul, apostles are legitimated only by the word they bear—and not by the form in which it is conveyed or by the amazing feats which may accompany it, but by the way it takes effect in the lives of those to whom it is addressed." But this suggests that Paul's apostleship would in Paul's view be nullified if the Corinthians failed to recognize his apostolic authority or accept his word as that of God (cf. Furnish, 578: "their obedience constitutes the only valid proof both of the genuineness of their faith and of the legitimacy of his apostolate"). I would be inclined to guess that Paul would feel his apostolic authority nullified only if *all* the churches rejected him. In Galatians I think he seriously accepts the possibility that the churches he addresses may permanently repudiate him; but he does not for all that suggest that this would bring his apostleship to an end! Cf. Bultmann, *Second Letter,* 248: the real standard of truth and of Paul's authenticity is simply the Gospel (there is an error in the English translation: Bultmann's German original reads "das Evangelium ist der einzige Maßstab seines Handelns"—which means "the gospel is the sole criterion of his [Paul's] action").

that his warrants will work with all readers. Yet he presents them with care and vehemence.

The terminology for warranting or verification varies considerably. One major term is συνίστημι (3:1; 4:2; 5:12; 6:4; 7:11; 10:12, 18; 12:11). Also of special interest are δοκιμάζω, δοκιμή, and δόκιμος (2:9; 8:2, 8, 22; 9:13; 10:18; 13:3, 5, 7). The warrants are not piled up woodenly. Paul's language is often metaphorical (consider 11:3!),[41] and his use of warrants (e.g., his references to the Jewish scriptures) can be evocative as well as denotative.[42] Yet most of 2 Corinthians consists of serious arguments designed to convince the addressees.

The various warrants can be grouped on the basis of content. Some might be called kerygmatic, pertaining especially to Christ (5:14–21; 8:9; 10:1, etc.). Others involve scriptural quotations or allusions. Many warrants refer to the apostolic authority and the conduct of Paul, past and present. Still others involve the Spirit and the Corinthians' experiences of its presence. It is worth noting, however, that all these warrants are directly related to Paul's implied claims to be an authoritative interpreter. It is Christ as Paul interprets him, the Jewish scriptures as Paul interprets them, Paul's authority and the Christian experiences of the Corinthians as seen through Pauline "spectacles." We cannot expect the apostle to step outside his skin when he presents these warrants, but we can well suppose that there were Corinthians who said in effect, "We recognize the authority of Christ and the scriptures, and we remember our previous interactions with Paul—we just don't look at these things the way he does!" None of Paul's warrants in 2 Corinthians would likely persuade readers absolutely disdainful of his authority. So it seems fair to infer that Paul imagines that his words still have some weight with the Corinthians, though not so much as he would like. Even in chaps. 10–13 he writes to persuade the only partially unpersuaded.[43]

In relation to the kerygma, Paul gives an authoritative interpretation of it in 5:14–6:1. It is one which overtly claims that God not only was in Christ but is in Paul and his associates as they preach reconciliation through Christ. Another key emphasis in the epistle is on Christ's death and resurrection as a paradoxical paradigm of true Christian authority, a pattern exemplified in Paul's ministry (4:7–11). This christological paradigm seems to underlie 6:8–10 and is central to (or presupposed in) the ironic argument in chaps. 10–13. It

[41] See Stephen B. Heiny, "2 Corinthians 2:14–4:6: The Motive for Metaphor," in *Society of Biblical Literature 1987 Seminar Papers* (ed. Kent H. Richards; Atlanta: Scholars Press, 1987) 1–22.

[42] As is forcefully demonstrated in Richard B. Hays, *Echoes of Scripture in the Letters of Paul* (New Haven: Yale University Press, 1989).

[43] See Meeks, *First Urban Christians*, 137: we have limited evidence about how Paul's letters were received, but there are hints (e.g., in the preservation of his letters) that the problems in Corinth diminished and that his authority was honored.

is interesting, however, that Paul does not make this explicit till quite late in those chapters (13:4).

About twenty-eight passages refer to Christ in important ways as a warrant. Often the point is to argue that Christ speaks through Paul or that Paul bears authentic witness to Christ. Paul's apostolic authority derives from "the Lord" (1:1; 10:7–8; 13:10). Paul preaches Christ, not himself (4:5–6), and Christ speaks in him to the churches (2:14–17; 3:2; 5:19–6:1; 11:4, 10; 12:19; 13:3). Just as Christ is the yes to God's promises, so Paul's communications to the Corinthians fundamentally have been a consistent yes (1:18–20). Paul carries out his ministry in such a way that he will be vindicated by Christ at the parousia and Last Judgment and will then be joined in Christ's presence with the Corinthians (1:14; 4:14; 5:9–11).[44] Paul's experiences of weakness and suffering mirror Christ's death and resurrection (4:7–11). Christ gave up wealth to become poor so that Christians might be made rich (8:9). Evidently this explains how "the grace of God" has recently been manifested in the Macedonian's generous contributions despite poverty and suffering (8:1–2). In 10:1 Paul says he speaks to the Corinthians "by the meekness and gentleness of Christ." This prepares us for the paradoxical assault on opponents for the sake of Christ (10:5–6) carried out with emphasis on weakness, since Christ's grace is perfected in weakness (12:9, a special revelation to Paul and, through Paul, to the Corinthians) and his power is manifested partly through his crucifixion (13:4, just as Paul is weak in Christ but will show strong authority in dealing with the Corinthians). Paul arranged the church's betrothal to Christ (11:2), and Christ will remain in the church so long as it is faithful (13:5; cf. 1:2).

The will of God is cited as undergirding the gift of the Macedonians, which arose from prayer and which helps to warrant Corinthian generosity (8:5). God is appealed to directly as a warrant for generous giving in 9:6–11. In that passage his will is understood especially through a formal quotation of Ps 111:9 LXX in v. 9, but there are quite clear allusions to other scriptural passages as well: Prov 11:24 (v. 6), Prov 22:8a LXX and Deut 15:10 (v. 7), Isa 55:10 and Hos 10:12 LXX (v. 10). 2 Corinthians indeed offers a very considerable number of scriptural allusions and quotations, often presented as unquestionable warrants for the conclusions Paul seeks to draw. When Christ is said to fulfill God's promises in general (1:18–20), the promises are probably understood to be largely defined in scripture (cf. Rom 9:4). Sometimes scriptural quotations are introduced directly as warrants with a formula like "God says" or "It is written" (4:13; 6:2, 16; 8:15; 9:9; cf. 4:3). Twice quotations are offered

---

[44] See Furnish, *II Corinthians*, 286 on 4:14: "To the resurrection credo (14a) Paul has added a comment about God's presentation of *us* with *you* (14b) . . . this being together with his converts in the presence of the Lord will be the crowning evidence not only of the authenticity of their faith but also of the authenticity of those by whom they have come to faith." Cf. 1:14 and Phil 2:16; 1 Thess 2:19.

without introduction (10:17; 13:1). The interpretation of the story of Moses in 3:3–16 assumes the permanent validity of the scriptural account, not least because Paul argues that Moses' self-veiling points to the superiority of the ministry connected with the new covenant.[45] In 11:3 an allusion to the story of Eve and the serpent warrants Paul's warning that the Corinthians may be corrupted. Obviously the apostle can assume that the Corinthians consider the Jewish scriptures authoritative and know them quite well. He readily boasts that he, too, is a descendant of Abraham (11:22), and this, together with his apparent concern to exhibit mastery of scriptural interpretation, suggests that Jewish credentials had high prestige for at least some Corinthians.[46]

Paul is an apostle by God's will and empowerment (1:1; 2:14–17; 3:5–6; 4:1, 6–7; 5:19–20; 6:4; 10:13; 13:4) and his gospel is God's (5:19–20; 11:7). God's Spirit attests Paul's ministry (1:22; 3:6, 8, 17–18; 5:5). Paul mentions special revelations (12:1–10)[47] and miracles he has performed (12:12), as though they are strong evidence of divine authorization (which is not to say that he thinks of revelations and miracles precisely as do his opponents). In all his decisions and communications he is conscious of acting in the sight of God (4:2; 5:11; 8:21; 12:19), and the Corinthians should recognize their own relation to God's omniscience and judgment (7:12). Paul repeatedly affirms his integrity as something known to God (1:23; 5:11; 11:11, 31).

Many warrants stem from Paul's own experiences and style of ministry. His missionary labors and successes (not least in Corinth) are fundamental warrants (6:5; 11:23, 27; and esp. 10:13–16).[48] His standing before God is directly affected by the spiritual health of his congregations (1:14; 3:2–3; 12:21), although he points out twice that the disbelief with which some respond to his message does not disconfirm his apostleship (2:15–16; 4:3).

Paul also argues for the legitimacy of his authority from his love for the Corinthians (2:4; 6:6; 7:3; 11:3; 12:14–15, 19; cf. 2:5–11) and the fact that he consistently acts for the good of the church (1:7; 11:7, 28; 13:9–10). His expressions of confidence in the church (1:15, 24; 2:3, 17; 3:2; 7:4, 11–16; 8:7; 9:1–2, 13–15; 10:15) and his boasting about them to other Christians (7:14;

---

[45] Some scholars have gone further and discerned in this passage a view of Moses as a direct witness to the glory of Christ; see now Hays, *Echoes*, 142–53. On the imagery and Paul's meaning, see further Linda L. Belleville, *Reflections of Glory: Paul's Polemical Use of the Moses-Doxa Tradition in 2 Corinthians 3.1–18* (JSNTSup 52; Sheffield: JSOT Press, 1991) 192–225.

[46] Though Paul also points out he has been persecuted for his apostolic efforts by Jews (11:24, 26).

[47] On the subtleties and irony in Paul's claims, see Tabor, *Things Unutterable*, 53 n. 79, 120–21.

[48] In a recent study, Scott Hafemann goes so far as to say that the existence of the church in Corinth is "the decisive divine attestation of his [Paul's] claim to authority as the Corinthians' apostle"; it is "*objective* evidence of divine activity" and constitutes "the only canon of commendation that Paul recognizes" ("'Self-Commendation' and Apostolic Legitimacy in 2 Corinthians: a Pauline Dialectic?" *NTS* 36 [1990] 83).

8:24; 9:2) further attest his good will. Purity, candor, and honesty (including financial honesty) are additional warrants (1:18; 2:6, 17–18; 4:2, 13; 6:6–7, 11–12). In line with this, he does not seek to give the Corinthians unnecessary pain (1:21; 2:1, 4) but demands that they acknowledge his authority over them for their own good (1:14; 12:19; cf. 5:12). They have asked that his power be demonstrated, and he claims that he will prove it in a way that will surprise them when he visits the church and punishes all offenders (12:21–13:4). His letters are powerful evidence of God's judgment, and his visit will confirm that judgment (10:9–11).[49]

The theme of reversal of the Corinthians' notions of legitimation is prominent. The distinction between appearance and reality is assumed as a basis for arguing that Paul's authority is better than the Corinthians may imagine (5:12, 16; 6:8–10). Paul's irony or sarcasm itself is a rhetorical device to support his claims, especially when he speaks of his "folly" (10:12; 11:1, 16, 21; 12:11, 13). His weakness and suffering, which are targets for his opponents' criticism or ridicule, are really proofs of his authority (1:4–7; 2:4; 4:7–11, 16–18; 6:5, 9; 12:8–10) since they constitute a platform on which God's power is revealed and because they show forth Paul's likeness to Christ (13:3–4). His financial policy toward the Corinthians, taken by them as an occasion for suspicion, really demonstrates his parental love (11:7–10; 12:13–15). He attacks his opponents, sometimes bitterly, and this attests his courage and willingness to pass judgment when necessary (2:17; 5:12; 11:12–15, 18–23; 12:11).[50] He points out the purposes and devices of Satan in order to support his exhortations (2:11; 4:4; 11:3, 14–15; 12:7).

Paul appeals to the Corinthians to let their own consciences judge him (5:11; cf. 4:2), and he reminds them of experiences in which they discerned his authority (3:2–3; 7:12, 15; 12:17–18). Sometimes Paul expresses general warrants in proverblike form, perhaps thinking of them as general Christian principles, perhaps regarding them as principles which right-minded people in general accept (4:18c; 7:10; 9:6, 7; 10:18; 11:14; 12:14c). He shows some concern for maintaining a good reputation with non-Christians as well as Christians (4:2; 8:20–21). He implies that bad believing leads to bad morals (6:14–7:1; 12:20–21). He can also mention the actions and opinions of other Christians as supporters of his position or concerns (1:1; 7:6, 13–15; 8:1–7, 16–24;[51] 9:2, 13–14; 11:9–10; 12:17–18; 13:13).

---

[49] Furnish (*II Corinthians,* 575), following Bultmann, argues persuasively that the "two or three witnesses" of 13:1 are a combination of Paul's visits and the letter of chaps. 10–13.

[50] On the rhetorical tradition presupposed, see Sampley, "Paul, His Opponents," 169–70.

[51] On the complex church diplomacy implied in this passage, see esp. Hans D. Betz, *2 Corinthians 8 and 9* (Hermeneia; Philadelphia: Fortress, 1985) 70–86.

A few general theological principles recur and might be described as primary warrants. The notion that divine power is revealed in human weakness is connected with Christ and Paul in passages like 4:7–11; 6:2–10; 12:8–10; and 13:3–4 and seems a special case of the appearance/reality distinction.[52] The affirmation that God seeks equality is articulated most prominently in the rationale for contributions in 8:13–15. But these two ideas may have been combined in Paul's mind, since he apparently thinks that all Christians, not just apostles, should share Christ's poverty and weakness in order to make others rich (cf. 6:10). Related to these two warrants is a third, to which both seem subordinate: the claim of 5:14–21 that the Gospel centers in a proclamation of divine love revealed through the death of Jesus, a love that then invites humanity to be reconciled to God and causes those who accept the invitation to participate in Christ's death and resurrection, his love, weakness, power and glory (5:14–15; 3:17–18). Paul and the Corinthians are equally subjected to the word of God revealed in Jesus. Equality is not identity, however: just as Paul is not identical with Christ, so the Corinthians are not called to share exactly Paul's experiences of death and resurrection. Their experiences do not precisely parallel those of the Macedonian Christians or the Jerusalem saints. But they and all who live in faith are equally summoned into the same sphere of obedience (5:14–15).

IV. CONCLUSION

Paul's arguments throughout 2 Corinthians are complex and of various types, and this reflects not only his own complex personality[53] but also a complex set of doubts to which he was responding. Doubts provide the occasion for the letter fragments that make up 2 Corinthians, and to a greater degree than is the case even in Galatians the focal point of the church's doubting is Paul himself. The apostle emphasizes, however, that, if the Corinthians have doubts about him, he also has doubts about them. The warrants he uses include bold and sometimes "foolish" assertions of his authority, reminders of past events

[52] This is not to say, however, that the appearance/reality distinction is applied in the same way throughout 2 Corinthians. In 4:7–18 and 6:8–10 Paul emphasizes the contrast between deceptive appearance and inner reality. In 8:20–21 he stresses the importance of financial integrity in both reality and appearance. In much of the argument of chaps. 10–13 the focus is on Paul's outward, visible conduct and experience (note 10:7a); at issue are essentially two divergent ways of assessing that conduct and experience. Of course these differences support theories of 2 Corinthians as a combination of letter fragments.

[53] Kennedy, New Testament Interpretation, 93, 96. I should be more inclined than Kennedy seems to stress the complicated pattern of doubting Paul faces as the explanation for the varied character of his arguments.

and messages, appeals to the right understanding of the kerygma and the Jewish scriptures, expressions of affection, and vigorous attacks on opponents. The particular conclusions he wishes the church to draw vary in the different sections of the letter, but the fundamental one is that the Corinthians are insufficiently reconciled to God.

Theology emerges as Paul listens to the doubts of others and those in his own mind, reflects on essential convictions, and ponders which warrants preserve "the fear of the Lord" and are likely to persuade. Rhetoric builds on epistemology, and Paul strives to communicate both what the Corinthians need to know and how in faith they can know it.

8 DEATH IN US, LIFE IN YOU

The Apostolic Medium

Steven J. Kraftchick
Princeton Theological Seminary

I. SITUATING THE PRESENT ATTEMPT

IT IS UNNECESSARY to rehearse the difficulties of producing a Pauline theology for this group; the hurdles are well known. The problems involved with creating historical settings for the letters, assessing their oblique portraits of Paul's opponents and the nature of his theological disputes are necessary elements of any attempt to explain the way in which the letters reflect a "coherency" in Paul's thought. That Paul's theological work in the letters is situation-dependent few of us deny, but the more a Pauline theology is predicated upon its historical and rhetorical circumstances the more just those things recede from our grasp.

Nowhere is this more the case than in 2 Corinthians. On the one hand, Paul is severely constrained by circumstances in Corinth in what he can say and how he can say it. The rift between Paul and the Corinthians (which must have been deep, because of his failure to make promised visits and the disastrous visit he did make) turns almost every statement into a form of "apology" or defense. He also seems to write with an eye toward his perceived opponents or rivals, which gives a polemic edge to the apologies and suggests that Paul sensed that his words would be taken in ways he did not intend. Any exposition of the epistle has to recognize the limiting factors under which the letter was written and read. On the other hand, the reasons for the Corin-thian-Pauline misunderstandings, the nature of the opposition to Paul, and the manner in which it affected the congregation are shrouded in historical and social mists.[1] Thus, even though every interpretation of this letter must

---

[1] Both the integrity of the letter and the nature and positions of Paul's opposition are immensely complex problems. For the purposes of this paper I assume the unity of chaps. 1–9 (except for 6:14–7:3) and that chaps. 10–13 form a separate letter, which followed the letter composed of

be a product of historical decisions made by the exegete, the questions about the letter's integrity, the possibility and nature of charges brought against Paul, and the oblique manner in which he refers to them make a detailed description of the historical-rhetorical situation extremely difficult. The result is that every analysis of the letter is necessarily tentative in both its historical and theological reconstruction. As such, every reconstruction is always open to radical revision; this one is no exception.

Recent work in this seminar reminds us that particular problems like these are compounded by a second, related set of hurdles. One former supposition was that (at least as a working hypothesis) Paul's beliefs could be treated as stable entities despite the provisional shape they assumed in individual letters. So we argued that, given sufficient time and insight, we could: (1) discern a comprehensive set of convictions and (2) produce a map of their internal relationships so that the expression of these convictions in the individual letters could be sufficiently accounted for. However, as we have moved from letter to letter that assumption has become increasingly difficult to maintain. While most of us have posited the coherency of Paul's thought (in some fashion), the actual demonstration of that coherency has been more difficult to produce than we imagined. The various categories and expressions of convictions which we took to be stable continued to shift, not only between letters but sometimes within a letter. With that came broader terms for coherency: narrative, apocalyptic framework, and so on. But these categories began to lose their heuristic value as they became less specific. The working hypothesis subsequently became difficult to maintain.

In response various members of the seminar have suggested that there be a shift in our focus away from coherency of structure to matters of process and function. Their point is that, even if we could agree on the set of convictions that make up Paul's beliefs we would still need to explain how he chooses among them in order to describe adequately his activity as a theologian. Thus, while continuing to seek the main contents of Paul's beliefs and thought, we have become increasingly aware that his use of such convictions is equally important in understanding them. The synergistic relationship between the convictions and the dynamic involved with their linguistic expression would have to be part of any account of Paul as a theologian.[2]

1-9. In this I have followed generally the comments of Victor Furnish, since they attempt to provide a judiciously contoured hypothesis about rival apostles and are helpful in their approach to the letter's literary integrity (Furnish, *II Corinthians* [AB 32A; Garden City, NY: Doubleday, 1984] 48–54 and 35–40 respectively).

[2] So especially Victor Furnish's formulations of the problem in "Theology in 1 Corinthians" (chapter 4 in this volume) 60; idem, "Paul the Theologian," in *The Conversation Continues: Studies in Paul and John in Honor of J. Louis Martyn* (ed. R. T. Fortna and B. R. Gaventa; Nashville: Abingdon,

The matter of which convictions, or combination of convictions, and how they are given expression is obviously complex and made more so by the fact that Paul was a complex human being. In the case of 2 Corinthians it is impossible to ignore the personal elements that must have played a role in his perception of the world and his choice of expression, even though such factors throw wild cards into the process. In her model, Jouette Bassler attempts to address this personal element by suggesting that Paul's foundational convictions underwent two transformations: they were refracted or filtered first through his experiences and then through "the prism" of the circumstances he faced when writing.[3]

Because it includes efforts to indicate the fluid nature of Paul's theologizing and because it satisfies the need to see Paul's thought as contingent on both his experience and the situation he addressed, the model is a helpful one. However, there were also times when his convictions made sense of Paul's experiences, so that the movement in the model is in the opposite direction: from convictions to experiences, thus producing a cyclical reinterpretation of both. Similarly, the "prism" of the perceived situation, while affecting the linguistic expression of his convictions, itself was shaped by them. In this regard Bassler's model needs modification.

To demonstrate how this occurs I suggest that we consider the conviction of Jesus' death and resurrection as an instance of conceptual metaphor. Using a theory of metaphor that distinguishes its ability to reconstrue our conceptions and offers some sense of its pragmatic nature, I will argue that metaphor can serve as a means of understanding how the conviction that Jesus died and was raised by God functions (1) to structure Paul's thought about himself and (2) to challenge and so restructure the evaluative framework of his hearers. In the second part of the paper I want to illustrate how this occurs by first providing the pattern of death–resurrection derived from 5:14–21 and then by analyzing how that pattern comes to expression in 4:7–15, part of Paul's discussion of the ministry. Then, in a briefer section I will suggest that the pattern prompts a new understanding of the collection for Jerusalem. I will try to show that the death and resurrection of Jesus can be well understood when it is considered as a conceptual or "generative" metaphor, that is, one which may take various forms of specific expression but which reflects a particular construction of relations between its constituent terms. This part of the paper depends on a particular view of metaphor as a linguistic expression.

1990) 19–34; and Jouette Bassler, "Paul's Theology: Whence and Whither?" (chapter 1 in this volume). These suggestions were followed by Calvin J. Roetzel, "The Grammar of Election in Four Pauline Letters" (chapter 11 in this volume).

[3] Bassler, "Whence and Whither?," 10–11.

However, since I also think that viewing religious expressions as metaphor helps to explain their function within a community of belief and so clarifies how such statements are used theologically, I offer in a third section some concluding thoughts on the nature of metaphorical statements for conceiving of Paul as a theologian.[4]

II. A WORKING THEORY OF METAPHOR

Since the term "metaphor" has such a contentious history and because it is often thought of as an ornamental use of language with no place in serious discussion, it is necessary for me to provide a brief explanation of how I am using the term. The overview is not complete, since the matter of defining metaphor, assessing its cognitive value, and determining the exact nature of its function in language has engendered significant debate among both philosophers of language and linguists.[5] Nevertheless, in order to clarify how the term functions in this essay some attention to the theory is in order.

Eva Kittay's discussion of metaphor is congenial for my purposes because her theory combines a semantic and a pragmatic understanding of metaphor.[6]

---

[4] It is obvious that this paper can be no more than a beginning point, but that is how I understand the intended function of our focal papers. This would be the case even if the paper dealt with death and resurrection using only more conventional methods, but, because of the disputes concerning the nature and function of metaphor, its inchoate status is even more true. A complete project of this sort would require an argument for at least the following: (1) the chosen working definition of metaphor, (2) a study of metaphor's cognitive status and how metaphors make reference, and (3) how metaphorical speech is used by theologians. All of these are beyond the scope of this present paper. Recent explorations into the use of metaphor in theological talk include W. Alston, "Irreducible Metaphors in Theology," in *Divine Nature and Human Language: Essays in Philosophical Theology* (Ithaca, NY: Cornell University Press, 1989) 17–38; Garrett Green, *Imagining God: Theology and the Religious Imagination* (New York: Harper & Row, 1989); and Sallie McFague, *Metaphorical Theology: Models of God in Religious Language* (Philadelphia: Fortress, 1982). I have also found the article by Ben C. Ollenburger, "We Believe in God . . . Maker of Heaven and Earth: Metaphor, Scripture, and Theology," *Horizons in Biblical Theology* 12 (1990) 64–96 quite helpful as a judicious critique of excessive claims made on behalf of metaphorical language.

[5] For a convenient and insightful overview of this debate see the introduction to *Philosophical Perspectives on Metaphor* (ed. Mark Johnson; Minneapolis: University of Minnesota Press, 1981) 3–47.

[6] Contemporary metaphor theory contains an ongoing debate about the cognitive status of metaphors. A case for the cognitive view is made by Eva Feder Kittay, *Metaphor: Its Cognitive Force and Linguistic Structure* (Oxford: Clarendon Press, 1987). The strongest case against a special cognitive view is made by Donald Davidson in "What Metaphors Mean," in *On Metaphor* (ed. S. Sacks; Chicago: University of Chicago Press, 1978) 29–46. Davidson argues that a metaphor has no special cognitive meaning apart from the literal meanings of its constituent parts; instead its efficacy comes from its pragmatic force. Kittay offers a considered rebuttal of Davidson's arguments along with a critique of this position (pp. 96–123). Even if Davidson's position turns out to be the correct one, I do not think the general thrust of this paper is greatly altered. However,

The semantic and therefore cognitive element of her thesis enables me to suggest how Paul's thinking and the interpretation of his experiences have been structured by the theme of death and resurrection. The pragmatic functions of metaphor she describes provide the reasons why such restructuring could be valuable for Paul as a tool for communication, especially in situations like those he faced in Corinth. Finally, because Kittay situates metaphor alongside literal language and argues that both are context-dependent for meaning she provides an approach that does not dismiss or denigrate metaphor as merely figurative language, which is therefore somehow less valuable or truthful than literal propositional language.[7]

Kittay starts from an argument for the contextual nature of all language. According to her, "language itself is a bringing together of diversities into a unity of meaning which is contextually supported."[8] In other words, *any* sentence or phrase (literal or figurative) brings discrete entities into a new constellation which takes on a meaning potentially different from any of the terms which make up that sentence. More prosaically, words and sentences are contextually dependent for meaning. Metaphor is a means of enhancing and distilling this process "by juxtaposing ideas which are distinct and incongruent . . . ."[9] In this way metaphor is distinct from, but continuous with, literal language.

On this account both literal and metaphorical language can perform operations of comparison. But, whereas literal comparison takes place within fixed

---

one would need to focus more closely on the fact that thought is prompted by metaphor and leave conceptions of how this occurs out of the discussion.

[7] The discussions of how metaphors may refer in any way are, to say the least, complex. See Mary Gerhart and Allan Russell, *Metaphoric Process: The Creation of Scientific and Religious Understanding* (Fort Worth: Texas Christian University Press, 1984), which provides some helpful guidelines for a discussion of this problem, as well as the more rigorous and intense analysis found in Paul Ricoeur, *The Rule of Metaphor* (London: Routledge & Kegan Paul, 1978). The issue of "truth claims" and metaphor as truthful expressions is made into a denser thicket when we turn to theological claims and statements. Colin Gunton provides an important discussion of metaphorical language and truth claims for theology in *The Actuality of the Atonement* (Grand Rapids: Eerdmans, 1989). In Nicholas Lash's view, reference and truth become matters of correspondence between belief statements and the harsh realities of existence. He states "that correspondence eludes theoretical demonstration. It can, however, be practically, imperfectly, partially and provisionally shown by the character and quality of Christian engagement in patterns of action and suffering, praise and endurance, that refuse to short-cut the quest by the erection of conceptual or institutional absolutes" (*Theology on the Way to Emmaus* [London: SCM, 1986] 116). For McFague truth is a matter of "fit" and metaphor as central to all constructive fields from science to poetry to theology is true depending on how it "gives a more apt, or fitting way of interpreting reality than did the traditional view" (*Metaphorical Theology*, 41). It is this sense in which I am suggesting that Paul could have understood his metaphors to be true; that is, they produced a more fitting and apt description of reality than the competing models of the Corinthian congregation.

[8] Kittay, *Metaphor*, 17.

[9] Ibid.

or given categories, metaphor conjoins categories normally kept distinct, making it "the paradigmatic device for pointing out analogies and making comparisons which cross the bounds of our usual categories and concepts."[10] Formally speaking, then, metaphor is a linguistic expression of a concept by which an object "n" is simultaneously presented in two modes A and B, where A and B are incompatible. In its typical usage the object is classified under category A, but in the metaphor it is also brought under the classification of category B and this produces an anomaly.[11]

The anomaly that metaphor creates is important for our study because of its potential to reorient one's conceptual framework. With the creation of anomaly metaphor not only transfers the unknown to a given context of learning but can change the context of learning itself.[12] Under usual conditions the statements we hear or read are assimilated into a context produced by our understanding of the conditions in the world, but with an unusual expression like a metaphor an incongruity disrupts those "default" assumptions and causes us to rethink the statement.[13] If there is no reason to assume that the statement is a lie or that the speaker is incompetent in the language, then we seek a proper context for interpretation. Thus we conclude that a statement is an indirect speech act, an instance of hyperbole or irony, etc. As Samuel Levin has suggested, usually,

> given an incompatibility between [an] utterance and conditions in the world, the conditions are taken as fixed, and it is the utterance that must be construed. Now this is not a logically necessary position. We may, if we like, assume that, in the face of an incompatibility between what is asserted in an utterance and conditions as they obtain in the world, we regard the utterance as fixed and construe the world. Instead, that is, of construing

---

[10] Ibid., 19.

[11] The categories A and B are best understood as semantic fields or content domains. In Kittay's analysis "[a]ny experiential, phenomenal, or conceptual domain may be a content domain, for example, colour, fishing, electricity, etc. In other words, anything we may want to talk about, and which would require a set of related terms to talk about it, could serve as a content domain" (*Metaphor,* 34). In a complementary fashion a *semantic field* is a content domain that is structured in some specifiable way by certain relations of affinity or contrast. These relations include but are not limited to synonymy, hyponymy, cyclical series, noncyclical series, and ranking. When such relations are applied to a content domain it becomes a semantic field. Kittay uses the distinctions in order to allow for cases of metaphor where the topic is not easily conceived. In her analysis, "the topic is also a part of a system of ideas. From the imposition of one system upon another system, we arrive at meaning" (p. 35). Despite the possibility of confusion with other descriptions of semantic field, I have used her terms because they help us realize that as a conceptual device the topic of a metaphor is not always well ordered. Kittay offers a full discussion of her understanding of semantic fields and content domains on pp. 224–30.

[12] H. Petrie, "Metaphor and Learning," in *Metaphor and Thought* (ed. Andrew Ortony; Cambridge: Cambridge University Press, 1979) 441.

[13] On the matter of usual and unusual speech utterances, see H. P. Grice, "Utterer's Meaning, Sentence-Meaning, and Word Meaning," *Foundations of Language* 4 (1968) 225–42.

the utterance so that it makes sense in the world, we construe the world so as to make sense of the utterance.[14]

Further, on this account, "'defectiveness' is located in the world (i.e., the actual world), not in the utterance. 'Deviant' utterances are taken literally; they mean what they say—what gives is the world."[15]

My proposal is that precisely this function of metaphor makes it valuable for Paul's problems with the Corinthians. Functioning within "normal" or given parameters his statements about himself and his ministry are conceived by the Corinthians in such a manner as to disqualify him as a proper representative of God. But with the metaphor of death and resurrection Paul disqualifies the given construction; what gives is not his ministry, but the criteria and framework the Corinthians have used to evaluate it.

As we have just noted, a metaphor's important feature is its ability to point out unseen similarities and analogies because it introduces an incongruity that causes us to reflect on our normal mode of evaluation. It is also the case that the introduction of this incongruity "is related to the fact that when we categorize metaphorically we are guided by special interests—interests different from those which guide our usual classifications."[16] The use of metaphor enables us to highlight some aspects of the structured field and diminish others; it creates certain connections among terms and disallows other relationships; in short, a metaphorical transfer is an intentional one made in order to structure the target domain in ways that accomplish the speaker's goals. Further, just as "classification and categorization are both orderings, the intrusion of an incongruity is a disordering—one that forces a reordering if the structure of our conceptual organization is to retain a coherency. A new perspective is achieved—a new, if tenuous, point of view on the issues in hand."[17] It is this intentional use of incongruity which allows Paul the reference point to continue his argument with the Corinthian understanding of the apostolic ministry.

In this description of metaphor I have suggested several reasons for seeing it as important in evaluating how death and resurrection function within the

[14] S. Levin, "Standard Approaches to Metaphor and a Proposal for Literary Metaphor," in *Metaphor and Thought,* ed. Ortony, 131.

[15] Ibid.

[16] Kittay, *Metaphor,* 22. Note here also Nelson Goodman's comments on how we make and remake our worlds in *Ways of Worldmaking* (Indianapolis: Hackett, 1978) 7–17. According to Goodman, we use mechanisms of composition and decomposition, relative weighting of kinds, orderings of entities, deletion and supplementation, and deformation, in order to construct the world in manners that suit our purposes for discussion or activity. Paul's use of the death and resurrection as criteria for evaluating the world can be understood as a combination of these methods in which the Corinthian perception of the world is altered and thus shown to be a made, not a given, reality.

[17] Kittay, *Metaphor,* 22.

letter's argument. I want to make these explicit now (1–3) and add two more (4 and 5) before turning to the analysis of 2 Corinthians:

(1) Metaphor has a cognitive value in that it results in a reconceptualization of the topic under discussion so that properties of that topic are made conspicuous which before were not noticed and concepts held about the topic are reorganized. Metaphors map one conceptual structure onto another, permitting the digitalization of information previously in analog form.[18] In this sense, metaphor, while a linguistic expression, is also a way of structuring thought and so not dismissible as "ornamental language."

(2) The introduction of an incongruity by metaphor causes us to pause and reconsider how we have conceived of the world, creating momentary disequilibrium in our cognitive framework. This in turn calls into question the default assumptions with which we normally interpret the data and experiences the world provides.[19] Further, metaphor not only creates cognitive disequilibrium but helps resolve it by providing new ways in which to interpret and organize our concepts and experience. The jolting of those default assumptions is crucial to the success or failure of Paul's letter.

(3) For the purposes of description I distinguish between "rhetorical metaphors"—those which appear within an argument at the level of explicit expression—and "generative metaphors," which are tacit in an argument and set the framework for seeing problems and solutions to those problems.[20] The disturbance of default assumptions brings generative metaphors into the open and allows a fresh description of the problem. The death and resurrection of Jesus is in this sense a "generative metaphor."

---

[18] Ibid., 170.

[19] Default assumptions are

> those assumptions upon which speakers rely, in both verbal and non-verbal behaviour, in the absence of any contextual evidence canceling or questioning such assumptions. Because speakers are scarcely conscious of employing such assumptions, they presume, again with little consciousness of making such presumptions, that their audience has the same assumptions. They are *default* assumptions because they are what we assume in the absence of any contradictory evidence. Therefore, they only become conscious when something occurs which jars, such as the use of "she" rather than "he" when the context does not indicate the gender of the subject. When attempts to communicate fail because the interlocutors each proceed from different (default) assumptions, or when the world as normally experienced is altered by social, economic, political, or natural (gradual or cataclysmic) forces, our assumptions may be jarred. (Kittay, *Metaphor*, 57)

[20]For a discussion of how generative metaphors work and are created, see Donald Schön, "Generative Metaphor: A Perspective on Problem-Setting in Social Policy," in *Metaphor and Thought*, ed. Ortony, 254–83. McFague's use of radical models, in which she follows Stephen Pepper's understanding of "root-metaphors" presents a perspective similar to the one I wish to suggest (McFague, *Metaphorical Theology*, 28). Pepper's discussions of metaphor are found in *World Hypotheses* (Los Angeles: University of California Press, 1942).

(4) One can extend metaphors in that they invite further reflection on the newly formed relations, and so can imply other relations that the metaphor does not make explicit. They are therefore expandable and productive, and so open-ended. In this sense metaphors invite participation on the part of the hearer. Understanding a metaphor means being able to use its analogies to broaden the structural model it provides and to make connections the author does not explicitly state.

(5) In their invitation to participation metaphors create what David Cooper refers to as "special intimacy": "the bond which unites those who are reasonably deemed capable of hearing [an utterance]—and indeed, uttering it—with understanding."[21] The other side of this coin is that metaphors are also a challenge to a hearer in that they may not be understood. This permits one to consider Paul's use of metaphor as both invitation to an intimate relationship with him and as a matter of challenging address. This is both pragmatically important, given the discord between Paul and the Corinthians, and theologically important in that it shows how metaphor can embody the essence of the gospel.[22]

I can now state my thesis with more precision. I am arguing that the structure by which terms such as death, life, the glory of God, and power are related to one another by the resurrection of Jesus from the dead is transferred by Paul to the terms of his ministry and by extension to the life of the Christian in the present time before the eschaton. This provides a structure for that ministry and a way in which it, or any other ministry claiming to represent the gospel, can be adequately evaluated. Further, the understanding of life as eschatological is structured by the understanding that the raised Christ is the crucified Lord or, as Käsemann states it:

> Christ, exalted above the cross in his sublimity, is misunderstood if one separates the exaltation from the cross, and so reduces the relationship to that of two merely consecutive events. The Risen and Exalted One remains the Crucified One; and his sovereignty is not understood and acknowledged if the cross is merely made the last station on his earthly way. . . .[23]

In concrete terms this pattern of life requires practical demonstration, and so Paul's call to the Corinthians for participation in the collection is not an optional request but a claim that truly understanding the nature of the gospel's soterio-

---

[21] David Cooper, *Metaphor* (Cambridge: Basil Blackwell, 1986) 156.

[22] Eberhard Jüngel discusses the way in which metaphors are appropriate forms of theological talk in "Metaphorical Truth: Reflections on Theological Metaphor as a Contribution to a Hermeneutics of Narrative Theology," in *Theological Essays* (Edinburgh: T. & T. Clark, 1989) 16–71. See also Nicholas Lash, "Ideology, Metaphor and Analogy," in *Theology on the Way to Emmaus,* 95–119.

[23] Ernst Käsemann, *Jesus Means Freedom* (Philadelphia: Fortress Press, 1968) 67.

logical faculty also means a commitment to its demands for a life lived for another. In other words, participation in the new existence results in actions that are embodiments of the crucified Lord, which can take place in an apostle as well as in other believers.

III. ANALYSIS OF 2 CORINTHIANS

Overview of the Problems

The letter reveals a deep breach in the relationship between Paul and the Corinthians, which seems to have been the result of a number of events and perceptions. On the one hand, the Corinthians are deeply disappointed by Paul's failure to visit them after receiving his promises to do so (1:15–2:2). They perceived this as a lack of affection on his behalf or perhaps as an indication that Paul was only a flatterer who promised one thing and did another. On the other hand, Paul was disappointed in the Corinthians' failure to support him when he was embarrassed and insulted on his last visit (2:5–11). Since then the relationship had become strained and the amount of reciprocal trust minimal.

There also appears to have been an element of distrust toward Paul as a sincere, competent messenger of God (1:12; 2:17; 3:5; 4:2; 5:11; and 6:3). For whatever reasons—perhaps a lack of success for his preaching (4:3), or his personal demeanor (4:7–15, 6:4–10), or perhaps an insufficient demonstration of charismatic signs which they thought appropriate to the apostolic office (5:12–13a), the Corinthians failed to see in him enough evidence of the power of God. This lack of trust also seems to extend to the collection and Paul's participation in it, about which the Corinthians had misgivings. Since he had so adamantly rejected their offers of financial help previously, they wondered why the sudden reversal (1 Cor 9:15; 2 Cor 8:16–24; 9:1–5). Finally, other teachers had come to Corinth who appeared to be better representatives of the gospel than Paul, and it was insinuated that his credentials were inadequate or inferior to theirs (2:14–3:6). For his part Paul perceived the activities of these other missionaries as potentially destructive of the community's well-being and implied that they preach the gospel in a "watered down version" for their own gain (2:17; 4:1).

The combination of these social and theological misgivings resulted in the shutdown of mutual affection between Paul and the Corinthians (6:11–13; 7:2–3). Paul writes to restore this relationship and to restore their understanding and trust in him as an apostle of God. This attempt forms the bulk of 2:14–7:4. If he were to be successful in that, he would desire the Corinthians to participate in the collection for Jerusalem, which will demonstrate their correct understanding of the gospel and the reestablishment of his relationship with him (9:13).

It is clear that to accomplish these goals Paul must produce a credible defense of his activity as an apostle. But this already difficult matter is complicated because there were no set criteria for determining apostolic legitimacy until after Paul's death.[24] Paul did not have an "objective" standard against which to be measured and matched against the missionaries now present in Corinth (against whom he did not compare well). Thus, Paul's major problem, from the standpoint of communication, is how to establish proper criteria without participating in the same self-commendation that he condemns in his rivals. Specifically this becomes clear when we consider how Paul answers the questions raised about his ministry.

In previous correspondence and preaching Paul had claimed that his preaching came with power (1 Cor 1:24; 2:4–5), and in this letter he argues that his ministry is one of surpassing glory (3:4–11); but there remained for the Corinthians a question of how this glory became manifest. Paul's discourse on apostolic ministry (2:14–5:21) is an attempt to answer that question, but, in order for it to be successful, he must establish a proper set of criteria for judging words and actions that demonstrates why standard connections between power and demeanor were not acceptable. It is incumbent upon him to demonstrate that his gospel and life are consonant with "the gospel," and to do that he must dislodge the framework of evaluation used by the Corinthians.

Paul cannot avoid these charges against him: what he must do is reorient the Corinthians' understanding of the presence and purpose of adversities in his life. He must demonstrate that these "disqualifiers" were actually direct manifestations of God's power. His success or failure in defense hangs on the ability to make the Corinthians realize that the charges are not grounds for disqualifying his ministry and that the critics who have made them are using the wrong criteria for passing judgment. His reflections on and use of the death and resurrection of Jesus as an interpretive key for his life and experiences as an apostle provide him with the needed criteria to do this. The manner in which he applies the death and resurrection of Jesus metaphorically to his ministry is best demonstrated by considering 4:7–15. As Furnish has suggested, analyzing Paul's theological reflection begins with those passages where Paul is most deliberate about developing a topic concerning the gospel and then moves to others in which these conceptions are developed.[25] It is my sense

---

[24] So John Schütz, *Paul and the Anatomy of Apostolic Authority* (Cambridge: Cambridge University Press, 1975) 21.

[25] Furnish, "Theology in 1 Corinthians" (61–63).

that 5:14 is one of those passages where a fundamental conception is reflected on and that it is developed in particular ways in 1:8–11 and 4:7–15.

The Metaphoric Structure
of Death and Resurrection (5:14–21)

In order to gain access to the interpretive structure which the death/ resurrection holds for Paul, a consideration of 5:11–21 would be helpful. In that passage one encounters the most specifically theological (in Furnish's use of the term, i.e., critical reflection on a belief) interpretation in 2 Corinthians and perhaps in the Pauline corpus. Admittedly this is a section that is at least partially controlled by apologetics, as vv. 11–13 suggest. Paul is still involved with demonstrating the legitimacy of his own mission and denying that legitimacy to his rivals. Thus, he continues to defend himself to the Corinthians and, if v. 13 refers to charismatic activities, explains why these manifestations are not featured in his proclamation. Nevertheless, the features that appear in this section seem to go beyond polemic or apologetic interests, and, as long as we are mindful of their apologetic tint, they serve our investigation well.

The explicit claims in vv. 18 and 19 and the ἵνα and ὥστε clauses of vv. 15, 16, 17, and 21 provide important keys for determining Paul's understanding of the scope, nature, and implications of Jesus's death and resurrection. At least these four things can be claimed: (1) God's reconciling action is given specific manifestation in the death and resurrection of Jesus, and according to 5:20 that same activity is presently manifested in the ministry of Paul. That is, the shape of his ministry is defined by its founding events, and God's appeal for reconciliation is extended through this ministry. Moreover, the giving of this ministry (to all believers, as the ἡμᾶς ["us"] in v. 18c shows) is part of God's reconciling activity.[26] (2) The reconciling action is cosmic in scope (5:19), which implies that proper understanding of soteriology cannot be privatistic. The "all" of v. 14b is emphasized, and then extended to v. 14c with the ἄρα οἱ πάντες ("therefore all"). The consequence is that an ontological shift on a universal scale has taken place; the death of the one means that all have died.[27]

As we may infer from 5:15, the eschatological purpose of Christ's death and resurrection is not simply for personal soteriological gain but so that the

---

[26] Thus the phrasing in 4:1: ἔχοντες τὴν διακονίαν ταύτην καθὼς ἠλεήθημεν ("having this ministry as we have received mercy") — the ministry is Paul's due to God's mercy.

[27] Furnish suggests: "It [v. 14] is perhaps better understood in relation to Paul's conviction that everything old has come to an end (v. 17). The perspective here, then, would be cosmic and eschatological: all have died in the sense that all without exception are the objects of God's love and as such have been drawn, quite apart from anything they have done (cf. Rom 5:6–11), into the sphere of God's saving purpose and power" (*II Corinthians*, 327–28).

"ones who live will no longer live for themselves, but for the one who died and was raised on their behalf."[28] Dying with Christ means dying to self, but living for Christ, following the clue in 4:5 (the διὰ 'Ιησοῦν—"for Jesus' sake") is given form when one takes up the mission of Christ and lives in the service of others.[29] (3) The ὥστε clause of v. 16, which follows the ontic shift in v. 15 (no longer living for themselves but for the Christ) means that a new way of understanding has been effected. And the ὥστε clause in v. 17, which also draws an inference from vv. 14 and 15, maintains that a cosmic transformation has occurred, thus claiming that the death and resurrection transform the world and its understanding of reality. Verses 16 and 17 are parallel statements, but the ontological shift of v. 17 provides the context and basis for the epistemological shift of v. 16. Thus, one can talk of a new epistemology, but only as a result of and consonant with a new ontology. Paul's point is not that a new knowing occurs (although it is a goal of the apology), but that knowing is now controlled by a new being, a new ontic reality. A new evaluative set of criteria has been established as a result of a new existence, and both are effected and demonstrated in the death and resurrection of Jesus. Proper knowing is, therefore, the result of proper being.[30] The ability to see κατὰ σταυρόν ("in accord with the cross") is predicated on living κατὰ σταυρόν. Thus, proper knowing is not based on externals or standards of the world; rather it is the ability to see κατὰ σταυρόν.[31] (4) Finally, the death/resurrection has as its ultimate góal the reconciliation of the entire cosmos to God (v. 19a). Though it is manifest in God's actions toward and for humanity (v. 21), the reconciling message is finally a message that extends to all of creation, and it is therefore the demonstration of God's power and sovereignty.

Thus, death and resurrection supply a metaphoric structure for Paul that clarifies the manner of present existence. It is an existence that is lived not for oneself but for Christ and therefore in service of others. Second, it directs one's manner of knowing and by extension shows how one makes known the

[28] I interpret the two participles ἀποθανόντι ("died") and ἐγερθέντι ("was raised") in 5:15 as both referring to events ὑπὲρ αὐτῶν ("for them").

[29] So also Furnish, who, after recourse to Galatians and Romans 14–15 as a means of explication, concludes: "This association of living for Christ and living for others gives point to the present passage as well. Paul wants his readers to recognize that apostleship is not demonstrated by external characteristics of the apostles themselves (v. 12b), even should those be of an impressively 'religious' sort, like ecstatic utterances (v. 13a). Rather, the apostle, like every believer, is called to serve Christ by serving others. That is one claim Paul can and does make for his apostolate" (II Corinthians, 328–29).

[30] So also R. C. Tannehill, Dying and Rising with Christ: A Study in Pauline Theology (BZNW 32; Berlin: Töpelmann, 1967) 69.

[31] So J. Louis Martyn, "Epistemology at the Turn of the Ages: 2 Corinthians 5:16," in Christian History and Interpretation: Studies Presented to John Knox (ed. W. Farmer, C. F. D. Moule, and R. R. Niebuhr; Cambridge: Cambridge University Press, 1967) 285.

truth. The founding events as redeeming events make clear that Christ's love is expressed in his death (v. 14). To the extent that one is controlled by that love (συνέχει) one will live in a manner in which his death is expressed. Similarly, the founding events serve as the canon by which one's life is shaped and one's ministry is conducted. It is on this structure that Paul conducted his own ministry, interpreted its circumstances, and argued for its truth.

The Metaphoric Structure
in the Human Form of Paul's Ministry (4:7-15)

The comparison between the prior ministry of Moses and the one now granted to the apostles culminates in the claim that those who have accepted this new message no longer have veiled minds, but behold the glory of the Lord and are being progressively transformed from one degree of its intensity to the next (3:16, 18). But given the relationship between Paul and the Corinthians and their perceptions of him, this claim could not be stated without explanation. This Paul attempts in 4:1-6 and 4:7-15. Shifting the metaphor's plane from the divine action in Christ, he applies it to the divine action in his ministry. The function of the Christ as a bringer of life through death is mapped onto Paul's own activity. The mapping is not isomorphic, given Paul's understanding of the death/resurrection of Jesus as a one-time event. Nevertheless, the mapping highlights the daily dying of the apostle as the means by which God continues the ministry of reconciliation to create new life.

The διὰ τοῦτο ("therefore") of 4:1 suggests that this transformation is the basis for the section that follows in 4:1-6.[32] Rather than shrink away from the gospel, the apostle and his associates speak as a result of the power that causes this transformation. Hence, Paul argues that he and his associates, by the full disclosure of the truth (τῇ φανερώσει τῆς ἀληθείας), continue to preach only that message without tampering with its content or adopting a style inconsonant with its shape (v. 2), thus demonstrating their sincerity. This is expressed in more detail with the contrast in v. 5b, where Paul interprets both the content of the preaching as Jesus Christ as Lord and the manner of the

---

[32] Bultmann points out the close connection of 3:7-18 to 4:1-6, noting that (1) the ἔχοντες ("we are engaged") in 4:1 takes up the ἔχοντες of 3:12; (2) the διακονία ("ministry") in 4:1 corresponds to that of 3:7; (3) the καθὼς ἠλεήθημεν ("we have received mercy") in 4:1 corresponds to the διὰ Χριστοῦ ("through Christ") of 3:4; (4) the κεκαλυμμένον ("veiled") in 4:3 refers back to the κάλυμμα ("veil") of 3:13-18 and (5) the blinded νοήματα ("minds") of 4:4 refer to the hardened minds of 3:14-15; and (6) the αὐγάσαι ("seeing") in 4:4 corresponds to the ἀτενίσαι ("gazing") in 3:13. See R. Bultmann, *The Second Letter to the Corinthians* (Minneapolis: Augsburg, 1985) 99.

apostolic presence as being a slave of others for Jesus' sake.[33] Thus the gospel
is presented in both the speech and bearing of the apostle who labors for the
Lord and the benefit of the Corinthians. Here the paradox, made more evident
in the next section, is initially expressed as the antithesis of those who are
deceitful in presenting the gospel. Thus, the combination of what Paul preaches
and how he conducts himself is what makes his ministry commendable both
to the conscience of all and before God, despite outward appearance to the
contrary.

This section also introduces once more the deeper paradox of the gospel.
Paul's gospel *is* and *is not* veiled depending on the manner in which it is received.
Paul, despite external indications to the contrary, claims not to veil but to reveal
the gospel. Proper understanding of the message and its form enables one to
see the glory of Christ; without it one remains blinded. The gospel as such
is equivocal only in that it does not yield to "this-world reasoning" but rather
calls that form of reasoning into question. Thus the gospel is the entity that
causes a judgment not on itself but on its hearers (v. 4). The "glory of Christ"
is seen when one accepts that it is the glory of the crucified Christ. God, who
illumines, causes knowledge and enlightenment in the hearts of believers (v. 6),
countering the god of this age, who blinds (v. 4). Those who are enlightened
by the knowledge of the splendor of God are just the ones who comprehend
the paradox — glory is in the face (the person) of the one who was crucified.
The structure of the message has implications for the apostolic role, and Paul
turns to those in vv. 7–15.

As most commentators note, 4:7–15 is part of the larger unit that extends
through 5:10.[34] Furnish refers to its subject as "apostolic confidence," and so
it is a continuation of the discussion begun in 2:14. Still, as he notes:

> beginning in 4:7 another and special subject is present, initially formulated
> as the suffering of apostles (4:8–9), then enlarged to the topic of mortality

---

[33] Furnish, following Bultmann's suggestion that it is questionable to see Paul as referring to
himself as part of the gospel, argues that Paul cannot intend to include the apostle's role as part
of the preaching given the statement in v. 5a, even though the phrase is grammatically dependent
on the κηρύσσομεν ("we proclaim") (*II Corinthians*, 223). However, taken as a statement of the apostle's
behavior with the Corinthians and not as a form of preaching about oneself, it seems to me that
the grammatical form can be followed. This Bultmann actually seems to allow; see C. K. Barrett,
A Commentary on the Second Letter to the Corinthians (HNTC; New York: Harper & Row, 1973) 134.

[34] The final three verses of chap. 4 provide a transition to the next section, which deals with
contrasts of permanence and transition. These verses, which introduce this section, also suggest
that the death–life mode of existence that Paul has been describing as the only fitting mode for
present ministry is not the only form of existence which the Christian will have. In the ultimate
temporal scheme the present existence is a "momentary affliction," a nice irony in itself compared
to his emphasis on sufferings. Nevertheless, at this present time Paul's point is that this momentary
affliction is necessary and dictates how the apostle is to live. Any attempt to rush to the "end
existence" prematurely results in a vitiation of the content of the gospel. For the connection of
4:16–18 to 5:1–5, see Furnish, *II Corinthians*, 288.

(4:11), and thereafter further extended to include the situation of all believers (4:18ff.). Here Paul acknowledges that the sufferings and generally inglorious careers of himself and his apostolic associates might be (and evidently have been) taken by some as invalidating their claim to be ministers of a new covenant of surpassing glory (3:7–4:6). These mortal adversities he now interprets as an integral and appropriate part of true apostleship (4:7–15). . . .[35]

The previous section has claimed that the δόξα τοῦ θεοῦ ("glory of God") is present in Paul's ministry; the question he now attempts to answer is how, given the fact that his life does not display the expected manifestations of God's glory, this can be so.

The pericope can be divided into four units: the thesis statement (v. 7), the catalogue of hardships presented by the antitheses in vv. 8–9, the theological interpretation of those adversities by vv. 10–12, and the implication and extension of that interpretation to show that these adversities are for the ultimate purpose of the overflowing of "thanksgiving to the glory of God" (vv. 13–15).[36] Two parts of the metaphoric structuring become evident in these verses: the reinterpretation of suffering as death and the understanding of the ministry as an extension of resurrection life. Paul as one who is dying is also the one in whom the power of God to produce life can be seen. As the crucified Christ was the locus of God's most significant demonstration, so too in his present afflicted existence is the apostle the visible manifestation of that power.

Paul uses a form of the peristasis catalogue, common in both Jewish apocalyptic and Hellenistic philosophy, to show that his ministry is located in, and by, God's power, despite appearances to the contrary.[37] However, in distinction from those catalogues, Paul does not deny the real nature of the adversity that he has endured, nor, as in Stoic forms, does he argue that this endurance was the result of his own efforts. Rather, here as in 1:8–10 Paul

---

[35] Furnish, *II Corinthians,* 277. J. Lambrecht refers to the section as

a meditation on the paradox of a process of death which bears within itself, and already manifests, life, and which, ultimately, through the resurrection will culminate in an eternally lasting and glorious existence. What is mortal will, finally, be swallowed up by what is life without further ado (cf. 5,4). Because Paul meditates here on the relationship between suffering and eventual glory, we can distinguish this section of his apology from what precedes (2,14–4,6) and follows (5,11–7,4).

("The Nekrôsis of Jesus' Ministry and Suffering in 2 Cor 4, 7–15," in *L'Apôtre Paul: Personnalité, style et conception du ministère* [ed. A. Vanhoye; BETL 73; Leuven: Leuven University Press, 1986] 122–23).

[36] Lambrecht makes another division: vv. 7–12, 13–14, and 15, arguing that separating v. 15 from vv. 13 and 14 emphasizes the ultimate purpose of apostolic service—God's glory ("The Nekrôsis of Jesus," 128).

[37] See on this Wolfgang Schrage, "Leid, Kreuz und Eschaton: Die Peristasenkataloge als Merkmale paulinischer theologia crucis und Eschatologie," *EvT* 34 (1974) 141–75; Robert Hodgson, "Paul the Apostle and First Century Tribulation Lists," *ZNW* 74 (1983) 59–80; and J. Fitzgerald, *Cracks in an Earthen Vessel: An Examination of the Catalogues of Hardships in the Corinthian Correspondence* (SBLDS 99; Atlanta: Scholars Press, 1988).

applies the structure of life from death and so interprets his deliverance in terms of the God who raises the dead. The same power that raised Jesus from the dead (1:10) is active in delivering Paul from peril and afflictions. In both passages, Paul's experiences are interpreted and given meaning by his conviction that God acts to bring life from death.[38] Though the afflictions are not Paul's desire, nor are they sought by him, they are intrinsic to his ministry because in them God shows the incomparable power which is God's alone. Thus, the afflictions are not only a demonstration of God's power but an actual manifestation of the gospel. For, in the apostle the embodied nature of God's redemptive power—strength in weakness, life in death, light from darkness—is revealed (4:10–12). What the Corinthians have interpreted as evidence that Paul's claim to apostleship is illegitimate is reconstrued by means of the metaphoric exchange as direct evidence of God's activity in his life. The evidence remains the same, but by means of the new structure its assessment is transformed.

The terms θησαυρόν ("treasure") and ὀστρακίνοις σκεύεσιν ("clay jars") (v. 7) reflect backward and forward respectively to 4:1–6 and 4:8–9. The treasure, whether taken to be the ministry or the gospel, is embodied in the mortality of the apostles. The primary idea of the phrasing is to conjoin the treasure and earthen vessels. That is, the concept Paul desires the Corinthians to grasp is the contrast between treasure and earthen vessels. A vessel's worth comes from what it holds, not from what it is. The treasure is found in vessels that are surprisingly different from their content. The outward appearance cannot be taken as a sure guide to the inner contents; rather the outward container must be judged by what it holds.

For Paul, however, this contrast is not only an illustration but a principle of the ministry. Guided by the relationship between death and power that is created by the resurrection, Paul argues not only that the treasure can be found in earthen vessels but that it must be. To be a message about this event and therefore to properly present it, the gospel requires a form consonant with its content, whether in the type of speech employed or in the one speaking. Both message and messenger must be shaped by the event. Here one sees the metaphor's effect. The bearer of the message cannot act on her or his own

---

[38] In 1:8–9 the phrasing "we despaired of life itself. Indeed, we felt that we had received the sentence of death" implies that from a human standpoint Paul was certainly dead. There existed no deliverance from the situation he faced. When he did survive, he understood it as an instance of God's power and an attestation that God raises the dead. Moreover, this is a continuing factor in God's being and in Paul's life as the future tense ῥύσεται ("he will deliver") (v. 10) shows. Paul learns in this incident that the ministry—indeed, his own life—is dependent at all times on the power of God, and that alone. Dependence on self or others is impossible. Thus, here he understands existentially the religious affirmation that it is God who raises the dead.

but only in obedience to the message's content. As the death/resurrection scheme maintains that the Christ must act in accord with the redemptive actions, so also the representative of God. Thus, as the metaphoric structure is transferred to the field of apostleship, an indispensable correlation between the mortality of the apostles and the message they proclaim is created. The gospel/ministry must be presented by those whose lives are fragile, in order to show that the power comes from God alone (v. 7b).

Here, the point Paul had made concerning his mode of preaching in 1 Cor 1:17–18, "For Christ did not send me to baptize but to proclaim the gospel, and not with eloquent wisdom, so that the cross of Christ might not be emptied of its power. For the message of the cross is foolishness to those who are perishing, but to us who are being saved it is the power of God" (see also 1 Cor 2:1–5) is directly applied to his life as an apostle. Not only the message but the speaker must convey the gospel, and this means that life proceeding out of death must be manifest in him. Only when the mode of speech and the presence of the speaker are consonant with the cruciform nature of the message can the word of the cross occur and so be the power of God (1 Cor 1:18). Any other manifestation robs the cross of its power; hence, Paul's innuendoes about "peddlers of God's word" and "tampering with the word of God" in 2:17 and 4:3, when striking out at his rivals.

The ἐν παντί ("in every way") of v. 8 governs all four of the contrasts made in vv. 8–9, and this shows how the treasure is borne in the mortal bodies of the apostles—the sufferings and limitations of the ministry are essential, not accidental. This reference to "in every way" is picked up in v. 10 with the use of the temporal adverb πάντοτε ("always") in v. 11 with the use of ἀεί ("always"). The result is that both in the report and in its interpretation the adversities are understood as a typical and constant part of Paul's ministry, not exceptions or anomalies. But why the adversities are always present as a part of the ministry is explained by the interpretations found in vv. 10–11 and the resulting conclusion given in v. 12, which ground them in death/resurrection and its present mode of manifestation.

The cognitive function of metaphoric structure mentioned above is evident in this construction of Paul's ministry. Paul's conception and understanding of adversity and its relationship to his life are shaped by the relationship of death and life found in the paradigm of the Christ-event. Thus, the instances of dying which the apostle experiences are no less necessary than the death that Christ experienced. For the life of the gospel to appear, dying is a necessary part of the ministry, both within the "logic" of the gospel and because it is the embodiment of that gospel. With these verses Paul interprets the adversities in light of the death and resurrection of Jesus and concludes that the afflictions of the apostle result in the life of the community of belief. In this way he embodies the founding events of the gospel, which produces new life by the dying of the Christ. The life and ministry is thus given shape and organized by the metaphoric structure of Christ's death and resurrection.

In effect the transfer of these relationships to the apostle's own existence shifts the relationship between his adversities and the demonstration of power. What was formerly disjoined is now conjoined. The dying of the apostle is the potential for life in others. As a sharer of death, Paul understands himself as a recipient of God's life, but not for himself alone. The life is given so that it may be engendered in others. The pattern found in 5:14–15 is here utilized to present the apostolic existence in a new light. Rather than a fraud, Paul is a paradigm of God's activity in Christ. As Christ died to bring life, so the apostle brings life through his "death." The adversities are not coincidental to Paul's life but a necessarily constant part of his ministry, for they give form to his preaching and are an integral part of his message. Indeed, they are visible manifestations of what he says. As v. 10 makes clear, the adversities are the "dying of Christ."[39] However, the ἵνα clause ("so that") of v. 10 (which is parallel to the those found in vv. 7 and 11) makes certain that the reason for this dying is not missed. Bearing the dying of Jesus in his body means that the life of Jesus is disclosed. This life is, of course, the resurrection life of Jesus, which is the incomparable demonstration of the power of God.[40] Thus, the apostle's manner of existence is a physical expression of the gospel's message. Bearing the dying of Jesus, he reveals the resurrection life of Jesus; and it is because of this belief in the resurrection that Paul makes such an audacious claim for his own calamities.[41] Thus, the belief functions to interpret the experiences so that the sufferings of Paul become, in the new structure, the νέκρωσις τοῦ Ἰησοῦ ("death of Jesus").

[39] The phrase ἡ νέκρωσις τοῦ Ἰησοῦ ("the death of Jesus"), though employing an unusual term for Paul (νέκρωσις elsewhere only in Rom 4:19), is used here in a way similar to θάνατος ("death") as v. 11 shows. Nevertheless, here the word takes on the aspect of the process of dying. Thus, as Bultmann suggests, "Paul uses . . . νέκρωσις instead of θάνατος, since in this passage dying with Christ is not meant in that basic sense of a once for all (anticipatory) event in the Baptism, but in the sense that it continually occurs in concrete historical life" (*Second Letter to the Corinthians,* 117).

[40] "The 'life of Jesus' of which Paul speaks in vs. 10 corresponds to the 'power of God' of vs. 7. Just as the power of God manifests itself in the experiences of physical deliverance summed up in vss. 8–9, so this 'life of Jesus' manifests itself 'in our body,' that is, in the same experiences of physical deliverance. Thus the 'life of Jesus' is another way of referring to this divine power." See Tannehill, *Dying and Rising,* 84.

[41] Note here the use of φανερωθῇ ("may be made visible"), which connects the apostle's life to his preaching (2:14; 4:2). Just as his preaching is an open statement of the truth, so is his "life of dying" an open manifestation of God's power to give life. The power of God, as expressed in the resurrection life, is revealed in the apostle's life. As the death of Jesus is a necessary part of the giving of life, so the apostle understands his own bearing of that dying to be a necessary part of the ministry.

This same thought is given further breadth in v. 11, which is structurally and materially parallel to v. 10. The "bearing of the dying in his body" is now explained. This life of constant dying happens because Paul's life follows the pattern established by the death of Jesus. It is in his mortal flesh that the resurrection life is made manifest. Thus διὰ 'Ιησοῦν does not mean for Jesus' sake, but because of Jesus. That is, just as the death of Jesus brings life, so must it be with those who are representatives of him.[42] Hence, on the apostle's understanding adversities cannot be avoided or seen as disqualifications because they are the necessary medium for the gospel's expression. The life of Jesus breaks through in this existence, not by overcoming it but by reinterpreting it. Thus Paul calls these afflictions and persecutions dying, metaphorically structuring them so that they are, therefore, not to be denied (nor sought in some form of Christo-masochism) but understood in light of the definitive action God has taken in the death and resurrection of Christ. Situated between the founding events and their future completion (4:14), the Christian resides now in hope, established and informed by the metaphorical use of those events.

It is also evident that this section exploits the interpretive and jarring nature of the metaphor which is a necessary part of Paul's rhetorical goals. The apostle's ministry and life are interpreted as manifestations of the death and resurrection of Jesus. Those foundational events produce the proper relationship between death and life — not as opposites but as necessary complementaries. This proposed understanding challenges the Corinthians' own manner of evaluation because it provides as proof of the apostle's legitimacy just that evidence which they understood as his disqualification. In so doing Paul provides a new way of interpreting the evidence of the apostle's life and, with this metaphoric structure of death in life, calls the Corinthians to reevaluate not Paul but themselves. That is, the cognitive framework in which they have understood apostleship and Christian life is rejected by the apostle. If before the Corinthians were able to assimilate his language and life into their conceptual framework, it is Paul's present contention that this framework is incompatible with the new existence. With the new metaphoric structure the roles have been reversed. Those whose value are threatened are not those who manifest the death of Christ, but those who refuse to do so. The new life, the transformation from glory to glory, is present and can be seen, but only by those who evaluate the evidence properly.

Thus Paul claims, the resurrection life, though it will not be perfectly materialized before the eschaton (4:14; 5:2-5), is nevertheless present now. The questions how the apostle can be a representative of the gospel and how the glory of God can be now present, are answered in these verses. The presence

---

[42] So also Furnish (*II Corinthians,* 257) against Barrett (*Second Letter to the Corinthians,* 140).

of God's power is most clearly expressed in the afflictions and adversities of this mortal existence. The pithy formulations of 12:10 and 13:4 are already foreshadowed here. The weakness of the apostle is a determinative proof of the presence of the power of God and an integral part of his ministry. As Furnish has stated:

> the labors, risks, and sufferings of the apostle are not to be regarded as just the unfortunate consequences of his Christian witness, or as impressive evidence of the strength of his faith. Rather, they constitute the very essence of his witness, because they disclose the life-giving death of Jesus. They are in and of themselves *kerygmatic*.[43]

In v. 12 the consequence of this existence is stated. God acts through death to cause life. The verb form ἐνεργεῖται ("is at work") is most likely a passive, like φανερωθῇ ("may be made visible") in vv. 10–11.[44] The meaning then becomes that God uses death to bring life and so uses the "dying lives" of the apostles to bring life to the Corinthians. Paul's ministry then extends to the Corinthians to give life through his death. Thus the thesis statement of v. 7 is once more brought into view. The external adversities have been interpreted not as happenstance occurrences but as the work of God in the apostle, which enables life to spread to the Corinthians. Here too the pattern of Christ is evident, for it is through the death of the Christ that God brings the world new life.

This understanding of his mission leads Paul to the concluding verses of the section. Drawing on Psalm 115 LXX, Paul compares his faithful actions to those of the psalmist. Using the terms "believing" and "speaking" he claims that, like the Psalmist he speaks in adversity. He preaches because it is just that action which demonstrates his faith. Believing in the God who raised Jesus means understanding God to be working now in his life; therefore Paul's preaching stems from faith. Though his outward appearance is that of dying, Paul understands this existence to be part of his faithful witness to the one who raises the dead and who will ultimately raise him together with the Corinthians on the final day. Thus, Paul claims that the legitimacy of his ministry will be known with a final test—that is, the readers' future resurrection with Jesus will demonstrate the faithfulness of his preaching to them. This leads him to the ultimate goal of the preaching which he expresses in v. 15. The syntax of this verse is quite convoluted, although its sense is generally clear.[45] It is true that all of Paul's ministry is for the sake of the Corinthians

---

[43] V. Furnish, "Paul the ΜΑΡΤΥΣ," in *Witness and Existence: Essays in Honor of Schubert M. Ogden* (ed. Philip E. Devenish and George L. Goodwin; Chicago: University of Chicago Press, 1989) 78.

[44] So too Furnish (*II Corinthians*, 257), following Norbert Baumert (*Täglich sterben und auferstehen: Der Literalsinn von 2 Kor 4,12–5,10* [Munich: Kösel, 1973] 72–73).

[45] For discussions of the syntactic difficulties, see Furnish, *II Corinthians*, 259–60.

(as opposed to the self-serving he perceives in his rivals), but this is not its ultimate aim, which, for Paul, must be seeking to give glory to God. This goal, however, is achieved as more and more of the creation recognizes God's saving purposes and so contributes to the thanksgiving which gives God the glory for that action. Here, then, as in 1:11, Paul insists that truly comprehending God's power means moving past an understanding of χάρις ("grace") "for me" to its expansion throughout the world.[46]

Thus, in this section of the letter Paul's conviction about the death and resurrection of Christ is used metaphorically to reconstitute his adversity-filled life by means of the death/resurrection life structure; his adversities are to be understood as a dying which brings life. He thus presents the main address of the gospel itself. As the cross will not be fitted into reigning understandings of reality, so also Paul's life will not be fitted into preset understandings of power and value. As an expression of God's actions in the death and resurrection of Christ, Paul's ministry forces a reexamination of the self. Here the pragmatic function of metaphors is evident. The anomalous nature of the gospel manifested in and through Paul's ministry cannot be assimilated into former world construals; they are incompetent to do so. Rather, the gospel claims that its reality is the framework for construing the world. Thus, understanding the gospel also means restructuring one's world. With his characterization of the ministry as a "dying life" Paul has produced a metaphor that forces the same decision. To recall Levin's words about metaphors, what gives is not the utterance, but the world. Like the gospel, Paul's ministry calls the hearer into question by its very form; and that is what provides its legitimacy.

The Metaphoric Structure Expanded (2 Corinthians 8–9)

Briefly I would like to suggest that the expandable nature of metaphor is also present in the epistle by considering Paul's oblique references to the collection as demonstrations of διακονία ("ministry"). In 8:1 a similar pattern to that of 4:7–15 is used to describe the Macedonian participation in the collection. Out of their affliction and depth of poverty comes a wealth of liberality. Just as life has come from death in Paul's ministry, so here the Macedonians give liberally from their scarce monetary resources. Interestingly, in 8:4 this is referred to as ἡ κοινωνία τῆς διακονίας ("sharing in the ministry"). Paul repeats this use of διακονία in 9:1 and especially in 9:12 and 13, each time as a reference

---

[46] Cf. George Boobyer, *Thanksgiving and the 'Glory of God' in Paul* (Borna-Leipzig: Universitätsverlag von Robert Noske, 1929) 79–80.

to the collection. Of particular note in the latter instance is that this participation results in increased thanksgiving to God (v. 12) and the glorifying of God by the Corinthians (v. 13). Moreover, this is a test of their service, a way in which they can bring glory to God and an acknowledgment of the gospel which is a display of their obedience to the pattern established by that gospel in Christ (cf. 8:8, 24). All of this suggests that the collection is itself structured by the generative metaphor that structures Paul's conceptions of his ministry. There is thus a double transfer of the metaphor's structure: from the field of the death and resurrection of Jesus, to the field of Paul's ministry, to the matter of the collection. The Macedonians give shape to their belief; they enact in their giving the pattern of the founding events. From their participation comes the confirmation that they belong to God and to Paul (8:5).

Casting the collection in this light makes the matter of the Corinthian participation more imperative than Paul's language appears to suggest at first sight. The collection was an obvious point of difficulty, and Paul chooses his language quite carefully in this section. Still, by creating the link between the collection and the form of ministry, which he argues is the only form proper to the gospel, Paul implies that it is through the collection that the Corinthians demonstrate their commitment to the gospel. Thus, in 8:8–9 he makes reference once more to the Christ-event and its consequences and suggests that this model is to be followed by the Corinthians, so that they may prove their love for others. The delicate matter of participation, about which Paul is deeply concerned, could not be approached directly by command (v. 8), but through the transitive use of the metaphor Paul's rhetorical objective can be achieved.[47]

In her discussion Kittay has suggested how this ability of metaphor to structure a distant field implicitly occurs. Referring to R. Buckminster Fuller's geodesic structures, she notes how three equilateral triangles can be situated contiguously to form two more: a fourth formed by the interior sides of the initial three, and a fifth that incorporates all four as one large triangle. With the appropriate placement of the first three triangles the others are formed. This she suggests can be an appropriate use of metaphor. Situating the boundaries of one field in a particular relation to another "yields a concept that

---

[47] So also John Koenig, who asks:

Is it merely a coincidence that in 2 Corinthians 8–9 Paul repeatedly names the collection for the poor believers in Jerusalem *he diakonia*—and always with the definite article (8:4, 9:1, 12, 13)? See also 9:13, where the apostle envisions that the Corinthians' help in this project will bring about a significant glorification of God by the Jerusalem church. It appears that for Paul the next step forward to be taken by the Corinthians in the ministry of reconciliation is the completion of their part in the collection. ("The Knowing of Glory and Its Consequences [2 Corinthians 3–5]," in *The Conversation Continues,* ed. Fortna and Gaventa, 169 n. 25)

need never be explicitly stated, and whose existence need not be explicitly asserted, for it to be operative in our understanding of the metaphor."[48] This I think is the logic of chaps. 8 and 9 in the letter. Though the explicit arguments of the first seven chapters are not specifically invoked, it is not because they are forgotten. Rather the understanding of ministry lies behind Paul's references to the collection in these chapters (and, behind the understanding of the ministry, the pattern of death/resurrection). Thus an understanding of the ministry which follows Paul's conception naturally results in the participation in the collection. By creating the double extension from death resurrection to the collection Paul makes his claim without an explicit demand.

Thus, the metaphor is extended and the invitation of interpretation broadened to include a praxis for the gospel. The gospel understood means the gospel embodied as living out the mission in the service of others. This implies that the collection is not an option that can be ignored. The giving of money (an eminently tangible symbol of power) is a visible display of not trusting in one's own means for sufficiency and reflects an understanding that all means of power are ultimately related to and dependent on God. Thus, Paul's hope that the glory of God will reach further and further is given concrete form when the Corinthians realize that their participation in the gospel is a faithful rendering of their own understanding of God's grace.

IV. METAPHOR AND THEOLOGY

It is clear that an analysis such as this is only a beginning point. Incomplete as this study is, I think it does suggest that metaphor is a fruitful way forward in assessing how the core convictions that Paul held could function in structuring his thought. This suggests three other matters that one would want to consider.

First, the open-ended nature of metaphor, which allows for its extendability, has positive and negative features. On the positive side, the manner in which metaphor provokes thought allows a "nonsyllogistic" logic to be proposed when we consider how Paul's thoughts cohere. There is an organic nature to Paul's thinking, and considering how metaphor plays a role in structuring thought allows us to see the links that Paul makes, even — and especially — when they do not appear to be syllogistically evident ones. On the negative side, metaphors can be taken in directions which the utterer had not intended. Here one sees how Paul's preaching, teaching, and letters could be interpreted in ways that differed from his desires or intent, not because of outside influence

---

[48] Kittay, *Metaphor,* 277.

or a desire to refute the apostle but because the metaphors themselves allow
for this. Thus, part of Paul's task as a "theologian" was to create contexts that
narrowed the possible avenues of interpretation to those consonant with other
aspects of the gospel.[49]

This suggests another feature of the theological task. The relationship of
one metaphor to another needs attention. Are there metaphors that are hier-
archically more important than others? More to the point, one would want
to consider which analogies are better interpretations of belief than others.
Metaphors, because they are structural reorderings, do not allow for complete paraphrase by their very nature. We can paraphrase some aspects of a
metaphor, but not all of them, and this point has important exegetical implications. Our exegeses must present adequate paraphrases, but we cannot forget
that they will inevitably be incomplete. This also reminds us of an important
theological condition provided by metaphor. Metaphor is a necessary part of
religious and theological language because it is a form of expression that will
not yield to a replacement expression. There are times when metaphor resists
complete paraphrase not only because it is intrinsic to this form of linguistic
expression but because it is theologically necessary. We want certain expressions to serve as challenges, to present address, and to invite the hearer to
participate in their understanding. As this occurs, the world of the hearer is
brought into question, allowing for its reorientation by the structure that the
metaphor provides. This means that we must remember the open-ended nature
of metaphoric expressions when we interpret them if we wish to fully grasp
their theological potential.

Finally, an exegetical approach that stresses the nature of metaphors is no
fool-proof therapy, despite its potential to capture much of what religious
language attempts. Offering a new metaphor to replace an older one that no
longer serves the community's needs, or proposing analogies for interpreting
metaphors that do, is an ongoing task. These attempts at expressing the beliefs
of the religion may fail, even when the metaphors are apt. Metaphorical
theology is not an alternative to interpretation, but an intrinsic part of interpretation; thus it cannot be forgotten in our attempts to discover Paul's theology
or write that theology anew. However, if the letter to the Corinthians is any
indication, even those metaphors that are expressed in a forceful and striking

[49] Ibid., 172:
   [E]ven if the utterer of the metaphor intended only one such contrast, the reader is
   free to construe as many as will in fact result in interesting induced relations. Such
   a reader will not properly be accused of misreading the metaphor. What we commonly say here is that the metaphor reveals more than what was intended by its creator.
   Our representation provides a nice mechanism by which to account for the multifarious
   and non-exclusive possibilities inherent in metaphorical interpretation.

manner may not result in the desired goal. As with all expressions that reflect the gospel, there is always the possibility that they will not be heard; but this, too, is in keeping with a gospel that insists on its nature as address.[50]

[50] I would like to thank J. C. Beker for discussions about this paper, Beverly Gaventa for her response to it, and especially Hendrikus Boers for his help in its construction.

9 APOSTLE AND CHURCH IN 2 CORINTHIANS

A Response to David M. Hay and Steven J. Kraftchick

Beverly Roberts Gaventa
Princeton Theological Seminary

"LOOK AT WHAT is before your eyes," Paul admonishes in one of his letters to believers in Corinth (2 Cor 10:7 NRSV). For the student of 2 Corinthians, who sees in that letter a veritable morass of historical, literary, and exegetical problems, Paul's challenge seems insurmountably difficult. The task of discussing theology in 2 Corinthians is complicated not only by questions the letter itself raises but by the recent proliferation of proposals for addressing what is called "Pauline theology." Where does one begin? What questions does one ask? What constitutes an answer to those questions?[1]

Both David M. Hay and Steven J. Kraftchick have accepted the challenge to "look at what is before your eyes," making fresh proposals about the way in which Paul goes about the task of interpreting the gospel in 2 Corinthians. My response addresses the methods and conclusions of each, and then turns to an issue I regard as neglected by each, as well as by much recent study of 2 Corinthians, namely, the theological connection between apostle and church in 2 Corinthians.

I. CONVICTIONS, DOUBTS, AND WARRANTS: A RESPONSE TO DAVID M. HAY

The title of David Hay's essay, "The Shaping of Theology," provides an important signal about the contribution that will follow. Hay consistently

---

[1] The question of what is included in the term "2 Corinthians" must be addressed at the outset. For the purposes of this paper, my assumption is that canonical 2 Corinthians consists of two letter fragments. Chapters 1–9 (probably without 6:14–7:1) contain most of one letter, and chaps. 10–13 contain most of a second, and later, letter. Since the second letter concerns many of the same issues and comes only a brief period after the first, they are treated together in what follows. For a review of the complicated scholarship on this question and defense of the position adopted here, see Victor Paul Furnish, *II Corinthians* (AB 32A; Garden City, NY: Doubleday, 1984) 30–41.

selects words of action with which to describe what has traditionally been referred to as "Paul's theology": develop, process, activity, practice, theologizing, interacting, dynamic, emerging. In this way, he draws attention to the fluidity of Paul's theological endeavors and reflects some of the significant issues raised in earlier discussions of the SBL Pauline Theology Group.[2]

Hay argues that the "theological activity" of Paul in 2 Corinthians can be analyzed by means of three constituent and dynamic components: convictions, doubts, and warrants. As Paul considers the doubts he faces at Corinth and within himself, he reflects on the convictions he regards as essential and considers which warrants will be effective in addressing and overcoming those doubts. Theology, then, emerges in this process. Rather than attempt a thorough explication of the argumentation of 2 Corinthians, which is clearly beyond the scope of his essay, Hay helpfully introduces some of the major examples of each dynamic component.

Convictions

Three types of convictions are identified, the distinctions being made among them on the basis of their place in Paul's argumentation rather than on the basis of their level of certainty or hierarchy of importance. Defining a conviction as a "self-evident truth,"[3] Hay differentiates: (1) convictions Paul and the Corinthians apparently share (e.g., the reconciling action of God in the death of Jesus, the bodily resurrection of believers, the authority of Jewish scriptures); (2) convictions Paul believes are in jeopardy at Corinth (e.g., Paul's authority as an apostle, Paul's love for the Corinthians, his good conscience in his dealing with the Corinthian church); and (3) emphatic assertions regarding the "principle of divine power revealed in weakness."[4]

This parsing out of convictions shared by both sides from those that remain contested is a helpful starting point in the study of Paul's argumentation, but reviewing the convictions does prompt the question whether they are all of the same order of importance. To take but one example, does Paul regard the Corinthians' affirmation of his own apostolic authority and his integrity in

---

[2] See esp. N. T. Wright, "Putting Paul Together Again: Toward a Synthesis of Pauline Theology (1 and 2 Thessalonians, Philippians, and Philemon)," in *Pauline Theology I,* 183–211; Richard B. Hays, "Crucified with Christ: A Synthesis of the Theology of 1 and 2 Thessalonians, Philemon, Philippians, and Galatians," *Pauline Theology I,* 227–46; Jouette M. Bassler, "Paul's Theology: Whence and Whither?" (chapter 1 in this volume); Steven J. Kraftchick, "Seeking a More Fluid Model: A Response to Jouette M. Bassler" (chapter 2 in this volume).

[3] Hay, "Shaping of Theology," 139.

[4] Ibid., 140–41.

dealing with them as of the *same level of importance* as their confidence in God's raising Jesus from the dead? If so, why is that the case, and what does it suggest about Paul's understanding of the apostle and the church and their interaction?

Another issue that emerges from Hay's distinction between shared and contested convictions in 2 Corinthians again concerns the standing of Paul. All of the convictions Hay identifies as contested have to do with Paul himself: his divinely authorized apostleship, his understanding of the folly of comparing apostles, his integrity, his love for the Corinthians. Yet, as Hay also observes, Paul insists throughout that he himself is not the issue. Hay explains this apparent anomaly as a conflict of perceptions; the Corinthians persist in making the apostle the issue, while Paul regards the church's relation to Christ as the issue.[5] Certainly there is a conflict of perceptions here, but in my judgment another of the convictions that Paul regards as threatened is the conviction that the bond between the gospel, the apostle, and the church is indissoluble.[6] This way of putting it provides a framework within which to understand the conflicting perceptions.

Doubts

Hay identifies five different types of doubt in 2 Corinthians: (1) Paul's despair as reflected in 1:8–9 and 4:7–12; (2) Paul's self-doubt; (3) Paul's doubt regarding the Corinthians; (4) the Corinthians' doubt regarding Paul; and (5) doubt as an inevitable part of faith.[7] Among these, the first, third, and fourth make the most important contributions to shaping theology as reflected in the letter.

The discussion of the despair of Paul in 1:8–9 and 4:7–12 is most suggestive, because it raises important questions about the way in which Paul's own experiences of privation, persecution, and failure influence his responses to the Corinthians (and, no doubt, to other Christians as well). What is less clear in this part of Hay's analysis is whether despair is best regarded as a form of doubt. When Paul writes that he "despaired of life itself" (2 Cor 1:8), of course, he could well mean that he doubted that his life would continue. But is that doubt in the same sense as his doubt about the constancy of the Corinthians or their doubt about his credentials? The passages Hay invokes strike me as

---

[5] Ibid., 141–42.

[6] One helpful feature of John Schütz's discussion of 2 Corinthians is his exploration of the difference between Paul's understanding of the apostle–gospel connection and that of his opponents (*Paul and the Anatomy of Apostolic Authority* [SNTSMS 26; Cambridge: Cambridge University Press, 1975] 165–86).

[7] Hay, "Shaping of Theology," 142–48.

having less to do with doubt than with what we conventionally think of as interpreting Paul's hardships in the light of the death of Jesus.[8]

A second question regarding this component of Paul's argumentation focuses on the clarity of the category itself. How are the doubts Hay identifies as Paul's doubts about the Corinthians and their doubts about him to be distinguished from the convictions he regards as contested? Paul's sense that the Corinthians do not sufficiently share his conviction about his own authority is difficult to separate from a doubt about them. Can these two components be distinguished from one another in a way that will clarify exactly how Paul sorts through convictions with which to combat the doubts of the Corinthians?

Warrants

Four groups of warrants are identified by Hay, based on their content; warrants appeal to (1) kerygma, (2) scripture, (3) apostolic authority and Paul's conduct, or (4) the activity of the Holy Spirit, particularly among the Corinthians.[9] Hay then explores some important examples of the working of individual warrants in specific texts. This initial probe of Paul's argumentative strategy in 2 Corinthians usefully identifies major ways in which he seeks to verify his claims and lays the groundwork for further discussion. What needs to be clarified, however, is the extent to which a warrant differs from a conviction. A warrant seems to be only a conviction that Paul draws on in a particular context, an "active" conviction, rather than one held in reserve. If my reading is correct, then a number of questions follow about how specific warrants are employed in certain instances and why.[10]

The General's Strategy

Drawing on the martial imagery of 2 Cor 10:1–6, Hay opens his essay with the comment that Paul's "goals [in 2 Corinthians] are as definite and as aggressively pursued as those of any soldier or general."[11] In this exploration of convictions, doubts, and warrants, Hay helpfully identifies the weapons

---

[8] This is in keeping with the line of interpretation of Kraftchick's "Death in Us, Life in You" (chapter 8 in this volume).

[9] Hay, "Shaping of Theology," 150–53.

[10] Here it may be that Hay too quickly sets aside the work of Stephen Toulmin (*The Uses of Argument* [Cambridge: Cambridge University Press, 1958] 94–145). See also the discussion in David H. Kelsey, *The Uses of Scripture in Recent Theology* (Philadelphia: Fortress, 1975) 125–34.

[11] Hay, "Shaping of Theology," 135.

at Paul's disposal. The question is whether he also throws light on Paul's battle plan. Does this model advance our understanding of Paul's way of working, his way of "shaping" theology?

Its active, fluid character is a feature of Paul's theologizing that Hay strongly asserts and with which many students of Paul would concur. The problem emerges, of course, when attempting to describe that activity. Despite Hay's depiction of the emergence of theology out of the dynamic components of convictions, doubts, and warrants, the impression of that theology left by the essay as a whole remains somewhat static. To overstate the matter for the sake of argument: Paul appears to approach battle by sifting among the available weapons, picking the ones best suited for the task, and authorizing their use. Although military strategy is far from my field of expertise, I doubt that a competent general equates strategy exclusively with weaponry. The question I am raising is simply whether the model Hay describes is sufficiently dynamic and substantially different from earlier understandings of Paul as drawing from his theological storehouse the appropriate items with which to address the problems of a particular community.

Certainty and Doubt
Versus Understanding and Misunderstanding

In Hay's study, the category of doubt serves double duty. On the one hand, doubt is a component of argumentation, as outlined above; it constitutes a problem that "gives rise to arguments (based on warrants) designed to persuade persons to move toward new or stronger convictions."[12] On the other hand, however, doubt is also a major dynamic in the content of 2 Corinthians; the dialectic between certainty and doubt becomes, on Hay's reading, a key issue in the letter. Among the doubts (i.e., problems) Paul addresses, then, is that of doubt and certainty.

At first consideration, this suggestion is an attractive one. Clearly Paul does have something we might call doubts about the Corinthians, and they about him. Whether 1:8–9 and 4:7–12 are rightly grouped with other doubts, at one level those texts can be said to concern Paul's doubt (see the discussion above). On the whole, however, I want to suggest a different framework within which to understand the evidence Hay adduces, and that is the dynamic of under-standing and misunderstanding. What is at stake in 2 Corinthians has less to do with *doubt* than it does with competing *understandings* of what God has accomplished in the death and resurrection of Jesus Christ and what implica-

---

[12] Ibid., 137.

tions that death and resurrection have for the way in which human beings understand God, themselves, and one another.[13]

Hay identifies a number of doubts Paul has regarding the Corinthians, including doubts about their affection for him, their convictions regarding the gospel, their mistaken thinking about the nature of his authority. Each of these "doubts," as well as others, can be seen as a symptom of the larger conflict of understandings between Paul and the Corinthians. Paul views the gospel as having to do with the one who "died for all" and whose death brings about a revolution in perception, indeed, a new cosmos, and reconciliation from God (5:16–21). In Paul's judgment, the Corinthians have not so much *doubted* that gospel as *misunderstood* it.

Of course, the Corinthians' interpretation of events would run along quite different lines, but I suspect the same dynamic would obtain. Hay rightly identifies their concerns about Paul's integrity regarding money, his sufferings, his access to charismatic gifts, his knowledge and speech. Even if these are, in some sense, doubts about Paul, they more fundamentally reflect a different understanding (for Paul, a misunderstanding) of the nature of the gospel.

II. METAPHOR AND METAPHORS:
A RESPONSE TO STEVEN J. KRAFTCHICK

The issue of conflicting understandings is also important in Steven Kraftchick's paper. Kraftchick employs contemporary discussion of metaphor in order to agree that Paul's underlying convictions about death and resurrection function metaphorically in 2 Corinthians. Specifically, Kraftchick concludes that, in 2 Corinthians, "the structure by which terms such as death, life, the glory of God, and power are related to one another by the resurrection of Jesus from the dead is transferred by Paul to the terms of his ministry and by extension to the life of the Christian in the present time before the eschaton."[14] What enables this transference, in Kraftchick's view, is Paul's metaphorical understanding of the death and resurrection of Jesus Christ.

Kraftchick proposes a promising way of thinking about the complex of issues we call Pauline theology. Both rhetorical and generative metaphors have received insufficient attention from students of Paul, and Kraftchick provides

---

[13] Here I am very much influenced by J. L. Martyn's essay "Epistemology at the Turn of the Ages: 2 Cor. 5:16," in *Christian History and Interpretation: Studies Presented to John Knox* (ed. W. R. Farmer, C. F. D. Moule, and R. R. Niebuhr; Cambridge: Cambridge University Press, 1967) 269–87.

[14] Kraftchick, "Death in Us, Life in You," 164.

a genuine contribution with this exploration. Metaphor theory should prove particularly useful in our consideration of 2 Corinthians, where metaphors (or, more precisely, what Kraftchick would refer to as rhetorical metaphors) figure prominently. Several other recent studies of 2 Corinthians focus on specific metaphors, suggesting that the time may be right for a broad discussion of metaphor and metaphors in Paul, or at least in 2 Corinthians.[15]

By way of response to Kraftchick's interpretation of the role metaphor plays in the theology of 2 Corinthians, I shall first address the model of metaphor being used here (especially the categories of generative and rhetorical metaphors) and then the particular conclusions that are drawn from it for understanding death and resurrection in 2 Corinthians.

Generative Metaphor and Rhetorical Metaphors

A crucial element in Kraftchick's argument is the distinction between generative metaphors, those tacit metaphors that "set the framework for seeing problems and solutions to those problems" and rhetorical metaphors, those that "appear within an argument at the level of explicit expression."[16] The concept of generative metaphor comes from the work of Donald A. Schön, who distinguishes two traditions in the study of metaphor. One tradition, certainly the one most dominant in biblical studies, sees metaphor primarily as a "species of figurative language which needs explaining, or explaining away." A different tradition

> treats metaphor as central to the task of accounting for our perspectives on the world: how we think about things, make sense of reality, and set the problems we later try to solve. In this second sense, "metaphor" refers both to a certain kind of product—a perspective or frame, a way of looking at things—and to a certain kind of process—a process by which new

---

[15] The essay by Stephen B. Heiny ("2 Corinthians 2:14–4:6: The Motive for Metaphor," in *Society of Biblical Literature 1987 Seminar Papers* [ed. K. H. Richards; Atlanta: Scholars Press, 1987] 1–22) is important for its attempt to understand Paul's use of metaphor within the statements about metaphor found in ancient rhetoricians. See also Peter Marshall, "A Metaphor of Social Shame: ΘΡΙΑΜΒΕΥΕΙΝ in 2 Cor. 2:14," *NovT* 25 (1983) 302–17; Daniel Patte, "A Structural Exegesis of 2 Corinthians 2:14–7:4 with Special Attention on 2:14–3:6 and 6:11–7:4," in *SBL 1987 Seminar Papers,* ed. Richards, 23–49; Frances Young and David F. Ford, *Meaning and Truth in 2 Corinthians* (Grand Rapids: Eerdmans, 1989) 166–85; and Paul B. Duff, "Metaphor, Motif, and Meaning: The Rhetorical Strategy behind the Image 'Led in Triumph' in 2 Corinthians 2:14," *CBQ* 53 (1991) 79–92. An earlier study that merits review is that of Herbert M. Gale, *The Use of Analogy in the Letters of Paul* (Philadelphia: Westminster, 1964). None of these studies addresses the larger methodological questions Kraftchick raises, but they do indicate the timeliness of his proposal.

[16] Kraftchick, "Death in Us, Life in You," 163.

perspectives on the world come into existence. In this tradition, metaphorical utterances . . . are significant only as symptoms of a particular kind of SEEING-AS, the "meta-pherein" or "carrying over" of frames or perspectives from one domain of experience to another.[17]

It is this second sense of metaphor that Schön refers to as "generative metaphor." He illustrates the concept by reference to conflicts over social policy, where unstated (and perhaps even unconscious) metaphors control the ways in which groups view a given situation. Hence, conflicts over social policy may be understood as reflecting deep-seated conflicts over the way in which problems should be viewed—the controlling (generative) metaphors.[18] By definition, then, if death and resurrection is Paul's "generative metaphor" in 2 Corinthians, it provides the framework through which Paul will see everything else. Death and resurrection becomes the lens through which Paul understands his own apostolic task as well as the life of the Christian.

One question this concept raises is whether a "generative metaphor" is really a metaphor at all. Discussion of metaphor in recent years has ranged widely, of course, and it is important not to limit the category so that it includes only one narrowly understood figurative device.[19] Nevertheless, it appears that Kraftchick's category of generative metaphor differs little from what we have earlier referred to as an underlying central conviction. Both notions allow us to explore the way in which one "lens" controls the way in which the world is viewed and "new perspectives on the world come into existence."

The specific generative metaphor that Kraftchick identifies in 2 Corinthians helpfully illustrates the question I am raising. To what extent is "death and resurrection" a metaphor (or, to what extent are "death" and "resurrection" metaphors, as I would prefer to distinguish between the two)? Paul is convinced that Jesus Christ died on the cross and that God raised him from the dead, and Paul has a particular understanding of that death and resurrection which he employs in a variety of crucial ways in 2 Corinthians. Does the central role which that understanding plays in 2 Corinthians constitute a metaphor? Or is it the case that Paul's understanding comes to expression by means of a variety of rhetorical metaphors? This question lurks in the paper itself, for

---

[17] Donald A. Schön, "Generative Metaphor: A Perspective on Problem-Setting in Social Policy," in *Metaphor and Thought* (ed. Andrew Ortony; Cambridge: Cambridge University Press, 1979) 254–55.

[18] For example, Schön describes conflicting generative metaphors at work in the arena of policy regarding public housing, where the same community may be viewed as "diseased" by one group and as a "natural community threatened with dislocation" by others ("Generative Metaphor," 262–68).

[19] See Wayne Booth's comments on this issue in "Metaphor as Rhetoric: The Problem of Evaluation," in *On Metaphor* (ed. Sheldon Sacks; Chicago: University of Chicago Press, 1979) 47–70.

Kraftchick sometimes speaks of death and resurrection *as* a metaphor[20] and sometimes of death and resurrection *functioning* metaphorically.[21] (One way of putting the question would be: Is metaphor here being used metaphorically?)

A second aspect of Kraftchick's understanding of metaphor that warrants further reflection is his discussion of the potential of metaphor, by virtue of bringing together categories that are "normally distinct," to "reorient one's conceptual framework."[22] By definition, metaphors create anomalies by bringing into juxtaposition categories that are not normally thought to belong together, but not all of the anomalies created thereby are of the same order. While some metaphors collide with prevailing views in such a way as to challenge or change them, others do not so much challenge as reinforce prevailing views. I am pointing here not to the customary distinction between "dead" metaphors and "vital" ones, but to the need for some discrimination among vital metaphors.

For example, when Paul writes that in Troas "a door" had been opened for him (2:12), he employs a metaphor, but one that does little to challenge or provoke. A listing of other metaphors of this sort might include the passages in which Paul employs paternal imagery to illumine his relationship to the churches he has established (e.g., 1 Cor 4:15; 1 Thess 2:11). On the other hand, as the complex history of exegesis itself confirms, the metaphor of the "veil" in 2 Cor 3:12–18 does force the hearer or reader to consider what comparison is being invoked and what suggestions are being made. Likewise the places in which Paul refers to himself with maternal imagery require considerable reflection.[23] Of course, given our historical and cultural distance from Paul, it sometimes proves difficult to identify which metaphors challenge and which reinforce. What I am after at this point is not the exegesis of any particular metaphor but the need for distinction among metaphors.

---

[20] The "death and resurrection of Jesus can be well understood when it is considered as a conceptual or 'generative' metaphor . . . " (Kraftchick, "Death in Us, Life in You," 158; see also 162, 163).

[21] Paul's "conviction about the death and resurrection of Christ is used metaphorically to reconstitute his adversity-filled life by means of the death/resurrection life structure . . . " (Kraftchick, "Death in Us, Life in You," 177).

[22] Ibid., 160–61.

[23] Since commentators frequently refer to Gal 4:19 and 1 Thess 2:7 as additional instances of Paul's use of "paternal imagery," this point is apparently not obvious. For further discussion of this issue, see Gaventa, "The Maternity of Paul: An Exegetical Study of Galatians 4:19," in *The Conversation Continues: Studies in Paul and John in Honor of J. Louis Martyn* (ed. R. T. Fortna and B. R. Gaventa; Nashville: Abingdon, 1990) 189–201; eadem, "Apostles as Babes and Nurses in 1 Thessalonians 2:7," in *Faith and History: Essays in Honor of Paul W. Meyer* (ed. John T. Carroll, Charles H. Cosgrove, and E. Elizabeth Johnson; Atlanta: Scholars Press, 1990) 193–207.

Death and Resurrection as Generative Metaphor
in 2 Corinthians

Turning aside for the moment from these questions about the theory of metaphor, I want to comment on the death and resurrection of Christ as the generative metaphor of 2 Corinthians. What I would press for here is what exactly is meant by "death and resurrection." Kraftchick comments that Paul's "reflections on and use of the death and resurrection of Jesus as an interpretive key for his life and experiences as an apostle provide him with the needed criteria" for making judgments and orienting his life.[24] Similarly, he writes that the "founding events serve as the canon by which one's life is shaped and one's ministry is conducted."[25] What Kraftchick articulates, and rightly so in my judgment, is the way in which Paul's generative metaphor exerts an impact on his understanding of his own apostolic task and the lives of all believers.

Can it not equally well be said that the Corinthians — or at least some groups of them — are also motivated by the generative metaphor of the death and resurrection of Jesus Christ? The problem is not that Paul and the Corinthians operate with two conflicting generative metaphors and that Paul here labors to substitute his own for theirs. The two sides share a generative metaphor, but they interpret that generative metaphor quite differently. While each side can speak about the death and resurrection of Jesus Christ, the same language conceals two very different ways of understanding.

If Paul's generative metaphor is one of death and resurrection, then surely it is the *death* of Jesus Christ that figures most prominently in that metaphor. In 5:14–21, Paul's interpretation of the death and resurrection opens by connecting the death of Christ with the death of all (ὅτι εἷς ὑπὲρ πάντες ἀπέθανεν, ἄρα οἱ πάντες ἀπέθανον). He then asserts that Christ's death means life for all, a life not for themselves but for the "one who died and was raised on their behalf" (καὶ ὑπὲρ πάντων ἀπέθανεν, ἵνα οἱ ζῶντες μηκέτι ἑαυτοῖς ζῶσιν ἀλλὰ τῷ ὑπὲρ αὐτῶν ἀποθανόντι καὶ ἐγερθέντι). Only in the final word of this statement is there any reference to resurrection. The passage likewise concludes with an indirect reference to Jesus' death (τὸν μὴ γνόντα ἁμαρτίαν ὑπὲρ ἡμῶν ἁμαρτίαν ἐποίησεν, ἵνα ἡμεῖς γενώμεθα δικαιοσύνη θεοῦ ἐν αὐτῷ) and here again connects that death with its consequences for humankind.

Perhaps Kraftchick and I are not actually in disagreement about this passage. Despite his use of "death and resurrection" as generative metaphor, Kraftchick's

---

[24] Kraftchick, "Death in Us, Life in You," 166.
[25] Ibid., 169.

discussion of this passage and of 4:7–15 seems to acknowledge Paul's emphasis on Christ's death. Where we clearly do agree is that Paul's understanding of the apostolate,[26] the Christian life, and indeed of the change in the cosmos itself, takes its structure from his understanding of the cross.

From Rhetorical Metaphors to Generative Metaphor

The broad movement in Kraftchick's paper is from generative metaphor to rhetorical metaphors. Based on the model of generative metaphor, he identifies "death and resurrection" as the generative metaphor and then explores the implications of that metaphor for understanding the rhetorical metaphors of 4:7–15. My question is what difference it would make if the procedure were reversed. Is it possible to see the rhetorical metaphors as symptoms of the underlying generative metaphor?[27]

Such an investigation goes well beyond the scope of this response, but a few preliminary observations might prove suggestive. In one section of 2 Corinthians, 2:14–5:10, the rhetorical metaphors are more prominent than elsewhere in the letter (and perhaps more prominent than in any of his letters). Here Paul employs an impressive, if also bewildering, array of rhetorical metaphors, including at least the following: triumphal procession, fragrance, aroma, letter of Christ, tablet of human hearts, veil of Moses, veil of the gospel, light of the gospel, treasure in clay jars, bearing the death of Jesus, the life of Jesus, earthly tent, building from God.[28] If this list provides clues to the generative metaphor that underlies Paul's theology in 2 Corinthians, what can we say about that metaphor? What is striking is that virtually all of these rhetorical metaphors turn on the conflict between understanding and misunderstanding the gospel. For those who understand, the apostles smell like life; the veil is removed; the treasure is visible; the death of Jesus is life itself. For those who do not understand, the apostles smell like death, and the veil remains.

To use Max Black's term, these are "strong metaphors"; they "are intended

---

[26] See Victor Paul Furnish, "Paul the ΜΑΡΤΥΣ," in *Witness and Existence: Essays in Honor of Schubert M. Ogden* (ed. Philip E. Devenish and George L. Goodwin; Chicago: University of Chicago Press, 1989) 73–88.

[27] If I have understood Schön's essay on generative metaphor correctly, this is in fact his procedure. He analyzes the statements of various groups to see how the images they use reflect their underlying metaphor.

[28] To call all of these rhetorical metaphors risks involvement in extensive discussion about the historical background and connotation of most, if not all, of these metaphors. I group them together simply in order to raise a methodological question about how one identifies a generative metaphor and not to suggest that they are all of one kind.

to be dwelt upon for the sake of their unstated implications."[29] They serve to prompt the question of exactly how understanding of the gospel comes into existence. In 5:16–17, Paul provides his answer to that question: by virtue of the death of Jesus Christ all old understandings die. To discern beneath the rhetorical metaphors of 2 Corinthians a generative metaphor requires some consideration of this conflict between understanding and misunderstanding. If we identify the generative metaphor as cross and resurrection, we need to modify that metaphor so as to take into account this dynamic of right understanding of death and resurrection over against misunderstanding.

III. APOSTLE AND CHURCH IN 2 CORINTHIANS

Kraftchick's treatment of the metaphorical function of the death and resurrection of Jesus highlights the centrality of that issue in 2 Corinthians. By virtue of the approach that he takes, Hay is less inclined to identify a central theological issue, although he does give particular attention to the need for reconciliation between the Corinthians and God. In my judgment, neither approach sufficiently considers the significance in 2 Corinthians of the theological connection between apostle and church.

Both Kraftchick and Hay touch on the congruence Paul assumes should exist between the gospel of Jesus Christ, on the one hand, and the work of the apostle and lives of believers, on the other hand. Hay identifies among the primary warrants "the notion that divine power is revealed in human weakness" and sees in 2 Corinthians Paul's argument that both the apostle and all believers are called upon to "share Christ's poverty and weakness in order to make others rich."[30] Kraftchick concludes that Paul transfers the generative metaphor of death and resurrection twice: first "from the field of the death and resurrection of Jesus, to the field of Paul's ministry," and then "to the matter of the collection."[31] The metaphor that shapes Paul's ministry also shapes the lives of believers.

Neither Hay nor Kraftchick explores this issue at length, which is understandable given the nature and scope of their contributions. What I want to suggest, however, is that we have not adequately depicted Paul's theologizing in 2 Corinthians unless we have attended to the profound connection he asserts between the apostle and the church, a connection that should be characterized as theological, although it is surely apologetic and pastoral as well. That

---

[29] Max Black, "More about Metaphor," in *Metaphor and Thought,* ed. Ortony, 26.
[30] Hay, "Shaping of Theology," 154.
[31] Kraftchick, "Death in Us, Life in You," 178.

is, among the important convictions that shape Paul's reflections in 2 Corinthians is his understanding that God has, in the gospel of Jesus Christ,
irretrievably bound together the apostle and the church. Neither party has
the option of abandoning this particular relationship. Proclamation of the
gospel depends on this connection, a connection that obtains until the eschaton
itself.

Before sketching the evidence for this connection in the letter, two closely
related objections need to be acknowledged and addressed in a preliminary
way: (1) The relationship between Paul and the Corinthians is so obviously
an issue at stake in this letter that it does not need to be asserted; and (2) Paul's
comments about his relationship with the Corinthians arise from his attempt
to heal the breach between them and win the Corinthians' adherence to his
understanding of the gospel, over against that of his opponents. These assertions are, therefore, rhetorical or pastoral in nature rather than theological.
Both these objections are right in what they affirm but wrong in what they
deny. First, the threatened rift between Paul and the church at Corinth so
massively dominates the letter that it can scarcely be overlooked; Paul is forced
to assert the connection in order to bring about reconciliation. Nevertheless,
little in recent scholarship acknowledges the specifically theological character
of the assertions Paul makes about the relationship between himself and the
Corinthians. Second, while Paul's comments about the connection between
himself and the Corinthians employ all of the rhetorical "weapons" at Paul's
disposal, and while he gives evidence of pastoral concern throughout the letter,
his assertions are not thereby to be characterized as exclusively strategic. Further
response to this particular objection will be considered following a survey
of Paul's comments in 2 Corinthians regarding the apostle–gospel connection.

Familial Language

Paul does not, in 2 Corinthians, explicitly characterize himself as the father
of the congregation, but in three important passages he does presuppose a
parental relationship with the Corinthians.[32] In 6:13, he writes "In return — I
speak as to children — open wide your hearts also" (NRSV). Consistent with
his use of the word τέκνον elsewhere (1 Cor 4:14, 17; Gal 4:19; Phil 2:22;
1 Thess 2:11; Phlm 10), Paul invokes the close relationship between the
Corinthians and himself at the conclusion of his discussion of his ministry

---

[32] For examples of paternal or maternal imagery elsewhere, see 1 Cor 4:15; 1 Thess 2:7, 11;
Gal 4:19. Victor Paul Furnish notes that parental imagery is especially prevalent in the Corinthian correspondence (*II Corinthians*, 361).

and in parallel with his plea for the Corinthians to be reconciled to God (5:20). In 11:2-3, he again presupposes his standing as father to the Corinthians with "I promised you in marriage to one husband, to present you as a chaste virgin to Christ" (NRSV). Just as custom makes the Jewish father responsible for his daughter's virginity until the finalization of the marriage, Paul understands himself to be responsible for the Corinthians, whose "sincere and pure devotion to Christ" (11:3) is threatened by the "superapostles."[33] In 12:14, in the context of defending his refusal to accept monetary support from the Corinthians, Paul asserts his responsibility "for children ought not to lay up for their parents, but parents for their children."[34] Similar to 11:2, this passage suggests that Paul's use of familial language does not arise from affection alone but from his powerful sense of responsibility to God for the standing of the Corinthians.

Love and Reconciliation

Any number of texts might be introduced as evidence of the love that Paul believes exists (or should exist) between himself and the Corinthians. Several times he speaks explicitly of his love for these people (2:4; 11:11; 8:7[35]; 12:15), and other passages might be said to refer indirectly to this affection (e.g., 1:6; 6:11-12; 7:2-4, 7-8). In 6:11-12 and 7:2-3, Paul directly appeals to the Corinthians to enlarge their affection for himself.[36] The context in which he makes this plea demonstrates its significance. Paul's comments about reconciliation with God come to an end in 5:20 with the words "we entreat you on behalf of Christ, be reconciled to God" (NRSV). There follows a characterization and defense of the ministry of Paul and his co-workers in the opening of chap. 6, which culminates in the direct appeal of 6:11-12 and 7:2-3.[37]

The call for reconciliation *with Paul*, therefore, stands in parallel with the call for reconciliation *with God*.[38] While it would be too much to say that these

---

[33] For a discussion of the imagery here and the relevant texts, see Furnish, *II Corinthians*, 499-501.

[34] On this saying, see especially the discussion in Peter Marshall, *Enmity in Corinth: Social Conventions in Paul's Relations with the Corinthians* (WUNT 2.23; Tübingen: Mohr [Siebeck], 1987) 247-51.

[35] I am here presupposing that the text reads "our love for you" (ἡμῶν ἐν ὑμῖν; with P⁴⁶ and B) rather than "your love for us" (ὑμῶν ἐν ἡμῖν; with ℵ, C, D and others). On the evidence, see B. M. Metzger, *A Textual Commentary on the Greek New Testament* (New York: United Bible Societies, 1971) 581; Furnish, *II Corinthians*, 403.

[36] As most commentators note, 6:11 is one of very few places in which Paul directly addresses a congregation ("Corinthians"; see also Gal 3:1; Phil 4:5). The result is to draw attention to the urgency and importance of what is being said.

[37] For my argument on this point, it makes little difference whether 6:14-7:1 is an interpolation, although I am inclined to think that it is.

[38] Furnish notes this connection between the two statements (*II Corinthians*, 14).

two forms of reconciliation are equally important, for Paul they are directly linked with one another.

"Ourselves as Your Slaves for Jesus' Sake"

In 2 Cor 4:5, Paul describes himself and his co-workers as "your slaves for Jesus' sake." This self-description merits attention, since Paul elsewhere describes himself as a δοῦλος Χριστοῦ (Rom 1:1; Gal 1:10; Phil 1:1) but never as a δοῦλος of anyone else. Indeed, this passage seems to contradict Paul's warning in 1 Cor 7:23 against submitting oneself as a slave to human beings. Of course, in 1 Cor 9:19 he asserts his enslavement to all people as part of his ministry and implicitly offers that slavery as a model to be imitated by others.[39] What makes the self-description in 2 Cor 4:5 the more remarkable is that it stands as a component of Christian proclamation "For we do not proclaim ourselves: we proclaim Jesus Christ as Lord and ourselves as your slaves for Jesus' sake" (NRSV). 2 Cor 4:5a sums up the apologetic strand of Paul's argument that extends back at least to 3:1: Paul is not preaching himself. 4:5b and c then make positive assertions about what Paul *does* proclaim: "Jesus Christ as Lord" *and* "ourselves as your slaves for Jesus' sake." Grammatically, "ourselves as your slaves for Jesus' sake" is part of Paul's description of the content of his preaching.[40] Even if we grant that Paul likely intends 4:5c to explicate the ἑαυτοὺς of 4:5a rather than to characterize the content of Christian preaching, the connection of 4:5c with the proclamation of Jesus' lordship is astonishing. The enslavement of the apostle to the churches stands alongside the gospel itself.[41]

Eschatological Boasting

At several points in 2 Corinthians 1–9, Paul refers to himself as boasting about the Corinthians or to the Corinthians as boasting about him (1:12–14; 5:12; 7:4; 8:24; 9:23). At first glance, these comments stand in some tension with the sharp attack on boasting found in chaps. 10–13 (10:15–18; 11:16–21,

---

[39] See also Gal 5:13, where Paul admonishes that the Galatians be mutually enslaved to one another.

[40] Commentators acknowledge this point but generally attempt to qualify its impact; see Bultmann, *The Second Letter to the Corinthians* (Minneapolis: Augsburg, 1985) 107; Furnish, *II Corinthians*, 223, 249–50.

[41] For differing assessments of the social significance of Paul's description of himself as a "slave of Christ," see Marshall, *Enmity in Corinth*, 295–306, 402–3; and Dale B. Martin, *Slavery as Salvation, the Metaphor of Slavery in Pauline Christianity* (New Haven: Yale University Press, 1990).

30; 12:1, 5–6); even if chaps. 10–13 do come from a later letter to Corinth, the contrast between the two sets of remarks is notable. Sorting through these varying remarks, 10:15–18 emerges as of particular importance, particularly because it recalls both 1 Cor 1:31 and 2 Cor 3:1. In 10:15–18, Paul provides guidelines within which boasting may be done, paramount among which is that boasting should be "in the Lord" (see Jer 9:22–23). Perhaps one explanation for Paul's boasting in the Corinthians (and theirs in him) is that he sees no conflict between boasting in the Lord and boasting in the Lord's church. Stated positively, the apostle's boast in the church and the church's boast in the apostle are both instances of boasting in God.

In addition, this mutual boasting, which is simultaneously boasting in the other and in God, occurs in an eschatological context. Admittedly, a number of Paul's comments about boasting pertain to boasting before other persons and in the present time (e.g., boasting to the Macedonians about the Corinthians' eagerness with respect to the collection, 9:2). 2 Cor 1:12–14, however, provides an important exception to this generalization, for there Paul asserts that "we are your boast and you ours in the day of the Lord Jesus" (author's trans.). A number of features of this text indicate its significance: (1) its location at the beginning of the letter; (2) the several references in v. 13 to the need for the Corinthians to understand this issue fully; (3) the fact of the prior eschatological reference in v. 13 (ἕως τέλους).[42] The reciprocal boasting of Paul and the Corinthians serves not merely to defend against the "superapostles" but to commend both parties before God and in the day of the Lord Jesus.[43]

Letter of Commendation

Introducing 2 Cor 3:1–3 into this discussion admittedly promises more confusion than clarification since debate continues unabated regarding virtually every word in this passage.[44] For my purposes at present, however, the importance of this text lies in what it conveys in a general way about the

[42] See also 7:2–3, which may reflect the eschatological character of the relationship between the Corinthians and Paul (note the order: "to die together and to live together").

[43] "The reciprocity of the subject of 'glorification' (you are my pride and I am yours) is emphatic, and it is made clear that both parties will play a part of 'the day of our Lord Jesus Christ' . . . (Jean Héring, *The Second Epistle of Saint Paul to the Corinthians* [London: Epworth, 1967] 8).

[44] In addition to the commentaries, see the following discussions of this passage: William Baird, "Letters of Recommendation: A Study of II Cor 3:1–3," *JBL* 80 (1961) 166–72; Earl Richard, "Polemics, Old Testament, and Theology: A Study of II Cor. 3:1–4:6," *RB* 88 (1981) 340–67; Richard B. Hays, *Echoes of Scripture in the Letters of Paul* (New Haven: Yale University Press, 1989) 125–31; Scott J. Hafemann, *Suffering and Ministry in the Spirit: Paul's Defense of His Ministry in II Corinthians 2:14–3:3* (Grand Rapids: Eerdmans, 1990) 180–225.

relationship between Paul and the Corinthians rather than in the resolution of the several exegetical problems. That the Corinthians are "our letter, written on our hearts"[45] demonstrates again the close emotional tie between Paul and the Corinthians. That this same letter is "known and read by all" moves the letter from the realm of private relationship into the realm of public proclamation. Furnish is undoubtedly right that we ought not "worry about how a letter written on someone's heart, the most interior dimension of one's being" can simultaneously be "known and read by all."[46] The metaphor of the letter is being made to serve two related purposes here; it conveys the intimate relationship between Paul and the Corinthians, *and* it conveys the status of that relationship as proclamation (cf. 1 Thess 1:8). Again Furnish puts it rightly: Paul holds the "members of his congregations in his *heart*, and by this he means . . . that they are shareholders with him in the gospel of Christ . . . ."[47] The description of this "letter" in 3:3 as a "letter of Christ, prepared by us"[48] ensures against the conclusion that Paul is himself the writer of the "letter" or the one finally responsible for the Corinthians. The letter has its origin in Christ, but Paul is irrevocably associated with it; and the letter itself serves to proclaim the gospel.

This survey of the apostle–church connection in 2 Corinthians has moved much too quickly over the landscape, dealing hastily with a number of texts and omitting a number of others that might well have been included. What it does demonstrate, nevertheless, is the theological character of the relationship between Paul and the Corinthians. Both the apostle and the church have their κλῆσις from God, but they live out that calling in relationship to one another. As their father in faith, Paul exercises certain authority and responsibility with respect to the Corinthians, but he is simultaneously their slave in Christ. At present their connection serves to proclaim the gospel itself, and their eschatological future includes boasting in one another before God.

We need now to return to one of the objections I identified earlier: Does this language in 2 Corinthians [merely] reflect Paul's strategy for overcoming

---

[45] In my judgment, this resolution of the text-critical problem (i.e., ἡμῶν rather than ὑμῶν) is the correct one, although my argument about the relationship between Paul and the Corinthians does not require this solution. For a careful review of the evidence, see Hafemann, *Suffering and Ministry in the Spirit*, 191–93.

[46] Furnish, *II Corinthians*, 194.

[47] Ibid.

[48] "Prepared by us" is the translation of the NRSV, but it needs to be acknowledged that translation of διακονηθεῖσα in this passage is difficult and disputed. C. K. Barrett translates "supplied by us," arguing that both "to write" and "to deliver" are too narrow since Paul's point is that his work brought this particular "letter of Christ" into being (Barrett, *A Commentary on the Second Epistle to the Corinthians* [HNTC; New York: Harper & Row, 1974] 108). Furnish suggests "cared for by us" in an attempt to leave ambiguous the question whether Paul himself serves as Christ's amanuensis or as Christ's courier (*II Corinthians*, 182).

the breach between himself and the Corinthians so that it has no real theological importance? Perhaps I am here flailing away at a straw opponent, but I can well imagine such a question being raised. First, by way of response, similar language in letters where the relationship does not stand in jeopardy (i.e., Philippians and 1 Thessalonians) strongly suggests that Paul is doing more than troubleshooting when he appeals to the relationship between himself and the Corinthians. Second, the overtly theological way in which he makes his appeal to the Corinthians supports my reading of the letter; that is, he might appeal to the pragmatic importance of their relationship (e.g., as a barrier against outsiders) but does not do so. Third, even if Paul's "intention" was only strategic, the letter as we have it now contains theological remarks that must be taken into account. The burden of proof rests with those who would place this relationship in the theological margins because it serves strategic purposes.

Whether we speak of the theology *of* 2 Corinthians or *in* 2 Corinthians or of Paul's *theologizing* in 2 Corinthians, or whatever formulation we employ, at the center stands the cross and the cosmic and epistemological crisis brought into being by that cross (5:11–16). Among the changes brought into being by that cross is the forging of a powerful, unbreakable connection between the apostle and the church. Neither stands independent of the other; neither has access to an exit from the relationship. The relationship itself proclaims the gospel in the present time and the relationship commends each party to God.

10 ON BECOMING
THE RIGHTEOUSNESS OF GOD

2 Corinthians 5:21

N. T. Wright
Worcester College, Oxford

I. INTRODUCTION: THE PROBLEM

2 CORINTHIANS 5:21 poses several problems for the interpreter; I shall here focus on one in particular. What does Paul mean when he says "that we might become the righteousness of God"? The text reads as follows:

τὸν μὴ γνόντα ἁμαρτίαν ὑπὲρ ἡμῶν ἁμαρτίαν ἐποίησεν, ἵνα ἡμεῖς γενώμεθα δικαιοσύνη θεοῦ ἐν αὐτῷ.

The NRSV translates this as follows:

> For our sake he [God] made him [Christ] to be sin who knew no sin, so that in him we might become the righteousness of God.

Many discussions of the verse assume one particular meaning for δικαιοσύνη θεοῦ here and work backwards to discuss what they see as the real problem, namely, the meaning of τὸν μὴ γνόντα ἁμαρτίαν ὑπὲρ ἡμῶν ἁμαρτίαν ἐποίησεν. I wish to examine, instead, the precise meaning, in this context, of the key final phrase.

The Regular Usage

There are two related reasons why this is problematic: the first to do with the regular meaning of the phrase in Paul, the second with the meaning of 2 Corinthians 5:21 in its context.

First, I regard it as an increasingly firm conclusion that Paul's other uses of the phrase (all in Romans) treat θεοῦ as referring to a δικαιοσύνη that is God's own, rather than a δικαιοσύνη that he gives, reckons, imparts, or

200

imputes to human beings. The debate has often been muddled, not least by misleading labeling of alternative views, but the following summary may help to clarify matters. The first question to be addressed concerning δικαιοσύνη θεοῦ is: Is the "righteousness" in question God's own, or is it a status or quality which, though relating to God in some way, is predicated of humans? Each possible answer divides into two further alternatives. (i) If the righteousness is, and remains, God's own, the genitive (θεοῦ) could then be seen as either possessive or subjective, depending on the meaning attached to δικαιοσύνη. If this "righteousness" is in some sense or other a quality or *attribute* of God, the genitive θεοῦ would be possessive, but if the "righteousness" is in some sense or other an *activity,* the genitive would be subjective. (This is often misunderstood, but it should be clear that a "subjective" genitive implies that the noun governed carries a verbal sense, without which the genitive lapses into its more regular possessive sense.) (ii) If the righteousness is, eventually at least, a status or quality attributed to humans, then the genitive θεοῦ could be seen either as objective or as a genitive of origin, depending once more on the sense attached to δικαιοσύνη. If the "righteousness" is something about humans (say, their faith) which somehow commends them before God, then the genitive is "objective," "a righteousness which counts before God," but if the righteousness is, rather, simply the human status which results from God's gracious action, the genitive is a genitive of origin, being equivalent to ἡ ἐκ θεοῦ δικαιοσύνη, as in Phil 3:9. (This too is often misunderstood, with the phrase "objective genitive" sometimes being used to designate the genitive of origin. Again, it should be clear that the phrase "objective genitive," strictly speaking, denotes a genitive which functions as the object of the verb implied in the noun which it governs.)[1]

Within the debate all four basic positions have been espoused. Luther's starting point was (what he saw as) the medieval view that the righteousness in question was God's *iustitia distributiva,* his even-handed rewarding of virtue and punishing of vice. Luther's classic response to this (which, he says, he subsequently discovered to have been Augustine's view as well) was that the righteousness of God was not a righteousness with which he himself is righteous, but rather a righteousness with which he makes others righteous. This, in other words, was a shift from a *possessive* reading of the genitive, and a "quality" understanding of δικαιοσύνη, to a grammatically complex double reading: it combined (a) the subjective/activity reading of the whole phrase (the "righteousness" remains God's, and denotes the activity whereby God reckons humans to be righteous), and (b) the genitive of origin/human status reading of the whole phrase (Luther could sometimes, not least with

---

[1] On these and other genitives, see BDF §§89–100.

2 Corinthians 5:21 in mind, refer to δικαιοσύνη θεοῦ as the status which humans have as a result of this reckoning).

The modern debate has reflected Luther's wrestling in several ways. The majority position until comparatively recently, expounded classically by R. Bultmann, H. Conzelmann, and C. E. B. Cranfield, was that the genitive denoted the origin of the status which humans then possessed as the result of God's gracious action in Christ.[2] E. Käsemann, on the other hand, pioneered the "subjective genitive" position in his paper "The 'Righteousness of God' in Paul," subsequently published in his New Testament Questions of Today;[3] for him, clearly, δικαιοσύνη θεοῦ was to be understood as an activity, namely, God's "salvation-creating power" by which he defeated the rebellious cosmos. This has become increasingly popular with scholars, though it is not well represented in modern English translations.[4]

My own view, suggested in various places and to be expanded elsewhere,[5] is that Käsemann is right in his critique of the prevailing reading (though even he does not see that Phil 3:9 should be excluded from the discussion), but wrong in his precise proposal. The righteousness does indeed remain God's; but this "righteousness" never leaves behind the all-important sense of covenant faithfulness. Nor does it need to, as Käsemann imagined, thinking thereby to defend Paul against the possibility of retaining any sense of Jewish particularism.

---

[2] For the debate, see C. Müller, Gottes Gerechtigkeit und Gottes Volk: Eine Untersuchung zu Römer 9–11 (FRLANT 86; Göttingen: Vandenhoeck & Ruprecht) 5–27; P. Stuhlmacher, Gerechtigkeit Gottes bei Paulus (FRLANT 87; Göttingen: Vandenhoeck & Ruprecht, 1966) 11–73; Manfred T. Brauch, "Perspectives on 'God's Righteousness' in Recent German Discussion," in E. P. Sanders, Paul and Palestinian Judaism: A Comparison of Patterns of Religion (London: SCM; Philadelphia: Fortress, 1977) 523–42; U. Wilckens, Die Brief an die Römer (EKKNT 6; Cologne: Benziger; Neukirchen-Vluyn: Neukirchener Verlag, 1978) 1. 202–33; C. E. B. Cranfield, A Critical and Exegetical Commentary on the Epistle to the Romans (ICC; Edinburgh: T. & T. Clark, 1975) 1. 92–99. The true "objective genitive" is rarely held today; an example is J. C. O'Neill, Paul's Letter to the Romans (Harmondsworth: Penguin, 1975) 38–39, 72, etc.

[3] E. Käsemann, New Testament Questions of Today (London: SCM, 1969) 168–82; see too his Commentary on Romans (Grand Rapids: Eerdmans, 1980) 23–30.

[4] The New International Version (NIV) persists in a most confusing rendering of Rom 3:21–26, in which δικαιοσύνη θεοῦ is rendered "a righteousness from God" in vv. 21–22, while v. 26 still clearly refers to God's own righteousness ("justice"!).

[5] See N. T. Wright, "The Messiah and the People of God" (D.Phil., Oxford, 1980) 57–85; idem, "Romans and the Theology of Paul," in Society of Biblical Literature 1992 Seminar Papers (ed. E. Lovering; Atlanta: Scholars Press, 1992); for the Jewish background, see N. T. Wright, The New Testament and the People of God (London: SPCK; Minneapolis: Fortress, 1992) 271f., showing that though the phrase was in some sense a technical term in biblical and postbiblical Judaism, it never left behind (pace Käsemann) its sense of "covenant faithfulness." For δικαιοσύνη θεοῦ in Romans 9–11, see N. T. Wright, The Climax of the Covenant: Christ and the Law in Pauline Theology (Edinburgh: T. & T. Clark; Minneapolis: Fortress, 1991) 234–46. I intend to offer a fuller version of these discussions in a forthcoming volume on Paul.

Paul's contention, supremely in Romans, is that in Christ Israel's God has indeed been faithful to the covenant made with Abraham, but precisely not in the nationalistic way which Israel imagined. A significant part of his whole argument in that letter is, I believe, that the nonethnic people of God in Christ really is, despite initial appearances, the family promised to Abraham. Into this picture fit, comfortably, not only the explicit references to δικαιοσύνη θεοῦ as such (1:17; 3:5, 21, 22; 10:3) but also the many other passages which attribute δικαιοσύνη to God in one way or another, or which discuss such attribution (3:25, 26; 9:6–29; etc.). There is thus, I contend, an excellent case to be made out for reading the phrase as a clear Pauline technical term meaning "the covenant-faithfulness of [Israel's] God."

To this apparently clear case 2 Cor 5:21 offers an apparently clear exception. The phrase is the same as that in Romans — that is, δικαιοσύνη θεοῦ itself — but the reference seems to be, unambiguously, to a status of δικαιοσύνη which is credited to "us," that is, Paul himself and, perhaps, his co-workers. Is this, then, the correct reading? If so, does it perhaps raise a question as to whether the emerging consensus on the usage in Romans is wrong, suggesting that we should after all read δικαιοσύνη θεοῦ there as a human status bestowed by God (the "genitive of origin") or perhaps a human status which counts before God (the "objective genitive")?

2 Corinthians 5:21 in Context

This would not itself, perhaps, be a very serious problem. It is important to stress that Paul is quite capable of using what seem to us technical terms in subtly different ways, as anyone who has studied his use of σάρξ ("flesh"), for instance, knows only too well. I would not, for my own part, go to any lengths to overturn the usual reading of 2 Cor 5:21, merely because of a search for a spurious harmony — which simply does not exist, at a terminological level, in the Pauline letters. But the second reason forces the question upon us. The verse has traditionally been read as a somewhat detached statement of atonement theology: we are sinners; God is righteous, but in Christ what Luther called a "wondrous exchange" takes place, in which Christ takes our sin and we his "righteousness."[6] And the difficulty with this, despite its being enshrined

---

[6] See, e.g., R. Bultmann, *The Second Letter to the Corinthians* (Minneapolis: Augsburg, 1985) 165 (commenting on this passage); also C. K. Barrett, *A Commentary on the Second Epistle to the Corinthians* (London: A. & C. Black, 1973) 180–81; M. D. Hooker, *From Adam to Christ: Essays on Paul* (Cambridge: Cambridge University Press, 1990) frequently, e.g., 17, 181. Victor Paul Furnish seems to accept this reading (*II Corinthians* [AB 32A; Garden City, NY: Doubleday, 1984] 351–53).

in a good many hymns and liturgies, as well as in popular devotion, is (a) that once again Paul never actually says this anywhere else;[7] (b) that here it is *God's* righteousness, not Christ's, that "we" apparently "become"; (c) that there seems to be no good reason why he suddenly inserts this statement into a discussion whose thrust is quite different, namely, a consideration of the paradoxical apostolic ministry in which Christ is portrayed in and through the humiliating weakness of the apostle (4:7–6:13); and (d) the verse, read in this way, seems to fall off the end of the preceding argument, so much so that some commentators have suggested that the real break in the thought comes not between 5:21 and 6:1 but between 5:19 and 5:20.[8]

II. PROPOSAL: COVENANT AND APOSTLESHIP

I suggest that these issues can be addressed simultaneously, and the problems resolved, by a consideration of the wider context within which the passage falls. From 2:14 on, Paul has been addressing the question of his own apostleship, and in chap. 3 in particular he has done so in relation to the *new covenant* which God has established in Christ and by the Spirit. I have argued elsewhere for a particular way of reading this chapter; the detail of this argument is incidental to my present purpose, since the overall drift, which is the important thing here, is less controversial.[9] Paul's argument, in a nutshell, is that he, as an apostle, is a minister of the new covenant (3:6) and that this ministry is not impugned by the fact that he suffers but is rather thereby enhanced (4:7–18), since Christ is in this way revealed the more clearly. This, he explains, is why he can use great "boldness" (παρρησία) (3:12–18).

The discussion of Paul's covenantal ministry then continues into chap. 5 (a fact sometimes obscured because much study of 5:1–5 has concentrated on it as an isolated fragment about personal eschatology, rather than as part of the sustained argument). It should be clear from the οὖν ("therefore") in v. 11 that vv. 1–10 contribute, as far as Paul is concerned, to the thrust of what follows: since all will appear before the judgment seat of Christ, with the prospect, for those who are Christ's, of receiving the "further clothing" of the glorious resurrection body, the apostle is spurred on to do the work of "persuading human beings." The link between 5:12 ("We are not commend-

---

[7] 1 Cor 1:30 is sometimes suggested as an exception, but there Paul sees not only δικαιοσύνη ("righteousness") but also σοφία ("wisdom"— the controlling category), ἁγιασμός ("sanctification"), and ἀπολύτρωσις ("redemption") as attributed to those "in Christ"; and, most importantly, the δικαιοσύνη in question is not spoken of as the δικαιοσύνη θεοῦ ("righteousness of God").

[8] E.g., Furnish, *II Corinthians,* ad loc.

[9] Wright, *Climax,* chap. 9.

ing ourselves to you again, but giving you an opportunity to boast about us") and 3:1; 4:2; and 6:4[10] makes it clear that we are still in the same ongoing argument: Paul is not "commending himself" in an unacceptable fashion, but merely explaining what it is that apostleship involves. Specifically, he is unpacking what it means, as he said in chap. 3, to be a "minister of the new covenant." The statements of 5:14–15, on the one hand, and 5:16–17, on the other, are not to be detached from this argument and treated as mere snippets of traditional soteriology. Both contribute directly to the statement of vv.18–19; this is what gives Paul's whole activity its specific focus:

> All this is from God, who reconciled us to himself through Christ, and has given us the ministry of reconciliation; that is, in Christ God was reconciling the world to himself, not counting their trespasses against them, and entrusting the message of reconciliation to us.

Here, then, is the focal point to which the long argument has been building up. Paul, having himself been reconciled to God by the death of Christ, has now been entrusted by God with the task of ministering to others that which he has himself received, in other words, reconciliation. Verse 20 then follows from this as a dramatic double statement of his conception of the task: "So we are ambassadors for Christ, since God is making his appeal through us; we entreat you on behalf of Christ, be reconciled to God." That is to say, when Paul preaches, his hearers ought to hear a voice from God, a voice which speaks on behalf of the Christ in whom God was reconciling the world. Astonishingly, the voice of the suffering apostle is to be regarded as the voice of God himself, the God who in Christ has established the new covenant, and who now desires to extend its reconciling work into all the world. The second half of the verse should not, I think, be taken as an address to the Corinthians specifically, but as a short and pithy statement of Paul's whole vocation: "On behalf of Christ, we make this appeal: 'Be reconciled to God!'"

In the light of this exegesis of chaps. 3–5, and this reading of 5:11–20 in particular, the thrust of 5:21 emerges into the light. It is not an aside, a soteriological statement thrown in here for good measure as though to explain how it is that people can in fact thus be reconciled. It is a climactic statement of the whole argument so far. The "earthen vessel" that Paul knows himself to be (4:7) has found the problem of his own earthiness dealt with, and has found itself filled, paradoxically, with treasure indeed: "for our sake

---

[10] 3:1: "Are we beginning to commend (συνιστάνειν) ourselves again?" 4:2: "We have renounced the shameful things that one hides; we refuse to practice cunning or to falsify God's word; but by the open statement of the truth we commend (συνιστάνοντες) ourselves to the conscience of everyone in the sight of God." 6:4: "But as servants of God we have commended (συνίσταντες) ourselves in every way."

God made Christ, who did not know sin, to be a sin-offering for us, *so that in him we might become God's covenant-faithfulness.*" The "righteousness of God" in this verse is not a human status in virtue of which the one who has "become" it stands "righteous" before God, as in Lutheran soteriology. It is the covenant faithfulness of the one true God, now active through the paradoxical Christ-shaped ministry of Paul, reaching out with the offer of reconciliation to all who hear his bold preaching.

What the whole passage involves, then, is the idea of the covenant ambassador, who represents the one for whom he speaks in such a full and thorough way that he actually *becomes* the living embodiment of his sovereign — or perhaps, in the light of 4:7–18 and 6:1–10, we should equally say the *dying* embodiment. Once this is grasped as the meaning of 5:21, it appears that this meaning fits very well with the graphic language of those other passages, especially 4:10–12. This in turn should play back into our understanding of chap. 3: the paradoxical boldness which Paul displays in addressing the Corinthians is organically related to his self-understanding as the "minister of the new covenant," the one who has "become the righteousness of God." Indeed, we can now suggest that those two phrases are mutually interpretative ways of saying substantially the same thing.

III. CONCLUSION

This conclusion may initially appear striking, even startling. However, one must insist that Paul has himself prepared the way for 5:21 with his metaphor of "ambassador" in the preceding verse. The whole point of the ambassadorial system, in the ancient as in the modern world, is that the sovereign himself (or herself) speaks through the agent. Paul stresses this: "God is making his appeal through us." It should therefore be no surprise that in his summing-up he should refer to himself as "becoming" the "righteousness," that is, the "covenant faithfulness," of God. If that covenant faithfulness was revealed climactically in the death of Jesus Christ, as Paul says in Romans 3:21–26, it is natural that the work of one who speaks "on behalf of Christ" (5:20 [bis]) should also be such a revelation, especially when the one so speaking is also acting out, in his own physical body, that same death (4:10, etc.). If Paul as an ambassador has any inadequacies, they are dealt with in the death of Christ; if he has a message to deliver, it is because he has become, by the Spirit, the incarnation of the covenant faithfulness of God. Indeed, it is Paul's strong pneumatology, coming on top of his strong *theologia crucis,* that rescues this striking idea from being in any way triumphalistic, except in the (highly paradoxical) sense of 2:14.[11]

---

[11] See C. F. D. Moule, "Reflections on So-Called 'Triumphalism,'" in *The Glory of Christ in*

This way of reading the verse, I submit, makes excellent sense of the overall context, answering the second of our original puzzles by showing that the verse is not an extra, added comment about something other than the subject of the previous paragraph. It also, by linking the discussion directly with that in chap. 3, actually emphasizes the meaning "the covenant faithfulness of God" for the key phrase δικαιοσύνη θεοῦ. This means that, so far from the verse proving to be a counterexample to the emerging consensus on the meaning of the phrase in Romans, it firmly supports the possessive or subjective reading of the genitive θεοῦ and suggests that δικαιοσύνη itself firmly retains its Jewish and covenantal associations. The "righteousness of God" is the divine covenant faithfulness, which is both a quality upon which God's people may rely and something visible in action in the great covenant-fulfilling actions of the death and resurrection of Jesus and the gift of the Spirit.

It should again be emphasized that this does not collapse Pauline theology into a "Jewish Christianity" of the sort from which E. Käsemann sought to free Paul when he argued that the phrase had lost its covenantal overtones and had become a technical term denoting God's "salvation-creating power," his victory over the cosmos. Rather, Paul's covenantal theology was thought through at every point, not least in our present passage, in the light of the death and resurrection of Jesus the Messiah, which revealed that God's covenant faithfulness was precisely the ground of the salvation of the whole world. As Romans 3 leads eventually to Romans 8, and to the renewal of all creation, so 2 Corinthians 3 (the new covenant) leads to 2 Cor 5:17 (καινὴ κτίσις, "new creation"). The two are, actually, inseparable: it was through the covenant with Abraham and his seed that God always intended to reconcile the world to himself, and in Christ that plan is now complete.[12] All that remains is for the apostolic ministry to be put into effect, through which this divine covenant faithfulness can become effective for any and all who will listen to the message.

Three final reflections. First, this way of reading the second half of the crucial verse *may* perhaps provide an additional reason for taking the second occurrence of ἁμαρτία in the verse as a reference not just to "sin" in general but to the "sin-offering."[13] I have argued elsewhere for this meaning for καὶ περὶ ἁμαρτίας in Rom 8:3, and I think it is likely, granted the more context-specific reading of the verse which I am proposing, that Paul would intend it here too.[14] This, if correct, would not water down the striking impression of the

---

the *New Testament: Studies in Christology in Memory of George Bradford Caird* (ed. L. D. Hurst and N. T. Wright; Oxford: Clarendon, 1987) 219–27.

[12] See now Wright, *The New Testament and the People of God*, chap. 9, esp. 259–79.

[13] Against, e.g., Barrett, *Second Epistle to the Corinthians*, 180; Hooker, *From Adam*, 13–14.

[14] ἁμαρτία is of course a regular LXX way of rendering the various phrases for "sin-offering"; see, e.g., Lev 4:8, 20, 24, etc.; see Wright, *Climax*, 221 n. 10, and, for the general argument, chap. 11.

first half of the verse, as is sometimes suggested, but would rather give it more specific direction. The verse is not an abstract, detached statement of atonement theology (Paul nowhere offers us such a thing); rather, it focuses very specifically on his own strange apostolic ministry. Insofar as this ministry is a thing of shame and dishonor, it is so despite Paul's intention, and the sin-offering is the right means of dealing with such a problem. Insofar as it is the means of the divine covenant faithfulness being held out to the world, it is because, in Christ, Paul has "become" the δικαιοσύνη θεοῦ ("righteousness of God"). This is only a suggestion, which could perhaps be taken up in subsequent discussion.

Second, some will no doubt object that I have missed the point entirely. Paul, it will be suggested, was here simply drawing on a traditional formula, only loosely integrated into his own flow of thought. In reply, I think it is certainly possible that behind our verse there lies a regular early Christian way of expressing something about Jesus' death and its effect. Almost all things are possible within the very shadowy world of pre-Pauline early Christian history. But I do not think it is very likely. The verse as I have read it fits so closely into Paul's argument, and employs such characteristic language in a characteristic way, that I think it far more probable that we have here an instance of something which scholars, even those who spend their lives in his company, are singularly slow to grant that Paul may have possessed: the ability to produce a pithy phrase on his own account and to draw together a complex line of thought in a telling and memorable epigram. We scholars, so often preferring learned obscurity to pungent clarity, sometimes project this image, among others, on to the apostle. It is not only the Corinthian church that tries to insist on the apostle's coming up to its ill-conceived expectations.

Third, this reading of 5:21 has tied it in quite tightly, I think, to the whole argument of chaps. 3–5. This suggests to me that, although of course the first half of chap. 6 grows organically out of just this conclusion, it is misleading to treat 5:19 as though it were the conclusion of the long preceding argument and 5:20 as though it were the start of the new one. When it is read in the way I have suggested, 5:20–21 forms the natural climax to the entire argument of the preceding three chapters, with 6:1 being the point where Paul turns to address a specific appeal to the Corinthians. They have, after all, already been reconciled to God (5:20);[15] now they need to be urged not to receive this grace in vain (6:1). Moreover, they now have a significant new motive to heed this appeal: the one who speaks is not simply an odd, shabby, battle-scarred jailbird, but one who, however surprisingly, is a revelation in person of the covenant faithfulness of God.

[15] It is wrong to import "you" into the translation as the object of δεόμεθα ("we appeal"). The point Paul is making is general: "this is the appeal we make." See above.

Part IV

Partial Syntheses
of Paul's Theology

11 THE GRAMMAR OF ELECTION IN FOUR PAULINE LETTERS

Calvin J. Roetzel
Macalester College

JOUETTE BASSLER'S ESSAY "Paul's Theology: Whence and Whither?" offers a superb critique of efforts so far to isolate the integrating center of Paul's theology. Her section "1 Thessalonians: Convictions" offers a summary of Paul's warranting statements relating to election that are "so basic that they can support an argument while requiring themselves no further confirmation."[1] Her study found evidence of Paul's view of election in four Pauline letters (1 Thessalonians, Philippians, Galatians, and 1 Corinthians), and generally agrees with the views of Tom Wright and Daniel Patte. With qualification she accepts Tom Wright's position that in monotheism and election the "truths to be celebrated as boundary markers round the community, as symbols of national [*sic*] and racial [*sic*] solidarity."[2] Further, she notes with guarded appreciation Daniel Patte's discussion of faith in which clues to Paul's theology appear as self-evident, foundational convictions which "because they cannot be demonstrated by argument . . . must remain in the background."[3] In spite of these agreements Bassler's position avoids the weaknesses of the views of Wright and Patte. Tom Wright's tendency toward visualizing Paul's theology as an integrated set of beliefs or "truths" which are already secure for Paul understates the dynamic character of Paul's theology and takes insufficient notice of the way various contingencies require new thinking by Paul which in turn shapes an emerging theology. Patte's position that Paul shares self-evident, foundational convictions that cannot be put into words causes one to wonder how one might

---

[1] Jouette Bassler, "Paul's Theology: Whence and Whither?" in *Society of Biblical Literature 1989 Seminar Papers* (ed. David J. Lull; Atlanta: Scholars Press, 1989) 420; see also her revised essay with the same title in this volume, pp. 12–14.

[2] N. T. Wright, "Putting Paul Together Again: Toward a Synthesis of Pauline Theology (1 and 2 Thessalonians, Philippians, and Philemon)," in *Pauline Theology I*, 195.

[3] See Daniel Patte, *Paul's Faith and the Power of the Gospel: A Structural Introduction to the Pauline Letters* (Philadelphia: Fortress, 1983) 12. See Bassler, "Paul's Theology" (in this volume), 12.

tease conclusions out of these convictions. If we cannot demonstrate these foundational convictions by argument or evidence, how would we know if we had discovered them?

Some tension exists in Bassler's position between her desire to trace a common thread or fundamental conviction of Paul through the letters and her concern with Paul's theology as an ongoing activity.[4] For even while she disavows any pretension that she has "uncovered the *center* of Paul's theology,"[5] she does appear to claim that she has uncovered the *foundation*. She sees in election a common "thread" running through all of the letters.[6] The thread metaphor, however, may suggest a certain consistency that works against construing Paul's theology as an ongoing, open-ended activity. On closer inspection the thread, though recognizable from one letter to the next, is hardly uniform. The common thread has many linguistic colors. For example, God's election (ἐκλογή) and appearance as the one "calling you" (καλοῦντος ὑμᾶς) in 1 Thess 1:4 and 2:12 give way to what is a very oblique allusion in Phil 1:7: "all of you share in God's grace with me" (NRSV) (συγκοινωνούς μου τῆς χάριτος πάντας ὑμᾶς ὄντας), and a unique autobiographical reference in Gal 1:15 in which Paul refers to being set aside from his mother's womb. The reference in Gal 1:6 to the one who "called you" (aorist καλέσαντος ὑμᾶς) shares a verb form with the reference in 1 Thess 2:12 and 1 Corinthians, but the tense and function are quite different in its context. The references in 1 Corinthians are the most varied of any of the letters, and Bassler correctly notes that here "it becomes clear that the concept of election or call no longer merely undergirds Paul's argument; it has instead become the focus of this argument."[7] The differences from letter to letter are significant enough to remind us that even a thread is hardly ever absolutely uniform. In its naked form it is a finely spun collection of fibers of varying length and coloration. Moreover, its association with other fibers, fabrics, threads, and stitching change its appearance, if not its character, from letter to letter.

At another level Bassler's treatment is most suggestive. In her association of election (ἐκλογή) with call, the Spirit, being set aside, and inclusion in a shared community of grace, she implicitly suggests that the term election is best viewed as part of a larger field of discourse. Moreover, her implicit recognition that election and call may have a different valence from letter to letter encouraged us to attend to that process more carefully. To those concerns we now turn under a rubric we have called the "grammar of election."

---

[4] See Bassler, "Paul's Theology," in this volume, p. 17: "I have argued that instead we should self-consciously begin to construe Paul's theology as an activity."

[5] Ibid.

[6] Ibid., 14–15.

[7] Ibid., 15.

I. THE GRAMMAR OF ELECTION

The reference to Paul's *grammar of election* requires some explanation. The word "grammar" carries at least three meanings: (1) It can refer to the rules by which subjects, objects, verbs, predicate adjectives, and other parts of speech relate to each other in a sentence. (2) It can signify the basic principles of the arts or sciences. For the past two centuries the word has been used in this manner, referring variously to a *"grammar* of assent," a *"grammar* of painting," a *"grammar* of ancient geography," a *"grammar* of music," and, more recently, a *"grammar* of film."[8] (3) As philosophers of language have shown, it can also refer to the way language, symbols, metaphors, cultic acts, and myths collaborate to shape a community's identity, its view of reality, its world construction, and its interaction with its context. A study of grammar in this sense is concerned with the way language *shapes* rather than merely *expresses* one's view of the world. It is in this latter sense that we use the term "grammar" here.

Relying on Wittgenstein, theologians like George A. Lindbeck, Wayne Proudfoot, D. Z. Phillips, and Paul Holmer increasingly speak of a *grammar* of faith as an alternative to the foundational approach to theology.[9] So far, however, the insights of these theologians have received scant use by New Testament scholars. Given the frustration of attempts in recent years to find a center of Pauline theology, this latter approach may have special relevance for our discussion.

In his treatment of "Theology as Grammar," Wittgenstein suggested that *"essence* is expressed by grammar" rather than the reverse — at least in a primary sense.[10] By this Wittgenstein meant that "essence" is not known as an independent entity in space but rather is apprehended through language. Even colors, he noted, are learned not through their separate independent existence, but through language. Under promptings from parents, teachers, siblings and friends who point to a color saying, "See! This is red," children learn their colors. He noted with satisfaction that color recognition is a linguistic phenomenon. For example, the color turquoise is known and experienced through

---

[8] *Oxford English Dictionary* (2d ed.; Oxford: Oxford University Press, 1989) 6. 743.

[9] For example, see the recent work of D. Z. Phillips, *Faith After Foundationalism* (London: Routledge, 1988). Especially germane are his discussions of "Grammar and Theology" (pp. 195–254) and "Manners without Grammar" (pp. 131–94). Important for this discussion is George A. Lindbeck, *The Nature of Doctrine: Religion and Theology in a Postliberal Age* (Philadelphia: Westminster, 1984) 79–84, and Wayne Proudfoot's *Religious Experience* (Berkeley: University of California Press, 1985). See also Paul Holmer's *The Grammar of Faith* (New York: Harper & Row, 1978).

[10] See Wittgenstein, *Philosophical Investigations* (trans. G. E. M. Anscombe; New York: Macmillan, 1968) 116. G. P. Baker and P. M. S. Hacker have a very useful discussion of grammar in Wittgenstein (*Wittgenstein, Rules, Grammar and Necessity* [Oxford: Basil Blackwell, 1985] 34–80).

language, and cultures without words for turquoise do not recognize the color. From this experience comes an interest in the way this color fits and works together with other hues—pink, brown, yellow, black, chartreuse, etc.—to form patterns, contrasts, and various cultural expressions. The way these fit and work together is their grammar. Inasmuch as the way things fit and work together is context-sensitive, Wittgenstein called this grammar "a language game" with its own rules, parts, actions, and goals. Even the parts that fit together function differently from game to game (in Paul's case from letter to letter?). The Queen of Spades, for example, means one thing in a game of Hearts and quite another in a game of Bridge. Dice function differently in Monopoly, Trivial Pursuit, and "Craps." The mistake made by theologians, according to Wittgenstein, is that they focus on the *form* of expressions and not on their *use* or their context (i.e., the game in which they are used). The word "game," as Wittgenstein used it, need not carry a pejorative or "trivial" sense but should suggest another way of looking at the rules of discourse Paul follows in different letters as he does theology. Observing this process is giving attention to the grammar of election.

George Lindbeck's adoption of elements of Wittgenstein's approach is instructive. Under the heading "Grammar and Doctrine, Continuity and Change," Lindbeck has explicitly noted that doctrine reflects the grammar of theology.[11] If one were to try to state what is absolutely basic for Paul might it not be God? Were that the case one would hardly be closer to understanding Paul's theology. According to Lindbeck, one would still need to determine what the word "God" meant for Paul, and one would learn that meaning by examining "how the word operates within [Paul's] religion and thereby shapes reality and experience rather than by first establishing its propositional or experiential meaning and reinterpreting or reformulating its use accordingly."[12]

By focusing on grammar, Wittgenstein and Lindbeck encourage us to look at all aspects of language in its human web—namely, symbols, actions, metaphors, and the way they fit together. We learn about one part of a web not by concentrating on the essence of that constituent element or even by isolating each element for examination but by observing how it works or fits with its other parts and context. This approach has at least two implications for our study of election in the Pauline letters: (1) It suggests that we focus not so much on what the text signifies in a propositional or foundational sense

---

[11] Lindbeck, *Nature of Doctrine*, 79–84.

[12] Ibid., 114. I am aware of the substantive criticism of Lindbeck offered by D. Z. Phillips (*Faith After Foundationalism*, 196–225); however, Phillips agrees with Lindbeck's critique of foundationalism in theology.

as on how election operates in the text to direct the community. The term "election" in the Hebrew Bible is an old symbol often referring to the choice of Israel as God's beloved. Even there, however, scholars note the different ways the Yahwist, Deuteronomist, Hosea, and Ezekiel understand election. It is insufficient, therefore, simply to note that Paul inherited the term and used it. We must note how Paul's thinking was shaped by this venerable and varied tradition, and how his context required fresh thinking about the tradition. In his specific response to his context the term election will likely acquire new meaning for Paul. (2) Attention must be given to the way the term "election" fits into a larger language field and the way that field fits in its epistolary context. By looking at the larger interpretative scheme, we witness Paul's composition of fresh combinations, his new thinking, and his innovation. Even while his thinking is shaped by such a storied tradition, his collision with new contrarieties opens the way to new theological formulations. The study of this process may give us a more reliable basis for guessing at the meaning of Paul's theologizing about election in the letters discussed below.

II. I THESSALONIANS

Context of Paul's Grammar of Election

The situation of the Thessalonians is hardly transparent. Even granting that Paul's letter may suppress conflicting voices and opinions, may mask skepticism about his gospel and may conceal ambivalence in the community, some things are obvious, nevertheless. First, believers were suffering for their association with Christ (1:4–6; 2:13–16; 3:3–4). Some baptized members of the church had died, but we cannot be certain if they were murdered by enemies or died of natural causes. In any case, discouragement bordering on despair is implied by Paul's strong contrary emphasis on hope and steadfastness (4:13–18; 1:3; 2:19; 4:13; 5:8). Second, although the danger of backsliding was real, we cannot be certain that Paul's exhortation to "abstain from immorality (πορνεία)" (my translation of 4:3) was provoked by eschatological enthusiasm, the allure of Hellenistic religion, or persecution. In spite of these uncertainties, his warnings against pollution and erection of discrete boundaries between the insiders and outsiders do suggest a level of ambiguity that threatened the health, if not existence, of the community (e.g., 4:5). Third, there was some problem with the ἀτάκτους that caused Paul to encourage their correction (5:14). Although the disorderly (ἀτάκτοι) have been identified with the God-taught (θεοδίδακτοι, 4:9) who have quit work to wait for Jesus' coming (παρουσία),[13]

---

[13] My own study of the *theodidaktoi* inclines me in that direction. See "*Theodidaktoi* and Handwork

certainty about their identity eludes us. For whatever reason, the disorderly or idle posed problems Paul recognized and presumably sought to address.

Paul's Language of Election

Outside of Romans Paul uses ἐκλογή ("election") only in 1 Thess 1:4 referring to "brothers and sisters beloved by God" whom God has chosen (NRSV). Synonymous with this language referring to God's election in warm, familial language, Paul used καλέω ("call") in a dual sense — referring to God's election of a people and to the status of that people as God's elect (2:12; 4:7; 5:24). Rarely Paul uses ἔθετο (aorist middle of τίθημι) meaning to appoint or destine a people for salvation (5:9). The richness and diversity of Paul's language about the identity of God's elite are masked from us by its familiarity. Some of that language is traditional (church, ἐκκλησία; saints, ἅγιοι; father, πατήρ; brothers, ἀδελφοί [1:1; 3:13; 3:11; and 2:14]) and some freshly minted referring to those in Christ (ἐν Χριστῷ), in the Lord (ἐν κυρίῳ), in God (ἐν θεῷ), and the God-taught (θεοδίδακτοι) (1:1; 4:16; 3:3; 5:18; 4:9). This language distinguishes them from pagan Gentiles (τὰ ἔθνη), who, as once did they, worship "dumb idols" (1:9).

Given the presence of traditional language referring to God's choice, the absence of a single reference to the community of Israel is amazing.[14] This omission poses a challenge for Tom Wright, who believes that the covenant community of Israel stands at the center of Paul's theology. Not only are there no references to Israel in 1 Thessalonians; there are also no citations from the Hebrew Scriptures, no allusions to God's covenant, or Torah or law (νόμος), and no appeal to God's historic promises. Surprisingly, the cascade of apocalyptic metaphors in 4:13–5:11 nowhere touches the experience of Israel. These omissions are especially puzzling in light of Paul's use of the term ἐκκλησία to name the elect community without any acknowledgment of its association with the ἐκκλησία κυρίου of the Septuagint (Deut 23:2; 1 Chr 28:8; Neh 13:1; Mic 2:5, etc.). Nowhere does Paul hint at the way this ἐκκλησία of Gentiles was grafted onto God's holy tree, Israel. Except for one fleeting reference to the prophets, the history of this community has its beginning with Jesus' word and death in the recent past and will find its resolution in Paul's own lifetime. This extreme foreshortening, so common in Jewish apocalyptic writings, may help explain this Pauline truncation, but if Paul's theology is in its early formative stages the difficult questions about the

---

in Philo and 1 Thessalonians," in *L'apôtre Paul: Personnalité, style et conception du ministère* (ed. A. Vanhoye; BETL 73; Leuven: Leuven University Press, 1986) 324–31.

[14] I use the term "elite" here in the French sense of *D'élite* meaning "choice, pick, or select."

relationship of the ἐκκλησία of the Gentiles to the ἐκκλησία of Israel have not yet been forced on him.

Paul's Discourse as Grammar

A sense of God forsakenness, abandonment, confusion, hopelessness, and helplessness lurks in the subtext of this letter. The danger of defection was real (4:3–8), and the need for encouragement was urgent. Paul's use of election language to address this issue reveals something of his pastoral heart.[15] Once Paul opens the letter, he immediately identifies the persecuted as the "beloved of God" whom God has chosen (τὴν ἐκλογὴν ὑμῶν, 1:4). Then after reminding them of their reception of the gospel (1:5), Paul includes the persecuted in a partnership of suffering that includes, most notably, "the Lord" (1:6), the apostles whom they imitate, and the churches in Macedonia and Achaia for whom they are an example (1:7). If it is genuine, 2:14–16 expands the circle of suffering by noting that "you suffered the same things from your compatriots as they did from the Jews" (2:14 NRSV). This allusion to persecution is preceded by a paragraph recalling his own tender care for the Thessalonians and an admonition to "lead a life worthy of God, who calls you (τοῦ καλοῦντος ὑμᾶς) into his own kingdom and glory" (2:12). The immediate reference to persecution in 2:12–16 again appears to associate election and persecution. At times it appears that it is the destiny of the elect to suffer persecution for Christ. Paul wants no one "to be shaken in these persecutions, because (γάρ) you yourselves know that we were destined (κείμεθα) for these things" (3:3, emphasis added, cf. 5:9). This huddling together against the cold is implicit also in Paul's in Christ, in God, and in the Lord (ἐν Χριστῷ, ἐν θεῷ, and ἐν Κυριῷ) language (1:1; 2:14; 4:16; 5:18; 4:1), in which he makes a pact with death through a presence that bridges the great divide. Paul's ἐν Χριστῷ language is striking and unusual in 1 Thessalonians in the way it unites the living and the dead in a common embrace. The emphasis on this "tie that binds" is obviously situational, for in the view of some that tie had been irrevocably sundered by the unexpected and shocking death of some believers (4:16). Through his recitation of the final apocalyptic scenario Paul thus joins the living elect with the departed saints (ἀγίων) in anticipation of Jesus' return (παρουσία).

---

[15] Even allowing for the presence of other concerns in the letter (e.g., 4:1–9), Karl Donfried's view that this letter is primarily a response to persecution deserves further discussion. His ideas were developed in "The Theology of 1 Thessalonians as a Reflection of its Purpose" (a paper distributed to the SBL Pauline Theology Consultation meeting in November 1986).

1 Thessalonians, however, is hardly one-dimensional, for Paul concerns himself not only with the destiny of the elect but also with the ethos of the elect. What led Paul to tie election and holiness so intimately in 1 Thessalonians? Was this association designed to counter confusion, uncertainty, and ambiguity rising from persecution (Donfried), eschatological enthusiasm (Jewett), or the appeal of Hellenistic religion and philosophy (Malherbe)? Or are the community's sense of its destiny and its ethos in the final analysis inseparable? If so, the question still would remain as to why Paul felt compelled to discuss both here? Although we cannot know the answers to any of these questions with certainty, we can say that this association sharply separated the elect from the "pagan" world and helped secure the identity of the addressees against challenge and compromise.

In any case, in 4:7–8 Paul emphatically linked the status of the elect with an ethos appropriate to that status. He begins by emphasizing holiness as a distinguishing mark of the elect: "For God has not called (ἐκάλεσεν) us for impurity (ἀκαθαρσίᾳ) but unto holiness (ἁγιασμῷ). Consequently, whoever disregards this, disregards not humankind but God who gives his holy spirit unto you." In so attempting to define the elect rather than merely subverting the opposition[16] Paul shares the outlook of the Holiness Code, in which Yahweh commands, "be holy as I am holy" (Lev 11:44, 45; 9:2; 20:26; etc.), but he makes no such association explicit. More than elsewhere Paul emphasizes the "*holy* spirit" (1:5, 6; 4:8), or spirit of the Holy One, as constitutive of the conduct of God's elect. This holiness sunders the holy from the unholy very broadly defined — from those acting immorally (πορνεία, 4:3), from "those not knowing God" (4:5), from the impure (4:7), from those "who have no hope" (4:13), from those who say "peace and security" during the eschatological crisis (5:2), from those of the darkness (5:4), from children of the night (5:5), from the sleeping (5:6), and from the drunk (5:7). And this separation, by giving the elect something to push against, defines them. Moreover, as in Jewish apocalyptic traditions, this separation not only *from* this pagan milieu but also *for* holiness is given an eschatological sanction: "whoever disregards this disregards not human things but God" (4:8). (Note a corresponding emphasis in 3:13 on holiness and blamelessness in light of the imminent coming (παρουσία) as the condition of the elect existence.)[17] In spite of these echoes

---

[16] The absence of subversive discourse and the presence of so much teaching, encouragement, reminding, and exhortation led Abraham Malherbe to call this a parenetic letter. Although he has argued this in many places, see his *Paul and the Thessalonians: The Philosophic Tradition of Pastoral Care* (Philadelphia: Fortress, 1987).

[17] Note the same association in *1 Enoch* 100:5; CD 4:4–6; and Dan 7:18, 22, 25, and 27. Donfried also noted the distinctive but not unique character of the holiness language in 1 Thessalonians and linked it with persecution in Jewish martyrological literature ("The Theology of 1 Thessalonians," 5–6).

of Jewish apocalypticism and martyrological traditions, however, Paul nowhere in this letter seeks to associate either the divine election or the status and behavior of the elect with God's choice of the Jewish people. Had Paul thought through that connection, or is it absent simply because it was irrelevant in this discourse with a Gentile community? There is some evidence that both factors were at work. As we shall soon see, if we assume that 1 Thessalonians was Paul's earliest letter, there is evidence that Paul's view of election develops as he faces new situations. That development, however, was evolutionary only from our perspective, for from Paul's angle of vision it was an attempt to understand the life of the elect in Christ in the revolution set in motion by the gospel of the end-time. We must recognize, however, that his strong emphasis on the communal aspects of election, holiness, and suffering may have suppressed conflicting voices and opinions. His stress on steadfastness in persecution may have masked both the nature of the resistance to his gospel and the degree of defection. And his unequivocal accentuation of cleanness, holiness, and morality may have concealed the level of ambivalence and doubt within the community about what one assigns to the world outside and what is tolerated inside. So even as we talk about development in Paul's theology we must be sensitive to the level of ambiguity and tension in this process that gives his theologizing a dynamic character.

III. PHILIPPIANS

Context of Paul's Grammar of Election

Even granting that no explicit reference to election appears in Philippians and only one reference to Paul's "upward call" (3:14), traces of a grammar of election do occur both in Paul's language and in his address of the context. As in 1 Thessalonians, Paul is less concerned here with the fact of election than with the status and marks of the elect. Whereas the epistolary context of the Thessalonians was suffused with uncertainty, hopelessness, and temptation to defect, inevitably associated with their persecutions, the letter(s) to the Philippians reveals a partnership of suffering shared by the Philippian converts and Paul. The letter is suffused with the horrors of Paul's imprisonment and the threat of an imminent execution. Even as Paul writes, multiple exchanges take place between the beloved church in Philippi and the shackled apostle in mortal peril. The Philippians have sent Epaphroditus to minister to him, and perhaps from him Paul learned that Judaizers were undermining his gospel in Philippi. To Paul's worry about his own fate and rivals competing for the loyalty of the converts in Philippi is added his concern for

Epaphroditus, who while ministering to the apostle has become critically ill. Meanwhile, the rivals back in Philippi advocated circumcision as the initiation rite of admission to the elect community. Their libertinism earned them the epithet "enemies of the cross of Christ" (3:18); their appeal to their ancestral Jewish traditions possibly encouraged the development of a spiritual hierarchy that Paul sought to overturn. Even as Paul writes he plans to dispatch Epaphroditus back to Philippi to offer a fuller report on the apostle and perhaps to bring a corrective and encouraging message from the apostle.

Paul's Language of Election

This context provoked Paul to appeal to the language of his Jewish traditions, which had shaped his outlook, and to use language crafted by the experience of his confinement to define the status of the messianist elect. In addition to the mystical language of identification so common in 1 Thessalonians — the "in" (ἐν) language (ἐν Χριστῷ, ἐν αὐτῷ, etc.) — this letter shares other parts of the Thessalonian language field. Even though the references to those ἐν Χριστῷ (1:1; 3:1, 9, 14; 4:21) parallel those in 1 Thessalonians, the emphasis on "partnership (κοινωνία) in the gospel" is markedly stronger in Philippians (1:5, 7). Three additional metaphors appear in Philippians that are decidedly important. The first is an apocalyptic metaphor that Paul invokes to designate the holy elect as those who "shine as lights in the cosmos" (2:15), an apparent metaphor that refers to the *maśkîlîm* as those who "shall shine like the brightness of the firmament" taken either from Daniel (12:3) or *1 Enoch* (104:2). This association with the heavenly elect is implicit also in the second metaphor, which affirms the status of the elect "in Christ" as marginal inasmuch as they are resident aliens in this world whose true colony (πολίτευμα) is in heaven (3:20). The final metaphor springs from the polemical context of the letter as Paul draws on the most important rite of his native religion addressing his church as the circumcision (περιτομή, 3:5). Notably, this small sample of language reveals a more direct appeal to the Jewish tradition than was the case in 1 Thessalonians, and the emphasis on the partnership of suffering, which was implicit in 1 Thessalonians, is more strongly emphasized here. Paul offers no reflection on the theological issue raised by his inclusion of Gentiles among the circumcision (not "true circumcision" as in the RSV), or among the heavenly luminaries. The solution to this theological conundrum is only latent and will later be developed by crisis.

Paul's Election Discourse as Grammar

The context noted above provoked Paul to draw explicitly on his own Jewish traditions and to introduce new language to interpret his own imprisonment and mortal peril and to define the status of his hearers, the messianist elect (cf. 4:21). He called up a vicious metaphor, κατατομήν (the "mutilation") to describe the "dogs" antithetical to the περιτομή (the "circumcision"), that is, the elect, who "worship in the spirit of God and boast in Christ Jesus and do not trust in the flesh" (3:3). Coopting the initiation rite of God's elect to refer to those ἐν Χριστῷ, Paul twisted the metaphor περιτομή into an ugly pun to condemn his rivals as "mutilators of the flesh" who were "confident in the flesh" (3:4). Although one might expect this metaphorical leap to cause him to reflect on the place of circumcision as a sign of God's covenant with Israel, it did not do so. Instead, he focused on the proper ground of confidence by autobiographically recalling his Jewish legacy—circumcised, an Israelite, a Benjaminite, a super Hebrew, a Pharisee blameless under the law (3:5–6)—to deconstruct the religious claims of the "mutilators of the flesh." But just when Paul appears to have been a victim of his own silliness, substituting his own status claims for theirs, he appears to realize what he has done. Instantaneously he draws back discarding them as "dung" in order that he may be found ἐν αὐτῷ, that is, in Christ (3:9). This spontaneous, visceral response to a serious challenge radically revalued the claims of the Judaizers and redefined "the circumcision" as those ἐν Χριστῷ. He was apparently unaware of the implications of his spiritualization of the sacral rite marking the elect or the bone of contention it would become in his relationship with the synagogue. It is stunning that this radical revaluation of circumcision did not lead to a repudiation of the physical circumcision of male initiates into the covenant community. If Paul failed to anticipate the angry explosion that his redefinition of circumcision would later ignite, he may be excused for lack of foresight, for the rules of the game in this setting had been set by the opposition with their appeal to circumcision as a definitive mark of the elect. In the absence of the Galatian challenge his thinking was incomplete, and consequently his more limited response aimed to reinterpret the rules made and followed by his rivals in Philippi.

Paul's own imprisonment dominates the circumstances of Philippians. Even while fearing his execution was imminent (1:20–26), Paul sought to honor Christ in his body "whether by life or by death" (1:20). In 2:17 he spoke metaphorically of his death as a sacrifice "as a libation upon the sacrificial offering of your faith." Through sharing in Christ's sufferings Paul hoped to become "like him in his death, if somehow I may attain the resurrection of the dead"

(3:10–11), and he interpreted this trajectory of suffering, death, and resurrection as the "upward call of God in Christ Jesus" (3:14). Giving these grim prospects a parenetic twist, Paul lifted them up as a model worthy of imitation by his addressees (3:17).[18] Thus his imprisonment became an occasion to urge the Philippians to "suffer for his [Christ's] sake, having the same struggle (ἀγῶνα) which you saw in me and which you now hear to be mine" (1:29–30). By appealing to his own suffering as a model and recalling the tradition of Christ's humiliation and death on a cross (2:5–11) Paul sought to deconstruct the teaching of "enemies of the cross of Christ" (3:17–18) and to offer a response to suffering very reminiscent of the martyrological traditions of Jewish apocalypticism. As an antidote to the fear, God forsakenness, alienation, and anger that persecution brought, Paul substituted a triumphant model and a partnership of suffering.[19]

Although Paul here relied on the language and cult of Judaism strikingly more than in 1 Thessalonians, he had not yet thought through the implications of his use of those traditions. Even though he calls those ἐν Χριστῷ the circumcision (περιτομή) and the Judaizers the mutilation (κατατομήν), he discounted his own circumcision and achievement as a Pharisee. Paul could call his own circumcision "dung" and the elect the "circumcision" in a wholly positive sense only because the metaphor "circumcision" expanded the reach of the traditional rite in quite unexpected ways. Paul had yet to realize the implications of his metaphorical construction for assessing the traditions of Yahweh's covenant with Israel. Paul had yet to understand the seriousness of the threat posed by the rival Jewish Christian missionaries. Paul was content here to excoriate the rivals without systematically contesting their teaching. As we shall see, that was soon to change.

IV. GALATIANS

Context of Paul's Grammar of Election in Galatia

Initially enthusiastic recipients of Paul's gospel, the Galatian church Paul founded from a sickbed cooled to the apostle and his message. After Paul's departure, the Galatian converts, either with external prompting or through internal disaffection, grew suspicious of the apostle and skeptical of the truth of his *kerygma*. Between the lines of the letter and mirrored in Paul's counter-

---

[18] I understand Paul to use ἄνω κλήσεως τοῦ θεοῦ in 3:14 not as a synonym of his election, that is, call into Christ, but as an expression of his elect status.

[19] For this insight I am indebted to Ralph Martin, *Carmen Christi: Philippians ii. 5–11 in Recent Interpretation and in the Setting of Early Christian Worship* (SNTSMS 4; Cambridge: Cambridge University Press, 1967).

charges we see the attacks of his critics. Apparently some had pointed to Paul's derivative status, his deference and subjection to the authority of the Jerusalem apostles, who claimed direct contact with the earthly Jesus. In the absence of any explicit instruction from Paul, the critics' emphasis on circumcision as the mark of election for Gentile male converts may have inclined the Galatians to take the command in Gen 17:10 ("Every male among you shall be circumcised" [RSV]) with utmost seriousness. The warning that any uncircumcised male was to be "cut off" from God's people (Gen 17:14) left little room for negotiation, and the threat, when linked with the practice of circumcision in Jerusalem by Jewish Christians, might have offered a warrant so compelling that the Galatian church felt obligated also to practice circumcision. If some such logic informed the Galatian practice and disagreement with Paul, we can better understand how the dispute between Paul and his converts was about the terms and marks of election rather than about the meaning of election itself.

In his response Paul expresses alarm over the Galatian understanding of the conditions of election. Rather than merely warning the Galatians about the circumcisers,[20] Paul uses some of his hottest rhetoric to contest their gospel. The difference between the situations in Galatia and Philippi was dramatic. In Philippi Paul enjoyed a warm and supportive partnership that existed from the beginning and continued with congregational support while he was in prison. Though Judaizers challenged his gospel in Philippi, the future of the congregation is hardly in doubt, and, therefore, Paul merely warns the Philippians about the "dogs" without attempting to refute them. In Galatia, on the other hand, the outcome is plainly in question. The opposition with its support of scripture and the Jerusalem circle was formidable. The erosion of his church's support triggered a savage response by Paul. In his fiery defense Paul's thinking about the distinguishing marks of election developed in some intriguing ways.

Paul's Language of Election

Galatians contains a rich collection of language that had previously shaped Paul's thinking and now is bent back onto the Galatian landscape in some ingenious ways. Space limits our discussion to three different though related language clusters dealing with the family, adoption, and calling. Interestingly,

---

[20] Of course the identity of these circumcisers and their provenance is hotly disputed. All of the possibilities have been carefully outlined for us by Hans Dieter Betz (*Galatians: A Commentary on Paul's Letter to the Churches in Galatia* [Hermeneia: Philadelphia: Fortress, 1979]). While that discussion is terribly important, the question of whether the circumcisers were local Gentiles, or emissaries from Jerusalem will have to be passed over for the moment.

his vocabulary about the family opens the letter, then disappears from the most polemical opening section of the body of the letter. For example, Paul addresses God as father (πατήρ) three times in the salutation (1:1, 3, 4) and does not again use the metaphor until 4:2, 6. Those who claim God as πατήρ are here for the first time recognized by Paul as children of God (υἱοὶ θεοῦ, 3:26; 4:6, 7) though he did call the elect children of light (υἱοὶ φωτός) in 1 Thess 5:51. Here also for the first time does Paul refer to the messianist believers as children of Abraham (υἱοὶ Ἀβραάμ, 3:7). Moreover, Paul turns the Abraham narrative to his advantage in chaps. 3 and 4 to emphasize the familial status of Gentile believers as heirs. Furthermore, here for the first time do his addressees become children of promise (τέκνα ἐπαγγελίας, 4:28) and children of freedom (τέκνα ἐλευθέρας, 4:31), though Paul uses the term τέκνα in other ways elsewhere (e.g., 1 Cor 4:14, 17; 7:14; 2 Cor 6:13; etc.). This privileged relationship with God expressed with familial metaphors has a quite logical extension in the copious use here of the brothers (ἀδελφοί) metaphor that universally appears in all of Paul's letters (Gal 1:2, 11, 19; 3:15; 4:12, 28, 31; 5:11, 13; 6:1, 18). Although this rich vocabulary had shaped Paul's identity from childhood, clearly he uses this language in some highly creative ways in Galatians. Nevertheless, his usage everywhere presumes a Jewish legacy. Intimately related to this metaphorical language field was Paul's novel discussion of adoption. And finally, his grammar of God's calling builds on the theology of election/calling that we have noted in earlier letters. It is to Paul's treatment of calling, family, and adoption that we now turn.

Paul's Discourse on the Grammar of Election/Calling

Four explicit references to calling appear in Galatians aimed at refuting the gospel of the Judaizers (1:6; 1:15; 5:8; 5:13). The reference in 1:15 is only indirectly relevant since it deals not with God's election of Galatian believers but with the divine appointment of Paul as an apostle before his birth. By appealing to the experience of Jeremiah and Isaiah, whom God also chose before birth, Paul hoped to gain additional authority for his apostleship in his struggle against his judaizing challengers, who obviously held quite a different theology of election. The first reference (1:6), however, enjoys pride of place. Expressing his astonishment that the Galatians were so quickly "turning from the One who called (καλέσαντος) you into the grace of Christ," Paul articulated what was to be the central theme of the letter—namely, that God included Gentiles in the elect community by grace rather than by law observance.

In the reference in 5:8 Paul mixed praise and blame to win the loyalty of his converts. He praised the Galatians for having run so well but scolded them for so quickly deserting the gospel: "who hindered you from following the truth?" Then Paul categorically boomed out that "This persuasion (πεισμονή) is not from the One calling you (καλοῦντος)" (5:8); in other words, it is a human and even a perverse invention separating its adherents from the company of the elect and the realm of grace. This unambiguous rejection of the truth claims of his rivals aptly summarizes a theme that informs the entire letter: In 3:4 he asks accusingly, "Have you experienced so much in vain?" In 4:11 he expresses the fear that his labor has been in vain and that they have fallen from grace. In 5:4 he reverses the warning of Gen 17:9–14, which his opponents evidently claimed as foundational. There God commands Abraham to circumcise "every male among you" as a sign of the covenant, and warns that "any uncircumcised male who is not circumcised in the flesh of his foreskin shall be cut off from his people; he has broken my covenant" (17:14). Radically reversing this warning, Paul holds instead that Gentile believers who accept circumcision *post facto* "who want to be justified by the law have cut yourselves off from Christ" (5:4). In 5:6 Paul offers the premise of his deconstruction of the rivals' preaching: "For in Christ Jesus (ἐν Χριστῷ ᾽Ιησοῦ) neither circumcision nor uncircumcision matters at all." To this Paul then juxtaposed his reconstructionist counterpart: "What matters is faith working through love." In 6:15 at the end of the letter, Paul in his own hand repeats this devaluation of the primal rite that had always served as a sign of God's covenant people: "For neither circumcision nor uncircumcision is anything, but a new creation." By so arguing, Paul aims not to establish Gentile Christianity as a new religion[21] but to undermine the practice of his adversaries, who sought to supplement his gospel to the Gentiles—which he judged to be sufficient in and of itself.

By taking love as the essence of election, Paul's final calling remark in 5:13 offers a positive balance to his earlier slashing attack on those who misunderstood both the nature and the ethos of election/calling: "For you were called (ἐκλήθητε) to freedom, brothers and sisters, only do not let the freedom become an opportunity for the flesh, but through love be a slave to one another. For the whole Law is fulfilled in one commandment: Namely, 'You shall love your neighbor as yourself.'"[22] Instead of his earlier worry about the Galatians'

---

[21] Betz, *Galatians,* 263.

[22] I am uncertain if ἐλευθερία ("freedom") and κτίσις ("new creation") are coterminous, as David Lull has suggested, but they are certainly complementary. Both clearly serve as descriptions of some aspect of the state of the believers. See David J. Lull, *The Spirit in Galatia: Paul's Interpretation of Pneuma as Divine Power* (SBLDS 49; Chico, CA: Scholars Press, 1978) 110.

deserting their calling, or his concern with their ignorance of the true precondition of election for Gentiles, paradoxically Paul now links freedom with communal obligation. After earlier denouncing those devoted to law observance, he now admonishes his hearers to rigorously keep a commandment from Lev 19:18 (5:14), and he does so without any evident sense that he is contradicting himself. How is one to understand this substitution of a prescription of law observance for his earlier rejection of law observance? Perhaps the answer lies in the role freedom (ἐλευθερία) played in the dispute. Paul's reminder of the call to freedom recalls and emphasizes the statement in 5:1: "For freedom Christ has set us free." Up to 5:13 ἐλευθερία had been the flashpoint of the conflict between Paul and his adversaries. In 5:13, however, Paul appears to anticipate charges that his law-free gospel was antinomian and encouraged immorality.[23] But here as elsewhere Paul associates calling and moral behavior in an entirely traditional way. What is new here is the use of calling as a warning against defection and as a legitimate and necessary concomitant of the freedom he continues to proclaim in Christ. At stake in this discussion was what was the appropriate mark and ethos of the elect.

Paul's Discourse on the Grammar of Election/Adoption

The rivals' requirement of circumcision as a condition of and a distinguishing mark of God's covenant people (*běrît mîlâ*) provoked a heated response from Paul that included an interesting display of inspired exegesis. As noted above, the extent of the exploitation of family metaphors in Galatians has no precedent in earlier Pauline letters. The repeated emphasis on the Galatian status as children or sons and daughters in Galatians is well known. The metaphor father (πατήρ) logically requires sons and daughters (υἱοί) or children (τέκνα). Now for the first time Paul thinks through how it is possible for Gentiles to be incorporated into God's family, Israel. Recalling Genesis 15–17, Paul offered a graphic and novel description of the election of the Gentiles. Through the faith of Christ, Abraham's σπέρμα, Paul argued, God found a way to include Gentiles as Abraham's offspring (3:15–19) by adoption (υἱοθεσίαν, 4:5). In the fullest sense of the term the adopted children become heirs (κληρονόμοι), a term that Paul here uses for the first time (Gal 3:29; 4:1, 7). Even as his argument unfolds, Paul's thinking on this enormously complex issue is developing. Just

---

[23] At this point I go with Heinrich Schlier, *Der Brief an die Galater* (5th ed.; MeyerK 7; Göttingen: Vandenhoeck & Ruprecht, 1971) 242–43, against Betz, *Galatians,* 272–73. Having grown up in a diaspora community, Paul could hardly have been unaware of these charges brought against Jews who drifted too close to or beyond the boundary.

exactly how this takes place Paul will only gradually realize. As he gropes his way through this question, the cross comes to have a nuance heretofore unrealized.

In 3:10 Paul's interpretation of Deut 27:26 LXX begins with the announcement of a curse on all those who do not "abide by all the things written in the book of the law." This was followed in 3:13 by a loose citation of Deut 21:23 in which Paul finds a witness for his statement that Christ became a "curse"[24] through his crucifixion ("hanging on a tree"), and the result of this "sin-offering" was that "he redeemed us [Gentiles?] from the curse of the law becoming a curse for us" (3:13). Paul's hermeneutic gives his reference to the cross an unmistakable inclusive sense: "in order that the blessing of Abraam might come upon the Gentiles (τὰ ἔθνη) in Christ Jesus, [and] in order that we might receive the spirit through faith (διὰ τῆς πίστεως)" (3:14). Here Paul expands the symbolism of the cross to argue for the legitimacy of the inclusion of the uncircumcised among the elect. Those included are none other than sons and daughters of God (3:26). These adopted children (4:5) address God as "Abba"; and even though adopted they are no less heirs than the natural born (4:7).

The main point of Paul's allegorization of the Sarah and Hagar story (4:21–5:1) is the insertion of those formerly excluded into the inner circle as "children of the promise" and "children, not of the slave but of the free woman" (4:28, 31). Focusing as he does on *inclusion,* Paul has not yet thought through the implications of excluding those belonging to the "present Jerusalem" (4:25) nor anticipated the profound theological questions raised by his inclusion of the predominantly Gentile church within "the Israel of God" (6:16).[25] These passages, however, are best read in light of the dispute in Galatia and Paul's feverish efforts to discredit the Judaizers and thereby to make the case for numbering uncircumcised Gentiles among the elect.

In these references we see how Paul's grammar of election was influenced by the traditions held in common by him and his adversaries. The battle,

---

[24] Instead of "Everyman hanged from a tree is cursed by God" (LXX), Paul has, "Cursed be everyone who hangs on a tree" (LXX: κεχατηραμένος ὑπὸ θεοῦ πᾶς κρεμάμενος ἐπὶ ξύλου. Paul: Ἐπιχατάρατος πᾶς ὁ κρεμάμενος ἐπὶ ξύλου). Paul removes the reference to God (cursed by God) and adds the definite article. Paul's change suggests that he was unwilling to say Jesus' crucifixion was due to God's curse.

[25] A voluminous secondary literature discusses the identity of Paul's addressee in this passage. The best summaries of contrary views are by Betz (*Galatians,* 322–23) and Peter Richardson (*Israel in the Apostolic Church* [Cambridge: Cambridge University Press, 1969] 79–84). Betz makes a strong case for reading this passage in its most restrictive and abrasive sense, namely, to apply only to believers in Christ. He notes precedents for such a reading in the Qumran literature. Richardson solves the problem in the passage by punctuating the sentence as follows: "may God give peace to all who will walk according to this criterion, and mercy also to his faithful people Israel."

however, was over the proper reading of these texts. His adversaries read them in light of Jewish rites and religious practice sanctioned by centuries of use; Paul read them in light of the "new creation."[26] Nevertheless, the theological implications of Paul's hermeneutic *vis-à-vis* his ancestral religion were undeveloped. His interpretations of the Christ traditions were also in a formative stage, as shown by the way his response to various contexts shaped his view of the cross. For example, his use in this letter of the passion of Christ as a symbol for the inclusion of Gentiles among the elect goes far beyond its mimetic character in 1 Thessalonians and Philippians.

Observing Paul's use of the cross to support the inclusion of Gentiles *qua* Gentiles among the elect is instructive. By noticing how Paul's Galatian cross symbolism differs markedly at points from cross symbolism in 1 Corinthians, Philippians, and 1 Thessalonians, we can see how our attempt to find what is foundational in Paul's theology is risky. For if the cross is at the core of Paul's theology, as many argue, it is simply inadequate to say the cross is foundational without noting the way the interpretation of the cross is changed by its context and then bends back onto the context to shape that as well. This dialectical relationship of symbol and setting is fundamentally unstable and resists our tendency to find a resolution in Paul's theology that has a "totalizing" impact.[27]

V. 1 CORINTHIANS

Context of Paul's Grammar of Election in Corinth

Although persecution was a brutal fact for the Thessalonians, Philippians, and Galatians, no such grisly presence frightened the Corinthians. No disillusionment clouded the outlook of the community, and no Judaizing rivals sought to discredit Paul's gospel. Instead, an eschatological enthusiasm prevailed, and the adventures in libertinism, boasting, spiritual elitism; claims to possess wisdom; and pretentions to holiness threatened to fragment the community.[28] Their spirituality may have virtually eclipsed any emphasis on

---

[26] On this point I agree with Beverly Gaventa, "The Singularity of the Gospel: A Reading of Galatians," in *Pauline Theology I*, 147–59.

[27] While deconstructionism ignores broad reconstructionist tendencies in Paul's theology, the warning of J. Hillis Miller is apt: "Deconstruction attempts to resist the totalizing and totalitarian tendencies of criticism. It attempts to resist its own tendencies to come to rest in some sense of mastery over the work" ("The Critic as Host," in *Deconstruction and Criticism* [ed. H. Bloom et al.; New York: Seabury, 1979] 252).

[28] I am aware of William Baird's recent article "'One Against the Other': Intra-Church Conflicts in 1 Corinthians," in *The Conversation Continues: Studies in Paul and John in Honor of J. Louis Martyn*

the cross (1:12–17). In place of an identification with the suffering and dying one was a mythic sharing through surrogate mystagogues in the power of the risen Lord (1:12). They may have claimed the status of angels through their celibate marriages (7:1–5; Luke 20:34–36) and an ability to speak the language of angels (γλώσσαις τῶν . . . ἀγγέλων, 13:1). Paul's sarcastic description of them as full, rich, ruling, wise, strong, and honored (4:9–10) obviously caricatures their claims, but a grain of truth is probably embedded in the distortion. This destructive individualism, religious puffery (4:6, 18, 19; 5:2; 8:1; 13:4), and extremely waspish behavior threatened to fracture the church and provoked a Pauline response unexcelled in its attention to holiness and election (calling).

Paul's Language of Election in 1 Corinthians

Our discussion of 1 Corinthians will focus on Paul's explicit discussion of election, calling, and holiness. The apostle's grammar of holiness will include temple allusions, references to unleavened bread, warning against participation in the rituals of idols, and reminders that his addressees belong to the company of the "saints." As elsewhere, Paul includes family metaphors and thirty-four references to ἀδελφοί that may have been intended to correct centrifugal forces threatening the unity if not the existence of the community. Nevertheless, in 1 Corinthians more than in any of the other letters Paul offers an explicit discussion of the meaning and significance of election/calling. Noteworthy also is the sparing but important use of πατήρ in this letter (1:3; 8:6; 15:24).

Paul's Discourse as Grammar—Election and Holiness

In the salutation and thanksgiving of the letter, the apostle telegraphs his concern with election and associates it with holiness. Paul's own call (κλῆτος) by God (1:1) is followed immediately by a reference to "the church of God in Corinth, those made holy (ἡγιασμένοις) in Christ Jesus, i.e., those called [by God] to be holy ones" (1:2). Paul then concludes the thanksgiving by affirming the faithfulness of God "through whom you were called into the κοινωνίαν of his son, Jesus Christ our Lord" (1:9). This conclusion of the

---

(ed. Robert T. Fortna and Beverly R. Gaventa; Nashville: Abingdon, 1990) 116–36. I am in sympathy with his basic point, but the considerations here do not require that fine distinctions between groups be drawn.

thanksgiving is preceded by an expression of Paul's hope that his addressees will be established as "blameless on the day of our Lord, Jesus Christ" (1:8). We see, therefore, that in both the salutation and the thanksgiving Paul links holiness and election, dual concerns that are related though not always explicitly linked throughout the letter. Now we consider them seriatim.

Holiness. In 1:18–2:5 Paul relativized wisdom, and in 3:5–17 he punctured the religious puffery with a barrage of metaphors—planting, irrigation, growing, building, and house burning. With this cluster of metaphors Paul warned his readers to exercise their vocation with care, realizing the coming judgment by fire. The climactic metaphor of this kaleidoscope of images is the temple in 3:16–17. As God's dwelling on earth, Jews historically viewed the temple as the epicenter of holiness, as the locus and authority for their sacral system, as the organizing center of the geography of the cosmos that stratified the social order, offered access to the divine presence, and mediated atonement through the sacrificial cult. Whatever this symbol lacked for the Corinthians, it throbbed with life for Paul. After conjuring up the temple metaphor, Paul tied it to the church, calling down God's curse on its desecrators: "Do you not know that you are the Temple of God and the spirit of God dwells in you [as the holy of holies]? If anyone destroys the Temple; God will destroy that person, because the Temple of God is holy [and] you are [that Temple]" (3:17). Thus in a symbolic rhetoric Paul undermines a rigorously individualistic holiness, and by redirecting it to communal ends affirms the mission of the holy ones (ἅγιοι).

A similar strategy appears elsewhere in 1 Corinthians. In 5:6–8 Paul appeals to the symbolic value of unleavened bread calling on a community in danger of fateful pollution to become what it is, that is, those "called to be holy ones" (1:2): "Cleanse out the old leaven so that you may be new dough as you really are unleavened" (5:7). In 6:1–11 he mocks the ἅγιοι for acting like the immoral, that is, ἄδικοι. In 6:12–20 he reminds those living by the slogan "All things are lawful for me" (6:12) that the holy spirit dwells in their bodily temple. Finally, in 10:14 he invokes a pagan temple metaphor warning some reckless adventurers to "flee idolatry" because they cannot "drink the cup of the Lord and the cup of demons" (10:21). All of these expansions of metaphor, appeals to rites, warnings, and admonitions aim to revise the Corinthian version of the holy life, which Paul sees as a sorry confusion of human urges with piety.

Election. Inasmuch as Paul's addressees are called, Paul urges them to behave in a way befitting their status by separating themselves wherever possible from pollution and to build up the "body." Only one paragraph after the thanksgiving Paul challenges his addressees to evaluate their claim to wisdom in light of their calling. Instead of appealing to the passion of Christ as an example (1 Thessalonians), Paul uses his own preaching of Christ crucified (1:18–25) and the election/calling of the Corinthians to undermine the Corinthian wisdom theology: "But we proclaim Christ crucified, to Jews a scandal and to Gentiles foolishness, but to those who are called (κλητοῖς), Jews and Greeks, Christ [crucified] the power of God and the wisdom of God" (1:23–24). From this summary of what Christ crucified means to the called, Paul moves directly into an ironic juxtaposition of human and divine wisdom, of human and divine strength (1:26–28).

Paul begins by ordering the Corinthians to consider (imperative βλέπετε) their calling (κλῆσις): "not many were wise [or learned] (σοφοί) by human standards (κατὰ σάρκα), not many powerful, not many nobly born" (1:27). He then concludes with a report on the divine action that radically reversed this human hierarchical order: "But God elected (ἐξελέξατο) the foolish things of the world to shame the wise, and God elected (ἐξελέξατο) the weak things of the world to shame the strong, and God elected (ἐξελέξατο) the baseborn and despised, even the things that are not, to bring to nought the things that are" (1:27–28).

In this construction Paul takes for granted the hierarchical structure of the world. Yet he notes that in the election of the dregs of that order God subverted the very order itself and by implication the Corinthian hierarchy of spiritual gifts. It is the election (or calling) that in and of itself undermines the Corinthian pretensions of wisdom (1:30). In light of God's calling, Paul recognizes the arbitrariness and emptiness of hierarchical categories and suggests that God's election turns this hierarchy on its head. This leads him to note the self-contradiction of the Corinthian substitution of a charismatic hierarchy for a social one. Ironically, the Corinthian reversal still depends on the world's hierarchy for its primary model.[29]

Later, in 12:27–31, Paul further challenges this charismatic hierarchy by constructing his own. And, as in 1:26–31, Paul links this construction with election language. Using ἔθετο, God appointed, instead of ἐξελέξατο, God elected, Paul assembles his model: "God appointed (ἔθετο) in the church first apostles, second prophets, third teachers, then miracle workers, then healers, helpers, administrators, and speakers in various kinds of tongues" (12:28). After asking rhetorically, "Are all apostles?" etc., Paul concludes with the admonition: "Earnestly desire the higher gifts" (12:31, presumably referring to those near the top of the list. It appears that Paul plans to use his own model to smash that of the Corinthians.

---

[29] This inversion resembles William Buckley's famous comment about the conservatives' reliance on the *New York Times*. Conservatives, he noted, read the *Times* and then simply think the opposite.

But just when the last piece of the new model is in place, Paul pulls back. In a flash he seems to realize that what he has done is a contradiction; he has invented a hierarchy to get rid of a hierarchy. Then in one stroke he dashes his model to bits: "I will show you a more excellent way. If I speak with the tongues of mortals and of angels and have not love (ἀγάπην) I am a noisy brass or a wailing cymbal. And if I have the gift of prophecy and understand all mysteries and all knowledge, and if I have all faith so that I can move mountains and have not ἀγάπην I am nothing . . . ." (13:1-2). So love, according to Paul, radically relativizes or devalues all spiritual gifts and the hierarchies they generate. This eschatological gift, ἀγάπην, makes a mash of the Corinthian charismatic hierarchy. Thus Paul chose not merely to smash one hierarchical model with another, but to show how love brings to light the arbitrariness and self-contradiction of the Corinthian model and his own as well. If Paul did do what I have suggested that he might have done, his conversation about election aimed to redirect the Corinthian claim to superiority, to remove their grounds for boasting, and to illumine how love creates a new order.

Scott Bartchy made much the same point in his work on 1 Cor 7:21.[30] There he showed how Paul's discussion of slavery, celibacy, and marriage was related to his understanding of calling. Nine times in eight verses Paul uses some variant of the word calling (καλέω). If Hurd is correct that 7:1 is a Corinthian slogan—"it is well for a man not to touch a woman"—then by appealing to Paul's celibacy some in the community made holiness and celibacy correlates.[31] Paul, however, seeks to correct that understanding of calling and holiness by arguing that God's call subverts all advantages of rank and position, even religious rank and position. Thus slavery was no handicap in one's relationship to God, and being free no advantage; being uncircumcised was no handicap, and being circumcised no advantage; marriage was no handicap and celibacy no advantage; not speaking in tongues was no handicap, and speaking in tongues no advantage. For they all, as Bartchy noted, were "radically relativized by God's call."[32] Paul here not only deconstructs an elitist Corinthian theology but reconstructs a theology of election that is both concerned for others and free from the tyranny of the social order (7:23). Paul secures the identity of the Corinthians in the call of God rather than in an order established by circumcision or uncircumcision, slavery or freedom, or marriage

---

[30] S. Scott Bartchy, *ΜΑΛΛΟΝ ΧΡΗΣΑΙ: First-century Slavery and the Interpretation of 1 Corinthians 7:21* (SBLDS 11; Missoula, MT: Scholars Press, 1973).

[31] John C. Hurd, *The Origin of 1 Corinthians* (London: SPCK, 1965) 158-62. The emphasis on spiritual marriages (7:5), celibacy (7:7), and separation from unbelievers (7:12-16) all point in the direction of some form of asceticism as the distinguishing mark of the elect.

[32] Bartchy, *First-century Slavery,* 152.

or celibacy. Paul urged the Corinthians to "walk" as God has called them (7:17). Paul's fuller explication of what this way of life meant was to come later; here he aims to overturn a strategy that linked identity to one's social or religious status.

VI. SUMMARY

We have seen above that Paul did not come to his context culturally naked. Paul's grammar of election emerged in part from the language of the church about God, sin, Jesus Christ, the Spirit, righteousness, and the death, resurrection, and return (παρουσία) of Jesus, and in part from the venerable traditions of Israel. The work of Paul the theologian, however, cannot be described by isolating these constituent elements as foundational. These elements are hardly bedrock for Paul, if by bedrock we mean a stable, static, unchangeable foundational element. We have seen how the language of Israel and of the Hellenistic church shaped the theological understanding of Paul and how that in turn was further shaped by the context of the churches' requiring a response from Paul. Paul did not begin with a developed theology that merely shifted its emphasis from place to place. To be sure, his emphases and tactics did change, but we have argued that in the letters we can actually see the process of theological formation and formulation taking place. We have noticed how Paul portrays the elect as those called to suffer with Christ (1 Thessalonians), as a community of believing Jews and Gentiles (Galatians), and as those chosen by God without regard for rank, position, or circumstance (1 Corinthians). We have observed also that concern with the grammar of election involves one not only in observing Paul in the act of doing theology but also in attending to the language field or larger field of discourse of election. We have seen how the cross, or Jesus' passion, which belongs to Paul's election grammar, may serve as a model for the persecuted (1 Thessalonians and Philippians), as a symbol of inclusion (Galatians), and as a wrecking bar to dismantle hierarchical models of spiritual elitists (1 Corinthians). Election, thus conceived, is viewed less as a key propositional or foundational element than as an emerging, dynamic element in Paul's larger field of discourse.

12 THE CONTRIBUTION OF TRADITIONS TO PAUL'S THEOLOGY

A Response to C. J. Roetzel

William S. Campbell
Westhill College

AT THE 1990 ANNUAL MEETING of the Society of Biblical Literature in New Orleans, I presented a response to a very innovative study by Professor Calvin J. Roetzel. This essay is based on that paper and on subsequent reflections on Professor Roetzel's contribution. He stresses that Paul's cross symbolism differs markedly and develops throughout his letters, making it difficult, if not risky, to identify what is foundational in the apostle's theology.

While being in general agreement with this finding, I have given myself the task in this response of considering to what extent Paul's theology arises from, and is indebted to, earlier and contemporary traditions. I endeavor to show that, while Paul's theology develops creatively and contextually, it does so in a loose dialectic with existing traditions.

I. THE NEED FOR A FRAMEWORK FOR INTERPRETATION

Paul, like his contemporaries, was born into a community with its own traditions, representing the accumulated wisdom of earlier generations and their attempts to make sense out of their experience. Like any other human, Paul had mediated to him via the community an authoritative total vision of what the world is ultimately like and the place of the individual within it. He learned to participate in the symbolic universe of his Pharisaic community—to perceive the world as that community perceived it, interpreting his experience from their perspective.

In making this particular point, we are simply stressing that the human being is not a *tabula rasa* covered little by little with new knowledge through new experiences. We are, on the contrary, affirming that all experience and all perception are deeply colored by existing theory.[1] So Paul learned the language of Pharisaism, and this process in itself prepared him to receive the world in a particular way in keeping with its tradition. Membership in this community provided Paul with a framework into which his experience as an individual could be integrated from the start. Within this system of shared meaning, Paul became familiar with the fundamental (Pharisaic) perceptions that had come so to ground and define the community's existence that they did not need to be debated or justified, let alone questioned. A tendency to adhere to or to develop a covenantal theology or a covenantal mode of thinking, if such there be, was probably one example of such perceptions.

As a young man, Paul had to relate and accommodate his own experience to these inherited values — most of this probably taking place unconsciously. Nevertheless, not all experiences can always be interpreted as fitting easily and harmoniously into the tradition, and at this point for Paul, as for others, a tension would emerge between tradition and experience. There are a number of specific examples in the New Testament in which we can see a group stressing their continuity with the past with, for example, the Old Testament scriptures — and seeking to legitimate (new) elements of their practice by insisting that it is their interpretation rather than that of (other) older communities that upholds true continuity with the great values of the past.[2]

Thus far we have simply outlined the normal communal constraints on human thinking and development to which Paul, his contemporaries, and we ourselves are subject. Through this, we can explain how he related to his own and other groups in his society. But one significant aspect of Paul's life does not fit in quite so easily with this or other attempts to describe normal human religious development. Paul's conversion implies a major watershed in his life and thought that has frequently, whether deliberately or inadvertently, caused Paul and his theological thought to be seen in terms of some immediate revelation rather than in any sense of continuity with his previous religious upbringing. The point at issue here is, of course, what understanding is to be given to a revelation of God. Is it simply a new self-understanding, or does it involve an introduction to, or a discovery of, new theological concepts or propositions?[3] Is it not rather a new point of departure that impacts all existing presuppositions?

Whatever our particular understanding of Paul's revelation on the Damascus road, one thing is clear: only those things could have been revealed to Paul

---

[1] See H. Räisänen, *Beyond New Testament Theology* (London: SCM/Trinity Press International, 1990) 129–31.

[2] See F. Watson, *Paul, Judaism and the Gentiles: A Sociological Approach* (SNTSMS 56; Cambridge: Cambridge University Press, 1986) 49–50.

[3] See S. Kim, *The Origin of Paul's Gospel* (WUNT 2/4; Tübingen: Mohr [Siebeck], 1981) 233–34.

which he and his new Christian community could understand. R. M. Hare points out that our conceptual language games, like group dances, assume intersubjective cooperation within a community. Proposals for conceptual renewal which deviate too far from the conceptual forms that are current within the community are not intelligible to others and thus make cooperation with them impossible.[4] For this reason, philosophers or theologians who make proposals for conceptual innovation must necessarily leave unchallenged and unchanged the greater part of the conceptual apparatus of the cultural community to which they are addressing themselves. Even Paul must be bound by this factor since he necessarily had both to understand and to communicate his message. Even the most revolutionary thinker must speak — and think — in the language of his day.[5]

A possible refuge from this kind of argument is to insist that Paul's religious experience on the Damascus road was self-authenticating and self-explanatory. This is not an adequate response. Paul's religious experience — and religious experience in general — is absolutely central to our discussion, and yet experience and its interpretation are closely connected and difficult to dissociate from each other.

Räisänen criticizes L. T. Johnson for talking of "resurrection experiences."

> Talk of Jesus' resurrection already implies a particular interpretation of the event in question. It would be correct to say that the disciples experienced something which they interpreted with the help of categories of resurrection belief. . . . Had they lacked the conceptual framework supplied by apocalyptic Jewish eschatology, they would have been bound to search for a different explanation of what they had seen. . . . Without this pre-existing interpretative frame of reference, the Easter experiences would have remained mute.[6]

The frame that provided the Easter appearances with meaning consisted of both traditional elements (the eschatological thought world) and recent ones (the experience with the earthly Jesus).

So too in our search for Paul's thinking we must presuppose this preexisting frame of reference, irrespective of how we evaluate his revelatory experience. Indeed, W. Van Orman Quine reminds us:

> The totality of our so-called knowledge or beliefs . . . is a man-made fabric which impinges on experience only along the edges. Or, to change the figure, total science is like a field of force whose boundary conditions are experience.

---

[4] R. M. Hare, *Essays in Philosophical Method* (London: Macmillan, 1971) 33. I am indebted for this reference and a good discussion of this issue to Vincent Brümmer's essay "Philosophy, Theology and the Reading of Texts," *Religious Studies* 27 (1991) 451–62.

[5] See Dennis Nineham, *The Use and Abuse of the Bible* (London: SPCK, 1976) 13–14.

[6] Räisänen, *Beyond New Testament Theology*, 127–28.

A conflict with experience at the periphery occasions readjustments in the interior of the field. . . . Re-evaluation of some statements entails re-evaluation of others, because of their logical interconnections. . . . But the total field is so underdetermined by its boundary conditions, experience, that there is much latitude of choice as to what statements to re-evaluate in the light of any single contrary experience.[7]

II. THE CULTURAL CONTEXT
THAT INFORMED PAUL'S EXPERIENCE

Räisänen is convinced that "core experiences" of themselves are not sufficient to explain why Christianity emerged. Why did Paul draw different conclusions from his ecstatic vision than the Jerusalemites? He is of the opinion that, though we are certain that Paul's values were changed (Phil 3:1–16), it is hard to distinguish the immediate consequences of the experience for Paul's life and thought from what dawned on him later on, under the influence of quite different experiences such as social conflict; for Räisänen the role of the latter — that is, of social conflict, seems much more important than "core experiences."[8]

The result of this inquiry leads us to consider afresh the inherited framework Paul had acquired prior to his Damascus road experience. Here the recent magisterial work of Alan Segal is most instructive. Although Segal believes that Paul's conversion and his mystical ascension form the basis of his theology, "his language shows the marks of a man who has learned the contemporary vocabulary for expressing a theophany and then has received one."[9]

There is now considerable agreement among scholars that Paul, like most Christians in his day, was profoundly apocalyptic in his thinking. Paul's most characteristic topics are typical of apocalypticism. Segal sees the distinction between apocalypticism and mysticism as being an artificial theoretical one not warranted by the realities of first-century religious experience. Apocalypticism and mysticism were inextricably bound up in first-century Judaism and Paul himself is a prime example of the way in which the two were united phenomenologically.

In his writings to his new Christian communities among the Gentiles, it is evident that the apostle's understanding is similar in some ways to that of the Qumran community. In both there is a rigorous distinction between the

---

[7] Willard Van Orman Quine, *From a Logical Point of View* (Cambridge, MA: Harvard University Press, 1961) 42–43.

[8] Räisänen, *Beyond New Testament Theology,* 125–26.

[9] Alan F. Segal, *Paul the Convert: The Apostolate and Apostasy of Saul the Pharisee* (New York and London: Yale University Press, 1990) 69.

community and the outside world. Paul sees Christians as a congregation united by their absorption into Christ, the angelic vice-regent of God. Segal concludes that Paul's understanding of this issue is exclusively mystical and apocalyptic, with one proviso. The activity of the end-time has already begun. In this and in his abrogation of the special laws of Judaism for his Gentile mission, Paul's view of community is unique.[10] But in the Pauline communities, high-group definition, as also in the extreme Torah-true apocalyptic groups, enforced the separation from the outside world. Both in Qumran and in early Christianity, the process of salvation was inaugurated by membership in a religious sect, which considered itself a new covenantal congregation.

Segal seeks to fill in the cultural context that informed Paul's experience. Ezekiel 1, though often ignored in this context, was one of the central scriptures that Paul and Luke used to understand Paul's conversion.

> The vision of the throne-chariot, with its attendant description of Glory (Kavod), God's Glory or form, for the human figure, is a central image of Jewish mysticism, which is closely related to the apocalyptic tradition. . . . Paul is an important witness to the kind of experience apocalyptic Jews were having and an important predecessor to merkabah mysticism.[11]

Stories of heavenly journeys, of angelic transformation, or even of the ascent of exemplary men to divinity by identification with, or transformation into, the enthroned figure abound in early apocalyptic texts. "The journeys here usually begin after a crisis of human confidence about God's intention to bring justice to the world, and they result in the discovery that the universe is indeed following God's moral plan—the ancient scriptures about God's providence are proved true." The narration of exotic and amazing events is a pragmatic one—to explain the structure of heaven, thus providing an eschatological verification that God's plan will come to fruition and also a mechanism by which immortality is achieved.

Segal maintains that in this context Paul did not have to be a religious innovator to posit an identification between a vindicated hero and the image of the *kābôd*, the manlike figure in heaven, although the identification of the figure with the risen Christ is obviously a uniquely Christian development.[12]

Segal comes to the conclusion that "the center of Paul's gospel is the identification of Christ as the Glory of God" and that "Paul's vocation is to make known the identification of Jesus Christ as the Glory of God."[13] This language of vision has informed his thought in a number of crucial respects. According

---

[10] Ibid., 158–61.
[11] Ibid., 39–40.
[12] Ibid., 51.
[13] Ibid., 156–57.

to Segal, it allowed Paul to develop a concept of the divinity of Christ or the Messiah both as a unique development within the Jewish mystical tradition and as characteristically Christian. He uses Jewish mystical vocabulary to express the transformation experienced by believers, and he uses the language of transformation to discuss the ultimate salvation and fulfillment of the apocalypse, raising believers to immortality. Paul's vision also allows him to describe his teaching as an "apocalypse"—a revelation of hidden knowledge through the Holy Spirit, though it is mediated through the mind, not through the speaking of tongues.

Although it was possible to go from Pharisaic Judaism to Christianity without having a conversion experience such as Paul's, Paul is not one of those Jews whose faith in Christ only completed a previous belief in Judaism. His conversion caused him to revalue his Judaism, in turn creating a new understanding of Jesus' mission. In addition to this, in contrast to the Jerusalem church's conception of apostolate as deriving from Jesus' personal appointment, Paul develops a charismatic idea of apostleship dependent on a vision of the risen Christ—exactly what modern psychology and sociology would call a conversion (despite Paul's frequent use of the concept of prophetic commissioning, e.g., κλητός in Galatians 1 and Romans 1).[14]

We are deeply indebted to Segal's creative and convincing understanding of Paul and particularly for this useful description of the cultural context that informed the apostle's experience. The broad outlines of his study have elicited our support, though there may be some residual tension in regarding Paul's conversion and mystical ascension as the basis of his theology—while at the same time stressing the inheritance that provided the language to interpret this theophany.

III. THE INFLUENCE OF SCRIPTURAL INTERPRETATION IN THE FORMULATION OF PAUL'S THEOLOGICAL STATEMENTS

A crucial question in the development of Paul's theology must be the actual role played by the scriptures both in his understanding of God's purpose and in his self-understanding. There is good reason to maintain that in the past scholars have not paid adequate attention either to Paul's explicit or implicit use of scripture.[15] Segal is quite clear that Paul does not forget his Jewish past;

---

[14] Ibid., 69–71.

[15] An exception to this is the late Professor A. T. Hanson, my esteemed teacher and friend, who throughout his life devoted much of his work to this theme. See his *Studies in Paul's Technique and Theology* (London: SPCK, 1974) and *The Living Utterances of God: The New Testament Exegesis of the Old* (London: Darton, Longman & Todd, 1983).

rather he bends his Pharisaic exegesis to new ends.[16] Paul describes social groupings on the basis of scripture and of his previously learned methodology, which he never abandoned. But we would wish to question Segal's conclusion that his conversion experience turns scripture on its head and makes it come true in an ironic, unexpected way.[17]

One would not wish to argue against the thesis that Paul's perspective on the meaning of scripture has changed, reflecting the change from one community to another. But how new are the new assumptions about the meaning of scripture, which Paul does not so much argue as present? It is important not to exaggerate the new perspective that Paul brings to scripture. We are, of course, aware that Paul cannot possibly be regarded as presenting a phenomenological description of Torah (rather Paul's statements are the result of cognitive changes in a man who has experienced dissonance in a sharper way than most Christians).[18]

Segal himself insists that Paul's doctrines are not to be understood merely as opposition to midrash or to the LXX—a more complicated and more subtle dynamic is operating. He points out that, although no other Jews in the first century distinguish faith and law in the way Paul does, it is in fact Paul's experience as a Christian that encourages the reformulation of biblical promises. However, he is not talking about Torah in general in these places; he talks only about the use of Torah to define the basic community. Faith, not Torah observance, defines the Christian community.[19] But we should not take this to mean that Paul concludes the Torah is wrong or completely irrelevant; it signifies rather a fresh understanding of the place of Torah in the divine purpose. He now realizes that there are specific limits to the Torah's scope and perhaps too that there are temporal limits now that the Messiah has come.

The earliest Christians understood the scriptures both as Torah and, eschatologically, as prophecy of the fullness of time. In a striking example of *pesher* interpretation, Luke reports Jesus as saying in the synagogue at Nazareth, "this day is the scripture fulfilled in your ears." For Paul, as for many of his contemporaries, the interpretation of the scriptures becomes at the same time the medium of self-understanding and self-disclosure (not to say self-authorization). The earliest Christians could interpret only in the medium of their own day. Their self-understanding was not independent of history and tradition, as if by the invention of a new language, but within tradition and in the very language tradition made available in their texts. The Gospel texts

---

[16] Segal, *Paul the Convert,* 117.

[17] Ibid., 122–23.

[18] Ibid., 148; see also pp. 120–22.

[19] Ibid., 128.

(but Luke especially) picture Christ as an observant Jew who enters into tradition, understands himself in it.

In a certain way he understands himself in front of the scriptures, standing before them and answering to them and to a form of life that they project. The basic hermeneutical principle of *pesher* interpretation is that scripture makes sense not by opening inwardly to an intention that lies behind the text but by laying open (in front of itself or into its future) a possibility which the community takes upon itself to actualize or fulfill in terms of action, that is, in its forms or way of life.[20]

There can be no doubt that Paul stands in this *pesher* tradition. The scriptures open up to the immediate future and challenge Paul and his communities to live the life of the end-time, the coming aeon. If we exaggerate Paul's distance from Pharisaism or see him in continual opposition to it or to Torah in general, we fail to give adequate significance to the obvious fact that the apostle still lives very much in this world of *pesher* interpretation. It is not so much a world that he creates or one that is peculiar to him or his communities; it is rather part of a wider world that influences both him and other widely divergent groups.

Paul's interpretive activity is not purely an individual activity. However socially distinct from Judaism the Pauline communities may have been, it is quite clear that both the Qumran and the Pauline communities saw themselves as new covenantal congregations.[21] Paul goes to great lengths to show that those who have faith can also count themselves part of the covenant relationship with Abraham. Granted that Paul's perspective on the meaning of scripture has changed, reflecting the change from one community to another, it is no surprise that his emphasis as apostle to the Gentiles is on the entry requirements for the new covenantal community, in which the performance of the special laws of Judaism are not binding. His emphasis is necessarily different from that of Judaism, which naturally assumed a prior faith commitment and a prior act on God's part in justifying that never needs to be discussed.

But despite this radical difference, we must not lose sight of what was held in common. Paul's perspective is different; his communities are not synagogal communities. Nevertheless, the common goal of becoming God's covenantal congregation has real significance. There is an air of expectancy in Paul's converts; there is a new creation. But at least some of the framework of this expectation is taken over from and shared with Pharisaism. The fact that Paul

---

[20] See Gerald L. Bruns, "Midrash and Allegory: The Beginnings of Scriptural Interpretation," in *The Literary Guide to the Bible* (ed. R. Alter and F. Kermode; Cambridge, MA: Harvard University Press, 1987) 634–35.

[21] See Segal, *Paul the Convert*, 180.

and other Jews shared and took seriously the exegetical tradition of scriptural interpretation of their own day is a powerful and pervasive influence, the significance of which is difficult both to estimate and to exaggerate.

We may illustrate this with one example. Terence Donaldson, in a careful study of how Paul in Gal 3:13–14 argues for the inclusion of the Gentiles, comes to the conclusion that in these two verses Paul sees the cross as the eschatological redemption of Israel that sets the stage for the inclusion of the Gentiles. Donaldson suggests that there may be here a radical reinterpretation, in the light of the cross event, of a Jewish pattern of thought in which the inclusion of the Gentiles is seen as a consequence of the eschatological redemption of Israel. The fact that the same eschatological model of the relationship between Jew and Gentile in salvation history underlies both Gal 3:1–4:7 and Romans 11 raises the possibility that this aspect of Jewish tradition played a more important part in Paul's thought than has hitherto been recognized. As Donaldson notes, "while the revision is radical, it is nonetheless a revision."[22]

IV. THE INTERACTION
BETWEEN SCRIPTURAL INTERPRETATION
AND EVENTS OF EVERYDAY LIFE

There is no need to argue that scriptural interpretation never takes place in a vacuum; there is an obvious dialectical relationship between ideas and their social context. In stressing that scriptural interpretive tradition influenced Paul and his communities, we need to be more explicit as to how this actually took place. Paul was certainly no "ivory-tower" academic, and we need to be careful lest we adopt a too academic model. In Qumran we can see that the disciplined study of scripture did occupy a specific place in the life of the community. But one factor that was influential in Paul's interpretation may easily be overlooked—that is, the interaction between interpretation and events, whether internal or external to the community, that impinged in some way on their daily life.

We could argue that the Pauline communities, like other similar groups, saw what they expected to see and filtered out what did not suit their theoretical view of the world and its operation. But their own experience of events in the daily life of the community could not easily be ignored. The practice was here, to some extent at least, the mother of the theory, and interpretation had

[22] T. L. Donaldson, "The 'Curse of the Law' and the Inclusion of the Gentiles; Galatians 3. 13–14," *NTS* 32 (1986) 106.

to provide an explanation of events in order to make sense of their experience. However, the fact that the Spirit was seen as leading and directing the life of the community underlined the need for this and ensured its recognition as a theological activity. In the tradition of the prophets, the events of political life also required interpretation to explain God's ways with His people.

We see this, then, as a two-way process. The interpretive framework of these communities helped them to make sense of contemporary events. But there was genuine interaction, especially in relation to events within the life of the community, and these events in turn were active in giving direction about the meaning of scripture. It was not simply that one text directly influenced in a literary way the interpretation of another text somehow associated with it. It was rather that the texts themselves were interpreted by living communities, and what was happening to these people in their daily life was a powerful influence in their interaction with the text.

What we have here, then, is not a static formulation of accepted propositions. It is rather a living scriptural tradition that gives meaning to, and receives meaning from, events in the daily life of the community. Because the group perceives itself, as it were, in transit, traveling onward to its destined goal of transformation into the image of Christ, its interpretation can never remain static. The interpretation is not fixed by its past, but its real meaning is discovered in the living dynamic of the Spirit at work in an ever-new and ever-changing present.

If this argument carries conviction, it would help to explain why Paul, as Professor Roetzel has clearly indicated, feels little compulsion to repeat previously stated formulas in any coherent systematic way.[23]

V. NEW AND OLD IN PAUL'S THEOLOGY

Depending on which aspects one emphasizes, it is possible to paint two contradictory pictures of Paul's theological statements. One can see him as a radical innovator who emphasizes the new creation, someone with little concern for the motifs or traditions of Judaism. On the other hand, these are sufficient Jewish elements in his writings for some to insist that he is a devout Jew for whom Jesus Messiah is the completion of his faith.[24]

We will not resolve this issue simply by noting the frequency of certain

---

[23] Roetzel, "The Grammar of Election" (chapter 11 in this volume).

[24] W. D. Davies speaks of "a covenantal nomism in Christ," which also incorporates Gentile believers. See the new preface to the fourth edition of *Paul and Rabbinic Judaism* (Philadelphia: Fortress, 1985) 30–31, in which Davies responds to criticisims of his views by E. P. Sanders in *Paul and Palestinian Judaism* (Philadelphia: Fortress, 1977) 422, 478–79.

motifs, however valuable this may be. Wider and more basic issues need to be considered. The first of these is how we should regard Paul's "conversion" experience. We have already outlined our views in this matter, but it will be instructive to look also at John Gager's contribution. He sees Paul's "conversion" as that type of conversion in which the fundamental system of values and commitments is preserved intact "but it is turned upside down, reversed and transvalued." "For Paul, the religious target remains the same but whereas the law had been the chosen path to the goal, and Christ the rejected one, beforehand, their order is reversed after the event."[25]

This is a perfectly appropriate model and useful in some respects, but it also has certain limitations. I am concerned at the use that may be made of the stark "reversal of values." Thinking of this kind may tend to support the view that Christ stands in absolute opposition to Judaism (since *nomos* is the law of the Jewish people and not simply an abstract concept).[26]

I prefer a paradigm that suggests a reorganization in one's priorities rather than a stark reversal. The latter view is too blunt an instrument to describe the complexity of the apostle's thinking. The primacy of Paul's experience has recently been given more significance. Associated with this is the attempt to relate experience to basic convictions that are so powerful they may even lead their exponents into contradictory arguments in order to support them.[27]

Räisänen sees some merit in Patte's fundamental distinction between "convictions" and ideas. Räisänen believes that the crucial line of demarcation should be drawn not between "convictions" and "ideas" (which cannot be neatly separated) but between experiences and their interpretations. Interpretations resulting from experience include a whole spectrum of ad hoc ideas that never

---

[25] John G. Gager, "Some Notes on Paul's Conversion," *NTS* 27 (1981) 700. For a good discussion of the issues at stake here, see B. Gaventa, *From Darkness to Light: Aspects of Conversion in the New Testament* (OBT 20; Philadelphia: Fortress, 1986) 36–40. See also H. Räisänen, "Paul's Conversion and the Development of His View of the Law," *NTS* 33 (1987) 404–19; and J. D. G. Dunn, "'A Light to the Gentiles' or 'The End of the Law'? The Significance of the Damascus Road Christophany for Paul," now in *Jesus, Paul and the Law* (Philadelphia: Westminster, 1990) 89–107.

[26] T. L. Donaldson points out that we all too readily see *nomos* as an abstract concept, hanging in the air and (especially) disconnected from the people who found their identity in it, whereas for Paul this was not possible—"a statement about the law was at the same time a statement about *hoi hupo nomou* or *hoi en to nomo*" ("Curse of the Law," 102). See also B. Gaventa's comment: "In Galatians, the historical locus of the Christ-event means that Christ is not some eternal aeon that exists in contrast to the realm of the flesh. Neither does Paul interpret Christ and the law as ontological opposites" ("The Singularity of the Gospel: A Reading of Galatians," in *Pauline Theology I*, 158.

[27] For the concept of a distinction between Paul's reasons (or fundamental convictions) and his arguments, and the idea that his arguments be seen as attempts to work out problems raised by conflicting convictions, see E. P. Sanders, *Paul, the Law, and the Jewish People* (Philadelphia: Fortress, 1983) 4, 144–48.

reappear in the person's writings. He continues: "instead of dividing Paul's thoughts into two different groups, one might wish to establish a hierarchy ranging from the all-important to the casual."[28]

It seems to me that Paul did experience a cognitive shift, but it meant a reordering of his ideas into a new hierarchy. This seems a much better model than that of reversal/inversion. What is also important is that the process of reordering can be seen as an ongoing one (to some extent), and this allows room for development in Paul's thought such as Professor Roetzel has indicated.[29] This model allows for sharing of traditions, for some commonality across group boundaries (though common motifs might not take on the same role in different communities). It allows for a much more fluid situation among religious groups impinging on one another.

Professor Roetzel's study of Paul's grammar of election found Paul's thinking in his letters to be very fluid indeed. In 1 Thessalonians, Roetzel notes that, in spite of Jewish apocalyptic and martyrological traditions, Paul nowhere in this letter seeks to associate either divine election or the status and behavior of the elect with God's election of the Jewish people. But Paul in this letter does tie election and holiness intimately together. In doing this, he not only uses Old Testament themes but also maintains the normal Old Testament link between the two. What is lacking, however, is any explicit connection between election and the Pauline Gentile community.

In Philippians, even though "no explicit reference to election appears," Roetzel finds that a vocabulary of election does appear nevertheless in metaphors, synonyms, and symbolic language drawn from Jewish traditions.[30] In Corinthians, he observes, Paul uses the word καλέω ("call") no fewer than nine times in the space of eight verses. The divine choice is also shown to reverse the normal human hierarchical order, thus preventing believers from linking their identity to social or religious status. He concludes: "Paul secures the identity of the Corinthians in the call of God rather than in an order established by circumcision or uncircumcision, slavery or freedom, marriage or celibacy."[31]

---

[28] H. Räisänen, *Beyond New Testament Theology*, 134–35, 198–99; and Daniel Patte, *Paul's Faith and the Power of the Gospel: A Structural Introduction to the Pauline Letters* (Philadelphia: Fortress, 1983) 268–69.

[29] See C. J. Roetzel, "Grammar of Election," 219. In an appendix entitled "Psychological Study of Paul's Conversion," Alan Segal writes:

> The most recent data on religious defection and disaffiliation shows how complex and individual the process of religious change can be. . . . The most important conclusion from these studies is to note all the kinds of interactions in values that an actively questing subject can provide. Thus, while Paul's conversion brought a high degree of commitment to his Christian group, and a disaffiliation from Pharisaism, he may still have valued his Jewish identity. . . . (*Paul the Convert,* 299)

[30] Roetzel, "Grammar of Election," 220–22.

[31] Ibid., 232–33.

It is Paul's use of the cross in Galatians to support the inclusion in the elect of Gentiles qua Gentiles that Roetzel finds most instructive.

> By noticing how Paul's Galatian cross symbolism differs markedly at points from cross symbolism in 1 Corinthians, Philippians, and 1 Thessalonians, we can see how our attempt to find what is foundational in Paul's theology is risky. For if the cross is at the core of Paul's theology, as many argue, it is simply inadequate to say the cross is foundational without noting the way the interpretation of the cross is changed by its context and then bends back onto the context to shape that as well. This dialectical relationship of symbol and setting is fundamentally unstable and resists our tendency to find a resolution in Paul's theology that has a "totalizing impact."[32]

Roetzel concludes that "Paul did not come to his context culturally naked. Paul's grammar of election emerged in part from the language of the church about God, sin, Jesus Christ . . . and in part from the venerable traditions of Israel."[33]

To describe Paul's grammar of election as a combination of church traditions and traditions concerning Israel is, we believe, a correct and useful assessment of the evidence. Professor Roetzel has clearly indicated the variability in Paul's theologizing and particularly how his theology develops en route. We acknowledge the validity of the latter conclusion, but feel that he underestimates the significance of Paul's inherited traditions.

VI. THE SHAPE OF PAUL'S THEOLOGY

To describe all or part of the origins of Paul's language of discourse is not sufficient. It is in the end not so much origins as usage that is unique to Paul. It is the peculiar combinations and transformations of language that are typical of the apostle. In this respect Roetzel's emphasis on a grammar of election is most apt. But if the language usage is so fluid and flexible, what, if anything, is constant in Paul? What is it, in fact, that determines how Paul uses his language?

Two candidates present themselves; we might describe these as (1) the singularity of the gospel and (2) the unity and upbuilding of the community.[34] It would appear that all use of symbols, all theological constructions had for Paul no ultimacy or abiding significance as formulations in and of themselves.

---

[32] Ibid., 228.

[33] Ibid., 233.

[34] See John H. Schütz, *Paul and the Anatomy of Apostolic Authority* (SNTSMS 26; Cambridge: Cambridge University Press, 1975) 154–55, 243–44, 281–82; and Gaventa, "The Singularity of the Gospel," 153–54.

Rather, the purpose they served was to ensure absolute obedience to the gospel and the ultimate unity and well-being of the believing community. What served these ends was useful and beneficial, and what hindered them was to be opposed or discarded. So Paul's language of discourse is as flexible as the varied situation of his communities demands; it is only an instrument of a greater good. As we have already noted, Paul believed himself to be living in the end-time, already begun with Jesus' resurrection. He did not expect things to remain static or constant; he expected new things. Thus, all our concern for creedal statements retaining their ancient meaning and constancy would have been lost on Paul. He lived at a time before Christian doctrines had had time to harden into fixed formulations, and he does not appear to share our concern that he should repeat again in identical form his earlier pronouncements.[35]

From a sociological perspective, it is indeed a blessing that Paul repeats himself as little as he actually does. The appearance of apparently similar arguments about justification by faith in Galatians and in Romans has often obscured the particularity of both these letters and the fact that the repetition of the same doctrine in a different context does not warrant the view that its function is identical in each instance.[36]

On the other hand, Paul is, as Professor Beker has emphasized, essentially a hermeneutic theologian — an interpreter whose thought is delimited by the tradition in which he stands and which he interprets. Our study of the scriptural interpretive tradition which Paul inherited and shared supports this emphasis.[37] As we noted, there was an expectancy to discover new things in the vital interaction between scripture and the everyday life of the community — the community lived in the scriptures and the scriptures lived in them! But their interpretation remains in some sense still bound to the (original) text,

[35] See also Schütz's comment on the topic "another gospel" in Galatians: "The problem is all the more difficult when we remember that there is virtually no evidence that Paul regards 'gospel' as coterminous with a body of information or propositions (*Paul and the Anatomy of Apostolic Authority*, 119).

[36] N. A. Dahl notes that "Paul does not present the doctrine of justification as a dogmatic abstraction" ("The Doctrine of Justification and its Implications," in *Studies in Paul* [Minneapolis: Augsburg, 1977] 115); see also my study, *Paul's Gospel in an Intercultural Context: Jew and Gentile in the Letter to the Romans* (Frankfurt: Peter Lang, 1991) 106–7; and H. C. Kee, *Knowing the Truth: A Sociological Approach to New Testament Interpretation* (Philadelphia: Fortress, 1989) 24.

[37] While being in general agreement with Beker's thesis that Paul is essentially an interpreter of the gospel, I would also stress that Paul is more than simply an interpreter of traditions: Paul interprets the gospel in the context of his daily mission work. That is, the subject matter of Paul's interpretive activity is not limited to traditions but includes the interpretation of divine activity in the course of his apostolic work. (I refer here to Beker's article "Paul the Theologian: Major Motifs in Pauline Theology," *Int* 43 (1989) 353.

although "the occasion that prompts it may be external to it, some kind of crisis that is historical and theological."[38]

It is the scriptures that provide such a powerful and meaningful link between Paul and his Jewish heritage.[39] But it is the apocalyptic worldview in which the scriptures are interpreted that sustains and heightens the expectancy for new things.[40] As Räisänen notes, it is "the dialectical interaction between tradition (symbolic universe), experience and [its] interpretation that governs the way in which the world is perceived and interpreted by groups and individuals."[41] Thus, this relation to, and understanding of, the scriptures interpreted in the light of the Christ-event operates in some respects at least as "a foundational story about what God has done to bring salvation to his elect people."[42] A further example of an underlying foundational story is identified by Jouette Bassler in a summary of the convictions that seem to undergird 1 Thessalonians: God through the Holy Spirit is working through Paul and in the church which God has called. This call is not only a call of election, but also a call to community and holiness.[43] She rightly concludes that, however interesting the kerygmatic story is in and for itself, it became important to Paul and his churches because it was their story. "By God's election they had been grafted into it, and their sense of being a part of this story of God's presence with God's people is the only reason for remembering the story and writing to the churches."[44]

Professor Roetzel has not found it permissible to regard election and calling as key propositional statements or even as foundational expressions in Paul.[45] Nevertheless, the presence and use of election calling convictions still

---

[38] See Marie Sabin, "Reading Mark 4 as Midrash," *JSNT* 45 (1992) 6. The failure of Israel to respond positively to the Gospel, the success of the mission to the Gentiles, and the fall of Jerusalem are obvious examples of such times of crisis.

[39] Writing about Galatians, B. Gaventa states, "Paul constantly uses biblical interpretation and imagery, not only in response to his opponents' claims about the law but in reference to his own apostolic role (1:15). This absorption in scripture indicates that the gospel's invasion does not negate the place of Israel" ("The Singularity of the Gospel," 159).

[40] There is some diversity still in the definition of "apocalyptic." We have concentrated here on the attitude of mind, rather than on the actual content of an apocalyptic outlook. On this, see Christopher Rowland, *The Open Heaven: A Study of Apocalyptic in Judaism and Early Christianity* (New York: Crossroad, 1983) 20: see also Richard E. Sturm, "Defining the Word 'Apocalyptic': A Problem in Biblical Criticism," in *Apocalyptic and the New Testament: Essays in Honour of J. Louis Martyn* (ed. Joel Marcus and Marion L. Soards; Sheffield: JSOT Press, 1989) 39–40. See also Martinus C. de Boer, "Paul and Jewish Apocalyptic Theology," in the same volume, 180–81.

[41] Räisänen, *Beyond New Testament Theology*, 131.

[42] See R. B. Hays, "Crucified with Christ: A Synthesis of the Theology of 1 and 2 Thessalonians, Philemon, Philippians, and Galatians," included in *Pauline Theology I*, 231–32.

[43] Jouette M. Bassler, "Paul's Theology: Whence and Whither?" (chapter 1 in this volume) 14.

[44] Ibid., 16.

[45] Roetzel, "Grammar of Election," 214, 233.

carries some significance. Thus, one way to account for Paul's continuing use of scripture, of election terminology, people of God motifs, and so on (however sparse this use may be in some instances) is to maintain that the apostle sees himself and his work as part of an ongoing activity of God in which the Spirit is ever leading into new paths and new experiences. For Paul it is presupposed that God is at work in Christian proclamation and witness and in the emerging communities of believers. The work inaugurated in the resurrection of Christ is being continually demonstrated and carried forward in the power of the Spirit.

To a great extent, this "story" is implicit in Paul; it does not need to be argued because the Spirit's presence is proof itself of God at work; but sometimes we get glimpses of it in elements of covenantal language. The issue remains as to how to evaluate the significance of those elements in Pauline statements that often have little or no explicit connection with the traditional language of first-century Judaism.

Richard Hays, in his study of five letters in the Pauline corpus, has drawn attention to the surprising frequency of the theme of God's calling. He suggests that the background of this imagery is to be found in Deutero-Isaiah, where there are repeated references to God's calling of the Servant/Israel. Hays argues:

> If one hears such echoes in Paul's use of *kalein,* the close association of the "calling" imagery with the idea of Israel as a covenant people becomes more evident. Just as God called the Servant/Israel by gathering them from the corners of the earth so that they might be "a covenant to the people, a light to the nations," so God now calls the "Israel of God" (= the church) for a similar reason, so that the gospel might be proclaimed.[46]

What we find in Paul is that the apostle has creatively appropriated scriptural imagery in his understanding of believers in Christ. However vague the allusions, or however flexible the terminology, it is arguable that Paul sees the believing community as somehow a continuation of a covenantal people.[47]

---

[46] Hays, "Crucified with Christ," 238. Hays is careful to note that Paul never speaks of the church as the "new Israel," as though the old one had been supplanted. "Rather, believers in Jesus simply are Israel" (p. 238 n. 25).

[47] I use "covenantal" here in a very general sense. I do not mean to refer to a specific system of theology (we have already demonstrated Paul's "apocalyptic" freedom in creating new theological approaches). Paul's use of election and calling terminology is difficult to evaluate precisely, but the presence of this terminology in his letters is sufficient to merit the description "covenantal" in this limited sense. R. D. Kaylor argues that "covenant as conviction rather than concept functions as a persistent presence and a dominant reality in Paul's life, work and thought. . . . Covenant was one of the primary but unconsciously worn lenses through which Paul perceived himself and his world" (*Paul's Covenant Community: Jew and Gentile in Romans* [Atlanta: John Knox, 1988] 2–3).

Just as God was working out his purpose in history through Israel, so now God is active in a special way in believers in Christ.

For Paul it would appear that God's activity through the Spirit is concentrated in the Christian community in that God is, at the moment,[48] working out his purpose in and through them. Perhaps this is because they especially represent the new thing that God is doing in the world: it is not that the rest of the world is outside the rule of God entirely; rather God has chosen to work in and through the believing community to bring the rest of creation back to his control.

The basis for this is probably to be found in Paul's understanding of the revelation of the divine righteousness. Paul saw the resurrection of Jesus as a source of power which is released through the gospel and thus activated among believers. He sometimes equates grace and power (e.g., 2 Cor 1:12; 12:10; 1 Cor 15:10). Since grace is the sphere in which all Christians exist (Gal 5:4), the territory of the divine deed's sway, any apostasy is a departure from power, a moving away from one's standing in the gospel.[49]

The gospel is the power of God that leads to salvation, and Paul himself has experienced that power in his own life. Yet he himself as apostle is subordinate to the gospel norm. The power is not Paul's power; he can only make it available since he himself does not provide or control it. It is nevertheless closely associated with the gospel. As Schütz observes, "all of this makes sense only where power and the gospel are thought of within the milieu of a history moving to fulfilment, where there is still a frontier to cross, a *telos* yet to arrive. The final judgement is the final and unmistakable manifestation of power."[50] Paul's ambition, therefore, despite his concentration on his believing communities, is not to subject others to his authority but to subject all, including himself, to the power which manifests itself in the gospel and which will be manifest in the eschaton.

It seems legitimate to conclude that Paul's theologizing takes place within the specific context of ongoing divine activity in relation to a people who are called. Within this context, which includes the scriptural imagery and traditions relating to Israel, Paul felt free to theologize as the Spirit led—apparently with a great degree of freedom. On the other hand, the outcome of the divine activity, which is his basic theme, is not entirely open-ended. Covenant faith

---

[48] See E. Krentz, "Tracking the Elusive Center: On Integrating Paul's Theology" (seminar paper presented at the 1990 SBL meeting, New Orleans) 23. On God's activity in the world, see Owen C. Thomas, "Recent Thought on Divine Agency" and Rodger Forsman, "Double Agency and Identifying Reference to God," in *Divine Action: Studies Inspired by the Philosophical Theology of Austin Farrer* (ed. Brian Hebbelthwaite and Edward Henderson; Edinburgh: T. & T. Clark, 1990) 35–50, 123–42.

[49] See Schütz, *Paul and the Anatomy of Apostolic Authority,* 116–17.

[50] Ibid., 285–86.

saw God's purpose as having a destined goal. The divine purpose will lead to a final transformation and consummation. As Dunn writes (in a different context) "the outworking of God's saving power will be consistent with its initial expression."[51]

Within this purpose and in pursuit of this goal, Paul works with a great sense of freedom, but it is not an absolute freedom; and to some extent the content of his theology is also fixed. It is about the purpose of God revealed in Christ, about the people of God, and about the apostle's commission to work toward the achievement of that divine purpose in the lives of his converts.

VII. CONCLUSION

In this paper I have sought to take Daniel Patte's advice not to interpret Paul from "a history of ideas" approach.[52] Hence I have sought to pay due regard to the interaction between tradition and experience of events in daily life — to show how the scriptures and Paul's daily life interact with and reciprocally interpret each other.I have sought to avoid a too-academic model lest Paul be portrayed simply as an interpreter of texts.

Attention has been focused also on Paul's apocalyptic outlook. Our thesis is that to view Paul as an apocalyptic is not to maintain that he adhered to a particular set of doctrines. It is rather a "mind-set," an expectancy that God is doing or is about to do new things. It is to view apocalyptic categories as the justification for the innovative in Paul's mission as a whole.[53] Thus, the Spirit is always revealing new truths and thereby transforming the tradition of the past; so, in effect, the scriptures themselves relate not to the ancient past but to the immediate present and its future. Paul, in contrast to his interpreters, is not interested in the past as such, nor even in a narrative of the past involving promise and election — nor even in a past Christ-event. For the apostle, continuity and consistency in God's relation with his people are presupposed, and in his earlier letters he does not even seem to be aware of any need to be explicit about this. We have concluded, therefore, that Professor Roetzel's study has correctly demonstrated Paul's freedom and flexibility of discourse in addressing his communities.

But we wish to insist that all of Paul's thinking takes place in the very specific context of God's purpose for his "called" people. Thus despite his radical

---

[51] J. D. G. Dunn, "The Theology of Galatians," in *Jesus, Paul and the Law*, 242.

[52] Patte, *Paul's Faith and the Power of the Gospel*, 11.

[53] See Wayne A. Meeks, *The First Urban Christians: The Social World of the Apostle Paul* (New Haven and London: Yale University Press, 1983) 117, 175.

theologizing, there are elements both old and new in his thought. We argued in section II that Paul, the convert, was dependent on Jewish cultural traditions in which and with which to interpret himself and his experience. Following the thesis of Alan Segal, we came to see the apostle's life as a prime example of how mysticism and apocalypticism could be united phenomenologically.

The combination in one person of these influences requires us to deal seriously with the whole of Paul, his mystical experience, his mission activity, his authority and pastoral care, not just his theological ideas. But the recognition of Paul's indebtedness to his cultural heritage also requires that it be not lightly dismissed or regarded merely as a foil for a contrary life-style. We refused to follow the route that seeks to explain all Paul's theology as emanating directly from his Damascus road experience.

We could have insisted that Paul received all his theology, implicitly at least, in his conversion. But this would be to deny the influence of his Pharisaic past and of Antiochene Christianity. If we stress only the radical newness of Paul's experience, we make him too much a Melchizedek figure without historical antecedent — and thereby render him inexplicable in either social or historical terms by cutting him off from his cultural and religious past.[54]

We have also rejected explanations of Paul's thought that posit a strong antithesis between Paul's Jewish past — for example, his former view of the law — and his adherence to Christ. Instead of radical reversal, we preferred to think of his conversion in terms of a cognitive shift in which a new hierarchy of values was established. We sought thereby to avoid a hermeneutic of antithesis with Judaism.[55]

We also sought to stress the dynamic and dialectical nature of Paul's thought. Some otherwise excellent publications on Paul present a wooden image of the apostle that is only a pale reflection of the living dynamic person, one who could not possibly achieve the eminence we know he did.[56] We are very much aware of the complexity of the apostle's life and thought and how difficult it is to understand him without a certain degree of anachronism; we too readily make Paul one of us in anticipating that he will share our interest in carefully formulated propositions or abstract theoretical concepts.

---

[54] See Dunn, "A Light to the Gentiles," 105–6.

[55] See Lloyd Gaston, "Retrospect," in *Anti-Judaism in Early Christianity: Volume 2, Separation and Polemic* (ed. S. G. Wilson; Waterloo, Ont.: Wilfrid Laurier University Press, 1986) 163–64.

[56] Perhaps it would be fairer to acknowledge here that most books concentrate only on certain aspects of Paul's work or thought. The result is that when scholars treat a topic such as "the law in Paul," one cannot escape the suspicion that this kind of abstract discussion inevitably distorts the image of the person under investigation. I am not sure that even Stephen Westerholm's useful study *Israel's Law and the Church's Faith: Paul and His Recent Interpreters* (Grand Rapids: Eerdmans, 1988) can be completely exonerated from this criticism.

Central to Paul's concern were obedience to the gospel and the unity of his communities. What promoted this concern determined the content of his pastoral writings. Because the apostle lived in a vital tradition of scriptural interpretation, he used the imagery of scripture, especially that relating to God's call of Israel, as a central theme in his letters. Though he used this scriptural tradition freely and loosely, it did provide a framework for the apostle's diverse theological activity.

We have come to the conclusion, therefore, that if we look for firm propositions or for repetition in a fixed form of major doctrinal statements, we have the wrong presuppositions. Nor should we be disappointed that the "dialectical relationship of symbol and setting is fundamentally unstable and resists our tendency to find a resolution in Paul's theology that has a 'totalizing' impact."[57]

If we set out to find propositional or foundational statements and failed to do so, this factor ought not to cause us to undervalue what we have found just because it is rather different from what might have been anticipated. Even the evaluation of Paul's theology as being in a formative state needs to be treated with a degree of suspicion. It is possible that if Paul had lived longer his theology would have continued to show this same quality; in fact, he might even have been proud of it. Accordingly, Beker insists that "the fluid boundaries between convictions and contingency belong to the essence of Paul's hermeneutic."[58]

Paul's theologizing takes place in a context of interaction with scripture and the everyday life of his communities. It is an inner-scriptural, intertextual type of thinking,[59] a world full of images and metaphors that can be used and re-used in differing settings. As already noted, it is not a world of propositional truths, of abstract theorizing, or even of precise concepts.

It was the peculiarity of Paul's cultural inheritance that contributed largely to this thought world. The twin elements of continuity of scriptural tradition, tending toward conserving the insights of the past, and of an apocalyptic-mystical outlook, tending toward creative and imaginative new perspectives, might actually be regarded as contradictory. But in Paul's creative mind, under the unifying impulse of his vision of Christ, a complex web of ideas was drawn together. This combination of apocalyptic and mystical in fact offered Paul the freedom to innovate. Moreover, the metaphorical imagery provided a creative and flexible language amenable to fresh combinations and associations

---

[57] Roetzel, "Grammar of Election," 228.

[58] Beker, "Paul the Theologian: Major Motifs in Pauline Theology," 353.

[59] For Paul's indebtedness to scripture generally and for the most recent discussion of this aspect of his thought, see R. B. Hays, *Echoes of Scripture in the Letters of Paul* (New Haven and London: Yale University Press, 1989) esp. 154–55.

ideal for the volatile early days of a new movement. For a group oriented to the present and future, this symbolic language was also essential in order for it to be able to develop its own vision.

What we wish to stress here is that it was Paul's cultural inheritance that provided him with a tradition in which creative freedom was valued and visibly present. His creative freedom was already inculcated in his religious up-bringing. This tradition gave Paul the language for expressing a theophany, and his vision of Christ provided a new point of departure within a traditional web of ideas.

Those scholars who have insisted that Paul is no systematic theologian are perfectly correct. We misunderstand his theological method when we abstract his statements and lay them side by side to check for contradictions. It is also probably wrong to look for any one key or central element to elucidate Paul's theology. It is a body of tradition rather than a system of theology with which Paul interacts. But if the creative reformulating and transforming of inherited images and metaphors are what constitutes doing theology, then Paul is certainly a theologian par excellence.

BIBLIOGRAPHIES

1 Corinthians
Compiled by Gordon D. Fee

Agrimson, J. Elmo, ed. *Gifts of the Spirit and the Body of Christ.* Minneapolis: Augsburg, 1974.

Ahern, B. M. "Christian's Union with the Body of Christ in Cor, Gal, and Rom." *CBQ* 23 (1961) 199–209.

Allo, E.-B. *Premiere Epître aux Corinthiens.* EBib. Paris: Gabalda, 1934.

——. "La Synthese du dogme eucharistique chez saint Paul." *RB* 18 (1921) 321–43.

Andrews, H. T. "The Place of the Sacraments in the Teaching of St. Paul." *Exp* 1:12 (1916) 353–72.

Arrington, French L. *Paul's Aeon Theology in 1 Corinthians.* Washington: University Press of America, 1978.

Audet, L. "L'organisation des communautés chrétiennes selon les grandes épîtres pauliniennes." *SR* 2 (1972) 235–50.

Aune, David E. *Prophecy in Early Christianity and the Ancient Mediterranean World.* Grand Rapids: Eerdmans, 1983.

Bachmann, Philipp. *Der erste Brief des Paulus an die Korinther.* Additions by Ethelbert Stauffer. KNT. Leipzig and Erlangen: Deichert, 1936.

Badke, William B. "Baptised into Moses—baptised into Christ: A Study in Doctrinal Development." *EvQ* 60 (1988) 23–29.

Baird, William. "Among the Mature—The Idea of Wisdom in 1 Corinthians 2.6." *Int* 13 (1959) 425–32.

——. "'One Against the Other': Intra-Church Conflict in 1 Corinthians." In *The Conversation Continues: Studies in Paul and John in Honor of J. Louis Martyn,* edited by R. T. Fortna and B. R. Gaventa, 116–36. Nashville: Abingdon, 1990.

Baker, David L. "The Interpretation of 1 Cor 12–14." *EvQ* 46 (1974) 224–34.

Balch, David L. "Backgrounds of I Cor. VII: Sayings of the Lord in Q; Moses as an Ascetic ΘΕΙΟΣ ANHP in II Cor. III." *NTS* 18 (1972) 351–64.

——. "1 Cor 7:32–35 and Stoic Debates about Marriage, Anxiety, and Distraction." *JBL* 102 (1983) 429–39.

Banks, Robert. *Paul's Idea of Community: The Early House Churches in Their Historical Setting.* Grand Rapids: Eerdmans, 1980.

255

———, and G. Moon. "Speaking in Tongues: A Survey of the New Testament Evidence." *Churchman* 80 (1966) 278–94.

Barbour, Robin S. "Wisdom and the Cross in 1 Cor 1–2." In *Theologia Crucis—Signum Crucis: Festschrift für Erich Dinkler zum 70 Geburtstag,* edited by C. Andresen and G. Klein, 57–71. Tübingen: Mohr (Siebeck), 1979.

Barefoot, H. E. "Discipline in the Corinthian Letter." *RevExp* 57 (1960) 438–49.

Barré, M. L. "Qumran and the 'Weakness' of Paul." *CBQ* 42 (1980) 216–27.

Barrett, C. K. "Cephas and Corinth." In *Abraham unser Vater: Festschrift für Otto Michel,* edited by O. Betz, M. Hengel, and P. Schmidt, 1–12. ABSU 5. Leiden: Brill, 1963.

———. "Christianity at Corinth." *BJRL* 46 (1964) 269–97.

———. *The First Epistle to the Corinthians.* HNTC. New York: Harper & Row, 1968.

———. *From First Adam to Last.* New York: Scribner's, 1962.

———. "Things Sacrificed to Idols." *NTS* 11 (1965) 138–53.

Bartchy, S. Scott. ΜΑΛΛΟΝ ΧΡΗΣΑΙ: First-century Slavery and the Interpretation of 1 Corinthians 7:21. SBLDS 11. Missoula, MT: Scholars Press, 1973.

———. "Table Fellowship with Jesus and the 'Lord's Meal' at Corinth." In *Increase in Learning: Essays in Honor of James G. Van Buren,* edited by R. J. Owens and B. Hamm, 45–61. Manhattan, KS: Christian College, 1979.

Barth, Karl. *The Resurrection of the Dead.* New York: Revell, 1933.

Barth, Markus. "A Chapter on the Church—the Body of Christ: Interpretation of I Corinthians 12." *Int* 12 (1958) 131–56.

Barton, Stephen C. "Paul's Sense of Place: An Anthropological Approach to Community Formation in Corinth." *NTS* 32 (1986) 235–46.

Bartsch, H. W. *Der korinthische Missbrauch des Abendmahls: Entmythologisierende Auslegung.* TF 26. Hamburg-Bergstedt: H. Reich, 1962.

Batey, R. "Paul's Interaction with the Corinthians." *NTS* 12 (1965) 56–69.

Baumann, R. *Mitte und Norm des Christlichen: Eine Auslegung von 1 Kor. 1.1–3.4.* Münster: Aschendorff, 1968.

Baur, F. C. "Die Christuspartei in der korinthischen Gemeinde: Der Gegensatz des petrinischen und paulinischen Christentums in der alten Kirche." *Tübingen Zeitschrift für Theologie* (1831) 61–136.

Beare, F. W. "Speaking with Tongues." *JBL* 83 (1964) 229–46.

Beasley-Murray, George R. *Baptism in the New Testament.* Grand Rapids: Eerdmans, 1962.

Best, Ernest. "The Interpretation of Tongues." *SJT* 28 (1975) 45–62.

———. *One Body in Christ.* London: SPCK, 1955.

———. "Prophets and Preachers." *SJT* 12 (1959) 129–50.

Bittlinger, A. *Gifts and Graces: A Commentary on 1 Corinthians 12–14.* Grand Rapids: Eerdmans, 1967.

Boers, H. W. "Apocalyptic Eschatology in I Corinthians 15: An Essay in Contemporary Interpretation." *Int* 21 (1967) 50–65.

Boismard, M.-É. "L'Eucharistie selon Saint Paul." *Lumen Vitae* 31 (1957) 93–106.

Bornkamm, G. "Lord's Supper and Church in Paul." In *Early Christian Experience,* 121–60. New York: Harper & Row, 1969.

Borchert, Gerald L. "The Resurrection: 1 Corinthians 15." *RevExp* 80 (1983) 401–15.

Boucher, Madeleine. "Some Unexplored Parallels to 1 Cor. 11,11–12 and Gal. 3,28: The New Testament on the Role of Women." *CBQ* 31 (1969) 50–58.

Bourke, Myles M. "The Eucharist and Wisdom in First Corinthians." In *Studiorum Paulinorum Congressus Internationalis Catholicus,* 367–81. AnBib 17, 18. Rome: Pontifical Biblical Institute, 1961.

———. "Reflections on Church Order in the New Testament." *CBQ* 30 (1968) 493–511.

Bousset, Wilhelm. *Die Hauptprobleme der Gnosis.* FRLANT 10. Göttingen: Vandenhoeck & Ruprecht, 1907.

Boyd, Donald G. "Spirit and Church in I Corinthians 12–14 and the Acts of the Apostles." In *Spirit Within Structure: Studies in Honor of George Johnston,* edited by E. J. Furcha, 55–66. Allison Park: Pickwick, 1983.

Brandenburger, Egon. *Adam und Christus.* WMANT 7. Neukirchen-Vluyn: Neukirchener Verlag, 1962.

Brockhaus, Ulrich. *Charisma und Amt: Die Paulinische Charismenlehre auf dem Hintergrund der frühchristlichen Gemeindefunktionen.* 2d ed. Wuppertal: Theologischer Verlag Rolf Brockhaus, 1972.

Brown, Raymond E. *The Semitic Background of the Term "Mystery" in the New Testament.* Facet Books, Biblical Series 21. Philadelphia: Fortress, 1968.

Bruce, F. F. *1 and 2 Corinthians.* NCB. Grand Rapids: Eerdmans, 1971.

Brunt, John C. "Love, Freedom, and Moral Responsibility: The Contribution of 1 Cor. 8–10 to an understanding of Paul's Ethical Thinking." In *Society of Biblical Literature 1981 Seminar Papers,* edited by K. H. Richards, 19–33. Chico, CA: Scholars Press, 1981.

Budillon, J. "La première épître aux Corinthiens et la controverse sur les ministères." *Istina* 16 (1971) 471–88.

Byrne, Brendan. "Eschatologies of Resurrection and Destruction: The Ethical Significance of Paul's Dispute with the Corinthians." *Downside Review* 104 (1986) 288–98.

———. "Ministry and Maturity in 1 Corinthians 3." *ABR* 35 (1987) 83–87.

Caird, G. B. "Everything to Everyone: The Theology of the Corinthian Epistles." *Int* 13 (1959) 387–99.

Callan, Terrance. "Prophecy and Ecstasy in Greco-Roman Religion and in 1 Corinthians." *NovT* 27 (1985) 125–40.

Calvin, John. *The First Epistle of Paul the Apostle to the Corinthians,* edited by D. W. Torrance and T. F. Torrance. Grand Rapids: Eerdmans, 1960.

Carrez, M. *Paul et l'Eglise de Corinthe.* Paris: Desclée, 1977.

Carson, D. A. "Pauline Inconsistency: Reflections on 1 Corinthians 9.19–23 and Galatians 2.11–14." *Churchman* 100 (1986) 6–45.

———. *Showing the Spirit: A Theological Exposition of 1 Corinthians 12–14.* Grand Rapids: Baker, 1987.

Cartlidge, David R. "1 Corinthians 7 as a Foundation for a Christian Sex Ethic." *JR* 55 (1975) 220–34.

Cavallin, H. C. C. *Life After Death: Paul's Argument for the Resurrection of the Dead in*

1 Cor 15. Part 1: An Enquiry into the Jewish Background. ConBNT 7/1. Lund: Gleerup, 1974.

Cerfaux, Lucien. *The Church in the Theology of St. Paul.* New York: Herder & Herder, 1959.

Chadwick, H. "'All Things to all Men.'" *NTS* 1 (1955) 261–75.

Chenderlin, Fritz. *"Do This as My Memorial": The Semantic and Conceptual Background and Value of* 'Ανάμνησις *in 1 Corinthians 11:24–25.* AnBib 99. Rome: Pontifical Biblical Institute, 1982.

Cipriani, Settimio. "La comunità di Corinto come 'stimolo' alla riflessione teologica di S. Paolo." *Lateranum* 50 (1984) 86–100.

———. "La risurrezione di Cristo e la nostra risurrezione nella prospettiva di 1 Cor 15." *Asprenas* 23 (1976) 112–35.

Cirignano, Giulio. "Carismi e ministeri in 1 e 2 Corinizi." *Parole di Vita* 26 (1981) 109–22.

Clark, G. H. "Wisdom in First Corinthians." *JETS* 15 (1972) 197–205.

Clavier, H. "Brèves remarques sur la notion de σῶμα πνευματικόν." In *The Background of the New Testament and Its Eschatology,* edited by W. D. Davies and D. Daube, 342–62. Cambridge: Cambridge University Press, 1954.

Collins, Adela Yarbro. "The Function of 'Excommunication' in Paul." *HTR* 73 (1980) 251–63.

Conzelmann, Hans. *1 Corinthians.* Hermeneia. Philadelphia: Fortress, 1975.

———. "On the Analysis of the Confessional Formula in I Corinthians 15:3–5." *Int* 20 (1966) 15–25.

———. "Paulus und die Weisheit," *NTS* 12 (1966) 231–44.

Cope, O. Lamar. "First Corinthians 8–10: Continuity or Contradiction?" *ATR* 11 (1990) 114–23.

Corrington, Gail P. "Paul and the Two Wisdoms: 1 Corinthians 1:18–31 and the Hellenistic Mission." *Proceedings of the Eastern Great Lakes and Midwest Bible Societies* 6 (1986) 72–84.

Craig, C. T. *First Epistle to the Corinthians.* IB 10. New York: Abingdon, 1954.

Crone, T. M. *Early Christian Prophecy: A Study of Its Origin and Function.* Baltimore: St. Mary's University Press, 1973.

Culliton, J. B. "Lucien Cerfaux's Contribution concerning 'The Body of Christ.'" *CBQ* 29 (1967) 41–59.

Cullmann, Oscar, and F. J. Leenhardt, *Essays on the Lord's Supper.* Ecumenical Studies in Worship 1. Richmond: John Knox, 1958.

Currie, S. D. "'Speaking in Tongues': Early Evidence Outside the New Testament Bearing on 'Glossais Lalein.'" *Int* 19 (1965) 274–94.

Dahl, Murdock E. *The Resurrection of the Body: A Study of 1 Corinthians 15.* SBT 36. London: SCM, 1962.

Dahl, Nils. "Paul and the Church at Corinth according to 1 Corinthians 1–4," in *Christian History and Interpretation: Studies Presented to John Knox,* edited by W. R. Farmer, C. F. D. Moule, and R. R. Niebuhr, 313–35. Cambridge: Cambridge University Press, 1967.

Daines, Brian. "Paul's Use of the Analogy of the Body of Christ—With Special Reference to 1 Corinthians 12." *EvQ* 50 (1978) 71–78.

Dautzenberg, Gerhard. *Urchristliche Prophetie: Ihre Erforschung, ihre Voraussetzung im Judentum und ihre Struktur im ersten Korintherbrief.* Stuttgart: W. Kohlhammer, 1975.

Davis, James A. "The Interaction between Individual Ethical Consciousness and Community Ethical Consciousness in 1 Corinthians." *HBT* 10 (1988) 1–18.

———. *Wisdom and Spirit: An Investigation of 1 Corinthians 1.18–3.20 Against the Background of Jewish Sapiential Traditions in the Greco-Roman Period.* Lanham, MD: University Press of America, 1984.

de Boer, Martinus C. *The Defeat of Death: Apocalyptic Eschatology in 1 Corinthians 15 and Romans 5.* JSNTSup 22. Sheffield: JSOT Press, 1988.

Delcor, Mathias. "The Courts of the Church of Corinth and the Courts of Qumran." In *Paul and Qumran: Studies in New Testament Exegesis,* edited by Jerome Murphy-O'Connor, 69–84. London: Chapman, 1968.

Delling, G. "Das Abendmahlsgeschehen nach Paulus." *KD* 10 (1964) 61–77.

Dennison, William D. *Paul's Two-Age Construction and Apologetics.* Lanham, MD: University Press of America, 1986.

Dominy, B. "Paul and Spiritual Gifts: Reflections on 1 Corinthians 12–14." *SWJT* 26 (1983) 49–68.

Doudelet, A. "L'Eucharistie chez Saint Paul." *Collectanea Mechliniensia* 54 (1969) 33–50.

Doughty, Darrell J. "The Presence and Future of Salvation in Corinth." *ZNW* 66 (1975) 61–90.

Duggan, M. W. "The Spirit in the Body in First Corinthians." *Bible Today* 18 (1980) 388–93.

Dulau, P. "Pauline Privilege: Is it Promulgated in the First Epistle to the Corinthians?" *CBQ* 13 (1951) 146–52.

Dunn, James D. G. *Baptism in the Holy Spirit: A Reexamination of the New Testament Teaching on the Gift of the Spirit in Relation to Pentecostalism Today.* SBT 2/15. London: SCM, 1970.

———. *Jesus and the Spirit.* Philadelphia: Westminster, 1975.

Dupont, Jacques. *Gnosis: La connaissance religieuse dans les épîtres de S. Paul.* Universitas Catholica Lovaniensis, Dissertationes in Facultate Theologica 2/40. Louvain: Nauwelaerts, 1960.

Edwards, Thomas Charles. *A Commentary on the First Epistle to the Corinthians.* London: Hodder & Stoughton, 1903.

Eichholz, Georg. *Was heisst charismatische Gemeinde? 1. Korinther 12.* Munich: Kaiser, 1960.

Elliott, J. K. "Paul's Teaching on Marriage in I Corinthians: Some Problems Considered." *NTS* 19 (1973) 219–25.

Ellis, E. E. "Christ and Spirit in 1 Corinthians." In *Christ and Spirit in the New Testament: Studies in Honour of Charles Francis Digby Moule,* edited by B. Lindars and S. S. Smalley, 269–77. Cambridge: Cambridge University Press, 1973.

———. "Christ Crucified." In *Reconciliation and Hope: New Testament Essays on Atonement and Eschatology Presented to L. L. Morris on His 60th Birthday,* edited by Robert Banks, 69–75. Grand Rapids: Eerdmans, 1974.

——. *Pauline Theology: Ministry and Society.* Grand Rapids: Eerdmans, 1989.

——. *Prophecy and Hermeneutic in Early Christianity: New Testament Essays.* Grand Rapids: Eerdmans, 1978.

——. "Traditions in 1 Corinthians." *NTS* 32 (1986) 481–502.

Engberg-Pedersen, Troels. "1 Corinthians 11:16 and the Character of Pauline Exhortation." *JBL* 110 (1991) 679–89.

——. "The Gospel and Social Practice according to I Corinthians." *NTS* 33 (1987) 557–84.

Fascher, Erich. *Der erste Brief des Paulus an die Korinther.* THKNT 7/1. 3d ed. Berlin: Evangelische Verlagsanstalt, 1984.

Fee, Gordon D. "Εἰδωλόθυτα Once Again: An Interpretation of 1 Corinthians 8–10." *Bib* 61 (1980) 172–97.

——. *The First Epistle to the Corinthians.* NICNT. Grand Rapids: Eerdmans, 1987.

Ferguson, M. "Theology of First Corinthians." *SWJT* 3 (1960) 25–38.

Feuillet, André. *Le Christ Sagesse de Dieu d'après les Epîtres pauliniennes.* EBib. Paris: Gabalda, 1966.

Findlay, George G. *St. Paul's First Epistle to the Corinthians.* EGT. London, 1900. Reprint, Grand Rapids: Eerdmans, 1983.

Fischer James A. "1 Cor. 7,8–24 — Marriage and Divorce." *BR* 23 (1978) 26–36.

Fisk, Bruce. "Eating Meat Offered to Idols: Corinthian Behavior and Pauline Response in 1 Corinthians 8–10 (a Response to G. D. Fee)." *Trinity Journal* 10 (1989) 49–70.

Fitzer, Gottfried. *"Das Weib schweige in der Gemeinde": Über den unpaulinischen Charakter der mulier-taceat-Verse in 1. Korinther 14.* Theologische Existenze Heute 10. Munich: Kaiser, 1963.

Fitzgerald, John T. *Cracks in an Earthen Vessel: An Examination of the Catalogues of Hardships in the Corinthian Correspondence.* SBLDS 99. Atlanta: Scholars Press, 1988.

Ford, J. Massyngberde. "Toward a Theology of 'Speaking in Tongues.'" *TS* 32 (1971) 3–29.

Fraeymann, M. "La Spiritualisation de L'Idée du Temple dans les Epîtres Pauliniennes." *ETL* 23 (1945) 378–412.

Fraiken, Daniel. "'Charismes et Ministères,' à la lumière de 1 Cor. 12–14." *Église et Théologie* 9 (1978) 455–63.

Friedrich, Gerhard. "Freiheit und Liebe im ersten Korintherbrief." *TZ* 26 (1970) 81–98.

Fung, Ronald Y.-K. "Justification by Faith in 1 & 2 Corinthians." In *Pauline Studies: Essays Presented to Professor F. F. Bruce on his 70th Birthday,* edited by D. A. Hagner and M. J. Harris, 246–61. Grand Rapids: Eerdmans, 1980.

Gaffin, Richard B., Jr. *Perspectives on Pentecost: New Testament Teaching on Gifts of the Holy Spirit.* Phillipsburg, NJ: Presbyterian and Reformed, 1979.

Garlatti, Guillermo J. "La Eucaristía como memoria y proclamación de la muerte del Señor (aspectos de la celebración de la cena del Señor según San Pablo)." *Revista Bíblica* 46 (1984) 11–20.

Gärtner, Bertil E. "Pauline and Johannine Idea of 'to Know God' against the

Hellenistic Background." *NTS* 14 (1968) 209–31.

Gaventa, Beverly R. "'You Proclaim the Lord's Death': 1 Corinthians 11:26 and Paul's Understanding of Worship." *RevExp* 80 (1983) 377–87.

Genest, Olivette. "L'interprétation de la mort de Jésus en situation discursive: un cas-type, l'articulation de figures de cette mort en 1-2 Corinthiens." *NTS* 34 (1988) 506–35.

Giblin, Charles H. "Three Monotheistic Texts in Paul." *CBQ* 37 (1975) 527–47.

Gillespie, T. W. "A Pattern of Prophetic Speech in First Corinthians." *JBL* 97 (1978) 74–95.

Glasswell, M. E. "Some Issues of Church and Society in the Light of Paul's Eschatology." In *Paul and Paulinism: Essays in honour of C. K. Barrett,* edited by M. Hooker and S. G. Wilson, 310–19. London: SPCK, 1982.

Godet, Frederick. *Commentary on St. Paul's First Epistle to the Corinthians.* Edinburgh: T. & T. Clark, 1886.

Gooch, Paul W. "Authority and Justification in Theological Ethics: A Study in 1 Corinthians 7." *Journal of Religion and Ethics* 11 (1983) 62–74.

Gressmann, Hugo. "Η ΚΟΙΝΩΝΙΑ ΤΩΝ ΔΑΙΜΟΝΙΩΝ." *ZNW* 20 (1962) 173–86.

Grosheide, F. W. *Commentary on the First Epistle to the Corinthians.* NICNT. Grand Rapids: Eerdmans, 1953.

Grudem, W. *The Gift of Prophecy in 1 Corinthians.* Washington, DC: University Press of America, 1982.

Gundry, Robert H. "'Ecstatic Utterance' (N.E.B.)?" *JTS* 17 (1966) 299–307.

———. ΣΩΜΑ *in Biblical Theology.* SNTSMS 29. Cambridge: University Press, 1976.

Guy, H. A. *New Testament Prophecy: Its Origin and Significance.* London: Epworth, 1947.

Hahn, F. "Charisma und Amt: Die Diskussion über das kirchliche Amt im Lichte der neutestamentlichen Charismenlehre." *ZTK* 76 (1979) 419–49.

Hall, Barbara. "All Things to All People: A Study of 1 Corinthians 9:19–23." In *The Conversation Continues: Studies in Paul and John in Honor of J. Louis Martyn,* edited by R. T. Fortna and B. R. Gaventa, 137–57. Nashville: Abingdon, 1990.

Hamilton, Neill Q. *The Holy Spirit and Eschatology in Paul.* SJT Occasional Papers 6. Edinburgh: Oliver & Boyd, 1957.

Hanson, A. T. *The Paradox of the Cross in the Thought of St Paul.* JSNTSup 17. Sheffield: JSOT Press, 1987.

Harpur, T. W. "The Gift of Tongues and Interpretation." *CJT* 12 (1966) 164–71.

Harris, B. F. "ΣΥΝΕΙΔΗΣΙΣ (Conscience) in the Pauline Writings." *WJT* 24 (1962) 173–86.

Harrisville, Roy A. *1 Corinthians.* Minneapolis: Augsburg, 1987.

———. "Speaking in Tongues: A Lexicographical Study." *CBQ* 38 (1976) 35–48.

Hassler, Victor. "Das Evangelium des Paulus in Korinth: Erwägungen zur Hermeneutik." *NTS* 30 (1984) 109–29.

Heinrici, C. F. G. *Der erste Brief an die Korinther.* MeyerK. Göttingen: Vandenhoeck & Ruprecht, 1896.

Héring, Jean. *The First Epistle of Saint Paul to the Corinthians.* London: Epworth, 1962.

Hermann, Ingo. *Kyrios und Pneuma.* SANT 2. Munich: Kösel, 1961.

Hill, C. E. "Paul's Understanding of Christ's Kingdom in 1 Cor 15:20–28." *NovT* 30 (1988) 297–320.

Hill, David. *New Testament Prophecy.* Atlanta: John Knox, 1979.

Hodge, Charles. *An Exposition of the First Epistle to the Corinthians.* New York, 1857. Reprint, Grand Rapids: Eerdmans, 1953.

Hodgson, Robert. "Paul the Apostle and First Century Tribulation Lists." *ZNW* 74 (1983) 59–80.

Hofius, Otfried. "Herrenmahl und Herrenmahlsparadosis: Erwägungen zu 1 Kor 11,23b–25." *ZTK* 85 (1988) 371–408.

Holladay, Carl R. *The First Letter of Paul to the Corinthians.* Austin: Sweet, 1979.

Holmberg, B. *Paul and Power: The Structure of Authority in the Primitive Church as Reflected in the Pauline Epistles.* Philadelphia: Fortress, 1980.

Horn, W. M. "Speaking in Tongues: A Retrospective Appraisal." *Lutheran Quarterly* 17 (1965) 316–29.

Horsley, R. A. "The Background of the Confessional Formula in 1 Kor 8:6." *ZNW* 69 (1978) 130–35.

———. "Consciousness and Freedom Among the Corinthians, 1 Corinthians 8–10." *CBQ* 40 (1978) 574–89.

———. "Gnosis in Corinth: 1 Corinthians 8.1–6." *NTS* 27 (1980) 32–51.

———. "'How can some of you say that there is no resurrection of the dead?': Spiritual Elitism in Corinth." *NovT* 20 (1978) 203–31.

———. "Pneumatikos vs. Psychikos: Distinctions of Spiritual Status among the Corinthians." *HTR* 69 (1976) 260–88.

———. "Wisdom of Words and Words of Wisdom in Corinth." *CBQ* 39 (1977) 224–39.

House, H. W. "Tongues and the Mystery Religions of Corinth." *BSac* 140 (1983) 134–50.

Howard, J. K. "Christ Our Passover: A Study of the Passover-Exodus Theme in I Corinthians." *EvQ* 41 (1969) 97–108.

Hurd, John C., Jr. *The Origin of I Corinthians.* 2d ed. Macon, GA: Mercer University Press, 1983.

Jansen, J. F. "1 Cor 15.24–28 and the Future of Jesus Christ." *SJT* 40 (1987) 543–70.

Jeremias, Joachim. "'Flesh and Blood cannot inherit the Kingdom of God' (1 Cor. xv.50)." *NTS* 2 (1956) 151–59.

———. "Das paulinische Abendmahl—eine opferdarbringung?" *TSK* 108 (1937–38) 124–41.

Jeske, Richard L. "The Rock Was Christ: The Ecclesiology of 1 Corinthians 10." In *Kirche: Festschrift für Günther Bornkamm zum 75. Geburtstag,* edited by Dieter Lührmann and Georg Strecker, 245–55. Tübingen: Mohr (Siebeck), 1980.

Johnson, L. T. "Norms for True and False Prophecy in First Corinthians." *American Benedictine Review* 22 (1971) 29–45.

Käsemann, Ernst. *Leib und Leib Christi.* BHT 9. Tübingen: Mohr (Siebeck), 1933.

———. "On Paul's Anthropology." In *Perspectives on Paul,* 1–31. London: SCM, 1969.

———. "The Pauline Doctrine of the Lord's Supper." In *Essays on New Testament Themes,* 108–35. SBT 1/41. London: SCM, 1964.

———. "The Theological Problems presented by the Motif of the Body of Christ." In *Perspectives on Paul,* 102–21. London: SCM, 1969.

Kendall, E. L. "Speaking with Tongues." *CQR* 168 (1967) 11–19.

Kertelge, K. "Das Apostelamt des Paulus, sein Ursprung und seine Bedeutung." *BZ* 2 (1970) 161–81.

Klauck, H.-J. "Eucharistie und Kirchengemeinschaft bei Paulus." *Wissenschaft und Weisheit* 49 (1986) 1–14.

———. "Der Gottesdienst in der Gemeinde von Korinth." *Pastoralblatt* (Cologne) 36 (1984) 11–29.

———. *Herrenmahl und hellenistischer Kult: Eine religionsgeschichtliche Untersuchung zum ersten Korintherbrief.* NTAbh 15. Münster: Aschendorff, 1982.

———. *1. Korintherbrief.* Würzburg: Echter, 1984.

Koenig, John. "From Mystery to Ministry: Paul as Interpreter of Charismatic Gifts." *USQR* 33 (1978) 167–74.

Kottackal, Joseph. *The Salvific Folly of God: A Biblical-Theological Study on the Paradox of God's Folly and the World's Wisdom.* Kottayam: Oriental Institute of Religious Studies, 1984.

Krajewski, Ekkehard. *Geistesgaben: Eine Bibelarbeit über 1. Korinther 12–14.* Kösel: Oncken, 1963.

Kreitzer, L. Joseph. "Baptism in the Pauline Epistles, with Special Reference to the Corinthian Letters." *Baptist Quarterly* 34 (1991) 67–78.

———. *Jesus and God in Paul's Eschatology.* JSNTSup 19. Sheffield: JSOT Press, 1987.

Kugelmann, Richard. "The First Letter to the Corinthians." *JBC,* 254–75. Englewood Cliffs, NJ: Prentice-Hall, 1968.

Laeuchli, S. "Monism and Dualism in the Pauline Anthropology." *BR* 3 (1958) 15–27.

Lambrecht, J. "Paul's Christological Use of Scripture in 1 Cor. 15.20–28." *NTS* 28 (1982) 502–27.

Lampe, G. W. H. "Church Discipline and the Interpretation of the Epistle to the Corinthians." In *Christian History and Interpretation: Studies Presented to John Knox,* edited by W. R. Farmer, C. F. D. Moule, and R. R. Niebuhr, 337–61. Cambridge: Cambridge University Press, 1967.

———. *The Seal of the Spirit.* New York: Longmans, Green & Co., 1951.

Lane, William L. "Covenant: The Key to Paul's Conflict with Corinth." *TynBul* 33 (1982) 3–29.

Lang, F. *Die Briefe an die Korinther, übersetzt und erklärt.* Göttingen: Vandenhoeck & Ruprecht, 1986.

———. "Die Gruppen in Korinth nach 1. Korinther 1–4." *TBei* 14 (1983) 68–79.

Leaney, A. R. C. "The Doctrine of Man in 1 Corinthians." *SJT* 15 (1962) 394–99.

Lias, J. J. *The First Epistle to the Corinthians.* Cambridge: Cambridge University Press, 1907.

Lietzmann, Hans. *Mass and Lord's Supper.* Leiden: Brill, 1953.

———. *An die Korinther.* Revised by W. G. Kümmel. HNT 9. Tübingen: Mohr (Siebeck), 1949.

Lührmann, Dieter. *Die Offenbarungsverständnis bei Paulus und in paulinischen Gemeinden.* WMANT 16. Neukirchen-Vluyn: Neukirchener Verlag, 1965.

Lütgert, W. *Freiheitspredigt und Schwarmgeister in Korinth.* BFCT 12/3. Gütersloh, 1908.

MacDonald, Margaret Y. *The Pauline Churches: A Socio-Historical Study of Institutionalization in the Pauline and Deutero-Pauline Writings.* SNTSMS 60. Cambridge: University Press, 1988.

MacGorman, Jack W. *The Gifts of the Spirit: An Exposition of 1 Corinthians 12–14.* Nashville: Broadman, 1974.

———. "Glossalalic Error and Its Corrections: 1 Corinthians 12–14." *RevExp* 80 (1983) 389–400.

Machalet, C. "Paulus und sein Gegner: Eine Untersuchung zu den Korintherbriefen." In *Theokratia: Jahrbuch des Institutum Judaicum Delitzschianum, II: Festgabe für Karl Heinrich Rengstorf zum 70. Geburtstag,* edited by W. Dietrich, P. Freimark, and H. Schreckenberg, 183–203. Leiden: Brill, 1973.

MacVean, W. C. "The Essential Oneness of Christ's Body: 'A Still More Excellent Way.'" *CJT* 5 (1959) 96–104.

Malherbe, Abraham J. "House Churches and Their Problems." In *Social Aspects of Early Christianity,* 60–91. Baton Rouge: Louisiana State University Press, 1977.

Maly, Karl. *Mündige Gemeinde: Untersuchungen zur Pastoralen Führung des Apostels Paulus im 1 Korintherbrief.* Stuttgart: Katholisches Bibelwerk, 1967.

Marshall, Peter. *Enmity in Corinth: Social Conventions in Paul's Relations with the Corinthians.* WUNT 2/23. Tübingen: Mohr (Siebeck), 1987.

Martin, D. W. "'Spirit' in the Second Chapter of First Corinthians." *CBQ* 5 (1943) 381–95.

Martin, Ralph P. *The Spirit and the Congregation: Studies in 1 Corinthians 12–15.* Grand Rapids: Eerdmans, 1984.

Masson, C. "L'Evangile et la Sagesse selon 1 Co 1.17–3.23." *RTP* 6 (1957) 95–110.

Maurer, C. "Sinn und Unsinn des Pluralismus — eine Paulusstudie." *Kirchenblatt für die reformierte Schweiz* 134 (1978) 322–25.

Meeks, Wayne A. *The First Urban Christians: The Social World of the Apostle Paul.* New Haven: Yale University Press, 1983.

Menzies, Allan. "The Lord's Supper: St. Mark or St. Paul?" *Exp* 5/10 (1899) 241–62.

Meyer, H. A. W. *Critical and Exegetical Handbook to the Epistles to the Corinthians.* ET. Edinburgh: T. & T. Clark, 1879.

Meyer, Lauree H., and Graydon F. Snyder. "Sexuality, Its Social Reality and Theological Understanding in 1 Corinthians 7." In *Society of Biblical Literature 1980 Seminar Papers,* edited by Kent H. Richards, 359–70. Chico, CA: Scholars Press, 1980.

Meyer, Paul W. "The Holy Spirit in the Pauline Letters: A Contextual Exploration." *Int* 33 (1979) 3–18.

Millon, G. *Les grâces de service: La manifestation de l'Esprit pour l'utilité: charismes, diaconies et opérations selon 1 Corinthiens 12:4–7.* Mulhouse: Centre de Culture Chrétienne, 1976.

Mills, Watson E. *A Theological/Exegetical Approach to Glossolalia.* Lanham, MD: University Press of America, 1985.

Minear, Paul S. "Christ and the Congregation: 1 Corinthians 5–6." *RevExp* 80 (1983) 341–50.

——. "Paul's Teaching on the Eucharist in First Corinthians." *Worship* 44 (1970) 83–92.

Mitchell, Margaret M. *Paul and the Rhetoric of Reconciliation: An Exegetical Investigation of the Language and Composition of 1 Corinthians.* HUT 28. Tübingen: Mohr (Siebeck), 1991.

Moffatt, James. *The First Epistle of Paul to the Corinthians.* MNTC. New York: Harper, 1938.

Moody, D. "Charismatic and Official Ministries: A Study of the New Testament Concept." *Int* 19 (1965) 168–81.

Moule, C. F. D. "St. Paul and Dualism." *NTS* 12 (1965–66) 106–23.

Mounce, R. H. "Continuity of Primitive Tradition: Some pre-Pauline Elements in I Corinthians." *Int* 13 (1959) 417–24.

Mühlberger, S. *Mitarbeiter Gottes: Ein Arbeitsheft zum 1. Korintherbrief.* Klosterneuburg: Osterreichisches Katholisches Biblewerk, 1978.

Mühlen, Heribert. *A Charismatic Theology: Initiation in the Spirit.* New York: Paulist, 1978.

Müller, K. "1 Kor 1:18–25: Die eschatologisch-kritische Funktion der Verkündigung des Kreuzes." *BZ* 10 (1966) 246–72.

Müller, U. B. *Prophetie und Predigt im Neuen Testament.* Gütersloh: Mohn, 1975.

Munck, Johannes. "The Church Without Factions: Studies in 1 Corinthians 1–4." In *Paul and the Salvation of Mankind,* 135–67. Richmond: John Knox, 1959.

Murphy-O'Connor, Jerome. *I Corinthians.* Wilmington, DE: Glazier, 1979.

——. "1 Cor 8:6: Cosmology or Soteriology?" *RB* 85 (1978) 253–67.

——. "Eucharist and Community in First Corinthians." *Worship* 50 (1976) 370–85.

——. "Freedom or the Ghetto (1 Cor. viii, 1–13; x, 23–xi.1)." *RB* 85 (1978) 543–74.

Neuenzeit, Paul. "Eucharistie und Gemeinde: Eine notwendige Relation nach paulinischer Theologie." *Una Sancta* 25 (1970) 116–30.

——. *Das Herrenmahl: Studien zur paulinischer Eucharistie-auffassung.* SANT 1. Munich: Kösel, 1960.

Neuhäusler, E. "Ruf Gottes und Stand des Christen: Bemerkungen zu 1 Kor 7." *BZ* 3 (1959) 43–60.

Neyrey, Jerome H. "Body Language in 1 Corinthians: The Use of Anthropological Models for Understanding Paul and his Opponents." *Semeia* 35 (1986) 127–70.

Nickle, Keith. *The Collection.* SBT 1/48. London: SCM, 1966.

Niederwimmer, K. "Erkennen und Lieben: Gedanken zum Verhältnis von Gnosis und Agape im ersten Korintherbrief." *KD* 11 (1965) 75–102.

O'Brien, J. F. "St. Paul on Charisma." *Cross and Crown* 22 (1970) 449–57.

Orbiso, Teofilo de. "La eucaristia en San Pablo." *EstBib* 5 (1946) 171–213.

Orr, William F., and James A. Walther. *I Corinthians.* AB 32. Garden City, NY: Doubleday, 1976.

Osborn, E. "Spirit and Charisma." *Colloquium* 7 (1974) 30–41.

Osty, E. *Les Epîtres de Saint Paul aux Corinthiens.* 3d ed. Paris: Cerf, 1959.

Oudersluys, R. C. "Charismatic Theology and the New Testament." *Reformed Review* 28 (1974) 48–59.

———. "The Purpose of Spiritual Gifts." *Reformed Review* 29 (1975) 212–21.

Padgett, Alan. "Feminism in First Corinthians: A Dialogue with Elisabeth Schüssler Fiorenza." *EvQ* 58 (1986) 121–32.

Pagels, E. H. "Paul and Women: A Response to Recent Discussion." *JAAR* 42 (1974) 538–49.

Painter, John. "Paul and the πνευματικοί at Corinth." In *Paul and Paulinism: Studies in Honour of C. K. Barrett,* edited by M. D. Hooker and S. G. Wilson, 237–50. London: SPCK, 1982.

Parratt, J. K. "The Holy Spirit and Baptism: Part II, The Pauline Evidence." *ExpTim* 82 (1970–71) 266–71.

Parry, Reginald St. John. *The First Epistle of Paul the Apostle to the Corinthians in Revised Version with Introduction and Notes.* Cambridge: Cambridge University Press, 1926.

Pearson, Birger. "Hellenistic-Jewish Wisdom Speculation and Paul." In *Aspects of Wisdom in Judaism and Early Christianity,* edited by R. L. Wilken, 43–66. Notre Dame, IN: University of Notre Dame Press, 1975.

———. *The Pneumatikos-Psychikos Terminology in I Corinthians.* SBLDS 12. Missoula, MT: Scholars Press, 1973.

Peters, E. H. "Saint Paul and the Eucharist." *CBQ* 10 (1948) 247–53.

Pfitzner, Victor C. *Paul and the Agon Motif.* NovTSup 16. Leiden: Brill, 1967.

———. "Proclaiming the Name: Cultic Narrative and Eucharistic Proclamation in First Corinthians." *Lutheran Theological Journal* 25 (1991) 15–25.

Pherigo, Lindsey P. "Paul and the Corinthian Church." *JBL* 68 (1949) 341–50.

Pierce, C. A. *Conscience in the New Testament.* SBT 15. London: SCM, 1957.

Plank, K. A. "Resurrection Theology: The Corinthian Controversy Reexamined." *Perspectives in Religious Studies* 8 (1981) 41–54.

Porter, Calvin L. "An Interpretation of Paul's Lord's Supper Texts: 1 Corinthians 10:14–22 and 11:17–34." *Encounter* 50 (1989) 29–45.

Poythress, V. S. "The Nature of Corinthian Glossolalia: Possible Options." *WTJ* 40 (1977) 130–35.

Prior, David. *The Message of 1 Corinthians.* Downers Grove, IL: InterVarsity, 1985.

Pritchard, N. M. "Profession of Faith and Admission to Communion in the Light of 1 Corinthians 11 and other Passages." *SJT* 33 (1980) 55–70.

Prümm, Karl. "Zur Neutestamentlichen Gnosis-Problematik: Gnostischer Hintergrund und Lehrenschlag in den beiden Eingangskapiteln von 1 Korintherbrief." *ZKT* 87 (1965) 339–442; 88 (1966) 1–50.

Radcliffe, Timothy. "'Glorify God in Your Bodies': 1 Corinthians 6,12–20 as a Sexual Ethic." *New Blackfriars* 67 (1986) 306–14.

Ramaroson, L. "'L'Église, corps du Christ' dans les écrits pauliniens: simples esquisses." *Science et Esprit* 30 (1978) 129–41.

Reese, J. M. "Paul Proclaims the Wisdom of the Cross: Scandal and Foolishness." *BTB* 9 (1979) 147–53.

Reumann, J. "Οἰκονομία-Terms in Paul in Comparison with Lucan *Heilsgeschichte.*" *NTS* 13 (1967) 147–67.

Richardson, Peter. "Pauline Inconsistency: 1 Corinthians 9:19–23 and Galatians 2:11–14. *NTS* 26 (1980) 347–62.

——, and Paul W. Gooch. "Accommodation Ethics." *TynBul* 29 (1978) 89–142.

Ringe, S. H. "Hospitality, Justice, and Community: Paul's Teaching on the Eucharist in 1 Corinthians 11:17–34." *Prism* 1/2 (1986) 59–68.

Robertson, Archibald T., and Alfred Plummer. *A Critical and Exegetical Commentary on the First Epistle of St Paul to the Corinthians.* ICC. Edinburgh: T. & T. Clark, 1914.

Robinson, D. W. B. "Charismata Versus Pneumatika: Paul's Method of Discussion." *Reformed Theological Review* 31 (1972) 49–55.

Robinson, James M. "The Sacraments in Corinth." *Journal of the Interseminary Movement of the Southwest* (1962) 21–32.

Robinson, John A. T. *The Body: A Study in Pauline Theology.* SBT 5. London: SCM, 1952.

Ruef, John. *Paul's First Letter to Corinth.* Philadelphia: Westminster, 1977.

Runia, K. "The 'Gifts of the Spirit.'" *Reformed Theological Review* 29 (1970) 82–94.

Saake, H. "Pneumatologia Paulina: Zur Katholizitat der Problematik des Charisma." *Catholica* 26 (1972) 212–23.

Scharlemann, M. H. *Qumran and Corinth.* New York: Bookman Associates, 1962.

Schelkle, K. H. "Charisma und Amt." *TQ* 159 (1979) 243–54.

Schlatter, Adolf. *Die Korintherbriefe.* Stuttgart: Calwer, 1962.

——. *Die Korinthische Theologie.* BFCT 18/2; Gütersloh: Bertelsmann, 1914.

Schlosser, Jacques. "Le corps en 1 Co 12, 12–31." In *Le corps et le corps du Christ dans la première épître aux Corinthiens,* edited by Victor Guénel, 97–110. Paris: du Cerf, 1983.

Schmithals, Walter. *Gnosticism in Corinth.* Nashville: Abingdon, 1971.

——. *The Office of Apostle in the Early Church.* Nashville: Abingdon, 1972.

Schnackenburg, Rudolf. *Baptism in the Thought of St. Paul: A Study in Pauline Theology.* New York: Herder & Herder, 1964.

Schrage, Wolfgang. "Leid, Kreuz und Eschaton: Die Peristasenkataloge als Merkmale paulinischer theologia crucis und Eschatologie." *EvT* 34 (1974) 141–75.

Schüssler Fiorenza, E. *In Memory of Her: A Feminist Theological Reconstruction of Christian Origins.* New York: Crossroad, 1983.

Schütz, J. H. "Charisma and Social Reality in Primitive Christianity." *JR* 54 (1974) 51–70.

Schweizer, Eduard. "The Service of Worship: An Exposition of I Corinthians 14." *Int* 13 (1959) 400–408.

Scroggs, Robin. "The Exaltation of the Spirit by Some Early Christians." *JBL* 84 (1965) 366–70.

——. *The Last Adam: A Study in Pauline Anthropology.* Philadelphia: Fortress, 1966.

——. "Paul and the Eschatological Woman." *JAAR* 40 (1972) 283–303.

——. "Paul and the Eschatological Woman: Revisited." *JAAR* 42 (1974) 532–37.

——. "Paul: Σόφος and Πνευματικός." *NovT* 14 (1967–68) 33–55.

Sellin, Gerhard. "Das 'Geheimnis' der Weisheit und das Rätsel der 'Christuspartei' (zu 1 Kor 1–4)." *ZNW* 73 (1982) 69–96.

——. "Hauptprobleme des ersten Korintherbriefes." In *ANRW* II.25.4, 2940–3044. Berlin: de Gruyter, 1987.

———. *Die Streit um die Auferstehung der Toten: Eine religionsgeschichtliche und exegetische Untersuchung von 1. Korinther 15.* FRLANT 138. Göttingen: Vandenhoeck & Ruprecht, 1986.

Senft, C. *La Première Epître de Saint Paul aux Corinthiens.* Paris: Delachaux & Nièstle, 1979.

Serra, D. "The Eschatological Role of the Spirit in the Lord's Supper." *Dunwoodie Review* 11 (1971) 185–202.

Sider, R. J. "The Pauline Conception of the Resurrection Body in I Corinthians 15:35–54." *NTS* 21 (1975) 428–39.

———. "St. Paul's Understanding of the Nature and Significance of the Resurrection in 1 Cor 15,1–29." *NovT* 18 (1977) 124–41.

Smalley, S. S. "Spiritual Gifts and 1 Corinthians 12–16." *JBL* 87 (1968) 427–33.

Smith, D. C. "Paul and the Non-Eschatological Woman." *Ohio Journal of Religious Studies* 4 (1976) 11–18.

Smith, D. M. "Glossolalia and Other Spiritual Gifts in a New Testament Perspective." *Int* 28 (1974) 307–20.

Smith, R. H. "Were the Early Christians Middle-Class? A Sociological Analysis of the New Testament." *CurTM* 5 (1980) 260–76.

Songer, Harold S. "Problems Arising from the Worship of Idols: 1 Corinthians 8:1–11:1." *RevExp* 80 (1983) 363–75.

Spicq, Ceslaus. "L'ἀγαπή de I Cor., XIII: Un example de contribution de la sémantique à l'exégèse néo-testamentaire." *ETL* 31 (1955) 357–70.

Stanley, D. M. "'Become Imitators of Me': The Pauline Conception of Apostolic Tradition." *Bib* 40 (1959) 859–87.

Stibbs, A. "Putting the Gift of Tongues in its Place." *Churchman* 80 (1966) 295–303.

Story, C. I. K. "The Nature of Paul's Stewardship with Special Reference to I and II Corinthians." *EvQ* 48 (1976) 212–29.

Stuhlmacher, P. "Das Bekenntnis zur Auferweckung Jesu von den Toten und die Biblische Theologie." *ZTK* 70 (1973) 365–403.

Suggit, J. N. "The Eucharist as Eschatological Proclamation, according to St. Paul." *Neot* 21 (1987) 11–24.

Sweet, J. P. M. "A Sign for Unbelievers: Paul's Attitude to Glossolalia." *NTS* 13 (1966–67) 240–57.

Talbert, Charles H. "Paul's Understanding of the Holy Spirit: The Evidence of 1 Corinthians 12–14." In *Perspectives on the New Testament: Studies in Honor of Frank Stagg,* edited by C. H. Talbert, 95–108. Macon, GA: Mercer University, 1985.

———. *Reading Corinthians: A Literary and Theological Commentary on 1 and 2 Corinthians.* New York: Crossroad, 1987.

Theissen, Gerd. *The Social Setting of Pauline Christianity: Essays on Corinth.* Philadelphia: Fortress, 1982.

Thiselton, A. C. "The 'Interpretation' of Tongues: A New Suggestion in the Light of Greek Usage in Philo and Josephus." *JTS* 30 (1979) 15–36.

———. "Realized Eschatology at Corinth." *NTS* 24 (1978) 510–26.

Thornton, L. S. "The Body of Christ in the New Testament." In *The Apostolic Ministry,* edited by K. E. Kirk, 53–111. London: Hodder & Stoughton, 1946.

Thrall, Margaret E. "Christ Crucified or Second Adam? A Christological Debate Between Paul and the Corinthians." In *Christ and Spirit in the New Testament: Studies in Honour of Charles Francis Digby Moule,* edited by B. Lindars and S. S. Smalley, 143–56. Cambridge: Cambridge University Press, 1973.

———. *The First and Second Letters of Paul to the Corinthians.* Cambridge: Cambridge University Press, 1965.

———. "The Pauline Uses of ΣΥΝΕΙΔΗΣΙΣ." *NTS* 14 (1968) 118–25.

Toews, John E. "The Role of Women in the Church: The Pauline Perspective." *Direction* 9 (1980) 25–35.

Trim, K. W. "Paul: Life after Death. An Analysis of 1 Cor 15." *Crux* 14 (1978) 129–50.

Trompf, G. W. "On Attitudes Toward Women in Paul and Paulinist Literature: 1 Corinthians 11:3–16 and Its Context." *CBQ* 42 (1980) 196–215.

Trummer, P. "Charismatischer Gottesdienst: Liturgische Impulse aus 1 Cor 12 und 14." *Bibel und Liturgie* 54 (1981) 173–78.

Van Linden, P. "Paul's Christology in First Corinthians." *TBT* 18 (1968) 379–86.

van Roon, A. "The Relation Between Christ and the Wisdom of God According to Paul." *NovT* 16 (1974) 207–39.

Vielhauer, P. "Paulus und die Kephaspartei in Korinth." In *Oikodome: Aufsätze zum Neuen Testament,* edited by G. Klein, 2. 169–82. TBü 65. Munich: Kaiser, 1979.

Visotzky, B. L. "Trinitarian Testimonies." *USQR* 42 (1988) 73–85.

von Soden, Hans. "Sacrament and Ethics in Paul." In *The Writings of St. Paul,* edited by W. Meeks, 257–68. New York: W. W. Norton, 1972.

Vos, J. S. *Traditionsgeschichtliche Untersuchungen zur paulinischen Pneumatologie.* Theologische Bibliotheek 47. Assen: Van Gorcum, 1973.

Wagner, C. "Gotteserkenntnis im Spiegel und Gottesliebe in den beiden Korintherbriefen." *Bijdragen* 19 (1958) 370–81.

Ward, W. E. "Theological Issues Raised in First Corinthians." *RevExp* 57 (1960) 422–37.

Wedderburn, A. J. M. *Baptism and Resurrection: Studies in Pauline Theology against its Greco-Roman Background.* WUNT 44. Tübingen: Mohr (Siebeck), 1987.

———. "The Body of Christ and Related Concepts in 1 Corinthians." *SJT* 24 (1971) 74–96.

———. "The Problem of the Denial of the Resurrection in 1 Cor 15." *NovT* 23 (1981) 229–41.

Wegenast, Klaus. *Das Verständnis der Tradition bei Paulus und in den Deuteropaulinen.* WMANT 8. Neukirchen-Vluyn: Neukirchener Verlag, 1962.

Weiss, Johannes. *Der erste Korintherbrief.* MeyerK 5. 9th ed. Göttingen: Vandenhoeck & Ruprecht, 1910.

Wendland, H.-D. *Die Briefe an die Korinther.* NTD. Göttingen: Vandenhoeck & Ruprecht, 1936.

Wengst, K. "Das Zusammenkommen der Gemeinde und ihr Gottesdienst nach Paulus." *EvT* 33 (1973) 547–59.

Wetter, Gillis P. "Die Auffassung des Apostels Paulus vom Abendmahl." *ZNW* 14 (1913) 202–15.

Wilckens, Ulrich. "Das Kreuz Christi als die Tiefe der Weisheit Gottes zu 1 Kor 2:1–16."

In Paolo a Una Chiesa Divisa, edited by L. de Lorenzi, 43–81. Rome: Abbazia di S. Paolo Fuori le Mura, 1980.

———. Weisheit und Torheit. BHT 26. Tübingen: Mohr (Siebeck), 1959.

Wilkinson, T. L. "Tongues and Prophecy in Acts and 1st Corinthians." Vox Reformata 31 (1978) 1–20.

Williams, C. G. "Glossolalia as a religious phenomenon: 'Tongues' at Corinth and Pentecost." Journal of Religion and Religions 5 (1975) 16–32.

Willis, Wendell Lee. Idol Meat in Corinth: The Pauline Argument in I Corinthians 8 and 10. SBLDS 68. Chico, CA: Scholars Press, 1985.

Wilson, Jack H. "The Corinthians Who Say There Is No Resurrection of the Dead." ZNW 59 (1968) 90–107.

Wilson, R. McL. "Gnosis at Corinth." In Paul and Paulinism: Essays in honour of C. K. Barrett, edited by M. Hooker and S. G. Wilson, 102–14. London: SPCK, 1982.

———. "How Gnostic were the Corinthians?" NTS 19 (1972) 65–74.

Wimbush, Vincent L. The Ascetic Paul. Macon, GA: Mercer University Press, 1987.

Winter, Bruce W. "The Lord's Supper at Corinth: An Alternative Reconstruction." Reformed Theological Review 37 (1978) 73–82.

———. "Theological and Ethical Responses to Religious Pluralism—1 Corinthians 8–10." TynBul 41 (1990) 209–26.

Winter, M. Pneumatiker und Psychiker in Korinth. Marburg: N. G. Elwert, 1975.

Wire, Antoinette Clark. The Corinthian Women Prophets: A Reconstruction through Paul's Rhetoric. Minneapolis: Fortress, 1990.

Wolff, Christian. Der erste Brief des Paulus an die Korinther. THKNT 7/2. Berlin: Evangelische Verlagsanstalt, 1982.

Wright, N. T. "Adam in Pauline Christology." In Society of Biblical Literature 1983 Seminar Papers, ed. David Lull, 359–89. Chico, CA: Scholars Press, 1983.

Wuellner, Wilhelm. "The Soteriological Implications of 1 Corinthians 1:26–28 Reconsidered." In SE 6, edited by E. A. Livingstone, 666–72. Berlin: Akademie, 1973.

Yorke, Gosnell L. O. R. The Church as the Body of Christ in the Pauline Corpus: A Re-examination. Lanham, MD: University Press of America, 1991.

2 Corinthians
Compiled by Victor Paul Furnish

Aejmelaeus, Lars. Streit und Versöhnung: Das Problem der Zusammensetzung des 2. Korintherbriefes. Suomen Eksegeetisen Seuran Julkaisuja 46. Helsinki: Suomen Eksegeetisen Seuran, 1987.

Allo, Ernest Bernard. *Seconde épître aux Corinthiens.* EBib. 2d ed. Paris: Gabalda, 1956.

Arrington, French L. *The Ministry of Reconciliation: A Study of 2 Corinthians.* Grand Rapids: Baker, 1980.

Bachmann, Philipp. *Der zweite Brief des Paulus an die Korinther.* Kommentar zum Neuen Testament 8. 1st and 2d ed. Leipzig: Deichert, 1909.

Baird, William. "Letters of Recommendation: A Study of 2 Cor 3:1–3." *JBL* 80 (1961) 166–72.

———. "Visions, Revelation, and Ministry: Reflections on 2 Cor 12:1–5 and Gal 1:11–17." *JBL* 104 (1985) 651–62.

Balch, David L. "Backgrounds of 1 Cor VII: Sayings of the Lord in Q; Moses as an Ascetic θεῖος ἀνήρ in II Cor III." *NTS* 18 (1972) 351–64.

Barnett, Paul W. *The Message of 2 Corinthians: Power in Weakness.* Leicester and Downers Grove, IL: InterVarsity Press, 1988.

Barré, Michael L. "Paul as 'Eschatologic Person': A New Look at 2 Cor 11:29." *CBQ* 37 (1975) 500–526.

———. "Qumran and the Weakness of Paul." *CBQ* 42 (1980) 216–27.

Barrett, C. K. "Boasting (καυχᾶσθαι, κτλ.) in the Pauline Epistles." In *L'Apôtre Paul: Personnalité, style et conception du ministère,* edited by A. Vanhoye, 363–68. BETL 73. Leuven: Leuven University Press, 1986.

———. *A Commentary on the Second Epistle to the Corinthians.* HNTC. New York: Harper, 1973.

———. "Paul's Opponents in II Corinthians." *NTS* 17 (1971) 233–54.

———. "Shaliah and Apostle." In *Donum Gentilicium: New Testament Studies in Honour of David Daube,* edited by E. Bammel et al., 88–102. Oxford: Clarendon, 1978.

Barth, Gerhard. "Die Eignung des Verkündigers in 2 Kor 2, 14–36." In *Kirche: Festschrift für Günther Bornkamm zum 75. Geburtstag,* edited by D. Lührmann and G. Strecker, 257–70. Tübingen: Mohr (Siebeck), 1980.

Bassler, Jouette M. "Perspectives from Paul, 1: Money and Mission; 2: The Great Collection." In *God and Mammon: Asking for Money in the New Testament,* 63–115. Nashville: Abingdon, 1991.

Baumert, Norbert. *Täglich sterben und auferstehen: Der Literalsinn von 2 Kor 4,12–5,10.* SANT 34. Munich: Kösel, 1973.

Belleville, Linda L. "A Letter of Apologetic Self-Commendation: 2 Cor 1:8–7:16." *NovT* 31 (1989) 142–63.

———. *Reflections of Glory: Paul's Polemical Use of the Moses-Doxa Tradition in 2 Corinthians 3.1–18.* JSNTSup 52. Sheffield: JSOT Press, 1991.

Best, Ernest. *Second Corinthians.* Interpretation. Atlanta: John Knox, 1987.

Betz, Hans Dieter. *Der Apostel Paulus und die sokratische Tradition: Eine exegetische Untersuchung zu seiner 'Apologie' 2 Korinther 10–13.* BHT 45. Tübingen: Mohr (Siebeck), 1972.

———. "Eine Christus-Aretalogie bei Paulus (2 Cor 12, 7–10)." *ZTK* 66 (1969) 288–305.

———. *2 Corinthians 8 and 9: A Commentary on Two Administrative Letters of the Apostle Paul.* Hermeneia. Philadelphia: Fortress, 1985.

Betz, Otto. "Fleischliche und 'geistliche' Christuserkenntnis nach 2. Korinther 5,16." *TBei* 14 (1983) 167–79.

Bieringer, Reimund. "2 Kor 5,19a und die Versöhnung der Welt." *ETL* 63 (1987) 295–326.

Binder, Hermann. "Versöhnung als die grosse Wende." *TZ* 29 (1973) 305–12.

Black, Matthew. "The New Creation in 1 Enoch." In *Creation, Christ and Culture: Studies in Honour of T. F. Torrance,* edited by R. W. A. McKinney, 13–21. Edinburgh: Clark, 1976.

Bornkamm, Günther. "Die Vorgeschichte des sogenannten Zweiten Korintherbriefes." In *Gesammelte Aufsätze,* 2. 162–94. BEvT 53. Munich: Evangelischer Verlag, 1971.

Bowker, John W. "'Merkabah' Visions and the Visions of Paul." *JSS* 16 (1971) 157–73.

Brändle, R. "Geld und Gnade (zu II Kor 8,9)." *TZ* 41 (1985) 264–71.

Breytenbach, Cilliers. "Paul's proclamation and God's 'thriambos' (Notes on 2 Corinthians 2:14–16b)." *Neot* 24 (1990) 257–71.

Bruce, Frederick Fyvie. *1 and 2 Corinthians.* NCB. Grand Rapids: Eerdmans, 1971.

Bultmann, Rudolf. *Exegetische Probleme des zweiten Korintherbriefes.* SEÅSup 9. Uppsala: Wretmans, 1947.

———. *The Second Letter to the Corinthians,* edited by E. Dinkler. Minneapolis: Fortress, 1985.

Caird, George B. "The Theology of the Corinthian Epistles." *Int* 13 (1959) 387–99.

Cambier, Jules. "Connaissance charnelle et spirituelle du Christ dans 2 Cor 5:16." In *Littérature et théologie pauliniennes,* 72–92. RechBib 5. Louvain: Desclée de Brouwer, 1960.

———. "Le Critère paulinien de l'apostolat en 2 Cor. 12, 6s." *Bib* 43 (1962) 481–518.

———. "Une Lecture de 2 Cor 12, 6-7a: Essai d'interprétation nouvelle." In *Studiorum Paulinorum Congressus Internationalis Catholicus, 1961,* 475–85. AnBib 17–18. Rome: Pontifical Biblical Institute, 1963.

Carrez, Maurice. *La deuxième Épître de Saint Paul aux Corinthiens.* CCNT 2/8. Geneva: Labor et Fides, 1986.

———. "Odeur de mort, Odeur de vie (à propos de 2 Co 2, 16)." *RHPR* 64 (1984) 135–42.

———. "Que représent la vie de Jésus pour l'apôtre Paul?" *RHPR* 68 (1988) 155–61.

———. "Réalité christologique et référence apostolique de l'apôtre Paul en présence d'une église divisée (2 Cor 10–13)." In *L'Apôtre Paul: Personnalité, style et conception du ministère,* edited by A. Vanhoye, 163–83. BETL 73. Leuven: Leuven University Press, 1986.

Carson, D. A. *From Triumphalism to Maturity: An Exposition of II Corinthians 10–13.* Grand Rapids: Baker, 1984.

Chevallier, Max Alian. "L'argumentation de Paul dans II Corinthiens 10 à 13." *RHPR* 70 (1990) 3–15.

Cohen, Boaz. "Note on Letter and Spirit in the New Testament." *HTR* 47 (1954) 197–203.

Collange, Jean-François. *Énigmes de la deuxième épître aux Corinthiens: Étude exégétique de 2 Cor. 2:14–7:4.* SNTSMS 18. Cambridge: Cambridge University Press, 1972.

Craddock, Fred B. "The Poverty of Christ: An Investigation of II Corinthians 8:9." *Int* 22 (1968) 158–70.

Crafton, Jeffrey. *The Agency of the Apostle: A Dramatistic Analysis of Paul's Responses to Conflict in 2 Corinthians.* JSNTSup 59. Sheffield: JSOT, 1991.

Craig, William Lane. "Paul's Dilemma in 2 Corinthians 5.1–10: A 'Catch-22'?" *NTS* 34 (1988) 145–47.

Dalton, W. J. "Is the Old Covenant Abrogated (2 Cor 3.14)?" *ABR* 35 (1987) 88–94.

Danker, Frederick W. "Consolation in 2 Cor. 5:1–10." *CTM* 39 (1968) 552–56.

———. *II Corinthians.* Augsburg Commentary on the New Testament. Minneapolis: Augsburg, 1989.

———. "The Mirror Metaphor in 1 Cor. 13:12 and 2 Cor. 3:18." *CTM* 31 (1960) 428–29.

Dautzenberg, G. "Motive der Selbstdarstellung des Paulus in 2 Cor 2,14–7,4." In *L'Apôtre Paul: Personnalité, style et conception du ministère,* edited by A. Vanhoye, 150–62. BETL 73. Leuven: Leuven University Press, 1986.

———. "Der zweite Korintherbrief als Briefsammlung: Zur Frage der literarischen Einheitlichkeit und des theologischen Gefüges von 2 Kor 1–8." In *Aufstieg und Niedergang der römischen Welt.* Principat 25, 4: Religion, edited by W. Haase, 3045–66. Berlin and New York: de Gruyter, 1987.

de Boor, Werner. *Der zweite Brief an die Korinther.* Wuppertaler Studienbibel. 4th ed. Wuppertal: Brockhaus, 1978.

De Lorenzi, Lorenzo, ed. *The Diakonia of the Spirit (2 Cor 4:7–7:4).* Série Monographique de "Benedictina," Section Bibl-Oec. 10. Rome: Abbaye de S. Paul, 1989.

Demke, Christoph. "Zur Auslegung von 2. Korinther 5,1–10." *EvT* 29 (1969) 589–602.

Dewey, Arthur J. "A Matter of Honor: A Social-Historical Analysis of 2 Corinthians 10." *HTR* 78 (1985) 209–17.

Dinkler, Erich. "Die Taufterminologie in 2 Kor. i 21f." In *Neotestamentica et Patristica: Eine Freundesgabe, Herrn Professor Dr. Oscar Cullmann zu seinem 60. Geburtstag Überreicht,* edited by W. C. van Unnik, 173–91. NovTSup 6. Leiden: Brill, 1962.

———. "Die Verkündigung als eschatologisch-sakramentales Geschehen: Auslegung von 2 Kor 5,14–6,2." In *Die Zeit Jesu: Festschrift für Heinrich Schlier,* edited by G. Bornkamm and K. Rahner, 169–89. Freiburg, Basel, and Vienna: Herder, 1970.

Duff, Paul Brooks. "Metaphor, Motif, and Meaning: The Rhetorical Strategy Behind the Image 'Led in Triumph' in 2 Corinthians 2:14." *CBQ* 53 (1991) 79–92.

———. "The Transformation of the Spectator: Power, Perception, and the Day of Salvation." In *SBL 1987 Seminar Papers,* edited by K. H. Richards, 233–43. Atlanta: Scholars Press, 1987.

Dugandzic, Ivan. *Das "Ja" Gottes in Christus: Eine Studie zur Bedeutung des Alten Testaments für das Christusverständnis des Paulus.* FB 26. Würzburg: Echter-Verlag, 1977.

Dumbrell, William J. "Paul's Use of Exodus 34 in 2 Corinthians." In *God Who Is Rich in Mercy: Essays Presented to Dr. D. B. Knox,* edited by P. T. O'Brien and D. G. Peterson, 179–94. Homebush West, New South Wales, Australia: Lancer [Anzea], 1986.

Dunn, James D. G. "2 Corinthians III.17 – 'The Lord is the Spirit.'" *JTS* 21 (1970) 309–20.

Dupont, Jacques. "Le Chrétien, miroir de la grâce divine, d'après 2 Cor. 3:18." *RB* 56 (1949) 392–411.

———. *La Réconciliation dans la théologie de saint Paul.* Louvain: Louvain University Press, 1953.

Ellis, E. Earle. "II Cor v.1–10 in Pauline Eschatology." *NTS* 6 (1960) 211–24.

Fallon, Francis T. "Self's Sufficiency or God's Sufficiency: 2 Corinthians 2:16." *HTR* 76 (1983) 369–74.

Findeis, H.-J. *Versöhnung—Apostolat—Kirche: Eine exegetisch-theologische und rezeptions-geschichtliche Studie zu den Versöhnungsaussagen des Neuen Testaments (2 Kor, Röm, Kol, Eph).* FB 40. Würzburg: Echter-Verlag, 1983.

Fitzgerald, John T. *Cracks in an Earthen Vessel: An Examination of the Catalogues of Hardships in the Corinthian Correspondence.* SBLDS 99. Atlanta: Scholars Press, 1988.

———. "Paul, the Ancient Epistolary Theorists, and 2 Corinthians 10–13." In *Greeks, Romans, and Christians: Essays in Honor of Abraham J. Malherbe,* edited by D. L. Balch, E. Ferguson, and W. A. Meeks, 201–15. Minneapolis: Fortress, 1990.

Fitzmyer, Joseph A. "Glory Reflected on the Face of Christ (2 Cor 3:7–4:6) and a Palestinian Jewish Motif." *TS* 42 (1981) 630–44.

———. "Reconciliation in Pauline Theology." In *No Famine in the Land: Studies in Honor of John L. McKenzie,* edited by J. Flanagan and A. Robinson, 155–77. Missoula, MT: Scholars Press, 1975.

Fraser, J. W. "Paul's Knowledge of Jesus: II Corinthians 5:16 Once More." *NTS* 17 (1971) 293–313.

Fridrichsen, Anton. "Peristasenkatalog und res gestae: Nachtrag zu 2 Cor. 11:23ff." *SO* 8 (1929) 78–82.

———. "Zum Stil des paulinischen Peristasenkatalogs 2 Cor. 11:23ff." *SO* 7 (1928) 25–29.

———. "Zum Thema 'Paulus und die Stoa,' eine stoische Stilparallele zu 2 Cor. 4.8f." *ConNT* 9 (1944) 27–31.

Fuchs, Eric. "La Faiblesse, gloire de l'apostolat selon Paul: Étude sur 2 Corinthiens 10–13." *ETR* 55 (1980) 231–53.

Furnish, Victor Paul. *II Corinthians: Translated with Introduction, Notes, and Commentary.* AB 32A. Garden City, NY: Doubleday, 1984.

Garland, David E. "Paul's Apostolic Authority: The Power of Christ Sustaining Weakness (2 Corinthians 10–13)." *RevExp* 86 (1989) 371–89.

Garrett, Susan R. "The God of This World and the Affliction of Paul: 2 Cor 4:1–12." In *Greeks, Romans, and Christians: Essays in Honor of Abraham J. Malherbe,* edited by D. L. Balch, E. Ferguson, and W. A. Meeks, 99–117. Minneapolis: Fortress, 1990.

Georgi, Dieter. *The Opponents of Paul in 2 Corinthians: A Study of Religious Propaganda in Late Antiquity.* Philadelphia: Fortress, 1985.

———. *Remembering the Poor: The History of Paul's Collection for Jerusalem.* Nashville: Abingdon, 1992.

Glasson, T. Francis. "2 Corinthians 5:1–10 versus Platonism." *SJT* 43 (1990) 145–55.

Godet, Georges Édouard. *La Seconde Épître aux Corinthiens.* Neuchâtel: Attinger, 1914.

Goppelt, Leonhard. "'Versöhnung durch Christus.'" In *Christologie und Ethik,* 147–64. Göttingen: Vandenhoeck & Ruprecht, 1968.

Goudge, Henry L. *The Second Epistle to the Corinthians.* Westminster Commentaries. London: Methuen, 1927.

Grech, Prosper. "2 Corinthians 3:17 and the Pauline Doctrine of Conversion to the Holy Spirit." *CBQ* 17 (1955) 420–37.

Grelot, P. "Note sur 2 Corinthiens 3.14." *NTS* 33 (1987) 135–44.

Güttgemanns, Erhardt. *Der leidende Apostel und sein Herr: Studien zur paulinischen Christologie.* FRLANT 90. Göttingen: Vandenhoeck & Ruprecht, 1966.

Hadidian, Dikran Y. "A Case in Study: 2 Cor 5:16." In *From Faith to Faith: Essays in Honor of Donald G. Miller on His Seventieth Birthday,* edited by D. Y. Hadidian, 107–25. PTMS 23. Pittsburgh: Pickwick, 1979.

Hafemann, Scott. "'Self-Commendation' and Apostolic Legitimacy in 2 Corinthians." *NTS* 36 (1990) 66–88.

——. *Suffering and the Spirit: An Exegetical Study of II Cor. 2:14–3:3 within the Context of the Corinthian Correspondence.* WUNT 2/19. Tübingen: Mohr (Siebeck), 1986.

Hahn, Ferdinand. "Der Apostolat im Urchristentum." *KD* 20 (1974) 54–77.

——. "Das Ja des Paulus und das Ja Gottes: Bemerkungen zu 2 Kor 1,12–2,1." In *Neues Testament und christliche Existenz: Festschrift für Herbert Braun zum 70. Geburtstag am 4. Mai 1973,* edited by H. D. Betz and L. Schottroff, 229–39. Tübingen: Mohr (Siebeck), 1973.

——. "'Siehe, jetzt ist der Tag des Heils': Neuschöpfung und Versöhnung nach 2. Korinther 5, 14–6, 2." *EvT* 33 (1973) 244–53.

Hamerton-Kelly, Robert G. "A Girardian Interpretation of Paul: Rivalry, Mimesis and Victimage in the Corinthian Correspondence." *Semeia* 33 (1985) 65–81.

Hanhart, Karel. "Paul's Hope in the Face of Death." *JBL* 88 (1969) 445–57.

Hanson, Anthony Tyrrell. "The Midrash in II Corinthians 3: A Reconsideration." *JSNT* 9 (1980) 2–28.

Harris, Murray J. "Paul's View of Death in 2 Corinthians 5:1–10." In *New Dimensions in New Testament Study,* edited by R. N. Longenecker and M. C. Tenney, 317–28. Grand Rapids: Zondervan, 1974.

Heiny, Stephen B. "2 Corinthians 2:14–4:6: The Motive for Metaphor." In *SBL 1987 Seminar Papers,* edited by K. H. Richards, 1–22. Atlanta: Scholars Press, 1987.

Hengel, Martin. "Das Bekenntnis zum dreieinigen Gott (2. Kor. 13,11–3)." *TBei* 16 (1985) 195–200.

Héring, Jean. *The Second Epistle of St. Paul to the Corinthians.* London: Epworth, 1967.

Hermann, Ingo. *Kyrios und Pneuma: Studien zur Christologie der paulinischen Hauptbriefe.* SANT 2. Munich: Kösel, 1961.

Hickling, Colin J. A. "The Sequence of Thought in II Corinthians Chapter Three." *NTS* 21 (1975) 380–95.

Hock, Ronald F. *The Social Context of Paul's Ministry: Tentmaking and Apostleship.* Philadelphia: Fortress, 1980.

Hodgson, Robert C. "Paul the Apostle and First Century Tribulation Lists." *ZNW* 74 (1983) 59–80.

Hofius, Otfried. "Erwägungen zur Gestalt und Herkunft des paulinischen Versöhnungsgedankens." *ZTK* 77 (1980) 186–99.

——. "Gesetz und Evangelium nach 2 Korinther 3." In *"Gesetz" als Thema biblischer Theologie,* edited by I. Baldermann, 105–49. Jahrbuch für Biblische Theologie 4; Neukirchen-Vluyn: Neukirchener Verlag, 1989.

——. "'Der Gott allen Trostes.' Paraklesis und parakalein in 2 Kor 1,3–7." *TBei* 14 (1983) 217–27.

———. "'Gott hat unter uns aufgerichtet das Wort von der Versöhnung' (2 Kor 5, 19)." *ZNW* 71 (1980) 3–20.

Hugedé, Norbert. *La Metaphore du Miroir dans les Épîtres de saint Paul aux Corinthiens.* Neuchâtel and Paris: Delachaux et Niestlé, 1957.

Hughes, Philip E. *Paul's Second Epistle to the Corinthians.* NICNT. Grand Rapids: Eerdmans, 1962.

Käsemann, Ernst. "Die Legitimität des Apostels: Eine Untersuchung zu II Korinther 10–13." *ZNW* 41 (1942) 33–71.

Kerr, A. J. "ΑΡΡΑΒΩΝ." *JTS* 39 (1988) 92–97.

Kertelge, Karl. "Das Apostelamt des Paulus, sein Ursprung und seine Bedeutung." *BZ* 14 (1970) 161–81.

———. "Jesus Christus verkündigen als den Herrn (2 Kor 4,5)." In *Christus Bezeugen: Festschrift für Wolfgang Trilling zum 65. Geburtstag,* edited by K. Kertelge, T. Holtz, and C.-P. März, 227–36. ETS 59. Leipzig: St. Benno, 1989.

Koenig, John. "The Knowing of Glory and Its Consequences (2 Corinthians 3–5)." In *The Conversation Continues: Studies in Paul and John: In Honor of J. Louis Martyn,* edited by R. T. Fortna and B. R. Gaventa, 158–69. Nashville: Abingdon, 1990.

Kremer, Jakob. "'Denn der Buchstabe tötet, der Geist aber macht lebendig.' Methodologische und hermeneutische Erwägungen zu 2 Kor 3, 6b." In *Begegnung mit dem Wort: Festschrift für Heinrich Zimmermann,* edited by J. Zmijewski and E. Nellesen, 219–50. BBB 53. Bonn: Hanstein, 1980.

Kruse, C. G. "The Offender and the Offence in 2 Corinthians 2:5 and 7:12." *EvQ* 60 (1988) 129–39.

———. "The Relationship between the Opposition to Paul Reflected in 2 Corinthians 1–7 and 10–13." *EvQ* 61 (1989) 195–202.

———. *The Second Epistle of Paul to the Corinthians: An Introduction and Commentary.* Tyndale New Testament Commentaries 8. Grand Rapids: Eerdmans, 1987.

Lambrecht, Jan. "The Favorable Time: A Study of 2 Cor 6,2a in Its Context." In *Vom Urchristentum zu Jesus: Für Joachim Gnilka,* edited by H. Frankemölle and K. Kertelge, 377–91. Freiburg, Basel, and Vienna: Herder, 1989.

———. "The nekrōsis of Jesus: Ministry and Suffering in 2 Cor 4, 7–15." In *L'Apôtre Paul: Personnalité, style et conception du ministère,* edited by A. Vanhoye, 120–43. BETL 73. Leuven: Leuven University Press, 1986.

———. "Philological and Exegetical Notes on 2 Cor 13,4." *Bijdragen* 46 (1985) 261–69.

———. "Structure and Line of Thought in 2 Cor 2,14–4,6." *Bib* 64 (1983) 344–80.

———. "La vie engloutit ce qui est mortel: Commentaire de 2 Co 5, 4c." In *La Paque du Christ. Mystère de Salut: Mélanges offerts au P. F.-X. Durrwell pour son 70e anniversaire,* edited by E. Charpentier et al., 237–48. LD 112. Paris: Cerf, 1982.

Lang, Friedrich. *Die Briefe an die Korinther.* NTD 7. Göttingen and Zurich: Vandenhoeck & Ruprecht, 1986.

Lang, Friedrich Gustav. *2. Korinther 5, 1–10 in der neueren Forschung.* BGBE 16. Tübingen: Mohr (Siebeck), 1973.

Lietzmann, Hans. *An die Korinther I/II,* edited and supplemented by W. G. Kümmel. HNT 9. 4th ed. Tübingen: Mohr (Siebeck), 1949.

Lillie, William. "Approach to II Corinthians 5:1–10." *SJT* 30 (1977) 59–70.

Lincoln, Andrew T. "2 Corinthians, the heavenly house and the third heaven." In *Paradise Now and Not Yet: Studies in the Role of the Heavenly Dimension in Paul's Thought with Special Reference to His Eschatology,* 55–86. Cambridge: Cambridge University Press, 1981.

———. "'Paul the Visionary': The Setting and Significance of the Rapture to Paradise in II Corinthians XII.1–10." *NTS* 25 (1979) 204–20.

Lindemann, Andreas. "Paulus und die korinthische Eschatologie: Zur These von einer 'Entwicklung' im paulinischen Denken." *NTS* 37 (1991) 373–99.

Lodge, J. G. "The Apostle's Appeal and Reader's Response: 2 Corinthians 8 and 9." *Chicago Studies* 30 (1991) 59–75.

Lohse, Eduard. "Ursprung und Prägung des christlichen Apostolates." *TZ* 9 (1953) 259–75.

Loubser, J. A. "Winning the Struggle (Or: How to Treat Heretics) (2 Corinthians 12:1–10)." *Journal of Theology for Southern Africa* 75 (1991) 75–83.

Lührmann, Dieter. "Rechtfertigung und Versöhnung." *ZTK* 67 (1970) 437–52.

Luz, Ulrich. "Der alte und der neue Bund bei Paulus und im Hebräerbrief." *EvT* 27 (1967) 318–36.

Machalet, Christian. "Paulus und seine Gegner: Eine Untersuchung zu den Korintherbriefen." In *Theokratia, Jahrbuch des Inst. Judaicum Delitzschianum II, 1970–72: Festgabe für Karl Heinrich Rengstorf zum 70. Geburtstag,* edited by W. Dietrich et al., 183–203. Leiden: Brill, 1973.

MacRae, George W. "Anti-Dualist Polemic in 2 Cor 4:6?" In *Studia Evangelica, IV/1: The New Testament Scriptures,* edited by F. L. Cross, 420–31. TU 102. Berlin: Akademie-Verlag, 1968.

Malherbe, Abraham J. "Antisthenes and Odysseus, and Paul at War." *HTR* 76 (1983) 143–73.

Manson, Thomas W. "2 Cor. 2:14–17: Suggestions Toward an Exegesis." In *Studia Paulina in Honorem Johannis de Zwaan,* 155–62. Haarlem: Bohn, 1953.

Manus, C. Ukachukwu. "2 Cor 10–11:23a: A Study in Paul's Stylistic Structures." *Bulletin de Théologie Africaine/Bulletin of African Theology/Boletím de Teología Africana* 5 (1983) 251–68.

Marguerat, Daniel. "2 Corinthiens 10–13: Paul et l'expérience de Dieu." *ETR* 63 (1988) 497–519.

Marshall, Peter. "A Metaphor of Social Shame: *thriambeuein* in 2 Cor. 2:14." *NovT* 25 (1983) 302–17.

———. *Enmity in Corinth: Social Conventions in Paul's Relations with the Corinthians.* WUNT 2/23. Tübingen: Mohr (Siebeck) 1987.

Martin, Ralph P. *2 Corinthians.* WBC 40. Waco: Word, 1986.

———. *2 Corinthians.* Word Biblical Themes. Dallas: Word, 1988.

———. "The Spirit in 2 Corinthians in Light of the 'Fellowship of the Holy Spirit.'" In *Eschatology and the New Testament: Essays in Honor of George Raymond Beasley-Murray,* edited by W. Gloer, 113–28. Peabody: Hendrickson, 1988.

Martyn, J. Louis. "Epistemology at the Turn of the Ages: 2 Corinthians 5:16." In *Christian History and Interpretation: Studies Presented to John Knox,* edited by W. R. Farmer,

C. F. D. Moule, and R. R. Niebuhr, 269–87. Cambridge: Cambridge University Press, 1967.

McCant, Jerry W. "Paul's Thorn of Rejected Apostleship." *NTS* 34 (1988) 550–72.

McDonald, J. I. H. "Paul and the Preaching Ministry: A reconsideration of 2 Cor 2:14–17 in its context." *JSNT* 17 (1983) 35–50.

Mealand, David L. "'As having nothing and yet possessing everything,' 2 Cor 6:10c." *ZNW* 67 (1976) 277–79.

Mell, U. *Neue Schöpfung: Eine traditionsgeschichtliche und exegetische Studie zu einem soteriologischen Grundsatz paulinischer Theologie.* BZNW 56. Berlin and New York: de Gruyter, 1989.

Menoud, Philippe H. "The Thorn in the Flesh and Satan's Angel (2 Cor. 12.7)." In *Jesus Christ and the Faith: A Collection of Studies,* 19–30. PTMS 18. Pittsburgh: Pickwick, 1978.

Meurer, Siegfried. *Das Recht im Dienst der Versöhnung und des Friedens.* ATANT 63. Zurich: Zwingli, 1972.

Michel, Otto. "'Erkennen dem Fleisch nach' (II Kor. 5,16)." *EvT* 14 (1954) 22–29.

Minear, Paul S. "Some Pauline Thoughts on Dying: A Study of 2 Corinthians." In *From Faith to Faith: Essays in Honor of Donald G. Miller on His Seventieth Birthday,* edited by D. Y. Hadidian, 91–106. PTMS 23. Pittsburgh: Pickwick, 1979.

Mott, Stephen C. "The Power of Giving and Receiving: Reciprocity in Hellenistic Benevolence." In *Current Issues in Biblical and Patristic Interpretation: Studies in Honor of Merrill C. Tenney,* edited by G. F. Hawthorne, 60–72. Grand Rapids: Eerdmans, 1975.

Moule, Charles F. D. "2 Cor 3, 18b." In *Neues Testament und Geschichte: Historisches Geschehen und Deutung im Neuen Testament. Oscar Cullmann zum 70. Geburtstag,* edited by H. Baltensweiler and B. Reicke, 231–38. Zurich: Theologischer Verlag, 1972.

Murphy-O'Connor, Jerome. "Another Jesus (2 Cor 11:4)." *RB* 97 (1990) 238–51.

———. "'Being at home in the body we are in exile from the Lord.' (2 Cor. 5:6b)." *RB* 93 (1986) 214–21.

———. "Faith and Resurrection in 2 Cor 4:13–14." *RB* 95 (1988) 543–50.

———. "A Ministry Beyond the Letter (2 Cor 3:1–6)." In *Paolo: Ministro del Nuovo Testamento (2 Co 2,14–4,6),* edited by Lorenzo de Lorenzi, 105–57. Serie Monografica di "Benedictina." Sezione Biblico Ecumenica 9. Rome: Abbazia di S. Paolo, 1987.

———. "Pneumatikoi in 2 Corinthians." *Proceedings of the Irish Biblical Association* 11 (1988) 59–66.

———. *The Theology of the Second Letter to the Corinthians.* New Testament Theology. Cambridge: Cambridge University Press, 1991.

O'Collins, Gerald G. "Power Made Perfect in Weakness: 2 Cor 12:9–10." *CBQ* 33 (1971) 528–37.

Oliveira, Anacleto de. *Die Diakonie der Gerechtigkeit und der Versöhnung in der Apologie des 2. Korintherbriefes: Analyse und Auslegung von 2. Kor 2,14–4,6; 5,11–6,10.* NTAbh new series 21. Münster: Aschendorff, 1990.

O'Neill, John C. "The Absence of the 'in Christ' Theology in 2 Corinthians 5." *ABR* 35 (1987) 99–106.

Oostendorp, Derk William. *Another Jesus: A Gospel of Jewish-Christian Superiority in II Corinthians.* Kampen: Kok, 1967.

Osei-Bonsu, Joseph. "Does 2 Cor 5:1-10 Teach the Reception of the Resurrection Body at the Moment of Death?" *JSNT* 28 (1986) 81-101.

Osten-Sacken, Peter von der. "Geist im Buchstaben: Vom Glanz des Mose und des Paulus." In *Evangelium und Tora: Aufsätze zu Paulus,* 150-55. TBü 77. Munich: Kaiser, 1987.

Pate, C. Marvin. *Adam Christology as the Exegetical and Theological Substructure of 2 Corinthians 4:7-5:21.* Lanham: University Press of America, 1991.

Pathrapankal, J. M. "'When I am Weak, then I am Strong' (2 Cor 12:10): Pauline Understanding of Apostolic Sufferings." *Jeevadhara* 18 (1988) 140-51.

Patte, Daniel. "A Structural Exegesis of 2 Corinthians 2:14-7:4, with Special Attention on 2:14-3:6 and 6:11-7:4." In *SBL 1987 Seminar Papers,* edited by K. H. Richards, 23-49. Atlanta: Scholars Press, 1987.

Penna, Romano. "Sofferenze Apostoliche, Antropologia ed Eschatologia in 2 Cor 4:7-5:10." In *Parola e Spirito,* edited by C. Marcheselli, 1. 402-31. Brescia: Paideia, 1982.

Perriman, A. C. "Paul and the Parousia: I Corinthians 15.50-57 and 2 Corinthians 5.1-7." *NTS* 35 (1989) 512-21.

Pesch, Rudolf, and Herbert A. Zwergel. "'Christus dem Fleische nach kennen' (2 Kor 5,16)? Zur theologischen Bedeutung der Frage nach dem historischen Jesus." In *Kontinuität in Jesus: Zugänge zu Leben, Tod und Auferstehung,* 9-34, 125-31. Freiburg: Herder, 1974.

Pfitzner, Victor C. *Strength in Weakness: A Commentary on 2 Corinthians.* Chi Rho Commentary. Adelaide: Lutheran Publishing House, 1992.

Plummer, Alfred. *A Critical and Exegetical Commentary on the Second Epistle of St. Paul to the Corinthians.* ICC. Edinburgh: Clark, 1915.

Price, James L. "Aspects of Paul's Theology and their Bearing on Literary Problems of Second Corinthians." In *Studies in the History and the Text of the New Testament in Honor of Kenneth Willis Clark, PhD,* edited by B. L. Daniels and M. J. Suggs, 95-106. SD 29. Salt Lake City: University of Utah Press, 1967.

Price, Robert M. "Punished in Paradise (An Exegetical Theory on II Corinthians 12:1-10)." *JSNT* 7 (1980) 33-40.

Provence, Thomas E. "'Who Is Sufficient for These Things?' An Exegesis of II Corinthians ii 15-iii 18." *NovT* 24 (1982) 54-81.

Prümm, Karl. *Diakonia Pneumatos: Der zweite Korintherbrief als Zugang zur apostolischen Botschaft. Auslegung und Theologie.* 2 vols. Rome, Freiburg, and Vienna: Herder, 1960, 1967.

Rebell, Walter. *Christologie und Existenz: Eine Auslegung von 2. Kor. 1,14-21.* Arbeiten zur Theologie 73. Stuttgart: Calwer Verlag, 1992.

Richard, Earl. "Polemics, Old Testament, and Theology: A Study of II Cor. III,1-IV,6." *RB* 88 (1981) 340-67.

Rissi, Matthias. *Studien zum zweiten Korintherbrief: Der alte Bund–Der Predigt–Der Tod.* ATANT 56. Zurich: Zwingli, 1969.

Roetzel, Calvin J. "'As Dying, and Behold We Live': Death and Resurrection in Paul's Theology." *Int* 46 (1992) 5-18.

Rolland, Philippe. "La structure littéraire de la Deuxième Épître aux Corinthiens." *Bib* 71 (1990) 73–84.

Roloff, Jürgen. *Apostolat–Verkündigung–Kirche.* Gütersloh: Mohn, 1965.

Romaniuk, Kazimierz. "Résurrection existentielle ou eschatologique en 2 Co 4, 13–14?" *BZ* 34 (1990) 248–52.

Saake, Helmut. "Paulus als Ekstatiker: Pneumatologische Beobachtungen zu 2 Kor. xii 1–10." *NovT* 15 (1973) 153–60.

Sampley, J. Paul. "Paul, His Opponents in 2 Corinthians 10–13, and the Rhetorical Handbooks." In *The Social World of Formative Christianity and Judaism: In Tribute to Howard Clark Kee,* edited by J. Neusner et al., 162–77. Philadelphia: Fortress, 1988.

Sánchez Bosch, Jorge. *"Gloriarse" según San Pablo: Sentido y teología de* καυχάομαι. AnBib 40. Rome: Pontifical Biblical Institute, 1970.

Schäfer, P. "New Testament and Hekhalot Literature: The Journey into Heaven in Paul and in Merkavah Mysticism." *JJS* 35 (1984) 19–35.

Schildenberger, Johannes. "2 Kor. 3:17a: 'Der Herr ist der Geist,' im Zusammenhang des Textes und der Theologie des hl. Paulus." In *Studiorum Paulinorum Congressus Internationalis Catholicus, 1961,* 451–60. AnBib 17–18, 1. Rome: Pontifical Biblical Institute, 1963.

Schlatter, Adolf. *Paulus, der Bote Jesus: Eine Deutung seiner Briefe an die Korinther.* 4th ed. Stuttgart: Calwer, 1934. Reprint 1969.

Schmithals, Walter. *Gnosticism in Corinth: An Investigation of the Letters to the Corinthians.* Nashville and New York: Abingdon, 1971.

———. *The Office of Apostle in the Early Church.* Nashville and New York: Abingdon, 1969.

Schneider, Bernardin. "HE KOINONIA TOU HAGIOU PNEUMATOS (II Cor. 13, 13)." In *Studies Honoring Ignatius Charles Brady, Friar Minor,* edited by R. S. Almagno and C. L. Harkins, 421–47. Franciscan Institute Publications, Theology Series 6. St. Bonaventure: Franciscan Institute, 1976.

———. "The Meaning of St. Paul's Antithesis 'the letter and the Spirit.'" *CBQ* 15 (1953) 163–207.

Schoenborn, Ulrich. "La Inversion de la Gracia: Apuntes Sobre 2 Corintios 8:9." *RevistB* 50 (1988) 207–18.

Schrage, Wolfgang. "Leid, Kreuz und Eschaton: Die Peristasenkataloge als Merkmale paulinischer theologia crucis und Eschatologie." *EvT* 34 (1974) 141–75.

Schulz, Siegfried. "Die Decke des Moses: Untersuchungen zu einer vorpaulinischen Überlieferung in II Cor. 3.7–18." *ZNW* 49 (1958) 1–30.

Schütz, John Howard. *Paul and the Anatomy of Apostolic Authority.* SNTSMS 26. Cambridge: Cambridge University Press, 1975.

Sevenster, Jan N. "Einige Bemerkungen über den 'Zwischenzustand' bei Paulus." *NTS* 1 (1955) 291–99.

———. "Some Remarks on the gumnos in 2 Cor. 5:3." In *Studia Paulina in Honorem Johannis de Zwaan,* 202–14. Haarlem: Bohn, 1953.

Souček, Josef B. "Wir erkennen Christus nicht mehr nach dem Fleisch." *EvT* 19 (1959) 300–314.

Spencer, Aida Besançon. "The Wise Fool (and the Foolish Wise): A Study of Irony in Paul." *NovT* 23 (1981) 349–60.

Spittler, Russell P. "The Limits of Ecstasy: An Exegesis of 2 Corinthians 12:1–10." In *Current Issues in Biblical and Patristic Interpretation: Studies in Honor of Merrill C. Tenney,* edited by G. F. Hawthorne, 259–66. Grand Rapids: Eerdmans, 1975.

Spörri, Theophil. *Alles im Dienste Christi: Studien über den zweiten Korintherbrief.* Zurich: Gotthelf, 1945.

Stählin, Gustav. "'Um mitzusterben und mitzuleben.' Bemerkungen zu 2 Kor, 7,3." In *Neues Testament und christliche Existenz: Festschrift für Herbert Braun zum 70. Geburtstag am 4. Mai 1973,* edited by H. D. Betz and L. Schottroff, 503–21. Tübingen: Mohr (Siebeck) 1973.

Stegemann, E. "Der Neue Bund im Alten: Zum Schriftverständnis des Paulus in II Kor 3." *TZ* 42 (1986) 97–114.

Stockhausen, Carol Kern. *Moses' Veil and the Glory of the New Covenant: The Exegetical Substructure of II Cor. 3,1–4,6.* AnBib 116. Rome: Pontifical Biblical Institute, 1989.

Stöger, A. "Amt und Amtsführung nach 2 Kor 10,1–13,10." *BLit* 58 (1985) 145–52.

Strachan, Robert H. *The Second Epistle of Paul to the Corinthians.* MNTC. New York and London: Harper, 1935.

Strecker, Georg. "Die Legitimität des paulinischen Apostolates nach 2 Korintherbrief 10–13." *NTS* 38 (1992) 566–86.

Stuhlmacher, Peter. "Erwägungen zum ontologischen Charakter der *kainē ktisis* bei Paulus." *EvT* 27 (1967) 1–35.

Sumney, Jerry L. *Identifying Paul's Opponents: The Question of Method in 2 Corinthians.* JSNTSup 40. Sheffield: JSOT Press, 1990.

Tabor, James D. *Things Unutterable: Paul's Ascent to Paradise in its Greco-Roman, Judaic, and Early Christian Contexts.* Studies in Judaism. Lanham, MD: University Press of America, 1986.

Talbert, Charles H. "Money Management in Early Mediterranean Christianity: 2 Corinthians 8–9." *RevExp* 86 (1989) 359–70.

———. *Reading Corinthians: A Literary and Theological Commentary on 1 and 2 Corinthians.* New York: Crossroad, 1987.

Theissen, Gerd. "The Veil of Moses and the Unconscious Aspects of the Law." In *Psychological Aspects of Pauline Theology,* 115–58. Philadelphia: Fortress, 1987.

Thrall, Margaret E. "'Putting on' and 'Stripping off' in 2 Corinthians 5:3." In *New Testament Textual Criticism: Its Significance for Exegesis: Essays in Honor of Bruce M. Metzger,* edited by E. J. Epp and G. D. Fee, 220–37. Oxford: Clarendon, 1981.

———. "Salvation Proclaimed: V. 2 Corinthians 5:18–21: Reconciliation with God." *ExpTim* 93 (1982) 227–32.

———. "A Second Thanksgiving Period in II Corinthians." *JSNT* 16 (1982) 101–24.

———. "Super-Apostles, Servants of Christ, and Servants of Satan." *JSNT* 6 (1980) 42–57.

Thüsing, Wilhelm. "Rechtfertigungsgedanke und Christologie in den Korintherbriefen." In *Neues Testament und Kirche: Für Rudolf Schnackenburg,* edited by J. Gnilka, 301–24. Freiburg and Vienna: Herder, 1974.

Travis, Stephen H. "Paul's Boasting in 2 Corinthians 10–12." In *Studia Evangelica* 6, edited by E. A. Livingstone, 527–32. TU 112. Berlin: Akademie-Verlag, 1973.

Treue, K. "Christliche Empfehlungs-Schemabriefe auf Papyrus." In *Zetesis: Album amicorum door vrienden en collega's aangeboden aan Prof. E. de Strycker ter gelegenheid van zijn 65e verjaardag*, 629–36. Antwerp: Nederlandsche Boekhandel, 1973.

Trocmé, Etienne. "Le rempart de Damas: un faux pas de Paul?" *RHPR* 69 (1989) 475–79.

Ulonska, Herbert. "Die Doxa des Mose." *EvT* 26 (1966) 378–88.

van Unnik, Willem C. "La Conception paulinienne de la nouvelle alliance." In *Littérature et théologie pauliniennes*, 109–26. RechBib 5. Louvain: Desclée de Brouwer, 1960.

———. "Reisepläne und Amen-sagen, Zusammenhang und Gedankenfolge in 2. Korinther i 15–25." In *Studia Paulina in Honorem Johannis de Zwaan*, 215–34. Haarlem: Bohn, 1953.

———. "'With Unveiled Face': An Exegesis of 2 Corinthians iii 12–18." *NovT* 6 (1964) 153–59.

Voight, G. *Die Kraft des Schwachen: Paulus an die Korinther II*. Biblisch-theologische Schwerpunkte 5. Göttingen: Vandenhoeck & Ruprecht, 1990.

Wagner, Guy. "Alliance de la lettre, Alliance de l'Esprit: Essai d'analyse de 2 Corinthiens 2/14 à 3/18." *ETR* 60 (1985) 55–65.

Ward, Richard F. "Pauline Voice and Presence as Strategic Communication." In *SBL 1990 Seminar Papers*, edited by D. J. Lull, 283–92. Atlanta: Scholars Press, 1990.

Watson, Francis. "2 Cor. x–xiii and Paul's Painful Letter to the Corinthians." *JTS* 35 (1984) 324–46.

Watson, Nigel M. "'To Make Us Rely Not on Ourselves but on God Who Raises the Dead': 2 Cor 1,9b as the Heart of Paul's Theology." In *Die Mitte des Neuen Testaments: Einheit und Vielfalt neutestamentlicher Theologie. Festschrift für Eduard Schweizer zum siebzigsten Geburtstag*, edited by U. Luz and H. Weder, 384–98. Göttingen: Vandenhoeck & Ruprecht, 1983.

Wendland, Heinz-Dietrich. *Die Briefe an die Korinther*. NTD 7. 15th ed. Göttingen: Vandenhoeck & Ruprecht, 1980.

Wenham, David. "Being 'Found' on the Last Day: New Light on 2 Peter 3.10 and 2 Corinthians 5.3." *NTS* 33 (1987) 477–79.

———. "2 Corinthians 1:17, 18: Echo of a Dominical Logion." *NovT* 28 (1986) 271–79.

Williamson, Lamar, Jr. "Led in Triumph: Paul's Use of Thriambeuo." *Int* 22 (1968) 317–32.

Wilson, R. McL. "Gnosis at Corinth." In *Paul and Paulinism: Essays in honour of C. K. Barrett*, edited by M. D. Hooker and S. G. Wilson, 102–14. London: SPCK, 1982.

Windisch, Hans. *Der zweite Korintherbrief*. MeyerK 6. 9th ed. Göttingen: Vandenhoeck & Ruprecht, 1924 (1970 reprint edited by G. Strecker).

Wolff, Christian. "True Apostolic Knowledge of Christ: Exegetical Reflections on 2 Corinthians 5:14ff." In *Paul and Jesus: Collected Essays*, edited by A. J. M. Wedderburn, 81–98. JSNTSup 37. Sheffield: JSOT Press, 1989.

———. *Der zweite Brief des Paulus an die Korinther*. THKNT 8. Berlin: Evangelische Verlagsanstalt, 1989.

Wong, E. "The Lord Is the Spirit (2 Cor 3,17a)." *ETL* 61 (1985) 48–72.

Wright, N. T. "Reflected Glory: 2 Corinthians 3.18." In *The Climax of the Covenant: Christ and the Law in Pauline Theology*, 175–92. Minneapolis: Fortress, 1992.

Yoder, John H. "The Apostle's Apology Revisited (2 Cor 5:11–15, 17)." In *The New*

Way of Jesus: Essays Presented to Howard Charles, edited by W. Klassen, 115–34. Newton: Faith and Life Press, 1980.

Young, Frances, and David F. Ford. *Meaning and Truth in 2 Corinthians.* Biblical Foundations in Theology. London: SPCK, 1987.

Zmijewski, Josef. "Kontextbezug und Deutung von 2 Kor 12, 7a." *BZ* 21 (1977) 265–72.

———. *Der Stil der paulinischen "Narrenrede": Analyse der Sprachgestaltung in 2 Kor 11, 1–12, 10 als Beitrag zur Methodik von Stiluntersuchungen neutestamentlicher Texts.* BBB 52. Bonn: Hanstein, 1978.

Zorn, R. O. "II Corinthians 5:1–10: Individual Eschatology or Corporate Solidarity, Which?" *Reformed Theological Review* 48 (1989) 93–104.

On 2 Cor 6:14–7:1

Beale, Greg K. "The Old Testament Background of Reconciliation in 2 Corinthians 5–7 and its Bearing on the Literary Problem of 2 Corinthians 6.14–7.1." *NTS* 35 (1989) 550–81.

Betz, Hans Dieter. "2 Corinthians 6:14–7:1: An Anti-Pauline Fragment?" *JBL* 92 (1973) 88–108.

Derrett, J. Duncan M. "2 Cor 6, 14ff. a Midrash on Dt 22, 10." *Bib* 59 (1978) 231–50.

Duff, Paul B. "The Mind of the Redactor: 2 Cor. 6:14–7:1 in Its Secondary Context." *NovT* 35 (1993) 160–80.

Fee, Gordon D. "II Corinthians vi.14–vii.1 and Food Offered to Idols." *NTS* 23 (1977) 140–61.

Fitzmyer, Joseph A. "Qumran and the interpolated paragraph in 2 Cor 6:14–7:1." In *Essays on the Semitic Background of the New Testament,* 205–17. Missoula, MT: Scholars Press, 1974.

Gnilka, Joachim. "2 Cor 6:14–7:1 in the Light of the Qumran Texts and the Testaments of the Twelve Patriarchs." In *Paul and Qumran: Studies in New Testament Exegesis,* edited by J. Murphy-O'Connor, 48–68. London: Chapman, 1968) 48–68.

Lambrecht, Jan. "The Fragment 2 Cor vi 14–vii 1: A Plea for Its Authenticity." In *Miscellanea Neotestamentica,* II, edited by T. Baarda, A. F. J. Klijn, and W. C. van Unnik, 143–61. NovTSup 47. Leiden: Brill, 1978.

Lategan, B. C. "'Moenie met ongelowiges in dieselfde juk trek nie' ('Do not be yoked together with unbelievers')." *Scriptura* 12 (1984) 20–34.

Murphy-O'Connor, Jerome. "Philo and 2 Cor 6:14–7:1." In *The Diakonia of the Spirit (2 Cor 4:7–7:4),* edited by Lorenzo de Lorenzi, 133–60. Série Monographique de "Benedictina," Section Bibl-Oec. 10. Rome: Abbaye de S. Paul, 1989. [See also *RB* 95 (1988) 55–69.]

———. "Relating 2 Corinthians 6.14–7.1 to its Context." *NTS* 33 (1987) 272–75.

Rensberger, David K. "2 Corinthians 6.14–7.1 — A Fresh Examination." *Studia Biblica et Theologica* 8/2 (1978) 25–49.

Saß, Gerhard. "Noch einmal: 2Kor 6,14–7,1: Literarkritische Waffen gegen einen >unpaulinischen< Paulius?" *ZNW* 84 (1993) 36–64.

Thrall, Margaret E. "The Problem of II Cor. vi.14–vii.1 in Some Recent Discussion." *NTS* 24 (1977) 132–48.

Waller, Elizabeth. "The Rhetorical Structure of 2 Cor 6:14–7:1: Is the So-Called 'Non-Pauline Interpolation' a Clue to the Redactor of 2 Corinthians?" *Proceedings of the Eastern Great Lakes and Midwest Biblical Society* 10 (1990) 151–65.

Zeilinger, Franz. "Die Echtheit von 2 Cor 6:14–7:1." *JBL* 112 (1993) 71–80.

▣ Scripture Index

▣ Name Index